The Penitential State

In 833 Emperor Louis the Pious, Charlemagne's son, submitted to a public penance in the wake of a rebellion by his three elder sons. This penance amounted to a deposition, for Louis was to atone for his sins for the rest of his life. Only half a year later, he was back on the throne again. In this major re-evaluation of Louis's reign, Mayke de Jong argues that his penance was the outcome of a political discourse and practice in which the accountability of the Frankish ruler to God played an increasingly central role. However heated their debates, this was a moral high ground Louis shared with churchmen and secular magnates. Through a profound re-reading of texts by contemporary authors who reflected on legitimate authority in times of crisis, this book reveals a world in which political crime was defined as sin, and royal authority was enhanced by atonement.

MAYKE DE JONG is Professor of Medieval History in the Department of History and Art History, Utrecht University.

Utrecht Psalter: The Psalmist admonishes Saul. The title of Psalm (51)52 – '...Doeg the Edomite came and told Saul, and said unto him, David is come to the house of Ahimelech' (cf. I Reg. 22.9) – is depicted at the lower left of the illustration. Doeg stands on one side of the enthroned Saul, and three retainers on the other. The Psalmist delivers a spirited admonition to the king (Ps. 51.3–9), pointing at Christ and His saints with one hand, and at Saul and his entourage with the other, which holds a razor (Ps. 51.4). (Utrecht, Universiteitsbibliotheek, MS 32, fol. 30r; by permission of the Utrecht University Library.)

The Penitential State

Authority and Atonement in the Age of Louis the Pious, 814–840

Mayke de Jong

CAMBRIDGE
UNIVERSITY PRESS

CAMBRIDGE UNIVERSITY PRESS
Cambridge, New York, Melbourne, Madrid, Cape Town, Singapore, São Paulo,
Delhi, Dubai, Tokyo

Cambridge University Press
The Edinburgh Building, Cambridge CB2 8RU, UK

Published in the United States of America by Cambridge University Press, New York

www.cambridge.org
Information on this title: www.cambridge.org/9780521881524

First published 2009
Reprinted 2010

Printed in the United Kingdom at the University Press, Cambridge

A catalogue record for this publication is available from the British Library

Library of Congress Cataloguing in Publication data
De Jong, Mayke.
The penitential state : authority and atonement in the age of Louis the Pious,
814–840 / Mayke de Jong.
   p.   cm.
Includes bibliographical references and index.
ISBN 978-0-521-88152-4 (hbk.)
1. Louis I, Emperor, 778–840.   2. Louis I, Emperor, 778–840 – Religion.
3. Repentance – Political aspects – France – History – To 1500.   4. Atonement –
Political aspects – France – History – To 1500.   5. Monarchy – France –
History – To 1500.   6. Church and state – France – History – To 1500.
7. France – Kings and rulers – Biography.   8. France – History – To 987 –
Sources.   9. France – Church history – To 987 – Sources.   10. France – Kings
and rulers – Religious aspects.   I. Title.
DC74.D4   2008
944'.014092–dc22
[B]
                                                              2008049138

ISBN 978-0-521-88152-4 hardback

For my students

Contents

Preface

This book started almost a decade ago, in 1999, when I was a Visiting Fellow Commoner at Trinity College, Cambridge. Having written some chapters, I realised that I had more work to do before I could do justice to a book with Louis's penance of 833 at its heart. After years of exploring the topic through articles, it was only during the academic year 2005–6 that I completed the first full draft of *The Penitential State*. I could do so thanks to a Fellowship at the Netherlands Institute for Advanced Studies (NIAS) in Wassenaar, and a replacement grant awarded by the Netherlands Organisation for Scientific Research (NWO). During this much-needed sabbatical year, my colleagues at Utrecht University generously enabled me to concentrate fully on writing. Particular thanks are due to Josine Blok, who took over from me as Chair of the History Department, and to Marco Mostert and Carine van Rhijn, who jointly held the fort in the section of Medieval History. At NIAS I had gathered a small theme group on 'The Formation of Carolingian Identity', consisting of Rosamond McKitterick, David Ganz and Els Rose. In our 'medieval attic', this Carolingianist nucleus was joined by Joseph Harris, Anu Mand, Arjo Vanderjagt and Jan Ziolkowski, with Helmut Reimitz as a regular visitor. To work shoulder to shoulder with this inspiring group of first-rate medievalists was a real privilege. As usual, NIAS provided the ideal environment for a joint project of this kind, with precisely the right mixture of solitude and sociability to keep us going. Rosamond McKitterick and I read each other's prose as soon as it rolled off the printer; other group members also offered helpful comments on first versions of various chapters, and so did assorted guests who attended our series of one-day workshops. In the summer of 2006, Stuart Airlie and Matthew Innes read the draft I had completed at NIAS. Their comments, and their confidence in the book-to-be, were invaluable.

Many factors then conspired against my finishing *The Penitential State* by the date stipulated in my CUP contract, such as moving to a new university building as well as to a new house in the autumn of 2006, and another two years of chairing what had suddenly become the Department of History *and* Art History. That I managed to complete the book only half a year behind schedule says a lot about the co-operative climate in the Utrecht Faculty of Humanities. I thank my fellow-administrators Maarten Prak, Wiljan van den Akker and Louise van der Kaaden for their support. Yet I sincerely doubt whether I would have managed to produce this baby without my two learned midwives across the Channel, Rosamond McKitterick and Jinty Nelson. Despite their own very busy lives, they found time to read and comment on the penultimate version of the entire manuscript. Their always prompt and pertinent feedback was tremendously encouraging, and, moreover, an act of real friendship. At the final stage and at short notice, I asked Stuart Airlie and Tom Noble to go over my last two chapters, which they did quickly and to my benefit; Tom also read the Introduction. I am grateful to them, and also to Jeroen Duindam, who shed an early modernist's light on chapter 5 and Carolingian court culture. Obviously, the final result remains entirely my own responsibility.

Throughout the years, I have incurred a great number of debts. Apart from those already mentioned, there are other colleagues and friends who, in various ways, have inspired me in the course of this project: Leslie Brubaker, Philippe Buc, Yitzhak Hen, Walter Pohl, Barbara Rosenwein and Chris Wickham. Since our days in the ESF programme *The Transformation of the Roman World*, Cristina La Rocca, Régine Le Jan, Julia Smith (members of 'group five', like Jinty Nelson and myself) and Ian Wood have been allies one can rely on. Furthermore, I have benefited from the generosity of Philippe Depreux, Albrecht Diem, Max Diesenberger, Gerda Heydemann, Conrad Leyser, Rob Meens, Christina Pössel, Steffen Patzold and Elina Screen, who have all shared ideas and unpublished work with me. On top of all this, I was blessed with a veritable support team in Utrecht: Carine van Rhijn, Irene van Renswoude, Erik Goosmann, Janneke Raaijmakers, Rutger Kramer and Bart Selten. They read various chapters at an early stage, gave me practical assistance, and generally cheered me on. At the proofreading stage, Janneke Raaijmakers came to the rescue, together with Wolfert van Egmond, Dorine van Espelo and Ruud Kroon. The map of the Carolingian world is Erik Goosmann's creation; Mariken Teeuwen kindly checked my translations for the Appendix. From California, Suzan Schönbeck masterminded the bibliography. To my infinite relief, the Utrecht undergraduate and graduate students who served as my guinea-pigs seemed to understand and enjoy what they read. This was perhaps the greatest boost of all, for it was mostly with such students in mind that I have written *The Penitential State*.

A note on annotation, citation and translation

For reasons of space, full titles of secondary literature can be found only in the bibliography. Throughout the footnotes, short titles have been used. Titles of frequently cited primary sources, editions and secondary literature have been abbreviated, and can be found in the list of abbreviations. Except for a few paraphrases within extracts from early medieval authors, biblical citations come from R. Weber's edition of the Vulgate, and translations of biblical texts from the Douai-Rheims Bible, in the version revised by Richard Challoner. I have gratefully made use of Tom Noble's unpublished working translation of the Thegan and the Astronomer, and of the translation of Ermold the Black by Carey Dolores Fleiner, annotated by Tom Noble. There are also excellent translations of Einhard's work by Paul E. Dutton, and of the *Annals of St-Bertin* by Janet L. Nelson. Unless indicated in the footnotes, I have usually made a translation of my own. To my regret, there was rarely room to complement these translations with the relevant Latin texts in the footnotes. I have resigned myself to this necessity, in the knowledge that the many primary editions are nowadays readily available on internet.

Abbreviations

AB	*Annales de Saint-Bertin*, ed. F. Grat, J. Vielliard and S. Clémencet (Paris, 1964)
AF	*Annales Fuldenses sive annales regni Francorum orientalis*, ed. F. Kurze, MGH *SRG* 7 (Hanover, 1891)
AfD	*Archiv für Diplomatik, Schriftgeschichte, Siegel- und Wappenkunde*
Agobard, *Epp.*	Agobard of Lyon, *Epistolae*, ed. E. Dümmler, MGH *Epp.* V (Berlin, 1898–9)
Agobard, *Cartula*	*Agobardi cartula de poenitentia ab imperatore acta* (833), MGH *Conc.* II/2, pp. 56–7
Agobard, *Opera*	Agobard of Lyons, ed. L. Van Acker, *Agobardi Lugdunensis Opera Omnia*, CCCM 52 (Turnhout, 1981)
AKG	*Archiv für Kulturgeschichte*
AMP	*Annales Mettenses Priores* 10, ed. B. von Simson, MGH *SRG* (Hanover, 1905)
Annales q.d. Einhardi	*Annales qui dicuntur Einhardi*, ed. F. Kurze, MGH *SRG* 6 (Hanover, 1895)
Ansegis	Ansegisus, *Collectio Capitularium*, ed. G. Schmitz, *Die Kapitulariensammlung des Ansegis*, MGH *Capit.* n.s. I (Hanover, 1996)
ARF	*Annales regni Francorum*, ed. F. Kurze, MGH *SRG* 6 (Hanover, 1895)
Astronomer	Astronomus, *Vita Hludowici imperatoris*, ed. E. Tremp, MGH *SRG* 64 (Hanover, 1995), pp. 280–554
BAV	Rome, Biblioteca apostolica Vaticana
BL	London, British Library
BM²	J. F. Böhmer and E. Mühlbacher, *Regesta Imperii*, I: *Die Regesten des Kaiserreichs unter den Karolingern, 751–918*, 2nd edn (Innsbruck, 1908)

BnF	Bibliothèque nationale de France
CCCM	Corpus Christianorum, Continuatio Mediævalis (Turnhout, 1966–)
CCSL	Corpus Christianorum, Series Latina (Turnhout, 1952–)
Charlemagne's Heir	P. Godman and R. Collins (eds.), *Charlemagne's Heir: New Perspectives on the Reign of Louis the Pious* (Oxford, 1990)
CSEL	Corpus Scriptorum Ecclesiasticorum Latinorum (Vienna, 1866–)
DA	*Deutsches Archiv für Erforschung des Mittelalters*
DOP	Adalhard/Hincmar, *De ordine palatii*, ed. Th. Gross and R. Schieffer, MGH *Fontes* 3 (Hanover, 1980)
Dutton, *CC*	P. E. Dutton, *Charlemagne's Courtier: The Complete Einhard*, Readings in Civilisations and Cultures 2 (Toronto, 1998)
EHR	*English Historical Review*
Einhard, *Epp.*	Einhard, *Epistolae*, ed. K. Hampe, MGH *Epp.* V (Berlin, 1898–9)
Einhard, *TMP*	Einhard, *Translatio et Miracula SS Marcellini et Petri*, ed. G. Waitz and W. Wattenbach, MGH *SS* XV (Hanover, 1888), pp. 238–64
Einhard, *VK*	Einhard, *Vita Karoli Magni*, ed. O. Holder-Egger, MGH *SRG* 25, 6th edn (Hanover and Leipzig, 1911)
EME	*Early Medieval Europe*
Epistola generalis (828)	*Hludowici et Hlotharii epistola generalis*, MGH *Conc.* II/2, pp. 599–601
Ermold	Ermoldus Nigellus, *In Honorem Hludowici Pii*, ed. (with French translation) E. Faral, in *Ermold le Noir: Poème sur Louis le Pieux et Épîtres au roi Pépin*, 2nd edn (Paris, 1964)
Flodoard	Flodoard, *Historia Remensis Ecclesiae*, ed. M. Stratmann, MGH *SS* 36 (Hanover, 1998)
FmSt	*Frühmittelalterliche Studien*
HJ	*Historisches Jahrbuch*
HZ	*Historische Zeitschrift*
JEH	*Journal of Ecclesiastical History*
LMA	*Le Moyen Âge*
MGH	Monumenta Germaniae Historica

Auct. Ant.	*Auctores antiquissimi*, 15 vols. (Berlin, 1877–1919)
Capit.	*Capitularia, legum sectio* II, *Capitularia regum Francorum*, ed. A. Boretius and V. Krause, 2 vols. (Hanover, 1883–97)
Capit. Episc.	*Capitula episcoporum* I–IV, ed. P. Brommer, R. Pokorny and M. Stratmann (Hanover, 1984–2005)
Conc.	*Concilia, legum sectio* III, *Concilia*: II, ed. A. Werminghoff (Hanover, 1906–8); III, ed. W. Hartmann (Hanover, 1984); IV, ed. W. Hartmann (Hanover, 1998)
Epp.	*Epistulae* III–VII (= *Epistulae merovingici et karolini aevi*, Hanover, 1892–1939)
Epp. sel.	*Epistulae selectae in usum scholarum*, 5 vols. (Hanover, 1887–91)
Fontes	*Fontes iuris germanici antiqui in usum scholarum separatim editi.*
Poet. lat.	*Poetae latini aevi carolini*, ed. E. Dummler, L. Traube, P. von Winterfeld and K. Strecker, 4 vols. (Hanover, 1881–99)
SRG	*Scriptores rerum Germanicarum in usum scholarum separatim editi, Scriptores rerum Germanicarum*, nova series
SRM	*Scriptores rerum Merovingicarum*, ed. B. Krusch and W. Levison, 7 vols. (Hanover, 1885–1951)
SS	*Scriptores* in folio, 30 vols. (Hanover, 1826–1924)
MIÖG	*Mitteilungen des Instituts für Österreichische Geschichtsforschung*
MS	manuscript
MMS	Monographien zur Geschichte des Mittelalters
NCMH II	*The New Cambridge Medieval History*, II, *c. 700–c. 900*, ed. R. McKitterick (Cambridge, 1995)
Nithard	Nithard, *Historiarum libri IV*, ed. and trans. P. Lauer, *Nithard: Histoire des fils de Louis le Pieux* (Paris, 1964)
Notker	Notker, *Gesta Karoli magni imperatoris*, ed. H. F. Haefele, MGH *SRG*, n.s. 12 (Berlin, 1959)
ÖNB	Österreichische Nationalbibliothek

PL	*Patrologiae cursus completus, series latina*, ed. J.-P. Migne, 221 vols. (Paris, 1841–64)
Radbert, *EA*	Paschasius Radbertus, *Epitaphium Arsenii*, ed. E. Dümmler, in *Abhandlungen der königlichen Akademie der Wissenschaften zu Berlin*, Phil.-Historische Abhandlungen 2 (1900), pp. 1–98
Radbert, *VA*	Paschasius Radbertus, *Vita Adalhardi*, *PL* 120, cols. 1507–82
RB	*Revue Bénédictine*
Relatio (833)	*Episcoporum de poenitentia, quam Hludowicus imperator professus est, relatio Compendiensis*, MGH *Conc.* II/2, pp. 51–5
RH	*Revue Historique*
SC	Sources Chrétiennes
Settimane	Settimane di studio del centro italiano di studi sull'alto medioevo (Spoleto, 1954–)
Thegan	Thegan, *Gesta Hludowici imperatoris*, ed. E. Tremp, MGH *SRG* 64 (Hanover, 1995), pp. 168–258
TRHS	*Transactions of the Royal Historical Society*

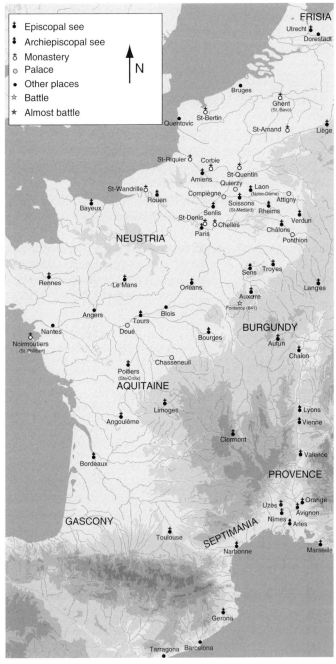

Map 1 The Carolingian world in the first half of the ninth century

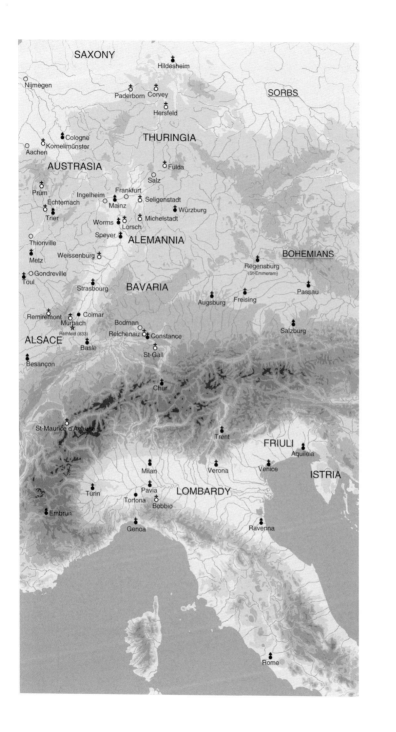

SAXONY

Hildesheim

Nijmegen

SORBS

Paderborn Corvey

Hersfeld

Cologne
Kornelimünster
Aachen

THURINGIA

AUSTRASIA

Fulda

Salz

Prüm

Ingelheim Frankfurt

Echternach Mainz Seligenstadt

Trier Würzburg

Worms Michelstadt

Lorsch

Speyer ALEMANNIA

Thionville

Metz Weissenburg

BOHEMIANS

Regensburg
(St-Emmeram)

Toul Gondreville

Strasbourg BAVARIA

Augsburg Freising Passau

Remiremont Colmar

Murbach

Rothfeld (833) Bodman

Reichenau Constance

ALSACE Basle

Besançon St-Gall

Salzburg

Chur

St-Maurice d'Agaune

Trent

FRIULI

Aquileia

Milan Verona Venice

ISTRIA

Turin Pavia LOMBARDY

Tortona Bobbio

Embrun

Genoa Ravenna

Rome

Map 2 Louis's succession arrangement of 817 (the so-called *Ordinatio imperii*)

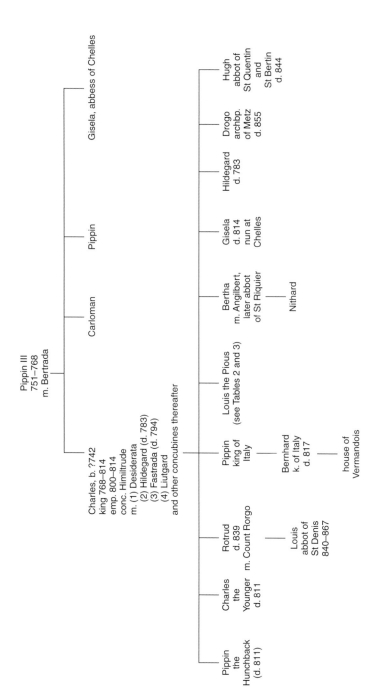

Pippin III
751–768
m. Bertrada

Charles, b. ?742
king 768–814
emp. 800–814
conc. Himiltrude
m. (1) Desiderata
    (2) Hildegard (d. 783)
    (3) Fastrada (d. 794)
    (4) Liutgard
and other concubines thereafter

Carloman

Pippin

Gisela, abbess of Chelles

Pippin
the
Hunchback
(d. 811)

Charles
the
Younger
d. 811

Rotrud
d. 839
m. Count Rorgo

Louis
abbot of
St Denis
840–867

Pippin
king of
Italy

Bernhard
k. of Italy
d. 817

house of
Vermandois

Louis the Pious
(see Tables 2 and 3)

Bertha
m. Angilbert,
later abbot
of St Riquier

Nithard

Gisela
d. 814
nun at
Chelles

Hildegard
d. 783

Drogo
archbp.
of Metz
d. 855

Hugh
abbot of
St Quentin
and
St Bertin
d. 844

Table 1 Pippin and Charlemagne

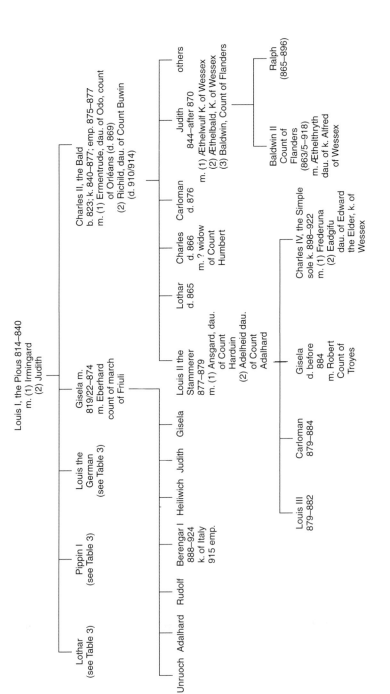

Table 2 The descendants of Louis the Pious I

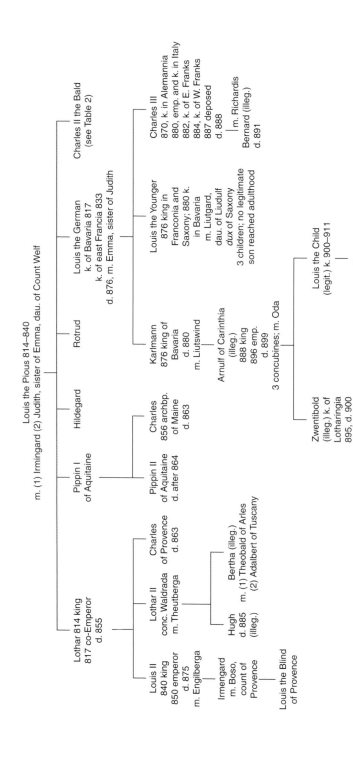

Louis the Pious 814–840
m. (1) Irmingard (2) Judith, sister of Emma, dau. of Count Welf

Lothar 814 king
817 co-Emperor
d. 855

Pippin I
of Aquitaine

Hildegard

Rotrud

Louis the German
k. of Bavaria 817
k. of east Francia 833
d. 876, m. Emma, sister of Judith

Charles II the Bald
(see Table 2)

Louis II
840 king
850 emperor
d. 875
m. Engilberga

Lothar II
814 king
conc. Waldrada
m. Theutberga

Charles of Provence
d. 863

Pippin II
of Aquitaine
d. after 864

Charles
856 archbp.
of Maine
d. 863

Karlmann
876 king of
Bavaria
d. 880
m. Liutswind

Louis the Younger
876 king in
Franconia and
Saxony; 880 k.
in Bavaria
m. Liutgard,
dau. of Liudulf
dux of Saxony
3 children; no legitimate
son reached adulthood

Charles III
870, k. in Alemannia
880, emp. and k. in Italy
882, k. of E. Franks
884, k. of W. Franks
887 deposed
d. 888
│ m. Richardis
Bernard (illeg.)
d. 891

Irmengard
m. Boso,
count of
Provence

Bertha (illeg.)
m. (1) Theobald of Arles
(2) Adalbert of Tuscany

Hugh
d. 885
(illeg.)

Arnulf of Carinthia
(illeg.)
888 king
896 emp.
d. 899
3 concubines; m. Oda

Louis the Child
(legit.) k. 900–911

Louis the Blind
of Provence

Zwentibold
(illeg.) k. of
Lotharingia
895, d. 900

no issue

Table 3 The descendants of Louis the Pious II

Introduction: The penitential state

In the autumn of 833, a crowd of prominent Franks gathered in the monastic church of St-Médard in Soissons. Those present witnessed the extraordinary spectacle of the mighty Emperor Louis prostrating himself in front of the altar, on a hair shirt, and publicly confessing 'that he had very unworthily handled the ministry that had been entrusted to him; that in so doing he had offended God in many ways and had put the church of Christ in public scandal, and that his neglect had led the people entrusted to him to multifarious disorder'.[1] Most of those present had come down from the nearby palace of Compiègne, where they were attending a royal assembly. This had been summoned for 1 October 833 by the Emperor Louis the Pious (814–40), yet it was not Louis himself, but his eldest son Lothar, who presided over the gathering. In June of that year, a military alliance of the emperor's three elder sons had confronted their father in the Alsace. Both sides were camped on either side of a wide-open space known as the Rothfeld. Before the armies could engage in battle, however, Louis's troops walked over to the sons' camp. Here, the massive desertion was taken as a sign that Louis's rule no longer enjoyed God's favour. After this divine judgement, as it was viewed by many, Lothar took over the leadership of the Frankish polity from his father. The assembly of Compiègne confirmed that he, Lothar, was now the legitimate emperor; the verdict of the bishops was that Louis should save his soul by submitting to a public penance. Lothar was among the witnesses in Soissons, with his retinue of great men, along with a throng of clerics and secular dignitaries, as many as the church would hold. They saw and heard Louis 'requesting' a public penance, so that he might atone for his sins and save his soul. Presenting the assembled bishops with a written confession, Louis exchanged his royal garb for that of a penitent. The public penance thus undertaken was intended to entail a definitive departure from secular office, which was effected by the bishops' imposition of hands, accompanied by the solemn

---

[1] *Relatio* (833), p. 53; see below, Appendix.

recitation of psalms and prayers. The emperor was to spend the rest of his life as a penitent, attempting to appease God, who had been offended.

This version of events comes from a document (*cartula*) in which the bishops who imposed this public penance painstakingly justified what they had done.[2] By voluntarily accepting this 'ecclesiastical' public penance, they claimed, Louis had definitively relinquished his imperial authority. He was to spend the rest of his life in atonement, placating God and saving his soul. From thenceforth, Louis's eldest son Lothar was to rule as sole emperor.[3] Things turned out differently, however. Within less than five months, Louis was back on the throne again: on Sunday 1 March 834, bishops solemnly reconciled him to the Church and reinstated him as a ruler. The rebellious alliance between Lothar and his brothers Pippin, king of Aquitaine, and Louis, king of Bavaria, had proved fragile. Their father cleverly made use of the fraternal rivalry that resurfaced almost immediately after the summer of revolt, secretly enlisting the support of his son Louis. A concerted offensive of paternal forgiveness was then unleashed on the rebellious sons. Louis and Pippin quickly returned to the fold. Lothar resisted, but in the course of 834 he too felt compelled to make an uneasy peace with his father. Bound by oaths that he would never rebel again, he was sent back to rule the kingdom of Italy, as he had before. None of those involved in the rebellion suffered bodily harm or loss of property. The only one of the bishops to be punished was Archbishop Ebo of Rheims, the ultimate scapegoat of this affair. It was now Ebo's turn to confess publicly and do penance.[4]

What is one to make of this imperial penance and its rapid undoing? Traditionally, Louis's humiliation has been viewed as one of the nadirs of Carolingian history. The great French medievalist Louis Halphen called the entire ceremony in Soissons an 'odious comedy', staged by the usurper Lothar and his accomplices.[5] More recently, the accusations against Louis and the penance imposed on him have been compared to the Stalinist show trials of the 1940s.[6] Did the emperor's authority ever recover from this profound onslaught? The general answer remains predominantly negative: the 'final years' from Louis's restoration in 834 until his death in 840 are usually presented as an unimportant epilogue to his reign.[7] Viewed from an

---

[2] See below, ch. 6.

[3] For a survey of the sources pertaining to the penance of 833, see BM[2], pp. 369–71; Simson, *Jahrbücher*, II, pp. 63–78. For a more extensive analysis of the penance and its context, see Halphen, 'La pénitence'; Noble, 'Louis the Pious', pp. 321–52.

[4] *AB*, s.a. 835, pp. 15–7.   [5] Halphen, *Charlemagne*, p. 252.

[6] Magnou-Nortier, 'La tentative', p. 640 ('le premier procès de type stalinien dans l'histoire de l'Occident').

[7] E.g. Boshof, *Ludwig*, p. 214; Kölzer, 'Kaiser Ludwig der Fromme', p. 16. The one explicit exception to this rule is Nelson, 'The last years'.

even more sombre perspective, the road which led to the battle of Fontenoy (841), and to the disintegration of the Carolingian empire, began at Soissons, where reform-minded bishops supported Lothar against his father. Having first gained far too much influence on Louis, this 'reform party' turned against the emperor when its ideals of political and religious unity were thwarted.[8] First, in 830, they drove the Empress Judith and her allies from the palace, and then, in 833, radical churchmen served as the instrument of Louis's deposition by cynically turning him into a public penitent. In short, it was the combination of ambitious churchmen and a weak emperor that succeeded in wrecking Charlemagne's inheritance. Bishops and other high-ranking clerics had their own goals, such as dominating laymen in general and rulers in particular, and they used their control of religion to achieve these aims.[9] This persistent view was sustained by a heritage of strident nineteenth-century anti-clericalism which has now largely vanished. It prevailed almost without challenge until the late 1970s, when a young American historian, Thomas Noble, argued that religion had not so much undermined Louis's empire as strengthened it.[10] At first, his arguments made little impression; even now, the notion that churchmen played a key role in undermining the Frankish state still lingers, and so does the idea that 'the Church' functioned as a separate and often antagonistic entity within the Carolingian body politic.[11]

When it comes to the impact of Christianity on the political theory and practice of this period, Louis's public penance in 833 is a test case, which poses some important questions. If this was indeed no more than the cynical deposition of a ruler who had become powerless, only thinly disguised as a religious ritual, why the need for such a disguise, and who exactly did Lothar and the bishops think they were fooling or convincing? If they claimed that Louis had offended God and scandalised the church, was this just empty rhetoric on the part of radical clerics? In my view, such rhetoric could work only if others shared its basic tenets as well. The imperial penance makes sense only if one accepts that there was an emperor who, together with his bishops and magnates, feared divine

---

[8] T. Schieffer, 'Krise'.

[9] Cf. Ullmann, *Carolingian Renaissance*, pp. 111–34, on the 'king's stunted sovereignty'; also Morrison, *The Two Kingdoms*, pp. 36–67.

[10] Noble, 'Monastic ideal' and 'Louis the Pious'; Noble built on his teacher François Louis Ganshof's article 'Louis the Pious reconsidered' (1957), which was more appreciative of Louis, but left religious aspects mostly aside; T. Schieffer, 'Krise', did integrate religion into his perspective, but blamed the reformers ('Reichseinheitspartei') for the break-up of the Carolingian empire.

[11] For a contrary view, see De Jong, '*Ecclesia*'.

retribution as the inevitable consequence of sin, and directed his policies accordingly. The notion that the leadership of this polity was accountable to God because of its divinely bestowed 'ministry' (*ministerium*) – as a ruler, a bishop, an abbot or abbess, or a count – was not just a figment of the clerical imagination, but a fascinating Carolingian adaptation of the ideas on ministry developed in Gregory the Great's *Regula Pastoralis*; by the ninth century, those with a *ministerium* included kings and counts. The implicit notion of accountability to God was shared by Louis (and Charlemagne, for that matter), the members of the ruling family, and their most trusted and high-ranking followers, the *proceres*. This expression often referred to lay magnates, but it would be a mistake to assume that this was always the case: a group of *proceres* could be headed by a bishop and three counts.[12] The ideal of exalted service held by this upper echelon was also being instilled into the ranks of the retainers and local sub-office-holders referred to as the *plebs*. The co-operation of such lesser men of honour, including the *Franci homines* and *centenarii*, and the *boni homines* judging at the royal/comital courts (*placita*), was crucial.[13] In the 830s, men from these middle ranks were to form the grumbling chorus that supported the rebellions against Louis, or suddenly stopped doing so.[14]

Although Carolingian authors distinguished between *clerici* and *laici*, theirs was not a vision of society that sharply opposed the clerical and the secular spheres. The different orders within the ninth-century leadership were thought to function in a complementary way, within a body politic that was modelled after the *ecclesia*. Just as Christ was the head of the body, his church, Louis was the head whose authority flowed into the various orders that were the limbs of this polity.[15] The emperor and his 'faithful men' (*fideles*), that is, the upper echelon of those who had sworn allegiance to Louis as lord, spoke the same kind of language and shared similar values.[16] Just as bishops needed to be at home in the world of high politics, high-born members of the laity needed to have access to the Latin Christian culture that was the norm at the court.[17] Even when opinions diverged and dissension was rife, this happened within a similar, or at least

[12] Astronomer, c. 61, pp. 534–6; the *proceres* who declared their loyalty to Louis in 814 (Astronomer, c. 21, p. 356, line 19) must also have comprised ecclesiastical magnates, or differently, Koziol, 'Is Robert I in hell?', pp. 250–1.
[13] MGH *Capit.* II, no. 260, p. 274; my thanks to Janet Nelson for making this important point.
[14] Astronomer, c. 48, p. 476, line 18; see also Astronomer, c. 7, p. 304, line 11.
[15] Fried, 'Herrschaftsverband', Guillot, 'Une *ordinatio* méconnue'.
[16] Nelson, 'The voice of Charlemagne'; Noble, 'Secular sanctity'.
[17] Patzold, 'Bischöfe'; McKitterick, *Carolingians*; Nelson, 'Literacy'; Wormald and Nelson (eds.), *Lay Intellectuals*.

mutually recognisable, frame of reference, which was not exclusively religious, but certainly heavily dominated by biblical and patristic thought. Regardless of their conflicting interpretations of Louis's penance in Soissons, contemporaries took this to be a religious ritual with potentially binding consequences. To eliminate God from early medieval narratives and their interpretation is to miss the point.[18]

At the court of Louis the Pious there existed a common agenda, a 'moral high ground' that was shared by and competed for by members of the emperor's inner circle. *Admonitio*, warning others of the dangers of sin, was a duty not just of bishops, but also of the ruler himself, and of the elite among his lay advisers. This moral high ground, and the way it was shared and competed for by those connected with Louis's court, including the ruler himself, is the focus of this study. Of Carolingian 'correction and emendation', the surveillance and social discipline which would ensure salvation, Michael Wallace-Hadrill remarked that, had this worked out, it would have resulted in a police state.[19] This is of course what the pre-modern Carolingian state could never become, even if its methods of defaming political opponents could at times be highly effective.[20] Rather than a police state, we are dealing with a political elite that was markedly preoccupied with sin and salvation – their own, and those of the 'Christian people' that made up the Frankish polity. The notion of *correctio* – otherwise known as 'reform' – was not a Carolingian invention, yet when Charlemagne seriously and systematically enlisted the co-operation of Alcuin and other learned courtiers, correction undeniably became a royal priority.[21] During Louis's reign, these ideas were tried and tested, and adapted accordingly. The turbulent years from 828 up to 834 are particularly interesting in this respect. Apart from a surge of texts during this brief period itself, an even more formidable body of narratives was produced in the next two decades, reflecting on the disturbing events of the recent past.

In writing this book, I have explored a substantial part of the historiography, biography, hagiography, letters and panegyrics of Louis's reign and shortly thereafter, trying to find out how this upper echelon of the Frankish polity aspiring to the moral high ground talked to each other, criticised each other and convinced each other. Put differently, what kind of political discourse prevailed in this period? To begin with, the

---

[18] As argued by Koziol, 'Is Robert I in hell?', pp. 236–8, 261–3, and Buc, 'The monster and the critics', pp. 444–6.
[19] Wallace-Hadrill, *Frankish Church*, p. 299. Wallace-Hadrill's views were inflected by his own life experiences, on which see I. N. Wood, 'John Michael Wallace-Hadrill'.
[20] See, for example, Airlie, 'Private bodies'.
[21] Ladner, *The Idea of Reform*; Brown, 'Introduction'.

contemporary expressions used to define Louis's penance in 833 merit further investigation, within their textual context. What, for example, was meant by notions such as *perturbatio populi*, *negligentia* or *scandalum*, the three key expressions in the accusations levelled at Louis in 833? This idiom mattered deeply, for it defined both reality as perceived collectively, and the limits of legitimate political action. My exploration of the political discourse at Louis's court includes the writings of the emperor's critics. Even when such men furiously rebuked Louis and those in his favour at the time, there was always the longing to be back at the court once more, as part of the inner circle. Whether authors criticised or supported the emperor, those who participated in the public debates of this period shared a common ground of ideals and values. Detecting the common ground of these debates and altercations has been another purpose of this project, and so has situating these debates within as precise a political context as possible.

What I do not offer, therefore, is pure 'discourse analysis'. Admittedly, I am interested in chronology, events and actions, and if there is enough information to do this, I cheerfully move back and forth between what happened and what was said about it. Neither is this book a full-scale study of Louis's reign, however, even though a study of this kind is long overdue, as is the critical edition of Louis's charters on which such a political biography should be based.[22] The continuity between Charlemagne's approach to governing the Christian people, now brought out in Rosamond McKitterick's new book on Charlemagne,[23] and that of Louis the Pious merits further investigation. In this book, however, I am mainly interested in a political community governed by the consciousness of having sinned, and by its search for strategies of atonement. To this community both Louis and those who opposed him belonged. Already in Charlemagne's reign, large-scale acts of collective expiation occurred with some regularity.[24] Louis returned to an older and more imperial model, however, exemplified by the Emperor Theodosius I and his public penance in 391: the emperor himself, admonished by Ambrose, publicly confessed his guilt in order to regain God's favour. At the assembly at Attigny in 822, the emperor voluntarily confessed his sins, especially those he had committed against members of his own family. During this public manifestation of atonement, Louis took the lead, while the bishops followed his 'salubrious example'. Together with their emperor, they were accountable to God for guiding their people to salvation.[25]

---

[22] Dickau, 'Kanzlei', I; Depreux, 'Kanzlei'; but see now Kölzer, 'Kaiser Ludwig de Fromme'.
[23] McKitterick, *Charlemagne*.
[24] Mordek, 'Zweites Kapitular von Herstal'; De Jong, 'Charlemagne's Church'.
[25] See below, chapter 3, pp. 122–9.

It is this fusion of a personal yet *ex officio* penance by political office-holders on the one hand, and the collective atonement they initiated in the polity at large on the other, that I have tried to capture in my title *The Penitential State*. Its connotations are deliberately ambiguous, referring to persons or groups who were penitents, and therefore in a 'state of penance', but also to a polity ('state') in which atonement had become one of the standard responses to adversity, disaster or endemic conflict. Whether wielded by the ruler, his bishops or his lay magnates, in this world authority was by definition of a religious nature. This is why my subtitle is simply 'Authority and Atonement in the Age of Louis the Pious': to add the qualification 'religious' would be superfluous.[26]

Research for this book started well over two decades ago, in 1986, when I still worked at the Catholic University of Nijmegen. With a group of advanced undergraduates, I began to study the texts generated by Louis's penance of 833. At the back of my mind, at the time, was Georges Duby's *Dimanche de Bouvines*, an admirable book in which one particular event, the battle of Bouvines of 27 July 1214, was put into its wider political, social and economic context, creating a window upon a society that experienced sweeping changes in all these areas. Likewise, we treated Louis's penance of October 833 as our access road into ninth-century politics and religion, but we also spent much time on the texts themselves: their structure, meaning and contradictory nature.[27] Increasingly fascinated, in the early 1990s I began to put Louis's public penance on my research agenda, to begin with in a pilot article addressing humility in the context of Christian kingship, and the way in which public penance in this period had worked as an instrument of royal discipline.[28] Subsequently, I set about exploring the wider context of 'Soissons, 833', investigating aspects such as the status of *paenitentia publica* in the post-Roman world, the structure of narrative texts on penance, biblical commentary as a hallmark of Christian kingship, the overlap between penance and monastic exile, and the changing connotations of *ecclesia* and *sacrum palatium*.[29]

An enduring interest during these years of circumnavigation was the semantic field I had explored with my students in Nijmegen: the Latin vocabulary used by ninth-century authors when they wrote about what

---

[26] My thanks to Conrad Leyser, who suggested this.
[27] In 1986, this resulted in an internal publication with fifteen articles and a translation of the key sources, notably the *Relatio* (833) and Agobard of Lyons's *Cartula*. This little grey book has accompanied me throughout my subsequent research.
[28] De Jong, 'Power and humility'.
[29] De Jong, *'Paenitentia publica'*, 'Transformations of penance', 'Pollution', 'The empire as *ecclesia*', 'Monastic prisoners' and *'Sacrum palatium'*.

really mattered in the world of politics and religion. My fascination with the construction of narratives owed very little to postmodernism, and almost everything to the *histoire des mentalités* of the 1970s. What interested me was how authors perceived their world, and what this revealed about a wider circle of men and women in their societies who shared this perspective. In the 1980s, I increasingly turned to British early medievalists for inspiring new approaches. For me, the outstanding model of how early medieval politics could be investigated effectively by the close reading of contemporary narratives was Janet Nelson's study of Nithard's *Histories*.[30] Nithard's history-writing was driven by the painful rhythm of the politics of 840–3, by an author who was part of the world he wrote about, and who tried to change it by his writings. In the second half of the 1990s there were others as well who inspired me to make narratives the basis of my work, as it had been before I got sidetracked by monasticism and child oblation.[31] Ian Wood's work on early medieval missionary hagiography was unabashedly text-oriented, and the same held true for Philippe Buc's *Dangers of Ritual*.[32] Reading fresh chapters as these books were completed, I increasingly felt that what we could know of the past was to be found in these multiple and complex narrative texts, and in the perspectives of their authors. This was also the general mood in the European research programme on the 'Transformation of the Roman World' (1992–7) in which I was privileged to take part. As Ian Wood concluded, in his summing up of our results, uncovering the ways in which individuals or communities represented themselves both consciously and unconsciously, in private and in public, had become one of the central concerns of this enterprise.[33] This approach, now with a firmer basis in manuscript studies, has been continued since 1997 in a research-student-oriented project called 'Texts and Identities in the Early Middle Ages'.[34] What interested and still interests us are the ways in which early medieval texts, narrative and otherwise, not just reflected but also affected perceptions of collective or individual identity, and how one might identify and understand such an impact. Our assumption is that texts can change human perceptions and conduct, and thereby, ultimately, the world as experienced by our authors and their audiences. It was mainly within the inspiring intellectual context of 'Texts and Identities' and those associated with it that I finally wrote this book.

---

[30] Nelson, 'Public *histories*'.   [31] De Jong, *In Samuel's Image*.
[32] I. N. Wood, *Missionary Life*; Buc, *Dangers of Ritual*.   [33] I. N. Wood, 'Report'.
[34] An enterprise founded by Walter Pohl, Ian Wood, Rosamond McKitterick and me in 1997, to ensure that what we had learned from the TRW project would be shared with a younger generation; since then, Régine Le Jan and her students have also joined in. The first collective publication is Corradini *et al.*, (eds.), *Texts and Identities*.

Back in 1986, when my students and I first studied the *dossier* of
Louis's public penance of 833, our guides into the topic were Thomas
Noble's two inspiring articles[35] and Rudolf Schieffer's highly informative survey of imperial penance from Theodosius the Great in Milan to
Henry IV in Canossa.[36] None of us was particularly worried by the
fact that for generations, Louis the Pious had been considered to be a
failure, for we were only dimly aware of it. What we saw was precisely
the opposite, namely a ruler who managed to regain his throne in less
than half a year, who simply bided his time and played along (as we
thought then), and had successfully bolstered his authority by atoning
publicly in 822, without being forced to do so by anybody. An important development at the time was the integration of that what had
once been 'church history', artificially segregated from political history,
into mainstream historical research, in its new guise as 'religious
history'.[37] Was this also on the minds of the organisers of a star-
studded international conference that met in Oxford in 1986, to reas-
sess 'Charlemagne's heir'? It is not clear from the proceedings, which
were published only in 1990 and lack an editorial introduction.[38]
Presumably, Karl-Ferdinand Werner's big, bold and beautiful overview
of Louis as a Christian ruler was meant to serve as such, but the fact
that this rich text comes to well over a hundred pages and, for reasons
unknown, was published in French, has not helped its dissemination.[39]
Whether consciously or not, the rebellions of 830 and 833 in general,
and Louis's penance in Soissons and its consequences in particular,
were not directly addressed by the Oxford conference. Even indirectly,
almost all participants to the conference managed to avoid the rebellions. Apart from Karl-Ferdinand Werner, who tried to include everything that might be remotely relevant to the reign of Louis in his
contribution, there was Janet Nelson, who wondered to what extent
the revolt of 833 and Louis's penance had impaired the last six years
of this emperor's reign. Hardly at all, was Nelson's conclusion, but she
seems to have delivered this message among a deafening silence of
disapproval.[40] In 1986, the turbulent early 830s were still too contentious for a revisionist agenda. As Philippe Depreux concluded in his
comprehensive historiographical overview of 1994, not much had
changed, despite all the decades of reconsidering Louis the Pious.[41]

---

[35] See above, n. 10.   [36] R. Schieffer, 'Von Mailand nach Canossa'.
[37] See the articles collected in Nelson, *Politics and Ritual*; Staubach, *Herrscherbild, Rex
christianus* and '*Cultus divinus*'. On these changes, see De Jong, 'Foreign past'.
[38] *Charlemagne's Heir*.   [39] Werner, '*Hludowicus Augustus*'.   [40] Nelson, 'The last years'.
[41] Depreux, 'Louis le Pieux reconsidéré?'

This can no longer be said. Over the past decade, the interest in 'Charlemagne's heir', his reign and his representation have been steadily growing. This has resulted, for example, in Matthew Innes's publications on royal representation and courtly socialisation,[42] as well as in Courtney Booker's investigation of the textual tradition and the long-term memory of Louis's penance in 833.[43] Not only has the once languishing edition of the charters of Louis the Pious received a new impetus;[44] there is now even an internationally funded project with the significant title 'The Productivity of a Crisis: The Reign of Louis the Pious and the Transformation of Carolingian Imperial Rule'.[45] This was a crisis that produced many texts, and yielded a transformation rather than a decline. Within the context of this project, some time-honoured concepts are in the process of being critically assessed, or even deconstructed, such as 'reform' or the 'party for the unity of the empire' (*Reichseinheitspartei*).[46] Here we touch upon a quintessentially German discussion, fuelled by the overwhelming importance of state formation in German history and historiography. For generations, German historians have tended to judge Carolingian political history by the measure of *Staatlichkeit* – or, rather, by the failure to live up to the ideals of modern state formation.[47] One of the key issues with regard to Louis's reign was the ideal of the unity of the Carolingian *Reich* (empire) as formulated in Louis's succession arrangement of 817, and the subsequent dissolution of this unity from the 830s onwards. Against the grim background of the ultimate failure of the Frankish state, different 'parties' were identified, which were pitted against each other, such as Judith's party, or Lothar's party, or the 'party for the unity of the empire' (*Reichseinheitspartei*) which, radicalised and turning against Louis, helped to undermine the very unity it had aspired to. To a large extent, these discussions have been an internal and German affair which the rest of the scholarly world has tended to steer clear of. It took a German historian, therefore, Steffen Patzold, to argue that there is

---

[42] Innes, 'Politics of humour' and 'Place of discipline'.

[43] Booker, 'A new prologue', 'Demanding drama', pp. 170–5, and 'Histrionic history'.

[44] As a project of the Nordrhein-Westfälische Akademie der Wissenschaften in Bonn; cf. Kölzer, 'Kaiser Ludwig der Fromme', with a provisional list of Louis's charters.

[45] 'Produktivität einer Krise: Die Regierungszeit Ludwigs des Frommen (814–840) und die Transformation des karolingischen Imperiums', funded by the Deutsche Forschungsgemeinschaft and the Agence nationale de la recherche, co-ordinated by Stefan Esders (Berlin) and Philippe Depreux (Limoges).

[46] Boshof, 'Einheitsidee' and *Ludwig* (with chapter headings such as 'The Reichseinheitspartei in die Defensive'. The notion of a 'Reichseinheitspartei' is central to T. Schieffer, 'Krise'; for an early critique of this concept, see Staubach, *Herrscherbild*, p. 45.

[47] E.g. Faulhaber, *Reichseinheitsgedanke*; Wehlen, *Geschichtsschreibung*. For a recent critical discussion, see Airlie, Pohl and Reimitz (eds.), *Staat*.

precious little in the narrative and documentary sources of the period
between 814 and 841 to indicate that political unity (*staatlich-politische
Einheit*) was an important issue for contemporaries, or any sign that a
threat to this ideal unity was the cause of the rebellions of 830 and 833.[48]
Reichseinheit was not so much a ninth-century ideal as a modern one,
which served the needs of historians preoccupied by state formation in
their own age.

Patzold's challenge to the older German historiography has
far-reaching consequences for our understanding of the rebellions of
830 and 833. If there was no clerical 'party' that, staunchly but unrealisti-
cally, defended a divinely sanctioned political unity, what then had the
entire conflict of the early 830s been about? Was it purely a matter of rival
factions pursuing their own interest under the cover of a lofty ideology?
Factional strife at Louis's court was indeed the motor that drove a series of
conflicts, but this is not to say that the religious idiom one encounters in
the sources can be understood as mere propaganda, or as a cover-up of the
secular and therefore more 'real' power politics underneath. God's will
and the way in which men related to it constituted the mightiest political
power in this world, and not one that should be reduced to a narrow
conception of clerical ideology.[49] This would suppose that these texts
were the result of deliberate manipulation, by authors who were not
only capable of lying – which of course they could, and did – but also of
positioning themselves completely outside the normative frame of their
society. But this was not the case. On the contrary, Ernst Tremp's expert
edition of the two biographies of Louis written by Thegan and the
so-called Astronomer reveals how much such authors relied on a broad
audience of court-connected clerics and laymen, and on the shared
values they could appeal to in order to mobilise this audience.[50]
Philippe Depreux's prosopography of the court of Louis the Pious has
become an indispensable instrument for the study of this elite.[51] The
ethos of faithful service to the king that imbued such high-ranking aristocrats and the sheer length of their service tended to be formidable. Louis
was surrounded not by a fickle and self-interested aristocracy, but by a
loyal upper echelon of magnates, the *proceres*, who derived at least a
considerable part of their stellar status from their and their predecessors'
record of royal service and their enduring access to the ruler. This typically
Carolingian aristocratic ethos of fidelity to the ruler and responsibility for

---

[48] Patzold, 'Eine "Loyale Palastrebellion"', with a bibliographical survey at p. 43, n. 3.
[49] As is argued, in different but equally illuminating ways, by Koziol, 'Is Robert I in hell?',
   pp. 236–8, 261–3, and Buc, 'The monster and the critics', pp. 444–6.
[50] Thegan, Astronomer.   [51] Depreux, *Prosopographie*.

the *respublica*, highlighted by both Stuart Airlie and Janet Nelson, should also be taken into consideration with regard to the rebellions of 830 and 833.[52] Rather than an inevitable conflict between the ruler and his always wayward aristocracy, ready to challenge their royal lord, what one encounters during the rebellions of the 830s was a disoriented aristocracy. Their core ideal of proper aristocratic conduct – *fides* – was undermined, as they anxiously decided to whom they should be loyal – Louis, or Lothar, or one of the other sons? Those who backed the wrong king and were banished from the court spent much time soul-searching and blaming others for their misfortune. When all is said and done, the rebellions of the 830s seem to have upset not only Louis himself but also everyone else who had been involved. First of all, there were the bishops who had to live down their collective responsibility for the imperial penance in Soissons in 833, and then there were the lay *fideles* who should have been faithful but were not, and had to suffer the consequences. Their diverse reflections after the event form the backbone of my own narrative.

This study is presented in six chapters, of which the first provides a succinct survey of Louis's life and reign. Although it has been written especially for newcomers to the subject, it is not a simple compilation of earlier surveys. Choices had to be made, and one of these was not to engage in protracted footnote wars with fellow specialists. I refer to the secondary literature only insofar as I have found it helpful; otherwise, I present my own view of the matter. The second chapter, 'Ninth-century narratives', is the result of my re-examination of the narrative texts that have had most impact on our modern understanding of Louis's reign. This chapter is also an introductory one, in that it aims to give those new to the topic some idea of the work and context of authors who figure frequently in the rest of this study. Yet here as well, I have blazed my own trail through scholarship, making new discoveries which reoriented the direction of my own research. Immersing myself once more in these ninth-century narratives in fact produced the next section, also consisting of two chapters, which explores the political and religious discourse of Louis's reign. Chapter 3 ('*Admonitio, correptio, increpatio*') investigates the idiom of admonition, warning and rebuke, attempting to provide a context for modes of address that too often have been understood as a one-sided and merely 'political' criticism of the ruler. 'The wages of sin' (chapter 4) discusses the emergence of a clear sense of a collective crisis, in the winter of 828–9, and investigates the way in which already existing perceptions of sin, divine retribution and atonement were further

---

[52] Airlie, 'Bonds of power' and '*Semper fideles?*'; Nelson, 'Ninth-century knighthood'.

articulated. The final and third section, again divided into two chapters, deals with the rebellions of the 830s. There is a relatively short chapter on the revolt of 830, not because this was an unimportant episode, but because I have already covered part of this ground before in some articles on the representation of the Empress Judith in contemporary exegesis and historiography.[53] The final and longest chapter (6) is, obviously, on Louis's penance of 833. All that we have is a wealth of contemporary and contradictory narratives after the event. From these, we may gather that Louis's tears belonged to public displays of humility,[54] but how the emperor coped with his own public penance (simply playing along, or feeling miserably guilty?) we can only imagine. As Thomas Noble saw very well when he wrote his dissertation in 1974, the presence of Pope Gregory IV on the scene of the conflict of 833 complicated matters considerably.[55] There was nothing quite so dramatic in terms of ecclesiastical intervention as a pope venturing north of the Alps in person. Admittedly, despite all the highly interesting theory on ritual, I have brought a minimal amount of this to bear upon the penances of Louis the Pious. What I mainly do in that last chapter is offer a close reading of the narratives concerning Louis's penance and reflect on what these may have meant to contemporaries who lived through these disturbing events, be it from a distance or, exceptionally, with a grandstand view. In a brief epilogue, finally, I try to finish a book that has not really ended. Even though no other medieval emperor ever submitted to a formal public penance, this kind of atonement by no means disappeared from the political arena – if only because Louis's penance of 833 was what every subsequent emperor or king wished to avoid.

---

[53] De Jong, 'Exegesis for an empress' and 'Bride shows'.   [54] Becher, 'Cum lacrimis'.
[55] Noble, *Louis the Pious*, pp. 321–52.

1   Louis the Pious (778–840)

A boy who became a king

Charlemagne's son Louis (*Hludowicus*) was born on 16 April 778 in the royal *villa* Chasseneuil, in Poitou.[1] His twin brother Lothar died as an infant, but Louis would survive his other brothers and become his father's sole successor to the Frankish empire. His mother, Hildegard, came from an ancient and leading Alemannian family, whose members had initially opposed the Carolingians, but then served the Frankish rulers continuously and well.[2] She was a fertile queen. Before these twins came along, she had already given birth to Charles and Carloman, and to two daughters, Adelaid and Rotrud. Three more daughters were to follow: Gisela, Hildegard and Bertha. There was nothing haphazard about the names chosen for Hildegard's sons: all were destined to rule. Whereas the elder boys were named after their royal father and uncle, the names of the twins – Louis/Clovis and Lothar/Chlothar, the most prestigious names of the Merovingian dynasty – underlined the continuity with a more distant Frankish royal past.[3] Already at this early stage, Charlemagne was developing a clear strategy for his succession. While the eldest, Charles, was to inherit the Frankish lands, the two younger brothers, Louis and Carloman, were to be the kings of two recently conquered *regna*, Aquitaine and Italy.[4] In the winter of 780 Charlemagne and Hildegard travelled to Italy with their two toddler sons and their baby daughter, Gisela. They celebrated Easter 781 in Rome, affirming the Franks' bond with the sacred city and its bishop, and the legitimacy of their two little sons as future rulers.[5] Pope Hadrian baptised Carloman,

---

[1] Astronomer, c. 3, p. 290, and c. 64, p. 554.
[2] Cf. Leyser, 'German aristocracy'; Airlie, '*Semper fideles?*', pp. 131–2, with further bibliography.
[3] Jarnut, 'Chlodweg und Chlotar'; Werner, '*Hludovicus Augustus*', pp. 20–1.
[4] By 768 Pippin III had managed to re-impose some measure of Frankish rule on Aquitaine; Italy became a Carolingian *regnum* in 774; see Fouracre, 'Frankish Gaul'.
[5] Angenendt, *Kaiserherrschaft*, pp. 64, 157; on relations between Charlemagne and Hadrian, see Noble, *Republic of St Peter*, pp. 138–83.

renaming him Pippin, after his grandfather who had saved the papacy from the Lombards – a suitable name for a future king of Italy. The pope then anointed Charlemagne's sons to be kings, Pippin of Italy and Louis of Aquitaine. Charlemagne and Hildegard dispensed their favours among ecclesiastical dignitaries according to proper hierarchy: Gisela was baptised in Milan, by Archbishop Thomas.[6]

A year later, at the age of four, Louis was 'sent to Aquitaine to rule as king'. His biographer, the Astronomer, gave a vivid portrayal of the *adventus* of the boy king in Aquitaine.[7] Louis was carried in a child's litter as far as Orléans, but there he was lifted on to a horse, girded with arms appropriate to his age, decked out in native Aquitanian dress and led 'according to God's will' to his new kingdom. The Astronomer's story highlights the imperial nature of Charles's expanding kingdom, full of different peoples with their own customs, as well as Louis's rootedness in Aquitaine. Louis was trained on the job, and Charlemagne closely monitored his youngest son's early education as king in Aquitaine.[8] In 785 his father summoned him to recently conquered Saxony, to attend an assembly in Paderborn. The entire royal family was present, arriving in the winter of 784/5, and remaining for Easter and most of the summer. Charlemagne's sons and daughters came, and his new wife Fastrada, whom he had married two years before, in 783, the very year in which Louis's mother Hildegard had died.[9] Charlemagne kept his son with him until the end of the autumn, the Astronomer explains, and then, with his father's leave, Louis returned to Aquitaine.

Both Thegan and the Astronomer depicted Louis as an exemplary and therefore obedient son, with Charlemagne ordering him hither and thither. In this way paternal dominance was emphasised, but so also was Louis's suitability for kingship; the relation between Louis and his own sons, be it negatively or positively, was to be portrayed in similar terms of paternal dominance and filial submission.[10] Not answering paternal summonses or leaving before getting express permission to do so were clear signs that the proper hierarchical order had been violated. When in 800 Louis invited his father to Aquitaine to inspect his realm, Charlemagne refused. He did so without publicly offending his son (*honorabiliter*), but he declined all the same, ordering Louis to come to him in Tours instead. Here Louis was received 'with great joy', and all was as it was supposed to

[6] *ARF*, s.a. 781, p. 56; *Annales q.d. Einhardi*, s.a. 781, p. 57.
[7] Astronomer, c. 4, pp. 294–6.
[8] Ibid., cc. 4 and 6, pp. 292–6, 300–4; Boshof, *Ludwig*, pp. 28–36.
[9] *ARF*, s.a. 785, pp. 68–70; Astronomer, c. 4, p. 296. This was the year in which Widukind and Abbio were baptised in Attigny.
[10] Kasten, *Königssöhne*, pp. 220–3.

be, with the son coming to the father instead of the other way around.[11] Observing the proper asymmetry in the relations between royal fathers and sons mattered deeply; in no way did a royal title entitle a son to any kind of equality with the senior monarch. He did, however, have the right to be treated with respect and dignity.

Adolescentia

King Louis was formally invested with his armour in 791 when he was fourteen years old, having travelled in his father's retinue from Ingelheim to Regensburg. He was allowed to accompany the campaign against the Avars up to the Wiener Wald, but no further; his father ordered him to stay in Regensburg with Queen Fastrada until he had returned.[12] Louis then got his marching orders for Italy, to help his brother Pippin fight Duke Grimoald of Benevento. All this was part of the life of the young king, whose father was busy fighting major wars of expansion against peoples perceived by the Franks as pagan enemies of their Christian kingdom, such as Saxons and Avars. Louis himself could fight like the best of them, a capacity he retained until the very end of his life, when he relentlessly fought the attempts of his third son, Louis the German, to assert his independent authority east of the Rhine.[13] At the very height of Louis's imperial power, shortly after 826, the poet Ermold the Black knew that nothing would please the emperor quite so much as singing the praises of the siege and capture of Barcelona (801/2), one of Louis's successful early military exploits. As Ermold claimed, the etymology of *Hludowicus* signified both the enjoyment of peace and the glory of warfare.[14]

When he married at the age of seventeen, the youthful king already had a daughter and a son by an earlier alliance.[15] Charles's judicious arrangement of this marriage was a step in the direction of a clearer distinction between so-called 'concubines' and legitimate wives. At the time, the idea of legitimacy was not yet stable, but a pattern was emerging that would become the norm during Louis's reign: only the offspring of a legitimate wife could succeed.[16] With hindsight, the legitimacy of Charlemagne's

---

[11] Astronomer, c. 12, p. 312; see also the preceding chapter on the year 804, when Louis was ordered up north to fight the Saxons, but they capitulated straight away; Louis was then dismissed.

[12] Nelson, 'The siting of the council at Frankfort' and 'Charlemagne – pater optimus?', pp. 275–6.

[13] Astronomer, cc. 60–2, pp. 532–46; cf. Goldberg, *Struggle*, pp. 87–94.

[14] Ermold, p. 10, lines 80–85.

[15] Alpais, who married Count Bego of Paris, and Arnulf, who became count of Sens; cf. Werner, 'Die Nachkommen', pp. 445–6, table 3.

[16] Konecny, *Frauen*, pp. 86–91.

real eldest son, Pippin, who was nicknamed 'The Hunchback', was contested, while his mother was dubbed a concubine.[17] Pippin's very name,
however, indicates that he had once been destined to be a king;
Hildegard's progeny, however, was given priority. A fruitless rebellion in
792 put an end to his royal aspirations; he was consigned to the monastery
of Prüm and did not return to the political arena, clearing the way for
Charles the Younger, who was to be groomed as the senior son and
successor. Meanwhile, Louis, like his father, married into the upper
echelon of the Frankish aristocracy. Louis's bride, Irmingard, was the
daughter of the Neustrian count Ingram, whose family had a long record
of serving the Pippinids. Irmingard was another prolific Carolingian
queen. As Thegan later observed, she gave birth to three sons 'while the
father was still alive' (patre vivente), and by this father Thegan meant
Charlemagne.[18] Lothar, who bore a Merovingian royal name, and also
the name of Louis's twin brother, was born in 795, Pippin in 797 and
Louis 'the German' in 806.

This was a royal family with a future ahead of it, yet nothing at this point
indicated that this future would lie outside Aquitaine. Louis energetically
set out to build his own kingdom, battling against Saracens and
(re)organising the Christian cult. In this respect as well, he was his father's
faithful son. Charles had in 789 proclaimed the overall restoration of the
cultus divinus in his kingdom by referring to King Josiah, who 'by visitation, correction and admonition, strove to recall the kingdom which God
had given him to the worship of the true God'.[19] Similarly, Louis's kingdom was bound together by royally regulated prayer.[20] With hindsight,
the Aquitanian Louis was hailed as a king who, because of his love of the
cult of God and the holy church, might well have been called a priest, and
who would have liked to enter a monastery, had not his father and, above
all, God's will, kept him from doing so.[21] This was a skilled author's
idealised image of a ruler who was equally at home in the world and the
cloister.[22] All the same, the impressive list of Aquitanian monasteries that
had been founded or reformed by Louis testifies to the very real energy
with which he set about 'reform' – that is, improving the efficacy of the cult
of God in general, and the quality of monastic prayer in particular. This
was also a matter of following in his father's footsteps: it was Charlemagne

[17] Einhard, VK, c. 20, p. 25; Nelson, 'The siting of the council at Frankfort', pp. 156–7. The
  only other text about the coniuratio Pippini is the Annales q.d. Einhardi, s.a. 792, p. 91.
[18] Thegan, c. 4, p. 178.
[19] Admonitio generalis (789), prologue, MGH Capit. I, no. 22, p. 54 ; Staubach, '"Cultus
  divinus"'; Brown, 'Introduction'.
[20] De Jong, 'Carolingian monasticism' and 'Charlemagne's church'.
[21] Astronomer, c. 19, p. 336.   [22] See below, chapter 2, pp. 83–4.

who began to impose the Rule of Benedict on all the monasteries of his realm. Louis followed suit, extending and intensifying observance of the *Regula Benedicti*, assisted by Witiza, a nobleman raised at the court of Pippin and Charlemagne. After his conversion to monastic life, Witiza was aptly renamed Benedict (of Aniane), for from that time he threw his weight behind making the Rule of Benedict of Nursia into the general norm for Frankish monastic life.[23] Louis set about the creation of an efficacious and unified army of prayer.[24] In 813 it was clear that he had succeeded better than any other Carolingian ruler, including his father.[25]

By then Charlemagne had lost his two eldest sons, and he himself was ailing. According to the poet Ermold the Black, it was Einhard, 'best loved by Charles, a man wise in intelligence and vibrant in goodness', who voiced the feelings of those who wished to see Louis designated and crowned as co-emperor before Charles died.[26] Using Einhard was strong ammunition indeed, for when Ermold wrote, Einhard was one of the most influential men at Louis's court. The *Royal Frankish Annals* give the short and non-panegyric version of the events of 813. After recovering from an attack of gout, 'he [Charles] then held the general assembly and placed a crown on the head of his son Louis, king of Aquitaine, whom he had summoned to him in Aachen, and he made him his partner in the imperial name; and he gave his grandson Bernard, son of Pippin his son, the rule of Italy and ordered that he be called king'.[27] At least since 811, when he had his will drawn up, the old emperor had been preparing for the end of his life.[28] The death of Charles the Younger towards the end of that year (4 December 811) did not make the father hasten to put Louis into position as the obvious replacement. The decision to do so took a lot of convincing from those who supported Louis; Charlemagne hesitated, and one year before he finally came round, he created real problems for his sole successor by setting up a rival dynasty in Italy.[29] Meanwhile, as the Astronomer observed, once Louis had learned of his brother Charles's death, 'the hope of ruling everything (*universitas*) welled up in him'. Louis put out feelers in Aachen, and even briefly considered acting upon the urgent call of 'both Franks and Germans' – meaning, everyone – to attend on his father at the court. Thus pressing a decision on the old emperor, but not wanting to arouse suspicion in his father, Louis held back, awaiting his

[23] Semmler, 'Benedictus II'; De Jong, 'Carolingian monasticism', pp. 629–34.
[24] Ardo, *Vita Benedicti*, c. 2, p. 201, line 37; Depreux, *Prosopographie*, pp. 123–9. Born in 751, Benedict died on 11 February 821. For a new working edition of Ardo's *Vita* by Gerhard Schmitz and collaborators, see www.rotula.de/aniane/text/praefatio.htm.
[25] Semmler, 'Karl der Große'.   [26] Ermold, lines 680–97, p. 54.
[27] *ARF*, s.a. 813, p. 138.   [28] Innes, 'Charlemagne's will'.
[29] Werner, 'Hludowicus Augustus', pp. 31–2.

father's summons. Eventually, this came. On 11 September 813, in the church of St Mary in Aachen, the old emperor made his only remaining son lift the golden crown and put it on his head, after Louis had solemnly promised to rule as his father admonished him to.[30] Louis had become a co-emperor in the style of Rome and Byzantium: he was now the 'consort of the imperial name' (*consors imperialis nominis*), as the court annalist expressed it.[31]

To Thegan we owe a detailed depiction of this coronation, highlighting the seamless continuity between father and son; to the Astronomer, a subtle evocation of a transition fraught with tension.[32] There was nothing strange about this, for Louis was an adult king who had his own network of loyal men. Now that the king of Aquitaine was in charge of the *universitas*, they expected their reward, while Charlemagne's inner circle worried about their entrenched positions at the court. Yet in this case, there was more than the usual anxiety surrounding a royal succession. Louis had not been his father's choice; for years on end, Charles the Younger had been the one to be crowned co-emperor, but he had suddenly died, and Charlemagne and his court could not adapt to this sudden change. Although nobody could deny that Louis was the legitimate heir, his rather sudden appearance in this role had the inner circle on tenterhooks.

The conquest of Aachen

Charlemagne died on 28 January 814, three months after Louis's coronation. His son had been waiting to take over. As if by premonition, the Astronomer claimed, Louis had called a general assembly in Doué, on the river Loire, for 2 February. On this significant day, the Feast of the Purification of the Virgin Mary, Louis would later summon the two general assemblies which confirmed his restoration to power after the rebellions of 830 and 833.[33] His solemn inauguration by his father in 813 did not guarantee a smooth transition, however. Some of the resistance to the newcomer is echoed in later stories in which Louis figured as the youngest son, overlooked and humble, who in the end turned out to be the best of the lot, precisely because of his humility. Apparently there were those who said that Louis should never have succeeded. Thegan parried these attacks by presenting Louis as the best of the three sons. He

---

[30] Thegan, c. 6, pp. 182–4; see also Ermold, lines 704–25, p. 56; Wendling, 'Die Erhebung Ludwigs'; see also Tremp, *Studien zu den Gesta Hludowici*, pp. 93–5, and Nelson, 'The Frankish kingdoms'.
[31] *ARF*, s.a. 813, p. 138. [32] Thegan, cc. 8–9, pp. 188–90; Astronomer, c. 21, pp. 346–50.
[33] Astronomer, c. 20, p. 344, c. 45, p. 464 (Aachen, 831), and c. 54, p. 500 (Thionville, 835).

contended that since the beginning of the world younger sons had surpassed their elder brothers, such as Abel, Isaac, Jacob and, most importantly, David, who had been elected and anointed king over all Israel at God's behest, and from whose seed came the incarnate Christ.[34] Other authors ascribed to great authorities from the *ancien régime*, such as Paulinus of Aquileia or Alcuin, the early insight that the youngest son was actually the most suitable successor.[35] These stories about Louis, the unlikely but perfect choice, also show that humility soon became a set ingredient of contemporary representations of this emperor.[36] For the Astronomer, Louis's mastering of his new empire meant gaining control of the palace in Aachen, first and foremost, as well as building a loyal inner circle on which he could rely. Upon learning the news of his father's death, the Astronomer suggested, Louis hurried north, as soon as he could assemble a decent retinue – but in fact his progress to Aachen was slow and hesitant, with messengers rushing to and fro in order to test the waters. The insecurity of Charlemagne's old entourage was embodied by Theodulf, bishop of Orléans, who, as Louis approached his city, anxiously asked for instructions: should he come and meet the emperor? Louis proceeded to Aachen,

for Wala, who held the highest place with Emperor Charles, was especially feared in case he might be organizing something sinister against the new emperor. But Wala came to him very quickly and with humble submission yielded to Louis's will, commending himself according to the custom of the Franks. After he had come to the emperor, all the Frankish nobles swiftly imitated him and a great crowd of them hurried to go and meet him.[37]

The atmosphere evoked by the Astronomer is one of suspicion and anxiety on both sides. Wala was the courtier with most authority in the realm, upon whom Louis was dependent for turning the opposition around – or did Wala have designs on the throne himself?[38] It is difficult to say, but Wala and his siblings, children of the youngest son of Charles Martel, did indeed constitute something like an alternative ruling family, from which some of Charlemagne's most trusted leadership had been drawn. All five of them were exiled in 814, or otherwise forced to leave the political arena. Adalhard, abbot of Corbie, was exiled to the monastery

---

[34] Thegan, c. 3, p. 178.
[35] Ermold, lines 599–633, pp. 48–9 (Paulinus); *Vita Alcuini*, c. 15, ed. Arndt, MGH *SS* XV/1, pp. 192–3 (Alcuin). See also Nithard, I, c. 2, pp. 4–6: 'Heres autem tante sublimitatis, Lodhuwicus filiorum eius justo matrimonio susceptorum novissimus, ceteris decedentibus, successit.' This is another variation on the theme of the youngest son.
[36] Glossed over completely by the *ARF*, s.a. 814, p. 148 ('summoque omnium Francorum consensu et favore'), and Thegan, c. 8, p. 188.
[37] Astronomer, c. 21, pp. 346–7.   [38] See Nelson, 'Women at the court'.

of St-Philibert on the island of Noirmoutiers, off the mouth of the Loire; Wala was tonsured and entered Corbie; Bernarius, a monk of Corbie, was sent to the community of Lérins, and Gundrada, prominent at Charlemagne's court, became a nun in Ste-Croix in Poitiers. Only Theodrada, abbess of the monastery of Notre-Dame in Soissons, could remain where she was.[39] Yet before all this happened and Wala was effectively barred from the court, it was up to him – Wala – and some other prominent men (*proceres*) to oust 'the entire troop of women – it was very large' from the palace at Aachen, 'only keeping a few that were useful for royal service'.[40]

By this vast troop of women Louis's many (half-) sisters and nieces were meant, plus other relatives who, like Gundrada, were female courtiers in their own right. Hinting darkly at the sexual misconduct of Louis's sisters, the Astronomer went on to portray the new emperor as a dutiful son carrying out his father's wishes, enabling his sisters to retire to their lands, or granting them lands if necessary.[41] And this was indeed what Louis was, to a large extent – a dutiful son who hastened to fulfil his father's last wishes. His young half-brothers Drogo, Hugh and Theoderic remained in the royal household,[42] and in the first years after Louis's accession, there was no sign of any friction with Bernard of Italy. In the Astronomer's narrative of Louis's early years in Aachen, Bernard surfaces time and again, invariably in a supportive role. Up to 816, he visited Louis's court regularly, contributing troops for Saxony.[43] Against those kinsmen he perceived as dangerous political opponents, he took swift and decisive action, removing them from the political arena. Monastic exile played a key role in this strategy. It had the advantage of being open-ended; if necessary, such exiles could be recalled, and reintegrated into public life.[44]

Upon his accession, Louis made his eldest son king of Bavaria, and Pippin succeeded him in Aquitaine. Here, the new emperor followed a strategy that was different from his father's. Rather than settling the younger sons in kingdoms and keeping the elder one with him at the court, it was the youngest, the later Louis 'the German', who stayed with his father. Inevitably, loyal men from Aquitaine were represented well in Louis's inner circle, such as his Archchancellor Helisachar, and

---

[39] Radbert, *VA*, cc. 33–5, cols. 1227A–1228B. Cf. Kasten, *Adalhard von Corbie*, pp. 103–4; Weinrich, *Wala*, pp. 28–33.

[40] Astronomer, c. 23, p. 352; see Nelson, 'Women at the court'.

[41] Astronomer, c. 21, p. 348: 'illud quod a sororibus illius in contubernio exercabatur paterno, quo solo domus paterna iniurebatur nevo'.

[42] Drogo, the eldest, was thirteen years old in 814.

[43] Werner, '*Hludovicus Augustus*', pp. 37–8.   [44] De Jong, 'Monastic prisoners'.

Bego, who became count of Paris in 814 and had married Alpais, Louis's firstborn daughter by a concubine.[45] His trusted monastic advisor Benedict of Aniane was summoned and established in the newly founded monastery of Inden (Kornelimünster), not far from Aachen.[46] Others connected with Louis's youth landed important positions. In 816 Ebo was appointed archbishop of the most important see of the realm, Rheims. This talented young cleric owed his freedom to Charlemagne and his training to Louis.[47] Ebo was no Aquitanian, for he came from *Germania*, on the other side of the Rhine, and neither were some other major figures in Louis's trusted entourage. In December 814 the formidable Hilduin became Louis's 'archchaplain of the sacred palace'. This nephew of Queen Hildegard was abbot of St-Denis, where he raised and educated Hincmar, the future archbishop of Rheims.[48] Whereas Charlemagne had appointed an archbishop to this position, that is, Hildebold of Cologne, Louis reverted to the habit of his grandfather Pippin, and selected an abbot for the function. Einhard is forever associated with Charlemagne because of his famous biography, yet he was as much Louis's as Charlemagne's courtier. Like other favoured 'men of the palace', as they referred to themselves, Einhard was the lay abbot of a handful of monasteries, which were all bestowed on him by Louis, not by Charlemagne. Moreover, in 815 Einhard and his wife Imma were richly endowed by the emperor with property in Seligenstadt, as a reward for his loyal service.[49] This service was to continue until Einhard's death in March 840, only some months before Louis himself died.[50]

In these first years the new emperor and his team made a flying start. The royal chancery worked overtime, producing more charters in one year than Charlemagne had issued in a decade. Admittedly many of these were confirmations of older privileges, but these also signalled the royal impact on regional and local affairs. In the years 814–17 Louis resided mostly in Aachen. There were assemblies in Frankfurt, Compiègne, Nijmegen and Paderborn, and, of course, hunting expeditions in the Ardennes; yet for Louis the palace in Aachen remained his main residence, as it had been for his father since his imperial coronation.[51] In the summers of 816 and 817, the ecclesiastical leadership of the realm gathered there in order to regulate the lives of monks, canons (*clerici canonici*) and canonesses (*sanctimoniales*), formulating the precise distinction between these

---

[45] Kasten, *Adalhard von Corbie*, pp. 88–91.   [46] Ardo, *Vita Benedicti*, c. 35, p. 215.
[47] See below, ch 6, p. 253.   [48] Depreux, *Prosopographie*, pp. 250–6.
[49] Smith, 'Einhard', pp. 57–67; Dutton, *CC*, xvii.
[50] Louis turned to Einhard for advice on the meaning of Halley's comet in 837; cf. Einhard, *Epp.*, no. 40, p. 130.
[51] On Charlemagne and Aachen, see Nelson, 'Aachen'. Werner, '*Hludowicus Augustus*', p. 8, notes that the majority of Louis's assemblies (fifteen in all) took place in Aachen.

different 'orders'. Not only abbots, monks and bishops took part in the debates, but also secular magnates and, above all, the emperor himself. In 816 Louis opened the meeting, admonishing those present to strive for unity of canonical life, even if authoritative texts on the topic were rare, and to ask for a sign from God by fervent prayer.[52] During the deliberations on the monastic office – should it be the Roman one followed since the days of Pippin, or the one prescribed by Benedict's Rule? – the emperor came down heavily in favour of the latter.[53] From now on, the Rule of Benedict not only was to become the only monastic rule, but also was to be followed in a unified fashion by all monks and nuns. The regularity of their life was a condition for the efficacy of their prayer; both should be 'correct' in order to please God. The rise of the *Regula Benedicti* as the only text governing monastic life had already begun during Charlemagne's reign. In 802, during a similar council at Aachen, Adalhard and Benedict of Aniane had publicly disagreed on the correct interpretation of the *Regula Benedicti*.[54] From 814 onwards, however, Adalhard was in monastic exile, and Benedict had become the dominant figure who helped Louis to correct and improve religious life in the realm.[55] With this reform offensive, Louis followed in his father's footsteps. In the last five years of his life, Charlemagne had intensified his efforts at creating a truly Christian polity, starting with an empire-wide inquiry on baptism, and culminating in the convocation of five councils in 813, which gathered in locations spread throughout the realm.[56] To aim not only for one monastic rule, but also for a unified monastic practice, was a logical step forward, and one, moreover, which had already been taken in Louis's kingdom of Aquitaine. All the same, Louis's brand of *correctio* and *emendatio*, the contemporary Latin expression for 'reform', was by no means limited to monasticism, or to the church in general. In many other areas as well, 'improvement' was the name of the game: judicial procedure, the levying of tolls, the protection of the poor and weak, the extension of markets and mints and, in general, the increase of the efficiency of local administration and its contact with the centre.[57] As

---

[52] *Institutio canonicorum Aquisgranensis*, prologue, MGH *Conc.* II/1, p. 312; cf. Semmler, 'Mönche und Kanoniker'.

[53] Hildemar of Corbie/Civate, *Expositio*, c. 14, p. 302. Hildemar, dictating his commentary around 840, remembered the 'synod in Francia' (Aachen 816) where these matters were discussed. 'Nam piissimus imperator Ludovicus voluit, ut monachi secundum regulam facerent officium.' Semmler, 'Die Beschlüsse'.

[54] Kasten, *Adalhard von Corbie*, pp. 93–100; De Jong, 'Carolingian monasticism', pp. 629–34.

[55] Semmler, 'Benedictus II'. See also De Jong, 'Carolingian monasticism', pp. 629–34.

[56] Keefe, *Water and the Word*; De Jong, 'Charlemagne's church', pp. 125–9; McKitterick, *Charlemagne*, pp. 306–15.

[57] Boshof, *Ludwig*, pp. 108–20; Werner, '*Hludowicus Augustus*', pp. 69–79.

during Charlemagne's reign, the ecclesiastical and secular domains were distinct, yet by no means separate. Because of the overriding importance of the divine cult, the so-called 'state of the church' (*status ecclesiae*) was perceived as a precondition for the prosperity of the polity (*regnum*). To rule properly was to work tirelessly and visibly for the betterment of these interlocking worlds. For Louis, 'reform' was not a change of course or an innovation. On the contrary, it meant proving one's mettle as a ruler and showing oneself a worthy successor of the great Charlemagne.

Dynasty

Consolidating his paternal inheritance in all possible ways, with himself and his own offspring firmly in charge, was at the top of Louis's agenda in those first years after he succeeded his father. Quite apart from all the business transacted and the networking conducted, assemblies and councils were ideal platforms for the representation of royal authority. Here, Louis publicly became the Christian emperor, responsible for the salvation of his people. The fact that in the autumn of 816 Pope Stephen IV rushed north to ensure the continued Frankish protection of Rome and its pontiffs is a clear indication of what had been accomplished in terms of the new ruler establishing himself. The meeting between the pope and the emperor in Rheims was the occasion for an abundance of mutual gestures of friendship. The festive anointing and coronation of Louis and Irmingard on 5 October also fell into this category. Louis was already an emperor, and the papal crowning could be seen as mere confirmation of this, and a *quid pro quo* for Louis's support of the papacy.[58] In Rome, the event did not make much impression, at least judging by the *Liber pontificalis*, which only recorded the many gifts that had been showered on the short-lived Pope Stephen IV.[59] In the north, however, where the ruler and his entourage benefited most from the association with Rome, a different perspective prevailed: Frankish authors made much of the imperial coronation, and of the wondrously beautiful golden crown brought from Rome.[60] It was, said the Astronomer, an imperial diadem.[61] Ermold,

---

[58] Boshof, *Ludwig*, p. 137, speaks of a 'Gegenleistung'. Noble, *Republic of St Peter*, pp. 302–8, on the resulting agreement, known as the *Pactum Ludovicianum*.

[59] *Liber pontificalis*, c. 99.2; Davis, *Lives of the Eighth-Century Popes*, p. 235. It is the Frankish sources that devote much attention to the coronation in Rheims.

[60] *Chronicon Moissacense*, s.a. 816, ed. Buc, 'Ritual and interpretation', p. 207; Ermold, lines 848–1137, pp. 66–88; Thegan, cc. 16–17, pp. 196–8; Astronomer, c. 26, pp. 366–8.

[61] Astronomer, c. 26, p. 368; see also *Ordinatio imperii* (817), prologue, MGH *Capit.* I, p. 271: 'more solemni imperiali diademate coronatum nobis et consortem et successorem imperii … constitui'. Louis is the subject of 'constitui'; as in 813, it was the reigning emperor who made his son into a co-emperor (*consors*).

who elaborated on what he expected would please the emperor, waxed eloquent, line after line, on the pope's arrival, the many mutual gifts and gracious speeches, and, above all, on the anointing and coronation of Louis and Irmingard. With poetic licence, Ermold claimed that the crown in question had been Constantine's, and a gift from St Peter himself.[62] That the Empress Irmingard was included in all depictions of the ceremony should not be overlooked.[63] The papal blessing of the *augusta*, the mother of the next emperor, ensured the continuity of the imperial dynasty. The lofty phrases Ermold put into Stephen's mouth reflected the Frankish understanding of what had happened in Rheims, the ancient city where Louis's namesake Clovis had once been baptised:

> May the Almighty, who increased the race of Abraham, grant that you may see the children by whom you will be called grandfather. May he grant you progeny, double and triple your descendants, so that from you a rich harvest will grow, which will rule the Franks as well as Roman might, as long as the Christian name resounds throughout the world.[64]

The seed of Louis and Irmingard alone received the papal benediction; from their descendants a harvest of rulers would spring forth. This is the stuff of panegyric, but it was also the view of the new emperor and his entourage, and of the empress herself, one may assume, whose progeny stood to inherit this vast realm as well as the purported crown of Constantine.

Given all this emphasis on Louis's lofty imperial status, it is understandable that he began to make arrangements for his succession. Charlemagne had done the same in 806, well before his death. Such measures, after all, were for the future, not for the present.[65] In July 817 Louis, aged thirty-nine, issued the *Ordinatio imperii*, as modern editors have called this text. This capitulary limited the succession to his three legitimate sons. The bulk of the realm was to go to his eldest son Lothar, who was made co-emperor; Pippin was to have the kingdom of Aquitaine, and Louis that of Bavaria, yet they were to exercise full royal power only upon the death of their father, and with due reverence for their elder brother, bringing him annual gifts and consulting him in crucial matters; similarly, Lothar would exercise his full imperial rights only once his father had died.[66]

---

[62] Ermold, lines 1076–7, p. 84.

[63] As Queen Bertrada was in 754; see Stoclet, 'La "clausula"'; Nelson, 'Bertrada'.

[64] Ermold, pp. 84–5, lines 1091–7.   [65] Kasten, *Königssöhne*, pp. 180–7.

[66] *Ordinatio imperii* (817), MGH *Capit.* I, no. 136, pp. 270–3. There is only one extant copy, which dates from *c.* 830: Paris, BNF, lat. 2718, fol. 76r–77v. On this manuscript and its close relation with the court, see McKitterick, 'Zur Herstellung von Kapitularien'; Patzold, 'Eine "loyale Palastrebellion"', pp. 58–9.

To nineteenth- and twentieth-century historians, preoccupied with state formation and political unity, this capitulary seemed a sudden break with tradition, favouring the unity of the empire over the traditional principle of partition.[67] Yet it should be kept in mind that *Ordinatio* is a modern title; in the one surviving manuscript it was called *divisio imperii*. This notion of 'division' was also central to Charlemagne's *divisio regnorum* of 806, not because this meant that anyone had the break-up of the Frankish polity in mind, but because contemporaries referred in these terms to a succession arrangement which provided for the participation in government of various sons.[68] The succession plan of 817 was presented as having occurred during an assembly held in Aachen 'as usual' (*more solito*),[69] following the example set by Charlemagne in 813: those present at the assembly consented to Louis's making one of his sons emperor during his lifetime, as Charles had done with Louis himself.[70] There were clear similarities with Charlemagne's *divisio* as well. Both settlements favoured the eldest of the three legitimate sons, giving the firstborn the undivided patrimony, while the younger brothers received only the more recently acquired *regna*.[71] Moreover, in both cases the father retained full control until his death; a son might be a king or even co-emperor, but he remained in all respects subordinate to the senior emperor.[72] But of course there were differences as well. Charlemagne had stipulated that, were his eldest son Charles to die, his inheritance should be divided between his brothers Pippin and Louis.[73] In 817, however, the succession was entirely vertical, with sons being favoured over brothers. The principle of a senior son succeeding to the majority of the realm, and exercising authority over his brothers, who received more modest shares, was applied all the way down. In the next generation, the senior brother was not necessarily to be the eldest; if there were more contenders, 'the people shall assemble and elect the one that God desires'.[74] In other words, what Louis prescribed in both the empire and the sub-kingdoms, at least in the generation after his sons, when he was no longer there to make the decisions, was succession by one son who was acknowledged as the most suitable and therefore legitimate heir by the leading men of the realm.

[67] For a brief survey and analysis of the German historiography on the issue of *Reichseinheit* versus *Teilungsprinzip*, see Patzold, 'Eine "loyale Palastrebellion"', pp. 43–6.
[68] Patzold, 'Eine "loyale Palastrebellion"', pp. 46–55.   [69] *ARF*, s.a. 817, p. 146.
[70] *Chronicle of Moissac*, BnF lat. 4886, fols. 52v–54v, ed. Buc, p. 208: 'Tunc omni populo placuit ut ipso se viventem constitueret unum ex filiis suis imperare sicut Karolus pater eius fecerat ipsum.'
[71] Nelson, *Charles the Bald*, p. 73; Classen, 'Karl der Große'.
[72] Kasten, *Königssöhne*, p. 172.   [73] *Divisio regnorum*, c. 4, MGH, *Capit.* I, no. 45, pp. 127–8.
[74] *Ordinatio imperii*, c. 14, MGH *Capit* I, no. 136, pp. 272–3; Kasten, *Königssöhne*, p. 180; what Louis prescribed, down to the grandsons, is one-son succession, not primogeniture.

This is not quite the 'unity of empire' it has been made out to be, with shades of modern state formation, yet Louis's concerted effort to create some real staying power for his own dynasty is unmistakable.

As Steffen Patzold has rightly argued, much confusion has been created by the modern proclivity to translate *imperium* as 'empire' in the territorial sense of the word, rather than as 'imperial rule', which was its predominant ninth-century meaning. The *unitas imperii* mentioned in 817 was not an indivisible empire, but the unanimity of imperial rule, of Louis with his co-emperor and younger sons, and of Lothar in a similar setting after Louis's death.[75] Thegan's rendering of the division of 817 is a good example of how the expression *imperium* could be employed by contemporaries, in a non-territorial sense: Louis gave Lothar the title of *imperator*, so that after his father's death he would receive all the kingdoms (*omnia regna*) which God had given him by his father's hand, and he would have the title and authority of his father (*nomen et imperium patris*).[76] Yet this very title and authority implied a tremendous responsibility, expressed during the 817 assembly in a way that made a deep impression on those present. Extensive deliberation, with mutual admonition of the emperor and his great men, yielded the view that it was not enough simply to regulate the succession 'according to paternal custom'. The reason offered was that the imperial authority granted by God could not be torn by human division, 'lest scandal arise in the holy church because of this and we incur the outrage of Him on whose might all rights to kingdoms are based'. Divine approval was then solicited, and received, by three days of fasting, prayers and almsgiving.[77] Involving God in the decision-making process was Louis's deviation from paternal custom, and so was, more generally, his public recognition that to be an emperor meant to prevent human discord from upsetting the cult of God or offending the divine Ruler of all kingdoms.[78] Above all, the assembly in 817 set out an ideal of a unanimous co-operation between the father, the senior son and co-emperor,

---

[75] Patzold, 'Eine "loyale Palastrebellion"', pp. 46–9.

[76] Thegan, c. 21, p. 211, with the usual exemplary translation by Ernst Tremp: 'den Titel und Herrschaft des Vaters'.

[77] *Ordinatio imperii* (817), MGH *Capit.* I, no. 136, p. 270–1: 'ne forte hac occasione scandalum in sancta ecclesia oriretur et offensam illius in cuius potestate omnium iura regnorum consistunt incurreremus. Idcirco necessarium duximus, ut ieiuniis et orationibus et elemosinarum largitionibus apud illum obtineremus quod nostra infirmitas non praesumebat. Quibus rite per triduum celebratis.' The other mention of the three-day fast is in the *Chronicon Moissacense*, p. 208: 'Tunc tribus diebus ieiunatum est ab omni populo. Hac lętanię factę post hęc iam dictus imperator Clotarium qui erat maior natum ymperatorem elegit.'

[78] Patzold, 'Eine "loyale Palastrebellion"', pp. 24–30, is right in seeing the three-day fast as an innovation which diverged from the *mos parentum*, but I fail to see why Benedict of Aniane should have been the one to introduce this.

and the junior royal brothers. What held this family firm together was their joint protection of the *sancta ecclesia*; conversely, the unity of 'the church' – that is, the community of those who worshipped God correctly – transcended incidental division, lending cohesion to the expanding Frankish polity. All this mattered deeply. For 821, the *Royal Frankish Annals* (followed by the Astronomer) relate that 'the partition of the kingdom between his sons that had been decided upon and recorded in previous years' was read aloud and confirmed by the oath of the leading men (*optimates*) during the assembly at Nijmegen.[79] This was the plan for the future.

One king who fell by the wayside was Bernard of Italy, Charlemagne's grandson and Louis's nephew. He was not mentioned in the *Ordinatio imperii*; Lothar would 'be our successor, if God wills it', and this included the kingdom of Italy. Thus, Bernard was written out of the story of succession: his son was not to be a king.[80] Upon his return to Aachen in the autumn of 817, only some months after the assembly that agreed on the new succession arrangements, Louis got news that Bernard, 'considering tyranny' under the influence of wicked men, had put troops on the passes that gave access to Italy, and had all the cities of Italy swear allegiance to him, 'which was partly true, but partly false'. Rumour ran rife.[81] After his failed revolt, all kind of accusations were levelled at Bernard: he intended to usurp the empire by tyranny,[82] he wanted to expel his uncle from his realm, and he had been born to a concubine.[83] So he may have been, but the problem with Bernard, at the time, was mainly that he was not a son of Louis; he could rule as king of Italy, but only on the authority of his uncle, and as long as the latter was alive.[84] What Bernard was fighting for, it seems, was the continuity of his own offspring as kings of Italy.

As swiftly as it started, Bernard's rebellion was suppressed. It ended in April 818 with most of the rebels being exiled or sent into 'internal exile' in monasteries. For good measure, this included Louis's half brothers Drogo, Hugh and Theoderic, not because they had been in league with Bernard, but because they were male family members now old enough to be a focus for opposition. As Thegan put it, they were tonsured and educated

---

[79] *ARF*, s.a. 821, p. 155; on the oaths sworn to the *Ordinatio* of 817, see also Astronomer, c. 34, pp. 400–2; Radbert, *EA* II, c. 10, p. 74; Agobard, *De divisione imperii* c. 4, p. 248, lines 23–7.
[80] *Ordinatio imperii*, c. 17, p. 273.
[81] *ARF*, s.a. 817, p. 147. The most extensive source for Bernard's rebellion, with mention of Bishop Theodulf of Orléans as part of the conspiration, is the *Chronicon Moissacense*, s.a. 817, ed. Buc, pp. 208–9.
[82] *Chronicon Moissacense*, s.a. 817, ed. Buc, p. 208: 'voluit in imperatorem et filios eius insurgere et per tyrannidem ymperium usurpare'.
[83] For the latter two accusations, see Thegan, c. 22, p. 210; cf. Werner, *Hludowicus Augustus*, pp. 34–7.
[84] See Classen, 'Thronfolge', pp. 227–8, who argues that the problem with Bernard had been created by Charlemagne; likewise, Werner, '*Hludowicus Augustus*', pp. 31–3.

in the liberal arts 'in order to mitigate discord'.[85] Drogo and Hugh were the sons of Charlemagne and Regina, a concubine. After the amnesty and reconciliation of 821, these two half-brothers became Louis's staunchest allies. Drogo became bishop of Metz in 823 and Louis's archchaplain in 834; Hugh was appointed abbot of St-Quentin and St-Bertin, shortly after Louis's restoration in 834.[86] Bernard's punishment, however, ended in a tragedy that would haunt Louis in years to come. By royal pardon Bernard's death sentence had been converted into the lesser punishment of blinding. In his succession arrangement of 806, Charlemagne had emphatically forbidden his sons to inflict this kind of disabling mutilation on their younger kinsmen, yet Louis (or his henchmen) resorted to it once more.[87] Within days Bernard died from the consequences.[88] At the assembly of Compiègne in 833 the first accusation brought against the emperor was that he had allowed his nephew to be killed, thereby violating the solemn promises he had made to his father in 813 to protect his younger siblings and relatives.[89] Was the emperor guilty of the murder of a kinsman, or had he been *piissimus* indeed, intending all along that Bernard's life should be spared? These were questions asked by contemporaries, and modern historians still tend to take sides along similar lines.[90] Both Louis's biographers were of course adamant that Louis had wished to spare Bernard, to the extent that the Astronomer blamed the victim himself: Bernard had brought death on himself by offering resistance while being blinded.[91] One strand of criticism, voiced in the 820s through visionary literature, blamed the Empress Irmingard, whose furthering of her sons' careers had caused Bernard's revolt, and thereby, indirectly, his death.[92] The empress's own demise, half a year later, was seen by some as a just punishment for her sins.[93]

---

[85] Thegan, c. 24, p. 214: 'discordiam ad mitigandam'.

[86] Depreux, *Prosopographie*, pp. 163–7, 265–8; Theoderic (born in 807) was the son of Charlemagne and Adallinde; after 818 he disappears from the sources, so he may well have died. Depreux, *Prosopographie*, pp. 382–3.

[87] *Divisio regnorum*, c. 18, MGH *Capit.* I, no. 45, pp. 129–30.

[88] Effectively summarised in *Chronicon Moissacense* s.a. 817, ed. Buc, 'Ritual and interpretation', p. 208: 'Sed piissimus imperator pepercit vitę eorum iussitque ipsi regi Barnardi oculos erui. Sed cum factum fuisset die tercius mortuus est.'

[89] MGH *Capit.* II, no. 195, p. 54.   [90] Noble, 'Revolt'; Jarnut, 'Kaiser Ludwig'.

[91] Astronomer, c. 30, p. 386; Thegan, c. 23, p. 212, who writes of Louis's grief and public confession in front of all the bishops, who imposed a penance on him. This is probably a reference to the penance of Attigny in 822, which Thegan situated directly after Bernard's death.

[92] Dutton, *The Politics of Dreaming*, pp. 72–3; Werner, '*Hludowicus Augustus*', pp. 43–8, who speaks of a 'clan of the empress'.

[93] Cf. Thegan, c. 23, p. 213, n. 275, with comments by Ernst Tremp on the subsequent tradition of Irmingard's responsibility for Bernard's death.

As Irmingard lay dying in Angers in the autumn of 818, the emperor conducted a successful campaign against the Bretons.[94] Louis returned to Aachen to spend the winter there, gathering in 819 a large assembly that generated an amazing legislative productivity aimed at the improvement (*emendatio*) of the realm in all possible domains: five major capitularies were drafted, along with a series of charters and letters.[95] If Louis was grieving for his dead wife, he was not giving himself much time to do so. On the contrary, one of the emperor's priorities seems to have been to find himself another spouse. The Astronomer claimed that many were afraid he might wish to give up the governance of the realm, but at the urging of his men Louis was compelled to give in, and chose a bride from the daughters of the nobility that had been brought to Aachen. This was Judith, the daughter of 'Count Welf', whom he married in February of that year. Judith was depicted as the emperor's own choice, hand-picked from the fairest and most high-born maidens in the land – a barely veiled reference to the book of Esther.[96] The real rise of what was to become the family of the 'Welfs' only came in the wake of Judith's illustrious marriage to the emperor, yet there is no doubt that this was a politically significant union. By marrying a bride from Alemannia, whose parents hailed from Saxon and Bavarian nobility,[97] Louis reinforced the connection with *Germania*, the lands on the right of the Rhine, just as his own father had done when he married Hildegard, Louis's mother. But was forging connections with the regional aristocracy of his realm the only reason for contracting this marriage? Why would one first regulate one's succession, as Louis had done only two years before, and then contract a new marriage with the risk of producing more heirs, upsetting this precious balance? As Janet Nelson observed: 'Louis was reconstituting the royal family, keeping his adult sons on tenterhooks.'[98]

---

[94] The empress died on 3 October 818; see *ARF*, s.a. 818, pp. 148–9; on the Breton campaign, see Smith, *Province and Empire*.

[95] *Capitulare ecclesiasticum*, MGH *Capit.* I, no. 138, pp. 275–80; *Capitula legibus addenda*, MGH *Capit.* I, no. 139, pp. 280–5; *Capitula per se scribenda*, MGH *Capit.* I, no. 140, pp. 285–8; *Capitulare missorum*, MGH *Capit.* I, no. 141, pp. 288–91; and probably also the *Capitula legi Salicae addita*, MGH *Capit.* I, no. 142, pp. 292–3. On this synod, see Hartmann, *Karolingerzeit*, pp. 161–7. Boshof, *Ludwig*, pp. 127–8.

[96] Astronomer, c. 32, p. 392; Thegan, c. 26, p. 214; Welf was called *comes* by the Astronomer, and *dux* by Thegan. The origins of his family are uncertain (Frankish or Bavarian?). He cannot be identified as an Alemannian count; cf. Borgolte, *Die Grafen*, pp. 288–9. On the representation of this marriage, see De Jong, 'Bride shows'; see also Koch, *Kaiserin Judith*.

[97] Thegan, c. 26, p. 214, who claims that Welf was 'de nobilissima progenie Baiariorum', and Heilwig, her mother, 'nobilissimi generis Saxonici'. Thegan may have raised their status somewhat, with hindsight, but he had no reason to be disingenuous about their origins.

[98] Nelson, *Charles the Bald*, p. 73.

Procreation

When Irmingard died, Louis was forty years old and far too young to retreat from public life. Like the capacity to fight and hunt, the ability to procreate was the hallmark of male power, and also of a king's capacity to rule (*utilitas*).[99] That the Astronomer credited Louis with a wish to retreat from public life, rather than to remarry, belongs to the repertoire of characterising the Christian ruler; for an emperor of high moral standards, a second marriage should be a matter of hesitation.[100] Not remarrying would have meant opting out of rulership, and, more importantly, a new marriage would hopefully bring another son. As Louis knew from experience, mortality could thwart the most carefully made plans for familial order and succession. His own two elder brothers had died unexpectedly, and so, very recently, had his wife Irmingard. One could have too many children, but also too few. At the time, nobody could predict Louis's own longevity and that of his sons. Only Pippin predeceased his father (in 838), which meant that from the mid-twenties onwards, Louis had to contend with three adult sons who were rulers in their own right, with ambitions to match their position.[101] Each of these sons could – and did – become a focus for discontented aristocrats looking for an alternative Carolingian ruler to further their interests. The elder sons themselves, constantly aiming for more autonomy as well as paternal recognition, found themselves faced with an autocratic father demanding total obedience, and with an emperor who tolerated no independent royal or imperial authority. Louis's battle to subdue his elder sons would continue to the very end of his life; after Easter 840 the old emperor advanced into Thuringia, on a forced march, in pursuit of his son Louis, who had invaded Saxony and Thuringia.[102]

All this was still in the future when Louis became a widower in 818. What he needed was another queen, capable of becoming her husband's support and the centre of his court, while affirming Louis's sexual prowess by giving him children. There is every indication that Judith fitted these requirements perfectly. Her few extant letters and charters reveal a queen who, together with her husband, held the 'reins of the realm'.[103] Those

[99] Peters, *Shadow King*.
[100] Astronomer, c. 32, p. 392; Kötting, 'Die Beurteilung der zweiten Ehe'.
[101] In 825 Louis sent his son Louis to Bavaria, which marked the beginning of the latter's kingship there; cf. Goldberg, *Struggle*, p. 47.
[102] Astronomer, 62, p. 542; Goldberg, *Struggle*, pp. 92–3.
[103] On the *gubernacula regni* that should be held by the king, see Agobard, *Liber apologeticus* I, c. 4, p. 311. See further Ward, 'Caesar's wife'; Dutton, *CC*, nos. 20–2 and 40–2, pp. 139 and 149–52. Biographical data in Depreux, *Prosopographie*, pp. 279–86; Koch, *Kaiserin Judith*.

who sought the emperor's ear would approach her, and her position as a go-between could lead to fierce envy on the part of prominent courtiers. Judith did not gain this great influence overnight, however. First a daughter was born, named Gisela, after Charlemagne's favourite sister; yet it was the birth of a son in 823, and his subsequent survival, which made Judith into the mother of a future king, a position which yielded both authority and anxiety. If anyone doubted that this boy was indeed meant to rule, they had only to think of his name: Charles.[104] Clearly his parents intended this boy to become a king; by making his eldest brother Lothar his godfather, they hoped to ensure the latter's protection and benevolence.[105] The stellar career of Judith and her family was now well and truly launched. From 825 onwards, her close relatives rose to prominent positions. Her mother Heilwig, presumably widowed by then, became abbess of the venerable royal nunnery of Chelles (825), and her sister Emma married Louis's son Louis the German (827).[106] Louis was the last of Irmingard's sons to get married. At the assembly of Thionville in 821, where the *Ordinatio imperii* was read out and confirmed by oath, Lothar solemnly wedded Irmingard, the daughter of Count Hugh of Tours.[107] Pippin's marriage to the daughter of Count Theodebert of Madrie took place in 822, in the aftermath of the important assembly of Attigny.[108] By 827, then, Louis's three elder sons had all established royal households of their own, with matching ambitions for themselves and their offspring.

For the time being, however, the heads of these three newly formed royal establishments were not independent agents. Although they were involved in the business of governance and thus had a certain measure of scope to build a power base of their own, Louis demanded strict obedience from his sons.[109] Lothar's position in particular was a difficult one. Crowned co-emperor and meant to be his father's *consors imperii*,[110] he was entrusted instead with ruling the kingdom of Italy in 822. He was sent here with his wife, with Wala and Gerung as advisers. Here, for all practical purposes, he operated as a sub-king comparable to his younger brothers; a festive imperial coronation by Paschal I in 823 did not change

---

[104] The birth is mentioned by the Astronomer, c. 422, but not by the *Royal Frankish Annals*. On Lothar being his half-brother's godfather, see Astronomer, c. 60, pp. 530–2, and Nithard, II, c. 1, p. 38.

[105] Nelson, *Charles the Bald*, pp. 76–7.

[106] Hartmann, *Ludwig der Deutsche*, p. 64; Goldberg, *Struggle*, pp. 55–6. Judith's brothers Conrad and Rudolf became sufficiently prominent to merit the punishment meted out to really powerful political opponents: they were tonsured and sent to a monastery; Thegan, c. 36, p. 222.

[107] *ARF*, s.a. 821, p. 156.   [108] *ARF*, s.a. 822, p. 159.

[109] Kasten, *Königssöhne*, pp. 181–9.   [110] Delogu, "'Consors regni'".

this situation very much.[111] Lothar's ambition was to expand his influence in the Frankish heartlands that would be his inheritance; significantly, between 822 and 829 he spent only one and a half years in Italy.[112] His aim was to exercise real imperial power, side by side with his father. For some time he did seem to manage this, with the support of his father, who allowed his imperial son considerable freedom of action in Italy, as well as high visibility during court ceremony.[113] From 825 until 829 imperial capitularies were issued jointly in Louis's and Lothar's name. Yet in the years of conflict that followed, 'Lothar was sent back to Italy' was a recurrent refrain in the *Royal Frankish Annals*. This was the kingdom to which his father restricted him when Lothar's imperial aspirations grew too threatening; at times, Italy must have seemed a place of exile. The three brothers vied for their father's approval, with Pippin consistently and regularly falling into disfavour, while Louis the German initially was the one who during rebellions first gave up resistance, swinging the balance in his father's favour. Towards the end of Louis's life, his son Louis would become his main opponent, refusing to dance to his father's tune.[114] There is nothing extraordinary about kings wishing to rule in their own right, commanding the respect and support of their own *fideles*. More surprising is an ageing emperor who in 839 significantly reduced the size of his son's Bavarian kingdom, and who threatened to invade unless Louis the German swore never to leave Bavaria without his father's explicit assent.[115] Albeit conditionally, the son did agree; such was the hold of the elderly Louis over his adult offspring in the year before his death.

These are some of the ingredients of the rebellions of 830 and 833, yet one should not project these tensions back on to the preceding decade. This saw the unfolding of the formidable might of which Louis's sons and inner circle remained in awe until the very end, and of a specific and new style of government, characterised by the kind of religious leadership and lofty humility that befitted a true Christian emperor.

---

[111] As Elina Screen observes: 'The Astronomer's whole account suggests that Louis, far from leaving Italy to his son's independent rule, saw Lothar more as a useful envoy, and a tool for the execution of his own policy in the kingdom.' See Screen, 'The Early Career of Lothar I'.

[112] Kasten, *Königssöhne*, p. 186.

[113] Lothar was baptismal sponsor for Harald's son in 826; see Ermold, pp. 174–6, and see also his positive portrayal in Walahfrid, *De imagine Tetrici*, ed. Herren, p. 126; ed. Dümmler, p. 375, lines 158–64.

[114] Astronomer, cc. 60–2, pp. 530–44; cf. Goldberg, *Struggle*, pp. 86–94.

[115] Goldberg, *Struggle*, p. 92; *AB*, s.a. 839, pp. 38–40.

Hludowicus Augustus

Louis's impact as a ruler did not depend on his regular presence throughout his realm. Apart from this being physically impossible, there was no need for it. A network of regional administrators, mostly counts and bishops supervised by *missi dominici*, received a regular stream of Louis's commands, sometimes in the shape of capitularies, but mostly as so-called 'mandates', imperial letters with binding instructions.[116] Already under Charlemagne, the use of the written word had become indispensable to the ruler's communication with, and control of, an expanding realm; in Louis's reign, written missives from the court became even more frequent and compelling. The raising of armies is a telling case in point; we owe our fairly detailed knowledge of the procedures and setbacks of the levying of troops to the written instructions to the *missi* that are still extant, as is a letter concerning the apportioning of supplies.[117] Unlike his father, this emperor did not travel far and wide on military campaigns. After 814 Louis ventured no further south than Chalon-sur-Saône, no further east than Paderborn, Remiremont and Salz, no further north than Nijmegen, and no further west than the Paris region, except for two campaigns against the Bretons. After his coronation in childhood, he never visited Rome, and neither did he return to Aquitaine after 814. Most often, the emperor operated in a restricted royal landscape. There were three areas with royal residences – palaces and *villae* – that Louis tended to favour, also as locations for assemblies: Frankfurt, Ingelheim and Worms (nine assemblies), Compiègne, Quierzy and Attigny (ten assemblies), and Aachen and its surroundings, where more than half of the assemblies took place: at least fifteen in all.[118]

At such gatherings, lay magnates and *fideles* appeared, as well as the ecclesiastical leadership. If the matter to be discussed required it, secular and clerical participants met separately, yet it would be misleading to make too much of a distinction between the 'assembly' as a secular institution and the 'synod' as a completely ecclesiastical affair. An assembly was usually referred to as a *conventus* or *placitum*, mostly specified as being *generalis* or *publicus*. For example, a predominantly ecclesiastical meeting might be called a *generalis et sanctus conventus*, but this did not

---

[116] Mersiowsky, 'Regierungspraxis', with reference to older literature, including McKitterick's groundbreaking *Carolingians and the Written Word*. On capitularies, see now Pössel, 'Authors'.

[117] Halsall, *Warfare*, pp. 95–6.

[118] Cf. Werner, '*Hludowicus Augustus*', pp. 7–8, who rightly argues that this was not a sign of weakness.

mean that other business could not be transacted as well.[119] Apart from such gatherings, the royal itinerary included ecclesiastical centres, where the Christian holidays were celebrated with proper splendour. Whenever the ruler and his household descended on a given location, be it a palace or a monastery, this produced a flurry of anticipatory activity, as well as much trepidation. All the same, it was not as if the physical presence of the ruler was necessary to make an impact on his subjects.[120] Assemblies allowed for high royal visibility, but above all, these were the occasions when the ruler could be approached, and men from far away could feel that they were at the heart of the polity, and part of it. Sons, *fideles*, envoys from Rome, Byzantium and even further afield, all flocked to the assembly in order to petition, to plead, to offer gifts, to negotiate, and to be seen in the presence of the ruler. Good kingship was being accessible to those seeking support and being seen to give it, inspiring confidence in others; it was also to command a numerous attendance, to admonish those present, and to involve them, however marginally, in the process of political decision-making. In short, assemblies were vital for the cohesion of the polity and consensus of 'the people', that is, the ruler's faithful men (*fideles*). When Louis failed to convene a major summer assembly, as was the case in 828, this was a sure sign of political trouble.

By all accounts, the assembly of Attigny (822) was a successful one, for here, Louis was 'in the presence of his entire people'.[121] The year before, during the assembly of Thionville in October 821, where Lothar was married, Louis initiated a general amnesty, recalling not only those of Bernard's supporters whom he had sent into exile, but also the siblings Adalhard, Wala and Bernarius, who had fallen from grace in 814. Furthermore, Louis was reconciled to his half-brothers Drogo and Hugh, who had been preventively tonsured in 818. All these men were quickly reintegrated into the corridors of power.[122] With Benedict of Aniane having died in February 821, there was a vacancy for a senior adviser, and Adalhard filled it within months. Wala, 'monk and kinsman', as he was referred to in the *Royal Frankish Annals*, became Lothar's counsellor when the latter was sent to Italy in 822.[123] When Adalhard died in 826, Wala succeeded his brother as abbot of Corbie, but this did not prevent him from being frequently present at the court, as one of Louis's most honoured advisers. Benedict's death seems to have created the political

---

[119] *Institutio canonicorum Aquisgranensis*, prologue, MGH *Conc.* II/1, p. 312; on the terminology for and overlap between assemblies and synods, see de Jong, '*Ecclesia*', pp. 124–9.
[120] Reuter, 'Assembly politics'; Airlie, 'Talking heads'; Pössel, 'Itinerant kingship'.
[121] *ARF*, s.a. 822, p. 158: 'in praesentia totius populi sui'.
[122] *ARF*, s.a. 821, p. 156; Astronomer, c. 34, pp. 404–6.
[123] *ARF*, s.a. 822, p. 159: 'Walahum monachum propinquum suum.'

space for the rehabilitation of this formidable pair. This did not mean, however, that Benedict's monastic dominance at the court now gave way to a more secular political mood. When it came to *correctio* in general and monastic reform in particular, Adalhard and Wala were as intransigent as Benedict had been.[124]

Louis's reconciliation with his political adversaries resulted from deliberations with his bishops and great men, said the court annalist, and the same held true for the emperor's public confession and his subsequent penance. This was no sudden whim, but part of a strategy planned well before October 821, intended to put a definitive end to the discord of the recent past, as publicly as possible, 'in the presence of all his people'. Significantly, the sins to which Louis confessed concerned strife within the family: apart from the half-brothers, Adalhard and Wala, 'Bernard, the son of his brother Pippin', was explicitly mentioned.[125] Harming one's kinsmen was a grievous sin, and, moreover, something Louis had expressly promised Charlemagne to refrain from when he was crowned co-emperor in 813. Louis was blamed for Bernard's death, and, for all we know, he blamed himself as well. Wiping the slate clean with God and his relatives was the aim of this operation, and it was meant to be comprehensive. Any similar sins committed either by Charlemagne or by himself were to be balanced by this sweeping public gesture, and by 'generous almsgiving, the continuous prayers of Christ's servants, and even by making amends himself'.[126] The huge claims for the effectiveness of this penance already indicate that Louis's reputation as a Christian emperor was enhanced, rather than diminished. By this penance, the Frankish emperor became the equal of a formidable Roman predecessor: Theodosius I, whose public penitence in 391 made him a particularly exemplary ruler, both in late antiquity and in the ninth century.[127] In Attigny in 822, Louis set an example, for the bishops present followed him with a confession of their negligence in life, doctrine and ministry.[128] The moral high ground during this assembly was undoubtedly dominated by the emperor himself.

The penance in Attigny inaugurated a new wave of imperial confidence. Liudewit, the rebellious *dux* of Lower Pannonia who had been a thorn in Louis's side since 818, was killed in 823, after many unsuccessful Frankish campaigns against him. There was systematic reflection upon

---

[124] Staubach, *Herrscherbild*, p. 34; cf. Weinrich, *Wala*, pp. 37–41.

[125] *ARF*, s.a. 822, p. 158.   [126] Astronomer, c. 35, p. 406.

[127] McLynn, *Ambrose of Milan*, pp. 316–29; R. Schieffer, 'Von Mailand nach Canossa'; for a discussion of the reception of Theodosius' penance in Carolingian sources, see below, ch. 4. On Louis's penance of 822, see also De Jong, 'Power and humility', pp. 31–2, and Guillot, 'Autour de la pénitence publique'.

[128] *Capitula ab episcopis Attiniaci data* (822), prologue, MGH *Capit.* I, no. 174, p. 357.

the nature of the Christian empire, as well as new ways of representing its meaning. In 822/3 Louis had new coins minted with a cross and the imperial title on one side and *religio christiana* on the other.[129] The year 823 brought the birth of Charles, and Lothar's baptismal sponsorship of his half-brother. The Frankish support of the papacy was clarified and guaranteed by the *Constitutio Romana* (824), a document issued by Louis and Lothar together. From now on, before their consecration, newly elected popes were to swear an oath of allegiance to the Frankish emperor.[130] The *Admonition to all orders of the realm* (825) is the capitulary that most clearly expresses Louis's views of what it meant to govern the *imperium christianum*. To him, Louis, God had entrusted the care of his holy church and this kingdom; this ministry (*ministerium*) was exercised by the ruler, yet by divine authority and human ordination all the different 'orders' of the realm participated in the royal office. Thus, the respective ministries of bishops, counts, abbots or abbesses were derived from that of the emperor, who declared: 'all of you should be our helpers'.[131] This was Louis's vision of the Christian body politic, in which kingship entailed sublime authority and heavy responsibility at the same time: the ruler was directly accountable to God. The importance of this vision was immediately recognised by Ansegis, the abbot of St-Wandrille, who in 827 put together a highly successful collection of the capitularies of Charlemagne and Louis. The second book, in which the ecclesiastical capitularies of Louis and Lothar were brought together, opens with this particular capitulary and its conception of the royal ministry.[132]

An important aspect of this was guarding the orthodoxy of the Christian polity, a matter that became pressing, for example, in 824 when the Byzantine co-emperors Michael II and Theophilos asked Louis to intervene in Rome with regard to the ongoing strife about the veneration of images. On 1 November 825 an expert meeting of Frankish bishops met in Paris, at Louis's behest. The committee worked fast, for its report to both

---

[129] Coupland, 'Money and coinage'; Garipzanov, 'Image of authority'.

[130] *Constitutio Romana*, MGH *Capit.* I, no. 161, pp. 322–4. Cf. Noble, *Republic of St Peter*, pp. 308–22. The *Constitutio* was issued when Paschalis I had died and had been succeeded by Wala's friend Eugenius II.

[131] *Admonitio ad omnes regni ordines*, c. 3, MGH *Capit.* I, no. 150, p. 303: 'omnes vos nostri adiutores esse debetis'. The title is not in any manuscript. Guillot, 'Une ordinatio méconnue', p. 457, opts for *ordinatio*, because in the last chapter Louis takes measures to ensure that his *voluntas et ordinatio* will be known to all; cf. *Admonitio*, c. 26, MGH *Capit.* I, p. 307; Ansegis II, c. 24.

[132] Ansegis, p. 65 on the transmission of the *Admonitio ad omnes regni ordines*) and pp. 521–41 for the text, divided into twenty-four *capitula* (Boretius' edition gives twenty-six). For Ansegis' biography, see ibid. pp. 4–10. The work was completed on 28 January 827; see ibid., p. 12.

the emperors, Louis and Lothar, was presented as soon as December of that year.[133] They ordered the bishops Jonas of Orléans and Jesse of Sens to check the biblical and patristic citations in the document, and to make and present a careful selection for Pope Eugenius II. In order to avoid controversy, the bishops were instructed to address the pope with proper patience and modesty.[134] Given that Louis took a firm stance of his own concerning the monastic office, there is no reason to suppose that he refrained from intervention in doctrinal affairs, even if this is difficult to ascertain. Whatever the case, the emperor's influence was decisive, and so was his sense of diplomacy. The proceedings of the council that gathered in November 826 in St Peter's, chaired by Eugenius, reveal the extent of the impact of Frankish ideals of 'correction and emendation' on Rome itself; the Northern reform agenda was adopted lock, stock and barrel.[135] In the same eventful year, the Danish king Harald, his queen and their son were baptised in Mainz, with Louis, Judith and Lothar acting as baptismal sponsors, and lavish celebrations following in Ingelheim. Shortly after the event, Ermold the Black provided a compelling vignette of the royal party about to enter the church for a truly imperial ceremony of baptism, glittering in their finery:

Triumphant Caesar, who often busily helped at the holy services, came through the wide entry into the hall. Resplendent in gold, sparkling with gems, he made his happy journey surrounded by his household. Hilduin was at his right hand, and Helisachar walked at his left; Gerung preceded him, carrying a staff, as was customary, guarding the path of the king, who wore a golden crown on his head. Dutiful Lothar, and Harald, in his robe, followed them in turn, gleaming with gifts. Coming before his father, the beautiful boy Charles, glorious in gold, walked happily, tapping the marble floor with his footsteps. Then came Judith, strong in regal duty, shining with marvellous gifts, attended by a pair of *proceres*: Matfrid and Hugh matched her steps, and so beside her, escorted their honourable lady; both of the distinguished men shone in gold clothes. Finally Harald's wife followed close behind, joyful because of the gifts of the pious empress. Then Fridugisus came out, followed by a wise group of disciples who shone white, both in their clothing and in their faith. Then the other youths followed, arranged appropriately according to their stations, each dressed in clothes bestowed by Caesar.[136]

Scapegoats and rebels

Less than two years later, cracks began to appear in this image of perfect harmony. Matfrid and Hugh, the two magnates portrayed as the empress's

[133]   Boshof, *Ludwig*, pp. 163–5.   [134] MGH *Conc.* II/2, no. 44 D, p. 533.
[135]   *Concilium Romanum*, a. 826, MGH *Conc.* II/2, pp. 559–92.
[136]   Ermold, p. 176, lines 2290–313; trans. Carey D. Fleiner.

retinue in 826, were banished from the court. When two crushing and shameful military defeats occurred in 827, one in the Spanish March and the other in Pannonia, those in charge fell from grace in February 828, losing their high offices and their lands – in short, all the *honores* they held from the emperor. Baldric, *dux* of Friuli, had been unable to stop Bulgars and Slavs from raiding upper Pannonia.[137] Compared to the two leaders of the failed Spanish campaign, he was a minor player in this drama. Count Hugh of Tours had served Charlemagne, and was Lothar's father-in-law; Count Matfrid of Orléans was one of Louis's highest-ranking courtiers.[138] Because of their alleged laxity and tardiness, they were turned into the scapegoats for the Spanish debacle. The impact of this particular defeat in Aachen was overwhelming. According to the court annalist, the disaster (*clades*) had been foretold by a terrible portent: fiery armies and terrible lightning had been observed in the skies.[139] The fact that Louis's former kingdom was involved, and the territory where he himself had been victorious in the early 800s, can only have made matters worse.

Louis's humiliating punishment of Hugh and Matfrid backfired in the years to come. These were men from powerful families in the Rhineland and the Moselle valley respectively, with a long record of royal service. To cut such men off from the court also meant that essential channels of patronage were suddenly blocked, and that entire networks that had relied on their protection and mediation now had to look elsewhere.[140] Instantly, Louis created two dangerous enemies, and also a sense of unease among his *fideles*: who would be next? The two men fought tooth and nail to regain their offices and lands, and attached themselves to Lothar's retinue, fuelling the latter's smouldering resentment. Apparently Louis was prepared to take the risk, against all these odds. One reason for this sudden action may have been a feeling of panic and fear caused by three major defeats against 'the pagans'. Apart from the Saracen Abu Marwan, who plundered the Spanish March with impunity, thanks to Aizo's treacherous dealings, and the Bulgars, who had devastated upper Pannonia, this disastrous year 827 also saw Harald, the newly baptised Danish king, ousted by pagan

---

[137] Krahwinkel, *Friaul im Frühmittelalter*, pp. 192–7.

[138] On Hugh, see Hummer, *Politics and Power*, pp. 157–65, with reference to older literature; on Matfrid, Depreux, 'Matfrid'. See also Depreux, *Prosopographie*, pp. 262–4, 329–31.

[139] *ARF*, s.a. 827: 'Quae tarditas in tantum noxia fuit ...' The word *clades* is significant, for this is a key term for disasters perceived as a punishment from God. See below, chapter 4, pp. 143–4.

[140] For an in-depth analysis of Matfrid's position at the court, see Depreux, 'Matfrid'.

Danes.[141] That the pagans were gaining the upper hand was taken as overwhelming evidence of God's displeasure. Matfrid, Hugh and Baldric not only were punished for their failure to defend Christian honour but also became scapegoats whose eviction from the palace was one of the first gestures of appeasement to the enraged deity.[142]

The seriousness of the situation, as perceived by Louis and his advisers, at least, is evident from the fact that all the adult royal sons were now deployed as military leaders. Louis the German was despatched to the Bulgars; Lothar was sent 'with many troops' to the Spanish March. In Lyons, together with his brother Pippin, Lothar concluded that there was no military threat from any Saracens. Nearby, the danger seemed less formidable than from afar.[143] Lothar returned to Aachen, where his father summoned a restricted winter meeting with his inner circle (*conventus procerum*) to discuss the containment of the crisis. Louis and Lothar acted together; the stream of written directives that started in December was issued in the name of both emperors. Already at an early stage of the deliberations, the gathering decided to convene four councils by the Sunday after Whitsun 829 (in Mainz, Paris, Lyons and Toulouse), which were to investigate current evils and their potential remedies; an empire-wide three-day fast was to support their endeavours. Moreover, all royal vassals and their troops were ordered to be on the alert. The remedies were time-honoured: prayer and atonement on the one hand and fighting on the other; yet in a novel manner, this winter meeting also addressed the problem of the 'negligence' of those in charge of a *ministerium*, that is, Louis, his bishops and lay magnates, and, in a more derivative way, his wife and sons. The key question was: what have we, the leadership, done to offend God? Both Einhard and Wala offered Louis 'booklets' (*libelli*) prescribing remedies of correction, bearing the authoritative stamp of divine inspiration: Scripture and the *patres*, angelic and demonic visions. During that winter, there was a consensus that the offended deity should and could be placated by an energetic correction of the sins that had upset the order in the realm. With this in mind, *missi* were sent into the empire and councils were convened. In June 829, at the council of Paris, the bishops did not spare themselves; their failures and transgressions, and those of the clergy, were listed first, followed by a second section devoted to 'kings, princes and the general populace'.[144] The optimism of the gathering and its confident trust in correction and penance are striking.

---

[141] *ARF*, s.a. 827, p. 173.   [142] See below, chapter 4.

[143] *ARF*, s.a. 828, p. 175; differently, Collins, 'Pippin I', pp. 380–1, who suspects foul play on the part of the two brothers, aided and abetted by Agobard.

[144] See below, chapter 4, pp. 176–9.

Because of all this hectic activity, Louis had to forgo hunting, and left Aachen only on 1 July for a general assembly in Worms.[145] Here, in the presence of Lothar and Louis the German (and, one may presume, of Judith as well), six-year-old Charles was granted a kingdom of his own, consisting of Alemannia, Alsace, Churrhaetia and parts of Burgundy.[146] Because of its supposed infraction of the 'unity of the empire', this grant has caused a lot of modern ink to flow. Fitting young Charles into the pre-existent arrangements for succession was no doubt a delicate operation, yet there is no sign in contemporary sources that the grant of 829 was either a momentous event or the cause of much fraternal envy.[147] Did anybody expect Charles *not* to be given a share of the inheritance? The really fateful measure taken in Worms, and a major affront to Lothar, was that Bernard of Septimania was made chamberlain. He soon assumed a position of authority second only to the emperor, and was entrusted with the care of young Charles. All this directly affected Lothar's position as co-emperor and his half-brother's official godfather.[148] After Lothar had been 'sent off to Italy', Bernard was installed as chamberlain, taking Lothar's place in the ranking of the palace.[149] The envy and frustration this engendered, among the elder sons and prominent courtiers alike, should not be underestimated. As the Astronomer reflected later on, by bringing in Bernard Louis wanted to create a buffer against those plotting against him, but it had only increased the discord.[150] Within a matter of months, the new chamberlain monopolised and manipulated access to the ruler, the worst and also the most common sin of heads of royal households.

Bernard also had the ear of the empress, and co-operated with her closely, as a chamberlain and a queen, who were jointly in charge of the royal household, were wont to do.[151] With Lothar in Italy, it was Pippin around whom the opposition clustered. Relations between Pippin and his

---

[145] *ARF*, s.a. 829, p. 177 ('in diversis occupationibus').

[146] *Annales Xantenses*, s.a. 829, p. 7. Cf. Nelson, *Charles the Bald*, p. 87, who rightly doubts whether this grant was particularly contentious.

[147] Only authors who wrote after 833 mention Lothar's anger about the grant: Thegan, c. 35, p. 220, on Lothar and Louis: 'Et inde illi indignati sunt tunc cum Pippino germano eorum' (but then again, Thegan also claimed that the younger brothers were 'indignant' in 817); for Nithard, Lothar was the villain of the piece, so always at loggerheads with his father and half-brother: Nithard, I, c. 3, p. 10. The *ARF* do not mention the grant, and neither does the Astronomer.

[148] Kasten, *Königssöhne*, p. 187.

[149] The court annalist juxtaposed the two events in a way that suggests a connection. *ARF* s.a. 829, p. 177: 'Hlotharium quoque filium suum finito illo conventu [Worms] in Italiam direxit ac Bernhardum comitem Barcinonae, qui eatenus in marca Hispaniae praesidebat, camerarium in palatio suo constituit.' On 6 September 829 the period of issuing imperial charters jointly with Lothar came to an end.

[150] Astronomer, c. 43, pp. 452–4.   [151] Ward, 'Caesar's wife'.

father had been strained for some time. Pippin had been implicated in the defeat of the Spanish March in 827. When Walahfrid Strabo came to the court in the spring of 829, Pippin was the absent son, of whom the poet could only praise the 'scented fragrance of his happy renown', for he had not seen him.[152] Neither was Pippin present at the assembly in Worms, which constituted another act of defiance. Many wounds festered: Matfrid's and Hugh's rancour, Lothar's confinement to Italy, Pippin's exasperation about his father's constant interference in Aquitaine.[153] Moreover, there was the frustration of leading courtiers with Judith and Bernard barring their access to the emperor, effectively closing his ears against the advice of others. These were the complex ingredients of a rebellion which, according to the Astronomer, began with the conspirators going to Pippin, claiming (*praetendentes*) that they had been humiliated, that Bernard's conduct was insolent and that he looked down on others; they also claimed that Bernard had, 'it is impious to say, committed incest in his [Pippin's] father's bed', and that Louis was so bewitched by sorcery that he could do nothing to avert this.[154] Through the centuries, adultery and witchcraft have been the two main accusations levelled at queens and courtiers who seemed too powerful for comfort; this was the first fully fledged instance in Western history.[155]

Under Pippin's aegis, the rebellion that had smouldered for months broke out during Lent 830. On Ash Wednesday Louis had departed on a badly timed campaign to Brittany, having left Judith behind. He received the news in St-Omer, and realized how serious the revolt was 'against himself, his wife and Bernard'.[156] Louis's position was a curious one. Although his room for manoeuvring was minimal, he remained a major player in the subsequent struggle for control. As soon as the rebellion broke out, shortly after Easter, Judith fled from Aachen through her husband's favourite hunting ground, the Ardennes, to the nunnery of St Mary in Laon. Judith's hiding-place determined the subsequent topography of the conflict. Louis proceeded to Compiègne, and Pippin, to whom the rebels initially looked for leadership, took his troops to nearby Verberie. Louis 'allowed Bernard to bring himself into safety by fleeing, but wished his wife to be in Laon and to remain in the monastery of St Mary', wrote the Astronomer, as if the emperor were still capable of taking such decisions.[157] Judith was veiled and sent to St Radegund's

---

[152] 'De imagine Tetrici', ed. Herren, p. 127 (lines 141–3) .
[153] Nelson, 'Frankish kingdoms', pp. 116–17.
[154] Astronomer, c. 44, p. 456.   [155] Bührer-Thierry, 'La reine adultère'.
[156] Astronomer, c. 44, p. 456. About the sequence of events, see Nelson, *Charles the Bald*, pp. 88–9.
[157] Astronomer, c. 44, pp. 456–8.

convent in Poitiers, while her two brothers, Conrad and Rudolf, were tonsured and shut away in monasteries.[158] During all this, Pippin was still in charge; only in May did Lothar come upon the scene, ready to take over. All the insurgents now clustered around him, with Hugh and Matfrid as his leading supporters. In that same month, during an assembly in Compiègne, the clock was turned back. Lothar once more issued charters together with his father, Matfrid was reinstated, and Bernard's brother Heribert was blinded. Louis himself passed the summer in Lothar's company and custody, 'an emperor in name only', as the Astronomer expressed it, with what may have been a deliberate reference to Einhard's characterisation of the last Merovingian king.[159]

Judging by the anger with which he was later accused of having feigned contrition and co-operation, Louis had handled the assembly in Compiègne with skill and tact.[160] First he agreed to a total rehabilitation of Lothar and his supporters, and then he managed to divert the location of the autumn assembly to Nijmegen, for he expected more support from the *Germani* than from the *Franci*.[161] Rightly so, for Louis, the king of Bavaria, backed his father. Once this was accomplished, Louis manipulated the attendance of this assembly, ordering his adversaries to come with only a limited retinue. In Nijmegen itself, there was a showdown with Archchaplain Hilduin, who had sided with the rebels, and now arrived *hostiliter* instead of *simpliciter* – that is, he came with his fighting men. Hilduin was ordered to spend the winter in Paderborn, in an army tent, and Wala, who had also been implicated, was sent back to Corbie, to live according to the Rule of Benedict – that is, to stop oscillating between the cloister and the court, and to stay put until his fate was decided on.[162] For a second time, the old courtier had been ousted from the corridors of power. The Astronomer's narrative underlines Louis's imperial self-control and mildness. Parental mercy prevailed over the sharp rebuke (*aspera increpatio*) that Lothar deserved; all the rebels were sentenced to death by the assembly, but then immediately pardoned by Louis, and committed to monastic custody.[163] He had regained imperial rule once more.[164] But, significantly, it was the renewed control of Aachen that

---

[158] *AB*, s.a. 830, p. 2.

[159] Astronomer, c. 45, p. 464: 'In talibus ergo consistens, solo nomine imperator aestatem transegit.' Cf. *AB*, s.a. 830, p. 2: 'omnem potestatem regiam uxoremque tulerunt'.

[160] Radbert, *EA* II, c. 10, p. 73: 'quamvis in corde aliud occuleret'.

[161] Astronomer, c. 45, p. 464: 'diffidens quidem Francis magisque se credens Germanis'. Cf. *AB*, s.a. 830, p. 2: 'ubi Saxones et orientales Franci convenire potuissent'.

[162] All these details about the Nijmegen assembly come from Astronomer, c. 45, pp. 460–4.

[163] Astronomer, c. 45, p. 464.   [164] *AB*, s.a. 830, p. 3: 'recuperato imperio'.

really made this clear. Louis returned there in the winter, taking Lothar along, and sent to Poitiers for Judith. As for her rehabilitation, this was not a foregone conclusion. One author depicted her return to Aachen as a triumphant *adventus;* as the empress approached the palace, she was met by her son Charles, Bishop Drogo of Metz, and other great men, and led to Louis, who restored Judith to her 'pristine honour'.[165] Yet before she was readmitted to the imperial bed, she had to clear herself from the charges against her, in the presence of all three of Louis's elder sons. Nobody dared to speak up as her accuser, so during an assembly in Aachen that coincided with the Purification of the Virgin Mary (2 February) she purged herself by oath, 'according to the judgement of the Franks'.[166] As for Bernard, later that year he was allowed to clear himself by oath as well; all his accusers had suddenly vanished.[167] Remarkably, the next phase of Bernard's career was spent in the service of Pippin of Aquitaine, the very king who had led the revolt that had toppled the short-lived chamberlain.[168] Staunch allegiance to the ruler was the ideal, but perhaps more of a reality for men lower down on the political ladder. Top dogs such as Bernard had multiple interests to take care of, and attached themselves to the ruler who would most enable them to wield political influence. This is one reason why one should not project modern notions of 'parties' on to this period; the other is that it is usually impossible to get at the nitty-gritty of actual political alliances and the way in which these changed. For magnates and other prominent *fideles* who had many others to protect, deep-seated ideals of loyalty coexisted – and at times conflicted – with the need to seek reliable and effective royal patronage. This was the normal situation, and well within the boundaries of what constituted honourable conduct, yet in the early 830s, this regular and flexible pattern of allegiances became too volatile for anyone's comfort.

Intermezzo

The three elder sons were dismissed to their respective kingdoms. Having weathered this storm quickly and efficiently, Louis pardoned his enemies with veritable lightning speed, no doubt in order to keep lingering

---

[165] *AMP*, s.a. 830, pp. 97–8; De Jong, 'Exegesis for an empress', pp. 78–9.

[166] *AB*, s.a. 831, pp. 4–5; Astronomer, c. 46, p. 464. The Purification of the Virgin Mary was a time at which assemblies were regularly convened: see Astronomer, c. 14, p. 320 (Charlemagne, 802, in Aachen); c. 20, p. 344; (Louis, 814, Doué, in anticipation of assuming full control), c. 54, p. 500 (Thionville, 835, punishment of Ebo of Rheims).

[167] At the assembly of Thionville; see Astronomer, c. 46, p. 466; Thegan, c. 38, p. 224; *AB*, s.a. 831, p. 4.

[168] Astronomer, c. 47, p. 468: Depreux, *Prosopographie*, p. 139.

resentment to a minimum. After Easter he proceeded from Aachen to Ingelheim, where he gathered another assembly. He received Lothar 'honourably' and recalled those he had sent into monastic exile,[169] leaving those who had been tonsured the choice of staying or leaving.[170] This flexible use of penitential exile in monasteries was what Ebo of Rheims was to call scathingly the 'modern authority of the palace'.[171] Hilduin was pardoned and regained two of his abbeys,[172] but Wala remained out of favour. All was well, as the Astronomer seems to suggest, for from Ingelheim the emperor went on to Remiremont to fish and hunt to his heart's delight, 'and his son Lothar he sent to Italy'.[173]

Yet the trouble was by no means over. Although the two rebellions of 830 and 833 were separate upheavals, with their own context and dynamics, the after-effects of the first revolt certainly helped to fuel the second one. One of the accusations levelled against the penitent emperor in 833 was that with his many changes of course, he had forced his sons and his *fideles* to swear conflicting oaths and thus to commit the sin of perjury.[174] The spring and summer of 831 were a case in point: filial disobedience was now punished by the drafting of new plans for succession. In February 831 in Aachen, an alternative was discussed that would split up the Frankish heartlands, conceding Neustria to Pippin; but the real beneficiaries were Louis the German (who had helped to end the short-lived revolt) and Charles.[175] Lothar was simply left with Italy. This partition had a tell-tale clause by which the father reserved the right to amend the arrangement, depending on the conduct of his sons.[176] For the time being, however, the new *divisio* was meant to gain the support of Pippin and the younger Louis, while Lothar was taught a lesson, but by May 831, when Louis was back in the saddle, he could once more afford to be on better terms with Lothar. Hence the honourable reception in Ingelheim in May, which was one of the reasons why Pippin challenged his father by refusing to attend an assembly in Thionville, the third assembly of that eventful year. He did turn up eventually, and was punished by being kept at Aachen against his will; not prepared to tolerate this dishonourable treatment, Pippin fled to Aquitaine, where an unlikely ally awaited him:

---

[169] *AB*, s.a. 831, p. 4.
[170] Astronomer, c. 46, p. 466; De Jong, 'Monastic prisoners'.
[171] Ebo, *Apologeticum, forma I* , MGH *Conc.* II/2, p. 799; de Jong, 'Paenitentia publica', pp. 885–6.
[172] Boshof, *Agobard*, pp. 211–14; probably St-Denis and St-Médard.
[173] Astronomer, c. 46, p. 466: 'et filium Hlotarium in Italiam direxit'.
[174] *Relatio* (833), no. 5, p. 54.
[175] *Regni divisio*, MGH *Capit.* II, no. 194, pp. 20–4. On the partitions of 831–2, see Nelson, *Charles the Bald*, pp. 89–91, and Kasten, *Königssöhne*, pp. 190–2.
[176] *Regni divisio*, MGH *Capit.* II, no. 194, c. 13, p. 23.

Bernard of Septimania.[177] Meanwhile, Louis the German could not accept his father's pardoning of Lothar and the possibilitity of losing the territories set aside for him in the 831 division. In late March 832, Louis meant to claim the latter and marched into Alemannia, but he had to withdraw swiftly when his father turned up with an army, accompanied by Charles, the rightful heir. On the Lechfeld, where Charlemagne had forced Tassilo into submission in 787, Louis was now duly forgiven, swearing never to rise up against his father again.[178] He was permitted to return peacefully to Bavaria, said the court annalist, while his father proceeded to Salz, where he was formally received by 'the lady empress'.[179] Order was restored, but not for long.

One plan for partition followed another, in rapid succession. In the summer of 832, once Louis the German was brought back into line, the emperor seems to have considered the exclusion of both Louis and Pippin, making Lothar and Charles the sole beneficiaries. Although the Astronomer is the only author to mention this particular division, it fits Louis's strategy of playing one son against the other. By October he was resolved to take away Aquitaine from Pippin and make the nine-year-old Charles its king. While Pippin was taken into custody in Trier, 'in order to correct his depraved behaviour',[180] at an assembly in Limoges the aristocracy of Aquitaine had sworn an oath of allegiance to the child who was to be their new ruler. Pippin escaped and returned to Aquitaine. Harsh winter weather put an end to the military campaign waged by his father, who had to withdraw from Aquitaine in a 'less than dignified fashion'.[181] In December Louis and Judith were present at the translation of Balthild's relics in Chelles, the nunnery of which Judith's mother was the abbess.[182] They could have done with some saintly support, for by now confusion was rife among the *fideles* of the emperor and his sons, whose future fate changed with every new partition. Louis had thoroughly antagonised Pippin and Louis the German, while negotiations with Lothar had not yet resulted in the latter's support. Over the past years, the father's deft manoeuvring had kept the sons divided, but now the spectre of a united front arose.

833 and all that

Writing to Pope Leo IV in 847–9, the Emperor Lothar reflected on this 'time of unhappy discord between us and our father, which, at the

---

[177] Astronomer, cc. 46–7, pp. 464–72.
[178] Goldberg, *Struggle*, pp. 62–8; *AB*, s.a. 832, p. 7; Thegan, c. 39, pp. 226–7.
[179] *AB*, s.a. 832, p. 7.   [180] Astronomer, c. 47, p. 470.
[181] Ibid., p. 472.   [182] *Ex translatione Balthechildis*, c. 1, p. 284.

instigation of the devil and his satellites, lasted for some time'.[183] The Astronomer would have agreed: he too blamed the devil and his helpers for a sequence of events that, in retrospect, seemed to have got completely out of the control of any of the main protagonists. The Astronomer's devil was aided and abetted by evil men who, like water shaping a stone, had persuaded the sons that their father wanted to ruin them even further.[184] A man who was so mild to strangers, would not have hurt his own off-spring, the Astronomer added, but one can see why the sons were on tenterhooks after the various succession arrangements of the past years. Still at Aachen after Christmas, the emperor received news that once more, united and like-minded, his sons intended to rebel against him.[185] After due consultation, Louis went to Worms at the beginning of Lent and remained there until Pentecost (1 June), celebrating these feasts and mustering troops. The sons, meanwhile, had congregated with their armies in Alsace, in a place called Rothfeld. Taking charge as the eldest son and legitimate emperor, Lothar had brought Pope Gregory IV from Rome, claiming that this was the only mediator who would be able to reconcile the hostile parties. This in itself promising strategy entirely misfired. As the Astronomer remarked, cynically, it would soon become clear that reconciliation was merely a pretext. The pope's assigned role was to legitimate the sons' attempt to depose their father by excommuni-cating him as well as all those bishops who would not co-operate; the Frankish episcopate, meanwhile, was furious at this intervention and maintained that he who had come to excommunicate would be excom-municated himself.[186] Rumour ran rife, and the presence of a Roman pontiff who did not observe the procedure of a proper *adventus* – that is, coming to Louis, rather than remaining in Lothar's camp – caused much nervousness in the senior emperor's quarters. The rest of the Astronomer's narrative, as well as a letter ascribed to Gregory, suggests that a well-meaning pope threw himself into the job of mediation without knowing what he had got himself into, and without getting anywhere. With the troops already preparing for battle, a hapless Gregory went back and forth between the two sides.[187]

Meanwhile, Louis's faithful men had begun to vote with their feet. Between St John and St Paul, that is, 24 June and 30 June, so many men had deserted the emperor that the common people (*plebs*), fawning on the

---

[183] *Epistolae selectae Leonis*, no. 46, MGH *Epp.* III, p. 610: 'cum tempore infelicissime discordiae, que operante diabolo per satellites suos inter nos genitoremque nostrum aliquandiu duravit'.

[184] Astronomer, c. 48, p. 472.   [185] *AB*, s.a. 833, p. 8.   [186] Astronomer, c. 48, p. 476.

[187] Noble, *Louis the Pious*, pp. 321–52.

sons, were ready to attack Louis. This was the Astronomer's derogatory way of referring to the lesser landowners who were the retainers of Louis's *fideles*. Others, more dramatically, claimed that all Louis's faithful men had gone over to the other side in one night.[188] In October, the bishops in Soissons would present this as firm evidence of a divine judgement, yet those condemning this desertion gave the place in question its enduring name: the 'Field of Lies' (*campus mentitus*).[189] Yet a hard core of loyal men stayed with the emperor, among whom was also his half-brother Drogo.[190] In order to avoid bloodshed, Louis gave himself up to his sons, extracting promises with regard to sparing his own life and that of Judith and Charles. Judith, who was put in the custody of her stepson and brother-in-law Louis, was exiled for a second time, much further away: she was taken to the Italian *civitas* of Tortona.[191] Lothar took his father and Charles via Metz to Soissons, where he ordered Louis to be kept under strict custody in the monastery of St-Médard. Charles was sent off to the monastery of Prüm, an experience he would remember well in adulthood. To Pope Nicholas I he later recounted that he, a boy of not yet ten years old, had been put into custody in Prüm 'as if I had committed many crimes'.[192]

On 1 October 833 the autumn assembly met according to plan in Compiègne, yet this time all the loyalty, gifts and embassies were destined for Lothar.[193] The Astronomer's view of this gathering was bleak: scores were settled, dissidents were bullied, and Louis was neither heard nor tried. While the assembly met and deliberated, Lothar kept his father in custody in St-Médard, some 40 kilometres away.[194] First, a delegation from Compiègne admonished Louis about his sins, and urged him to be mindful of saving his soul, and then all the bishops descended collectively on the emperor, urging him to submit to a public penance. Once they succeeded, Lothar was called from Compiègne to Soissons, to witness together with a crowd how Louis took off his belt of office (*cingulum militiae*) and placed it on the altar, exchanging his royal robes for the garb of a penitent. This conversion to the penitential state was effected

---

[188] Astronomer, c. 48, p. 474. Defection in one night: Thegan, c. 42, p. 228, and Radbert, *EA*, II, c. 18, p. 88 ('in eadem nocte reliquerunt (omnes) augustum').
[189] Astronomer, c. 48, p. 474, with n. 713.
[190] Nelson, *Annals of St-Bertin*, p. 27, n. 23, on an addition in the 'O' manuscript which says that Drogo, Modoin of Autun, Wiliric of Bremen and Alderic of Le Mans stayed, together with some other bishops, counts, abbots and other faithful men.
[191] Situated in northern Italy, between Genoa and Pavia.
[192] Council of Troyes (867), MGH *Conc.* IV, p. 240, lines 13–14: 'nos quoque, non adhuc decennem, quasi multorum criminum obnoxium'; Nelson, *Charles the Bald*, p. 91.
[193] *AB*, s.a. 833, p. 20; cf. Astronomer c. 49, p. 480.
[194] Astronomer c. 49, p. 482: 'Adiudicatum ergo eum absentem et inauditum.'

by an episcopal blessing. 'Let no one after a penance of this scope and kind dare to return to his worldly office (*militia saecularis*)', said the joint declaration of the bishops in which their version of the proceedings was elaborately established.[195] This was the obvious aim of the operation: that Louis would withdraw permanently from his royal office, leading the life of a public penitent who had laid down his arms and was therefore unfit for worldly rule. For all practical purposes, this amounted to a deposition, for the bishops announced themselves to be 'under the rule of the Emperor Lothar' and dated the document to the first year of his reign as sole emperor.[196] They took extreme care with documenting the formal aspects of this ecclesiastical *paenitentia publica*, to make sure there would be no technical mistakes that would render Louis's conversion invalid – so much so that their insecurity is obvious: this was a novelty dressed up as ancient canonical tradition, and they knew it. On 11 November, St Martin's, Lothar dismissed the assembly in Compiègne and went to Aachen for the winter, taking his father with him.[197]

The three brothers now made their own partition. Louis the German claimed all lands across the Rhine, while Pippin received Neustria between the Seine and the Rhine, and Lothar the rest.[198] Yet this was not the fraternal co-operation under Lothar's leadership that had been planned in 817. A full partition of territory and men was now envisaged.[199] Louis the German had not come to the assembly of Compiègne, making his opposition to Lothar clear. Not quite trusting the permanence of public penance either, Lothar and his allies tried to get Louis to make a monastic profession voluntarily, while the emperor staunchly refused: as long as he had no power over his own actions, he would not commit himself by any vow.[200] Everyone concerned knew that, unlike being tonsured a *clericus* and sent off to a monastery for temporary atonement, a monastic profession was irrevocable.[201] Louis's firm refusal to take this step shows that for him the situation was not exactly desperate; there was a fair chance that the fragile alliance between three competitive rulers would not last. The first cracks appeared before the year was out, with Pippin and

---

[195] *Relatio* (833), p. 55: 'ut post tantam talemque poenitentiam nemo ultra ad militiam saecularem redeat'.

[196] *Relatio* (833), p. 52. The date: 'in the month of October of the year of the Incarnation of [our] Lord Jesus Christ 830, in the twelfth indiction, that is, in the first year of [the reign of] this emperor.' Lothar issued his first charter as sole emperor from Soissons.

[197] Astronomer, c. 49, p. 482.

[198] Kasten, *Königssöhne*, pp. 192–3; Goldberg, *Struggle*, p. 70.

[199] Astronomer, c. 48, p. 478 ('imperium inter se fratres trina sectione partiuntur'); *Annales Xantenses*, s.a. 833, p. 8 ('tripertitum est regnum Francorum').

[200] *AB*, s.a. 834, trans. Nelson, p. 28; see also Thegan, c. 43.

[201] See below, ch. 6, pp. 234–41.

especially Louis the German allegedly pleading with Lothar to treat their father kindly.[202] Plans for the emperor's reinstatement were hatched all winter, and when Lothar learned that his brothers' armies were on their way, he left Aachen for Paris, taking his father with him and committing him to the monastery of St-Denis.[203] During the first week of Lent 834, envoys made it clear to Lothar that he was cornered by armies that would not hesistate to fight in order to free his father. Leaving Louis behind, Lothar and his allies fled south to Vienne, where he established a camp.[204] According to Nithard, Charles had already been taken from Prüm to St-Denis, and was liberated there with his father, a view confirmed by the Astronomer.[205] In Aachen, Louis received Judith, back from exile in Tortona. Having ensured the empress's safe return was a feat with which various rescuers were credited, but none more eloquently and charmingly than Ruadbern, the young laymen praised by Walahfrid Strabo for having risked his own life to liberate Judith: 'Your mind was filled with a loyalty that no hardship could weary.'[206]

Restoration

Within less than four months after his public penance, the scene for Louis's restoration was set. Just like the bishops who had performed this ritual, those who portrayed his reconciliation made sure that everything was seen to have been done by the book. The Astronomer stressed that Louis himself insisted on a proper reconciliation performed by bishops:

> Those who had remained with the emperor were urging that he had to take up the imperial insignia. But the emperor, since he had been removed from communion with the church in the way already described, and even though he did not wish to acquiesce in that hasty judgement, because the next day was Sunday, wanted to be reconciled in the church of St-Denis by episcopal ministration and consented to be girded with his arms at the hand of the bishops.[207]

For Louis, this was to be the first of a series of reconciliations and reinstatements. As for Lothar, vicious revenge was followed by humiliation. Having resisted until the summer, Lothar took a horrible revenge on Chalon-sur-Saône, burning the city and drowning Bernard's sister

---

[202] *AB*, s.a. 834, p. 11; Thegan, cc. 45–7, pp. 238–40.
[203] Astronomer, c. 50, p. 484; *AB*, s.a. 834, p. 12.
[204] Astronomer, c. 50, p. 488. Lothar fled on 28 February; cf. *BM* 926o.
[205] Nithard, I, c. 4, p. 18; cf. Astronomer, c. 52, p. 492.
[206] Godman, *Poetry*, pp. 216–21, at p. 219; Walahfrid Strabo, *Carmina*, MGH *Poet. Lat.* II, pp. 388–90. Cf. Astronomer, c. 52, p. 492, who envisaged a more sedate rescue party of Italian *fideles*.
[207] Astronomer, c. 51, p. 488.

Gerberga in a barrel in the river, as if she were a witch. But then he had to concede defeat.[208] The eldest son came to his father as a supplicant, throwing himself on the latter's mercy, and was granted Italy, 'just as Pippin, the Lord Emperor's brother, had held it at the time of the Lord Charles' – that is, Lothar was back to square one.[209] Louis the German ended up with the lands on the right of the Rhine as well as the Alsace, while Pippin's kingship of Aquitaine was confirmed. The contours of an arrangement that would leave Charles in possession of the central part of the patrimony now became visible.[210] The message in contemporary narrative sources was 'business as usual', with Louis taking public order and *correctio* firmly in hand, cracking down on brigands as well as on his son Pippin, who had usurped ecclesiastical property.[211] Sons were ordered about as if nothing had happened, and hunting – always a signal that matters were in control – was presented as having resumed with clockwork regularity. Christmas was celebrated in Metz with Louis's half-brother Drogo, who had stood by him, and would be rewarded by being made archchaplain in 834. For 2 February 835, a date that had marked a return to normality in 831 as well, the emperor summoned a council 'of nearly all the bishops and abbots' to Thionville, where the imperial penance was declared uncanonical, in a way that accurately mir-rored the proceedings of Compiègne: a detailed report of the proceedings was drawn up, signed by all those present.[212] As in 831, this settling of scores with his enemies took place on the feast of the Purification of the Virgin, the date of Louis's accession in 814 as well as a time of symbolic purification.[213] In 834, the bishops who had been instrumental in impo-sing the infamous penance were called to account, but they had either fled to Italy, or, like Agobard, failed to answer the imperial summons.[214] Only Ebo of Rheims had decided to face the imperial wrath, and thus it was he who became the scapegoat of the entire affair.[215] The church of St Stephen in Metz was the scene of Louis's solemn reconciliation (a mass celebrated by seven archbishops!) and coronation,[216] but also of Ebo's humiliation. Publicly and voluntarily, the court annalist insisted, Ebo declared that the emperor had been unjustly deposed, that this had

---

[208] *AB*, s.a. 834, p. 14; Thegan, c. 52, p. 244; Astronomer, c. 52, pp. 494–6. On witchcraft accusations, see below, chapter 5, pp. 200–2.
[209] *AB*, s.a. 834, p. 15; Thegan, c. 55, p. 250; Astronomer, c. 53, p. 498.
[210] Nelson, *Charles the Bald*, pp. 94–5, on the settlement of 837, which gave Charles a great expanse of territory north-east of the Seine.
[211] Astronomer, c. 53, pp. 498–500.   [212] *AB*, s.a. 835, pp. 26–8.
[213] See above, n. 166.   [214] Astronomer, c. 54, pp. 500–2.
[215] Cf. Thegan, c. 44, pp. 232–8.
[216] *AB*, s.a. 835, p. 28 (coronation); Astronomer, c. 54, p. 502 (seven archbishops sang seven psalms of reconciliation).

been perpetrated wickedly and against all sense of equity, and that Louis had been justly and deservedly restored to the throne.[217] In a restricted meeting of the council, the archbishop of Rheims confessed to a 'capital crime'; declaring himself unworthy of his high office, he resigned.[218] The rebellion of 833 was well and truly over. All that remained was the long-term memory of this tragic event, and also, in the decades directly there-after, a great deal of effort to shift the blame elsewhere. In the end, it was all the fault of the devil.

'The last years'

The prelate who presided over Louis's restoration in Thionville and Metz, making sure that all these rites and judgements were canonical to the hilt, was Drogo, the bishop of Metz. Once the rebellion was over, Louis tended to rely on his ecclesiastical half-brothers for support, rather than on his elder sons. Drogo was also the one who officiated at Louis's deathbed in the summer of 840, controlling the access to the dying emperor and hearing his daily confession.[219] What of the intervening six years – the 'last years of Louis the Pious'? Was Soissons indeed the moral undoing of Louis, and was Frankish history from 833 set on a course that led directly to the partition of Verdun in 843?[220] Janet Nelson has answered these questions with an emphatic negative, pointing out that, despite the hind-sight of his later historians, Louis could foresee neither his death nor subsequent developments. From 834 onwards, Nelson argues, the emperor ruled with vigour and authority. Lothar did not dare to come north, but concentrated on making something of his kingdom of Italy, except for his appearance in 839, when he consented to Charles receiving a share of the Frankish heartlands. Pippin was pacified by receiving Anjou and did not create any real trouble until his death in December 838; Louis the German, the bane of what turned out to be the emperor's real last years (839–40), was dealt with swiftly and decisively by a ruler who had now passed sixty and was suffering from a weakness of his lungs, but not so much that it prevented him from quickly mounting a campaign to chase his son out of Alemannia. Unlike Charlemagne, Louis did not retire as a warrior.[221] Nelson points to the skilful way in which Louis constructed alliances for Charles by arranging judicious marriages, and to his strict handling of real enemies. Neither Hugh nor Matfrid ever held lands above

---

[217] *AB*, s.a. 835, p. 28: 'eundem augustum iniuste depositum'.
[218] *AB*, s.a. 835, p. 28: 'ibique Ebo in plenaria sinodo capitale crimen confessus'.
[219] Astronomer, c. 63–4, pp. 546–54.   [220] T. Schieffer, 'Krise', pp. 13–14.
[221] Nelson, 'The last years', p. 156.

the Alps, Ebo and Agobard did not get reinstated, and Jonas of Orléans and Hilduin had become completely loyal once more. Only a small group of bishops imposed the public penance of 833; once this painful episode was over, yet other bishops reinstated Louis, and then concentrated on rebuilding consensus, together with their emperor. If Soissons was traumatic for anybody, it was for the bishops, who also had to suffer the shock of seeing Pope Gregory turning up in Lothar's retinue.[222] The real trauma for the Franks, Nelson concludes, was the battle of Fontenoy (841) and its fraternal bloodshed, not Soissons.

One of the arguments in favour of Louis's authority having been impaired is that the production of capitularies dropped drastically, showing that there was not much left of the emperor's former zest for reform. Yet, as Rosamond McKitterick has pointed out, capitularies are but one form of royal communication, so a drop in quantity may be less significant than has been thought.[223] Furthermore, the capitularies of Charlemagne and Louis put together in 827 by Ansegis, abbot of St-Wandrille, were also widely used after 834, and must have partly satisfied the demand for such texts. The *Admonitio* of 825, for example, owes its diffusion almost entirely to having been incorporated in Ansegis' collection.[224] Like Charlemagne in 803/5, Louis had peaks in the production of his capitularies that reflect an intensification of reform, such as the years 818/9 or 828/9. In other words, a period of relatively limited activity on the capitulary front was nothing out of the ordinary.[225] To this, one might add that too sharp a distinction between capitularies and conciliar acts distorts the picture; the empire-wide council that gathered at Aachen in 836, with its elaborate acts which harked back to the reform councils of 829, was as much a sign of the emperor's continued vigour as any capitulary.[226] Finally, there is the possibility of loss of vital documents, which cannot be used as an *argumentum e silentio*, but cannot be entirely discounted either. The *Ordinatio imperii* of 817, the knowledge of which was certainly spread far and wide, is extant in only one manuscript, and the same holds true for the highly influential 'programmatic' capitulary issued by Charlemagne in 802.[227]

---

[222] Ibid., p. 155.
[223] McKitterick, *Charlemagne*, pp. 228–63; Nelson, 'The last years', pp. 147–8: 'But there is a temptation to correlate lack of capitulary evidence with absence of significant goings-on, or lack of legislation with weak government.' See also Pössel, 'Authors'.
[224] See above, n. 131.   [225] Bühler, 'Capitularia relecta', p. 468.
[226] MGH *Conc.* II/2, pp. 704–67.
[227] BnF lat. 2718; see Mordek, *Biblioteca*, p. 425; *Capitulare missorum* (a. 802), MGH *Capit.* I, no. 33, pp. 91–9; BnF lat. 4613, cf. Mordek, *Biblioteca*, p. 474. On the spread of knowledge of the *Ordinatio imperii*, see McKitterick, *History and Memory*, pp. 265–70.

Another matter is Louis's control over his sons. The fact that Lothar did not venture north until 839 may be not just a sign of his dutiful concentration on Italy, but also a gesture of defiance. The Astronomer in particular highlights the diplomatic offensive mounted by Judith and her advisors to get on such good terms with Lothar that he would once more extend his protection and patronage to his young half-brother. This would indeed have been a good solution, but Lothar did not co-operate – in other words, he refused to come north, pleading illness or other obstacles. That relations were not exactly friendly is revealed by the Astronomer, who usually tended to be relatively positive about Lothar, but not in a chapter about the years 836–7, when Louis's negotiations with his eldest son (through Wala) had foundered. In Italy an epidemic broke out, which killed Wala and affected Lothar. Louis, solicitous about his son, was compared with David, who could hardly bear the death of his son Absalom, however much the latter had offended him.[228] Clearly it was Lothar who was in the role of Absalom here, for in 837 Louis got word that Lothar had broken his oaths, 'and that his men were disturbing with the cruelest attacks the great church of St Peter which his grandfather Pippin, and his father Charles, and he himself had taken under their protection' – that is, Lothar allowed his *fideles* to be compensated for lost lands north of the Alps by means of ecclesiastical property.[229]

Without having the opportunity to intervene in person, Louis had to deal with an elder son who refused to toe the line. All the sons predictably became more independent from their father as time went on, consolidating their own power base, yet Louis the German, the one who rescued his father, did his utmost to remain on good terms with the emperor throughout the 830s, hoping to be rewarded by favourable succession arrangements.[230] Meanwhile, Louis continued to endow his youngest son with a suitable inheritance. In 837 Charles was meant to receive the *optima pars regni Francorum*, as the *Annals of Fulda* expressed it.[231] In September 838, at Quierzy, the apple of his father's eye was invested with a sword belt, receiving a grant 'with immediate effect, of the Duchy of Le Mans and the western shores between Seine and Loire'.[232] With Lothar still in a contrary mood, Pippin, who could do nothing but assent, was turned into Charles's protector, a position Louis the German had hoped for.[233]

[228] Astronomer, c. 55, p. 508: 'imitatus videlicet beatum David, qui multis insectationibus lacessitus a filio, mortem tamen eius egerrime tulit'.
[229] Astronomer, c. 55, pp. 508–9, with n. 837.   [230] Goldberg, *Struggle*, pp. 76–7.
[231] *AF*, s.a. 838, p. 28; Kasten, *Königssöhne*, pp. 193–4: Frisia, the counties on the lower Rhine, Hamaland and the area between Meuse and Seine, Verdun, Northern Burgundy with fourteen counties and Paris.
[232] *AB*, s.a. 838, p. 36.   [233] Goldberg, *Struggle*, pp. 87–8.

Earlier that year, having ordered his son to Nijmegen, Louis had a frightful row with Louis the German.[234] The lands on this side of the Rhine (as seen from Aachen) that the latter had wrongfully wrested from his father's authority were taken in hand once more, with Louis having to restrict himself to the kingdom of Bavaria. This meant a huge loss for Louis the German.

This was the beginning of a conflict that would drag on until the very end of Louis's life.[235] The son who had remained most loyal during the rebellions of 830 and 833 now turned into an enemy, disappointed in the rewards that his fidelity had earned him: all his efforts to claim an expanded kingdom east of the Rhine were thwarted either by his father or, later on, by his brother Lothar. When Pippin died in December 838, Louis moved Charles to the fore as the future king of Aquitaine, instead of Pippin's two sons. This reallocation of Aquitaine would be a bone of contention in the following years; Louis had to spend the autumn campaigning in the south against Pippin II, who claimed to be the rightful king.[236] Charles, the youngest, had now become the favourite son who was to inherit the coveted Frankish heartlands. The very last partition occurred in 839, this time in the presence of Lothar, who had been made an offer he could not refuse: he was to receive the eastern half of the realm minus Bavaria, Louis the German's allotted kingdom, and Charles the western part.[237] To the very end, re-dividing the realm was Louis's way of punishing a wayward son.

Did the rebellion of 833 break Louis's hold over his elder sons? After 834, it has been argued, Lothar, Pippin and Louis were rapidly developing into relatively independent kings, who inserted themselves as an extra layer of authority (*Zwischengewalt*) between their father and the latter's *fideles*. In Charles's case, something new happened, in that in 838 his rule was meant to be effective immediately, rather than after his father's death; elsewhere, the elder sons had already drawn all power to themselves, operating as *de facto* kings on their own authority, not on that of their father.[238] Yet Louis's autocratic behaviour, the relentless partitions of the realm and his fierce military conflict with Louis the German in his old age all indicate that he was not just a lame duck, faced with sons who grew ever mightier. The balance of power shifted in more subtle ways. In many ways, the confrontation of 833 had been a bridge too far: all concerned were shocked by what had happened, and the repetition of a united front

---

[234] *AB*, s.a. 838, p. 36.   [235] Goldberg, *Struggle*, pp. 87–94.
[236] *AB*, s.a. 839, pp. 48–9; on Charles's position and Pippin's rebellion, see Nelson, *Charles the Bald*, pp. 97–102.
[237] Nelson, *Charles the Bald*, pp. 99–100.   [238] Kasten, *Königssöhne*, pp. 194–7.

of sons was therefore unlikely. This gave a considerable leverage to Louis, who could continue to divide and rule.

However shaky the family firm might have become, it was precisely Louis's forgiveness that allowed this difficult co-operation to continue; and it was the emperor's penance in 833 that had prevented violence and bloodshed within the family. Louis himself was certainly aware of his public penance as a crucial event: after February, his *intitulatio* expressed the sentiment that it was God's mercy that had returned him to power.[239] For Charles and Lothar the events of 833 became a painful memory, but it did not prevent them from cherishing the memory of their father. Modern historiography has made too much of the supposedly disastrous effects of this *paenitentia publica*, as if the shame of this humiliation had permanently impaired Louis's authority and reputation, and too little of its potential as a way out of an impossible deadlock.[240] Janet Nelson is right: this event was not the watershed that radically altered Louis's position. As his elder sons grew older and more experienced in government, they inevitably received more recognition as rulers in their own right, especially within their own kingdoms.[241] That this relative independence had been attained by conflict and opposition was inevitable in a world that viewed total obedience as the filial duty *par excellence*. If the father lived long, this stringent norm began to chafe.[242] In any case, in Constantinople nobody seems to have noticed that the western emperor lacked power and authority. On 18 May 839 a Byzantine embassy arrived in Ingelheim to confirm the perpetual peace and friendship between the two emperors and their peoples.[243]

Another matter altogether is the constant changing of succession arrangements throughout the 830s, which must have bred an atmosphere of mutual suspicion among the sons, and increasing uncertainty among their followers. The conflict between Louis and his sons did have real repercussions for the high aristocracy, whose prestige and self-esteem hinged upon royal service. Serving the ruler made these magnates part of a privileged elite, yet they were no longer sure which ruler they should serve.[244] All this became much worse during the inter-fraternal war that broke out after Louis's death in 840; as I said earlier, Fontenoy (841), where Louis's sons fought a bloody battle, was more of a trauma than the

---

[239] 'Divina repropriante clementia'; Dickau, 'Kanzlei', II, p. 46; Boshof, *Ludwig*, p. 206, n. 172. The first charter in which this intitulation was used was for Corvey, dated 15 May 834 (BM ^{2} 927).

[240] See below, chapter 6.

[241] Kasten, *Königssohne*, pp. 193–200; Goldberg, *Struggle*, pp. 77–94.

[242] Cf. Nelson, 'Charlemagne – pater optimus?'

[243] *AB*, s.a. 839, p. 42.   [244] Airlie, '*Semper fideles*', p. 133.

rebellion of 833, where Louis's men walked over peacefully, albeit treacherously, to Lothar's camp. On the one hand, by ruling his sons by means of division, playing them against one another and keeping them in suspense about their ultimate inheritance, Louis certainly contributed to the *Bruderkrieg* that followed his death. On the other, it is difficult to see what alternative he had; apportioning blame with hindsight is simply out of order.

The Astronomer's account of the last months of Louis's life should disabuse anyone of the illusion of Louis as a feeble peacemaker. After Lent 840, when Louis the German rebelled once more, a furious Louis 'took himself off to meet this storm and to calm it'.[245] Leaving Judith and Charles in Poitiers, where he had been crushing Aquitanian rebels, he hit back effectively, rushing back to Aachen for Easter, then chasing a fleeing son and summoning an assembly in Worms for 1 July. A widely recorded eclipse of the sun occurred on 5 May 840.[246] Then the emperor's health failed him. Increasingly ill, Louis lay dying in a military tent on the island of Petersau in the Rhine, between Ingelheim and Mainz. The Astronomer, to whom we owe a dramatic depiction of the emperor's last days, stressed the presence of 'many bishops and servants of God' gathered there, and notably Louis's half-brother Drogo, the bishop of Metz.[247] The latter was portrayed as entirely in charge of this model death, punctuated by confessions, masses and vigils. Louis divided his possessions between the churches, the poor and his sons Lothar and Charles. He sent Lothar a crown and a sword embellished with gold and gems to keep on the condition that he would protect Charles and Judith.[248] Towards the end, Louis had regained faith in his original plan of making his eldest son Lothar the guardian of the youngest, something Judith had done her utmost to bring about.[249]

The one shadow over this image of an exemplary death was the emperor's difficulty in forgiving his son Louis. A grudging declaration of pardon was extracted by Drogo, who was told to admonish the wayward son for his bad conduct. Louis chased off an evil spirit, in the confident fashion of someone who shoos off a dog. Was this merely an imitation of the *Life of St Martin*, or was this the demon of decades of discord with his elder sons? Some anxiety about the question whether this had been an altogether 'good death' seems to underly the Astronomer's narrative. But

---

[245] Astronomer, c. 62, pp. 540–2; on Louis's fury ('admodum ... motus'), see *AB*, s.a. 840, p. 48.

[246] Astronomer, c. 62, p. 545, n. 962.

[247] Astronomer, cc. 63–4, pp. 546–54; on this death scene, which was inspired by Sulpicius Severus' *Vita Martini*, see Tremp, 'Die letzten Worte'.

[248] Astronomer, c. 63, p. 548.   [249] Ibid., c. 59, p. 528.

in the end, Louis turned his eyes to heaven, and he seemed to laugh. The shadows of sin were dispelled. As the Astronomer wrote, citing Augustine: 'He cannot die badly who has lived well.'[250] This conclusion is followed by the very last sentences of the *Vita Hludowici*:

He died on the twentieth of June in the sixty-fourth year of his life.[251] He ruled over Aquitaine for thirty-seven years and was emperor for twenty-seven years. After his soul departed, the emperor's brother Drogo, the bishop of Metz, along with the other bishops, abbots, counts, vassals, and a large mass of clergy and people took the emperor's remains and with great honour had them transported to Metz where he was nobly buried in the basilica of St Arnulf, where his mother was also buried.[252]

That Louis's mother had been buried in Metz may have been as important for the choice of his burial site as the loyalty of his half-brother Drogo, or the fame of a sainted Carolingian ancestor, Arnulf. Neither Judith nor Charles was at his side when Louis died, but someone who rushed to Metz quickly was Lothar, who immediately founded an altar for his father, a gesture of filial piety mentioned in an anonymous epitaph commemorating the deceased emperor.[253] Lothar was finally ready to become the 'senior emperor', but once Louis had died, there was no more containment of fraternal discord.

---

[250] Ibid., c. 64, p. 552; Augustine, *De disciplina christiania* II, c. 13, p. 221.
[251] Louis was actually sixty-two or sixty-three, yet his epitaph and Nithard, I, c. 8, pp. 36, give his age as sixty-four, both making the same mistake.
[252] Astronomer, c. 64, p. 554; cf. Nelson, 'Carolingian royal funerals', pp. 155–60.
[253] MGH *Poet. lat.* II, pp. 653–4.

Ninth-century narratives

The court and its narratives

'It is in the reign of Louis the Pious above all that the courtly historiography played such a crucial role in deliberately enhancing the public and political image of the ruler.'[1] This is the point of departure for this chapter on ninth-century narratives produced during or shortly after Louis's reign, in which new images of kingship were created and articulated. This period saw a real upsurge of the writing of history, biography, hagiography, panegyrics, poetry and polemics centred upon the ruler. The most influential of these texts will be discussed separately in this chapter, for together they form the foundation of the grand narrative of Louis's reign. With a deliberate lack of precision, I have gathered these texts together under the title 'ninth-century narratives'. They are 'ninth-century' in that they all recorded and com- mented on (near-)contemporary events, with contemporary audiences in mind. For all their protestations that they wrote for posterity, the authors in question tended to be deeply involved in the political action of their day and age. In one way or another, they had some kind of a connection with the court of Louis the Pious. Either they were part of or had belonged to the emperor's inner circle of courtiers, or, residing elsewhere, they avidly followed events in and around the royal household. None of the works discussed here can count as 'official' biography or historiography, not even those in which the emperor was most loyally defended.

Even if the intended readership of these court-connected texts is more difficult to identify, it clearly shared these royal interests, in that the ruler was expected to be centre stage in the narrative.[2] Well-informed insiders at the court must have noticed, far better than we can now, how the authors in question took their position in specific power struggles among the 'men of the palace', and how competition between courtiers found its way into

---

[1] Innes and McKitterick, 'Writing of history', p. 209.
[2] On Frankish historiography, see above all McKitterick, *History and Memory*, especially chapters 2 ('Carolingian history books') and 5 ('History and politics'); see further Nelson, 'History-writing'.

what looked, at first sight, like a dispassionate or even official record. In the *Royal Frankish Annals*, for example, much is made of the arrival of Hilduin's Roman relics in 826, and significantly less of the translation of Einhard's martyrs the year thereafter.[3] Most of these nuances are now lost, yet in order to understand and use these texts, one needs to keep in mind that they originated from a world that consisted of men and women who, be it closely or tenuously, felt themselves connected with the royal household, measuring their status and privilege in terms of their proximity to the ruler and their loyalty in his service.[4]

The court was a community with a composition that changed in the course of the year.[5] The king's *fideles*, the faithful men from the regions, flocked there in droves for the big spring and summer assemblies, but in winter the court was reduced to the ruler's family and his inner circle of courtiers, the *homines palatini*. This hard core of men who remained 'of the palace', regardless whether they had left it for royal duty elsewhere, was largely recruited from the young aristocrats who, as warriors or clerics, received training in the royal household.[6] Together with those magnates who enjoyed the ruler's special favour (the *proceres palatii*) and those with special functions in the royal household (*ministri*), they formed the court in the strict sense of the word. Following late antique models, Einhard called this the *comitatus*, because these men were a regular or permanent part of the king's entourage.[7] The most important magnates, including Einhard himself, kept a house in Aachen. They remained at this palace throughout the winter of 828–9, deliberating with Louis and Lothar on ways to placate an offended deity, and in July 829 they accompanied the emperor to the palace at Worms, for a general assembly where 'the court' would be substantially enlarged with counts, bishops, abbots and other faithful men from all over the realm.[8]

When I refer to court-connected authors and their audiences, I therefore have a varied context in mind, with a geography that includes palaces as well as monasteries, and with a human membership that far exceeded the inner circle of the 'men of the palace', much as they may have wished to keep their proximity to the ruler and his family an exclusive privilege. In its broadest possible sense, 'the court' consisted of a network of elite men

---

[3] Cf. *ARF*, s.a. 826 and 827, pp. 172–4.
[4] Airlie, '*Semper fideles*'.   [5] Innes, 'Place of discipline', p. 61.
[6] Those whom Adalhard called the *pueri et vasalli*; see Innes, 'Place of discipline', p. 61.
[7] For an excellent introduction to the palace of Louis the Pious, see Depreux, *Prosopographie*, pp. 9–39, as well as Fleckenstein's classic study *Die Hofkapelle*.
[8] Einhard, *TMP*, I, c. 1; II, cc. 1, 6, 11; III, cc. 11, 12, 19. See also *ARF*, s.a. 829, p. 177, with regard to Louis breaking up *cum comitatu suo* from Aachen, to join the *generalem conventum* in Worms.

and women – lay magnates and their households, bishops and their clerics, abbots and abbesses and their communities – who owed their wealth and privilege to the ruler.[9] When Archbishop Leidrad of Lyons had a house near his episcopal residence rebuilt so that it would make a fitting place to lodge Charlemagne, should he ever come to visit Lyons, he mentally incorporated the court into his episcopal residence.[10] For Leidrad's successor, Agobard, the court in the restricted sense – the ruler and his entourage – was the undisputed centre of his world, and the intended audience of much of his fiery prose.[11] This world of those with access to the ruler, which could be referred to in passing as 'the palace', was a place of moral discipline, which required and instilled a special code of conduct, governed by restraint in speech, comportment and dress. It served as a model household for the magnates on whose loyalty the Carolingian polity depended, and whose prestige in turn depended on royal favour. With all the well-informed conviction of their own experience, two *homines palatini*, Adalhard of Corbie (d. 826) and Hincmar of Rheims (d. 882), described this normative order of the palace in detail, and thus helped to spread an ideal that was shared across generations: Adalhard had been educated at the court of Pippin III, Louis's grandfather, and Hincmar, as Hilduin's pupil, visited Louis's court. Hincmar claimed that as a youth he had seen Adalhard, 'the old and wise kinsman of the elder Charles, the emperor, and first among his first counsellors'. As he said himself, Hincmar had read and copied Adalhard's treatise on the palace, which thus became the core of his own *De ordine palatii*.[12] *De ordine*, then, spans the experience of six generations of Carolingian court culture in development. Such explicit reflection on the proper conduct of those who formed 'the palace' was no doubt influential, but it was the unrecorded memories of all these future counts, bishops and abbots who had been trained as youths in the palace, which turned the court into a frame of mind that could be shared throughout the realm.[13]

---

[9] I use the word 'elite' in the broad and flexible sense employed by Régine Le Jan and her working group: those who, within their world, exercise social power due to high birth and inherited status, or to the use of knowledge. See Feller, 'Introduction', p. 8.

[10] Leidrad, *Epistola ad Carolum* (812–14), ed. E. Dümmler, *Epistolae Karolini aevi* III, MGH *Epp.* IV (Hanover, 1895), pp. 542–4; on this letter, see De Jong, 'Charlemagne's church', pp. 103–4.

[11] See below, chapter 3, pp. 142–7.

[12] *De ordine palatii*, c. III, p. 54: 'Adalardum senem et sapientem domni Karoli magni imperatoris propinquum ... inter primos consiliarios primum, in adolescentia mea vidi. Cuius libellum de ordine palatii legi et scripsi.' On the dating of Adalhard's part of *De ordine palatii* to 810–14, or possibly 812, see Nelson, 'Aachen', pp. 226–8, and now McKitterick, *Charlemagne*, pp. 144–5, who makes a case for the 780s.

[13] For the expression 'frame of mind', see Nelson, 'History-writing', p. 439; cf. also Airlie, 'Palace of memory'.

Such men remained 'of the palace' throughout their lives, carrying the courtly *habitus* with them, wherever they happened to serve in later life. They shared an awareness of collective interests, but also had their factional or individual goals to pursue, in competition with others. Ninth-century historical writing contributed to consensus, but it also reflected and framed ongoing debates at the court; it was 'produced and consumed as a means of critique and contestation', and bound up with public affairs as they unfolded.[14] This was not 'court history' in the sense of a dutiful product written at the ruler's behest. If Charlemagne and Louis commissioned anything, it was biblical exegesis and astronomy, not historiography, biography or panegyrics.[15] Yet these narratives were court-connected in that they were composed by men (and occasionally women) who often enjoyed sufficient 'familiarity' with their lord and king to take the risk of speaking the truth about contemporary events and admonishing their ruler to learn from them. Often, as we shall see, authors wrote themselves into their own narratives, portraying themselves as trusted members of the king's inner circle. This was a claim to veracity and to having intimate knowledge of the ruler and his doings, but it was also a form of posturing for an audience of insiders as someone who belonged to the in-crowd.

The authors of the narratives discussed in this chapter came from the top echelon of Carolingian society. They were usually a part of the contemporary history they wrote, and it is of vital importance to remember that, however diverse their positions may have been in the strife within the imperial family, they shared fundamental values to which they appealed constantly in their narratives. Relating the significant actions (*gesta*) of rulers and magnates, these authors interpreted and evaluated the conduct of their main players, sometimes explicitly, but mostly by picturing their protagonists in the course of their actions. Relying on a set of shared notions of commendable behaviour or its opposite, authors sent out a constant bombardment of messages to their audience on who had lived up to expectations and who had not.[16] These expectations might concern any kind of public and formalised behaviour – the *adventus* of a ruler or a pope, the conduct of an assembly – but also the essential values of this particular elite: fidelity (*fides*) towards one's ruler but also towards God, obedience to one's father, fearless veracity, bravery in battle. Ninth-century

[14] Nelson, 'History-writing', p. 437.
[15] On exegesis for rulers: De Jong, 'The empire as *ecclesia*' and 'Monastic writing'; on astronomy and its importance for rulers, see Dutton, *Charlemagne's Mustache*, pp. 93–127 ('Of Carolingian kings and their stars').
[16] Buc, *Dangers of Ritual*; Pössel, 'Symbolic communication'.

narratives charted and redefined this high moral ground, with a sharp eye on the compass of divine authority: who had a right to stay on this ground, and who should fall? Radbert, the very last author discussed here, said that for him writing history was to draw a 'moral image' (*imago morum*) of his age and subjects. He was more explicit about this than most, but even in the annals that appear succinct and entirely matter-of-fact, there was a moral grid that invited contemporaries whose opinion mattered to subscribe to a common view of the past.

The message from inside: annals

The most influential narrative on Carolingian history, in the ninth century as well as nowadays, are the so-called *Royal Frankish Annals*, a compilation which spans the years between 741 and 829. The title *Annales regni Francorum* (henceforth, *ARF*), is a modern construct; these are not the official reports from the court they were once thought to be. Nonetheless, recent research on the process of redaction and adaptation of annals has confirmed that the impact of the *ARF* on the Carolingian world was considerable.[17] Another traditional view that this was a blow-by-blow account by scribes who were ultra-brief in the beginning and then found their voice, becoming more elaborate as they went on, is no longer tenable either; instead, the different versions as they are now known were at least in part the product of careful construction. Silence and omission could be as meaningful as explicit prose; neither did such texts remain stable, once they had been conceived. The meaning of annals could subtly change as they were combined with other works in special collections that highlighted certain aspects of the Frankish past, often in a specific political context.[18] All the same, some parts of the *ARF* may be less reconstructed than others; the section of 814–29 seems to be one of these, but this requires more investigation.

All this precludes any use of the *ARF* as a set of annals representing the official view from the court. Even if rulers had wanted to control the message of the annals, of which there is no indication whatsoever, they

---

[17] McKitterick, *History and Memory*, pp. 28–35, 101–13, 120–32, and *Perceptions of the Past*, pp. 63–90. On annals and nineteenth-century scholarship, Reimitz, 'Der Weg zum Königtum' and "*Nomen Francorum obscuratum*".

[18] Becher, *Eid und Herrschaft*, esp. pp. 21–77, on the *ARF* until 788 (Kurze's 'A class') reflecting Charlemagne's political agenda of 790; McKitterick, *History and Memory*, pp. 102–3, and Reimitz, 'Der Weg zum Königtum', on the silence regarding 751–2 and its function in representing the rise of Carolingian royal authority; on a compendium of historical texts, possibly compiled for the coronation of Charles the Bald as king of Lotharingia in 869 (Vienna, ÖNB cod. 473), see Reimitz, 'Geschichtsbuch'; McKitterick, *History and Memory*, pp. 121–3.

could not have done so. As soon as sets of annals were diffused throughout the realm, they could be used, edited or rewritten. If one wishes to be very sceptical, one could maintain that annals purporting to come from the court may very well have been produced elsewhere, for all we have to go on is the oldest manuscript and its provenance; any amount of tinkering may have been going on before the text as we have it was written down. On the other hand, it is precisely the widespread and unruly diffusion of the *ARF* that indicates that these annals and their derivatives had the special authority of a text thought to have been produced by the leadership at the court. In other words, the *ARF* may not represent official history in any modern sense of the word, but the text was produced by authoritative insiders at the court, and others wanted to know what they had to say.

This becomes more clear if one considers the annals stemming from the reign of Louis the Pious. First, there is the so-called Revised Version of the *ARF* up to 801. This text is no longer attributed to Einhard but is nonetheless considered the product of Louis's court; Einhard probably knew and relied on it when he wrote his *Vita Karoli*.[19] And then, of course, there is the section of the *ARF* from 814 to 829, which represents a unified view of Frankish history that is also reflected in its manuscript tradition. On the one hand, this unified view represents Louis in all his glory as a Christian emperor, taking care of the divine cult (*status ecclesiae*) and its material sustenance, receiving embassies from far and wide, and relentlessly fighting against the enemies of Christendom.[20] On the other hand, from the early 820s onwards, such triumphalist prose was increasingly punctuated by natural disasters, epidemics and other 'signs from heaven' which may or may not have been taken as indications of God's displeasure. Because of their wide and relatively uniform dissemination, the annals of 814–29 had a long-term impact, yet in the short term, as Helmut Reimitz has pointed out, the consensus of these years proved to be extremely fragile. From 830 onwards, the view of the Frankish past became more fragmented.[21] In the early 840s, however, the annals of 814–29 served the Astronomer as a basis for his account of this period,[22] and the same text found its way into ÖNB cod. 473 under the title *Gesta Hludowici*

---

[19] My thanks to David Ganz for this information. On the Reviser, see McKitterick, *History and Memory*, pp. 27–31 and 113–19; also Collins, 'The "Reviser" revisited'. On the section of the *ARF* from 801 to 814, see McKitterick, *Charlemagne*, pp. 31–49.

[20] See *ARF*, s.a. 819, for just one example.   [21] Reimitz, '*Nomen Francorum obscuratum*'.

[22] Tremp, Introduction to Astronomer, p. 80. The text used by the Astronomer resembles Kurze's C2 and C3, the two manuscripts considered to be 'closest to the court'. C3 (Petersburg lat. F.v.Iv.4) is the oldest textual witness to the *Annals of St-Bertin*; C2 has the best version of the *Vita Hludowici*, probably derived from a special festive copy made for Charles the Bald.

imperatoris.[23] Clearly this particular section of the annals was perceived as an entity by near contemporaries and the next generation, to be used as a building block in subsequent historical compilations. This was the kind of history of Louis the Pious that provided an authoritative account for his biographer, and that could in due course be renamed 'the Deeds of the emperor Louis'. By contrast, the continuation of the *ARF* known as the *Annales Bertiniani*, named after the monastery of St-Bertin, whence the most important manuscript derives, had a much more limited impact.[24] Only a few manuscripts survive, and it is doubtful whether the Astronomer knew and used the text.[25] Nonetheless, until Louis's death in 840 these annals were probably kept at the court, possibly as a group product under the general oversight of the archchaplain, first Hilduin's successor Fulco, and from 835 onwards Drogo of Metz. The latter's palace chaplain Prudentius then gradually took over the actual keeping of the annals. When Prudentius was rewarded with the episcopal see of Troyes in 843, the annals moved there with him.[26] These so-called *Annals of St-Bertin* (*AB*) offer a well-informed narrative about Louis's last decade, as observed by annalists who were part of the royal entourage. In the few extant manuscripts this text is presented as a seamless continuation of the *ARF*, yet these manuscripts are very few indeed, certainly compared to the ample transmission of the *ARF* up to 829, and this continuation lacked the wide-ranging influence of its predecessor.[27]

Judging by this development of what I shall call, for better or worse, the court annals, the rebellions against Louis the Pious put an end to what was perceived by contemporaries as one set of authoritative annals, which ran from Louis's succession in 814 to the year 829. This was not to say, however, that when the authors of the *Annals of St-Bertin* took over, this spelled a fundamental reorientation of anyone's mental horizon. It is not as if the perspective of the annalists who worked after 830 had suddenly shrunk, nor is there any significant break in the presentation of the material. Throughout the early 830s, the annals are staunchly on the side of the 'Lord Emperor', as Louis is consistently called, and are well informed about his movements throughout the troubles: this was the

---

[23] ÖNB, cod. 473. According to Reimitz and McKitterick, this is a compilation made for Charles the Bald on the occasion of his coronation as king of Lotharingia in 869; Reimitz, 'Geschichtsbuch'; McKitterick, *History and Memory*, pp. 121–3, 215–6.

[24] See *AB*, pp. xvi–lxxiv; Nelson, *Annals of St-Bertin*; see also Nelson, 'Annals of St. Bertin'.

[25] Nelson, *Annals of St-Bertin*, pp. 15–16. On the Astronomer and *AB*, see Tremp, Introduction to Astronomer, pp. 92–3.

[26] Nelson, *Annals of St-Bertin*, pp. 6–7, who sees Prudentius as someone who initially was a member of an authorial team, but who in due course became the main author.

[27] Ibid., pp. 15–6.

record of Louis's restoration. The real break in continuity came only later, with Louis's death on 20 June 840. Its impact is reflected in the annalistic record by a dearth of evidence for the period immediately thereafter, until the battle of Fontenoy (21 June 841).[28]

This leaves us with the question of why the *ARF* until 829 were so widely disseminated, while their continuation known as the *Annals of St-Bertin* was not. Should either Archchaplain Hilduin or Archchancellor Helisachar be considered as the author of the *ARF*, as has been argued,[29] with the result that when these men fell from royal grace in 830 and were banished from the court, the annals collapsed as well? It seems best to think of the *ARF* as a collective venture, presumably overseen by the archchaplain or archchancellor, without either of them – Hilduin, Helisachar or someone else – necessarily being 'the author' in the strict sense. Yet one cannot discount the impetus of such leading men when it came to spreading the view from the palace far and wide. The actual diffusion of annals from the court is difficult to grasp, yet there are some indications of activity of this kind.[30] The wide dissemination of the *ARF* and their many subsequent 'combinations and permutations'[31] was not just a matter of the ideological conviction of some high-ranking palace clerics who effectively imposed their view of the world on to other members of the elite. For the recipients of those texts outside the inner circle of the ruler, it must have mattered deeply who were associated with the court annals. To them, the authority with which this text was invested must have been dependent not just on an abstract 'palace' but above all on the men who ran it, who supervised the production of annals, and who were powerful patrons, as well as on those members of the elite, clerical and otherwise, who took a keen interest in the court and its records. To put it another way: the annalists who took over after 829 were obviously as able as their predecessors, but they probably did not have the public standing and political clout of men such as Einhard, Hilduin or Helisachar. Meanwhile, it should be kept in mind that their contemporaries thought

---

[28] Ibid., pp. 7–8.
[29] For Hilduin: Monod, *Études critiques*, pp. 136–41; Heinzelmann, 'Translatio', pp. 270–1; in favour of Helisachar, Malbos, 'L'annaliste royale'. For a biographical sketch of both men and their careers, see Depreux, *Prosopographie*, pp. 235–40, 250–6.
[30] McKitterick, *History and Memory*, pp. 21–2, discusses a little-known fragment of a 'class E' manuscript in a script associated with the court of Louis the Pious and concludes cautiously that 'it raises the possibility, therefore, of the royal court being directly associated with the dissemination of at least one version of the Frankish past'. This concerns Cologne, Sankt Maria im Kapitol A II/18, s. IX 1/3; a single and very frail leaf containing the E text entry for 824. The complete manuscript would have contained the Revised Version and the later section of the *ARF*, like others in this class.
[31] McKitterick, *History and Memory*, pp. 20–1.

of annals as a royal genre. As Ardo/Smaragdus maintained in his *Life* of Benedict of Aniane, 'no learned men would doubt, I think, that it is most ancient practice, habitual for kings from then to now to have their deeds and the events [of their reign] committed to annals for posterity to learn about'.[32] During the reign of Louis the Pious, those who participated in the composition of court annals by definition walked the corridors of power; explanations for ruptures and variations in annalistic strategy, to my mind, should first of all be looked for in the changing position and fate of the prominent courtiers who occupied themselves with this 'habit of kings'.

Imperial imagery: Einhard

With his *Vita Karoli*, Einhard (d. 840) set a standard for royal biography for others to aspire to, even if they could not live up to it. Both Thegan and the Astronomer knew Einhard's famous work, built on it, and at times engaged with it in a critical fashion. Moreover, even though in the early 830s Einhard retired from active duty at Louis's court, he remained an influential figure, who continued to enjoy royal favour.[33] To him, for example, the emperor turned for expert advice on the meaning of an ominous portent, the comet of 837.[34] The *Vita Karoli* has become so famous and familiar that it is difficult to keep in mind that this was once a pioneering work – the daring experiment of an author who did not rely on the well-known model of the hagiographical *vita*, but who chose Suetonius, Cicero and possibly also Tacitus as his examples to fashion a thematic biography of the king who had been his lord and patron (*dominus et nutritor*).[35]

The lack of early manuscripts has led to a long and still unresolved controversy about the date of the *Vita Karoli*. Another complicating factor is the fact that the extensive manuscript tradition has three strands: one without the preface which identifies Einhard as the author, one with the preface, and one with a verse dedication to Louis by his librarian Gerward. This suggests that the work was completed in various stages.[36]

---

[32] Ardo/Smaragdus, *Vita Benedicti*, Preface, MGH *SS* XV, p. 201; cf. Nelson, 'History-writing', on court-oriented historigraphy that is not necessarily 'official' or propagandistic.
[33] On Einhard's biography, see Schefers, *Einhard*; Depreux, *Prosopographie*, pp. 177–82; Dutton, *CC*, pp. xi–xli; Smith, 'Einhard'.
[34] Einhard, *Epistolae*, no. 40, ed. Hampe, pp. 129–30; Dutton, *CC*, no. 61, pp. 160–1. Another expert was the Astronomer (cf. Astronomer, c. 58, p. 522).
[35] Einhard, *VK*, prologue, p. 1. The best introductions to the *Vita Karoli*, its structure and its literary models, with references to older literature, are Ganz, 'Einhard's Charlemagne' and 'Einhardus peccator'.
[36] Ganz, 'Einhard's Charlemagne', p. 51, n. 19 (who identified 112 manuscripts of the work) thinks the *VK* already circulated in the mid-820s and was later revised.

Proponents of a relatively late date tend to exclude the possibility of this slow genesis of the work, and have furthermore agreed on two related and questionable assumptions. The first is that, by writing a *Life* of the great father, Einhard intended to criticise the unsatisfactory son; the second is that the work should therefore be part of the crisis of Louis's reign, which began in 828, so the work should be dated from this year onwards. This position has recently been defended by Matthias Tischler in his massive study of the *Vita Karoli*, who views Einhard's preface, especially, as a statement of 'resignation and hidden *Kulturkritik*'.[37] In Tischler's view, Louis was the main recipient of his father's *Life*, in the 'official' version to which Gerward, sometime between 829 and 830 when both men were still at the court, added his approval and dedication.[38] Why would praise of Charlemagne amount to critique of Louis, and if so, why would such critique be dedicated to the emperor with laudatory verse from his librarian? The only answer one gets is that evoking the image of Charlemagne was politically relevant, and that reform usually concentrated on Louis.[39] Presumably, Einhard's own preface was deliberately withheld from the emperor because its author called Charlemagne his *nutritor* and said that men now alive could scarcely equal this great ruler's deeds.[40] One fails to see why Louis would be in any way offended by these two statements.

All this is predicated on an antiquated view of Louis as a weak ruler, and also on an anachronistic notion of the function of criticism at Louis's court, to which I shall return in the next chapter. There is no reason to take the *Vita Karoli* as anything other than a testimony to the greatness of the father, of the sort which would have pleased the son. A date as early as 817 or shortly thereafter has been suggested, on the ground that Einhard's work would have supported Louis during the early years of his reign, and in the aftermath of the *Ordinatio imperii*.[41] This cannot be excluded, yet I am inclined to follow those who see a connection between the conception of this biography and the birth of Charles, the grandson who was the only one of Louis's sons who had not known the grandfather whose name he was given. He needed the kind of information that could be supplied only

---

[37] Tischler, *Einharts 'Vita Karoli'*, pp. 152–87 and 163 ('resignativen Tenor und versteckten Kulturkritik'); see the review by Julia M. H. Smith in *Speculum* 79 (2004), pp. 846–8, which is a fair assessment of the book's strengths and weaknesses.

[38] Tischler, *Einharts 'Vita Karoli'*, pp. 161–2.

[39] Ibid., p. 161, 'sondern daß das Bild dieses Kaisers politische Relevanz besaß und die zeitgenössischen Reformmechanismen im Reich stark auf den aktuellen Herrscher bezogen waren, begründete dieses Widmungsmodel.'

[40] Ibid., p. 158; Einhard, *VK*, prologue, p. 1: 'moderni temporis hominibus vix imitabiles actus'.

[41] Innes and McKitterick, 'Writing of history', pp. 202–8. McKitterick, *Charlemagne*, pp. 11–14.

by Einhard, an older courtier of great authority, who had known Charlemagne better than most, including his own son Louis.[42] Einhard may well have followed a procedure that was not uncommon at the time: before dedicating a work to the ruler himself, one first circulated it among friends, and then tried it out on a prominent courtier. Vetted and favourably received, the text was then deemed ready for royal consumption.[43] Along these lines, the *Vita Karoli* and its preface may first have been sent to Gerward, who then sent it on with a brief verse preface presenting the *Vita* to the emperor, praising him and identifying the work as Einhard's.[44]

In his other and less well-known work, the *Translation and Miracles of Sts Marcellinus and Peter*, Einhard wrote about the triumphant entry of the relics of Roman martyrs into the Frankish empire.[45] He had these brought (or, rather, stolen) from Rome in 827 for the churches he had built on his own property, in fierce competition with his fellow-courtier Hilduin of St-Denis, who had installed the Roman relics of St Sebastian in his monastery of St-Médard of Soissons the year before. The work relates the fetching of the relics from Rome, their arrival at the palace in Aachen, Hilduin's fruitless efforts to divert Einhard's martyrs to St-Médard, and their safe landing, by November 828, in their resting place in Seligenstadt.[46] With his martyrs in place, at the end of the second book, Einhard could embark upon a systematic presentation of his martyrs' miracles. His original plan was to conform to a geographical structure. First, he would describe the miracles performed in the saints' resting place in Seligenstadt, then those witnessed in Aachen by the courtiers (*aulici*) themselves, and finally those worked in various other places (*per diversa loca facta*). In this way, Einhard argued, he could not overlook any of their *signa atque miracula*.[47] This basic structure was loosely adhered to: eventually, it was the third book that began with miracles performed in Seligenstadt, yet the palace and its concerns repeatedly surface in this section of the *Translatio*. When Einhard attended the winter meeting of

---

[42] Krüger, 'Neue Beobachtungen'; David Ganz, in a paper presented at NIAS in 2006.

[43] Other instances are Hraban Maur, who dedicated his commentary on the Books of Kings first to Hilduin in 829, and then in 832 to Louis the Pious; see De Jong, 'The empire as *ecclesia*', pp. 203–4; likewise, Helisachar was the recipient of the first book of *Histories* of Frcculf of Lisieux, who then in 829 dedicated the second book to the Empress Judith, for the instruction of her son Charles; cf. Frcculf, *Historiae*, pp. 17–20, 435–9.

[44] Einhard, *VK*, p. xxix: 'Hos tibi versiculos ad laudem, maxime princeps / Edidit aeternam memoriam tuam / Gerwardus supplex famulus, qui mente benigna / Egregrium extollit nomen ad astra tuum / Hanc prudens gestam noris tu scribere, lector / Einhardum Magni magnificum Karoli.'

[45] Einhard, *TMP*, trans. Dutton, *CC*, pp. 198–246; Heinzelmann, '"Translatio"'; Smith, '"Emending evil ways"'.

[46] Einhard, *TMP*, II, c. 6, p. 247.   [47] Ibid., III, c. 1, p. 248.

828–9 at Aachen that discussed God's displeasure with the Frankish leadership, his martyrs acted as an effective channel of communication with Heaven, causing visions to occur that were then reported to Einhard in Aachen. The miracles performed in Aachen itself were grouped at the beginning of the fourth book, with a preface that reminded the reader that the miracles now to be described came to the attention of the ruler, his magnates and, indeed, all the courtiers.[48] At the end of this sequence Einhard related with pride that the emperor himself had informed him of a miracle that had occurred in his, Einhard's, house, while he was unaware of it. This was the apotheosis of this series of court-connected miracles: Louis himself had become more conscious of the powers of these saints than Einhard himself.[49]

His *Translation of Sts Marcellinus and Peter* was completed towards the end of 830 or the beginning of 831. I follow Matthias Tischler in this respect, but not in his view that this work embodied a more radical and explicit manifestation of the kind of criticism that Einhard had shortly before voiced in his *Vita Karoli*.[50] According to the traditional perspective, Einhard had by then retired from the court to lead a semi-monastic life on his own property in Seligenstadt, disillusioned with the direction in which the Frankish polity was heading under Louis's erratic leadership. Yet there are other ways of looking at Einhard's retirement. His letters to Judith and Louis from the spring of 830, in which he excused himself from the royal presence because of bad health, cannot be automatically taken as proof that the grand old man disapproved of the imperial couple, and therefore opted out. By 830, when Einhard was around sixty years old, he may well have had health problems.[51] In a letter written probably towards the end of 833, he declared himself to be so shocked about 'the revolution that has recently been brought about in this realm' that he did not know where to turn, except to God.[52] He was not the only one, and much of Einhard's exasperation must have been reserved for Lothar, whom in 830 he had admonished not to rebel against his father.[53]

Recent research has opened up new perspectives on Einhard. His wish to withdraw from the court and devote himself to a religious life in the proximity of his saints has been reinterpreted by Julia Smith as a revival of late antique forms of ascetic life which found expression in the household, rather than in a formal monastic conversion.[54] And as David Ganz

---

[48] Ibid., IV, c. 1, p. 256.   [49] Ibid., c. 7, p. 258; Heinzelmann, 'Translatio', p. 287.
[50] Tischler, *Einharts 'Vita Karoli'*, pp. 169–84.
[51] Einhard, *Epp.*, nos. 13–15, pp. 116–18; Stratmann, 'Einhards letzte Lebensjahre'.
[52] Einhard, *Epp.*, no. 31, p. 125: 'mutatio rerum, quae nuper in hoc regno facta est'.
[53] Ibid., no. 11, pp. 114–15; trans. Dutton, *CC*, pp. 147–8.
[54] Smith, 'Einhard', pp. 68–9.

pointed out, Einhard identified himself as 'the sinner' (*Einhardus peccator*) and 'set himself in a world of redemption, achieved by the prayers both of the living and of the saints in heaven'.[55] As he grew older, this courtier's main interest was with his abbeys, his churches, and especially the cult of his martyrs in the churches he had founded on land granted by Louis. When his wife Imma died in 835 Einhard grieved deeply for her. Was Louis's visit in 836 to Seligenstadt and Einhard's martyrs also a visit of condolence to his faithful courtier? It is a tempting thought.[56] Einhard followed his Imma on 14 March 840, and was buried in the same grave, *ad sanctos*, with the saints he had taken so much trouble to transport from Rome to a sacred landscape that was at least partly of his own making. In other words, Einhard had left the centre of the political arena, yet he remained keenly interested in what went on there, and continued to be a distant presence. His narrative about the Roman martyrs sang the praises of his saints, first and foremost, but it was also written to settle a score with his competitor Hilduin. Furthermore, through this work Einhard tried to create a favourable image of his own prominent role during the winter meeting of 828–9, taking part in an ongoing debate after the event. In 830, with surprising energy, the already ageing courtier harnessed both his literary skills and his formidable relics to the cause of steering back his royal and courtly readership to the cause of *correctio*. Preparing to retire from active duty at the court, Einhard now engaged in high-level admonition from Seligenstadt, a sacred place he had created himself. He clearly took his role as a go-between seriously: the palace could not be the moral hub it should be without being bolstered by Einhard's martyrs and their visionary information. It is this ongoing relationship and sense of public duty that are expressed in Einhard's *Translatio*, not his wish to retire from the world. He came from the palace and continued to belong to it, even if he was now to be found mostly in the proximity of his saints.

Understandably, the contrast between the two works has baffled historians. In his *Vita Karoli*, Einhard consciously embarked on a novel venture, imitating classical models and emulating their impressively polished style. Except for the preface that was added later, the author himself was absent from the text. By contrast, in the *Translatio* Einhard is present throughout the narrative, highlighting his own special relation to the martyrs, his prominent position at the court, and how the one reinforced the other.[57] This authorial presence is essential to the entire structure of the work, and is signalled in the very first chapter, when Einhard introduced himself as

---

[55] Ganz, 'Einhardus peccator', p. 41.   [56] Dutton, *CC*, p. xxxv.
[57] Concerning Einhard's authorial strategy in the *Translatio*, I have learned much from Gerda Heydemann. See Heydemann, 'Text und Translation'.

'still with a position in the palace and occupied with the business of the world', referring to the time before he decided to devote himself to his saints.[58] This is one of the reasons why this text is so informative about the deliberations that went on in Aachen in that particular winter; another is that the *Translatio* itself was part of the debate about *correctio* that had started in the winter of 828. Einhard's two major works show that he made deliberate choices as to the medium which was to convey the message. Judging by his *Translatio*, Einhard knew very well how to work as a hagiographer, extolling the miracle-working efficacy of his saints, but in his biography of Charlemagne he explored a different kind of genre. Everything he had learned in life, both as a boy in Fulda and as an adolescent at Charlemagne's court, went into the daring experiment called the *Vita Karoli*.[59] By modern standards, the text may not have been an exemplary biography of a Christian ruler, yet to contemporaries, it came fairly close to the ideal. Apart from a widely known and copied text, Einhard's *Life* became an important source of inspiration for Louis's two biographers, Thegan and the Astronomer.

A bishop's view: Thegan

By 836–7, when Thegan wrote his *Deeds of Louis*, Einhard's *Life of Charles* had apparently become the model that no aspiring royal biographer could afford to ignore. Whether any of them could live up to it was another matter altogether. Thegan could not, whether according to modern appraisals, or in the view of some of his contemporaries. As he had done for Einhard's *Life*, Walahfrid Strabo wrote a preface to Thegan's *Gesta Hludowici*, and called it a 'little work in the manner of annals, … succinct, and more truthful than elegant'.[60] Walahfrid explained that one should welcome this work for its good intentions, rather than discard it because of a certain 'rusticity', that is, lack of literary polish. Its author, Walahfrid explained, was a hot-tempered man, who could not keep silent about the indignity of unworthy men; his love for the most Christian emperor had further fuelled his natural ardour. He had been well educated, but now, heavily preoccupied with preaching and *correctio* – read 'pastoral care' – he had concentrated more on the heart of the matter than on its exterior form. And Walahfrid continued: 'Wishing to hear or recite the deeds and praise of the emperor Louis of sainted memory more often, I, Strabo, have inserted in this little work some chapter divisions and headings, so that by

---

[58] Einhard, *TMP*, I, c. 1, p. 239: 'adhuc in palatio positus et negotiis saecularibus occupatus'.
[59] Ganz, 'Einhard's Charlemagne', pp. 40, 44.
[60] Thegan, p. 168. See Tremp, *Studien* and 'Thegan und Astronomus'.

this table of contents specific items will be easier to find for those who wish to know.' His edition of Thegan was part of a small dossier of texts in which Walahfrid expressed his loyalty to Louis and his condemnation of Ebo. As Courtney Booker has now discovered, Walahfrid appended a copy of the bishops' report of Louis's public penance in 833, with a disapproving preface warning his reader that these were not the decrees of an authoritative synod, but a 'deadly attempt at fabrication' (*exitalis commenti molimina*).[61]

This preface to Thegan's *Deeds of Louis* was composed after the emperor's death, between 840 and 849.[62] As a young man, however, in 825, Walahfrid enthusiastically praised Thegan's stature, wisdom, orthodoxy, poetry and eloquence.[63] Thegan was a scion of the Frankish aristocracy from the area between Meuse, Moselle and middle Rhine; by 825 he was already an auxiliary bishop (*chorepiscopus*) of Trier.[64] Had he indeed forgotten his former learning in the course of his pastoral duties,[65] or did young Walahfrid praise him for qualities he never possessed? It has been claimed that Thegan's only literary quality was that his style was as biblical and virtuous as the contents of his work; especially when the hapless bishop tried to imitate Einhard, his weakness became particularly apparent.[66] But did Thegan indeed set out in Einhard's footsteps to produce a ruler's biography according to Einhard's model? Certainly, Thegan's portrait of Louis was based on Einhard's image of Charlemagne, which in turn was modelled on Suetonius' description of various emperors' public appearance and *habitus*.[67] Einhard's portrait of Charlemagne not only includes the emperor's features, physical prowess and expertise at hunting and swimming, his attire and his moderation in food and drink, but also four chapters on Charlemagne's public activity: his gifts as a speaker and his assiduous pursuit of the liberal arts, and, finally, his great devotion to the Christian cult, as exemplified by his building of the church in Aachen, his concern for correct worship there, his wide-ranging charity and his many gifts to St Peter's in Rome.[68]

---

[61] Thegan, p. 168; cf. Booker, 'A new prologue', p. 91.
[62] Together with an *accessus*, interpretative chapter headings; Berschin, *Biographie und Epochenstil* 3, p. 223.
[63] Tremp (ed.), Introduction to Thegan, p. 4. Walahfrid, *Carmen* no. 5, 2–3, MGH *Poet. Lat.* II, pp. 351–3.
[64] On Thegan's biography, see Tremp, *Studien*, pp. 4–18.
[65] Tremp (ed.), Introduction to Thegan, p. 5.
[66] Berschin, *Biographie und Epochenstil*, III, p. 226.
[67] Einhard, *VK*, cc. 22–7, pp. 26–32, with reference to the many relevant passages from Suetonius; on the organisation of the *Vita Karoli*, see Staubach, '*Cultus divinus*'; Thegan, c. 19, pp. 200–4; Tremp, *Studien*, pp. 57–63; Innes, 'Politics of humour'.
[68] Chapters 26–7 are usually seen as belonging to a third part of the *Vita Karoli* which deals with the administration of his realm, as announced in c. 4 (*De administratione*). Tremp, *Studien*, p. 60.

If one considers Einhard's portrait in its entirety, that is, including his praise of Charlemagne's involvement in the divine cult in Aachen and beyond, the contrast with Thegan's image of Louis becomes less marked than it has often been made out to be. Thegan responded to Einhard's text, freely changing elements of his model to evoke the image of a ruler who was a skilful handler of arms, proficient in Latin and only a little less so in Greek, skilful at allegorical exegesis and wary of profane epics (*carmina gentilia*), who was self-controlled, easily moved to mercy, devout, generous, moderate in food, drink and external display, in control of his emotions, caring towards the poor and pilgrims, and nobody's fool when it came to choosing the best times for hunting. Above all, Thegan emphasised Louis's truly imperial self-governance, which enabled him to govern others:

> He never *raised his voice in laughter* [Eccli. 21.23], not even when on the highest feasts musicians, jesters, mimes, flautists, and zither-players proceeded before his table in his presence to entertain his faithful men. His entourage used to laugh appropriately in his presence, but he himself never even allowed his white teeth to be bared in laughter.[69]

This was Thegan's unsmiling Louis presiding over a court where, in the presence of the emperor, loud and uncontrolled laughter was frowned upon. Matthew Innes has rightly stressed that such ideals of imperial self-control are reminiscent of the public persona of late antique and contemporary Byzantine emperors, as well as of the norms of monastic culture.[70] Both influences, reinforcing each other, are present in Thegan's portrait; as we shall see, royal/imperial self-control was a central issue in the public debate of the early 830s, to which Thegan responded. Did he also take on board 'Einhard's classicising and humanistic tendencies, and his reliance on a pagan antique model', as Innes argues, restating the conventional image of the ruler in the process?[71] This takes intertextuality one step too far, and I am inclined to side with Ernst Tremp, who has pointed out that Thegan used the *Vita Karoli* more as a checklist (what do I need to write about?) than as a model to follow or to distance himself from.[72] Furthermore, the notion that Thegan came up with a consciously Christian alternative presupposes that he and other contemporaries recognised Einhard's model as explicitly non-Christian, and therefore in need of being supplanted by something more suitable. There are many differences between the two texts, but these do not pertain to the contrast between these emperors being more, or less, Christian.[73] This alleged contrast is largely a

---

[69] Thegan, c. 19, p. 204.   [70] Innes, 'Politics of humour', pp. 140–7.
[71] Ibid., p. 138.   [72] Tremp, *Überlieferung*, pp. 61–2.
[73] As argued convincingly by Innes, 'Politics of humour', and Smith, 'Einhard'.

modern construct. Charlemagne's piety has been argued out of Einhard's portrait by relegating it to the domain of *administratio*, or by pointing out that this was public piety because the emperor was involved in the proper celebration of the Mass, unlike Louis's devotion, which was supposedly more personal because he went to church to pray, and prostrated himself, often in tears. The notional opposition between an early medieval ruler's praying privately in a church, and the public nature of mass, is a modern prejudice: Louis's prayer was as public as his father's preoccupation with the purity of St Mary's church, his creation in Aachen. Charlemagne's careful correction of the ways in which the lessons and psalms were read was echoed and enhanced by Thegan's vision of Charlemagne correcting the Gospels on his deathbed; similarly, the father's study of the liberal arts was elevated to a higher level, namely the son's proficiency in the allegorical interpretation of Scripture, for which the liberal arts were an essential preparation.[74]

So much has been made of the antithesis between these two authors, and of the superiority of one over the other, that one might almost forget that it was primarily for his portrait of Louis that Thegan relied on Einhard, and hardly at all in the rest of his work. Rather than extolling the greatness of a dead emperor, breaking new ground by applying the principles of classical biography and rhetoric, Thegan wrote in the aftermath of the crisis of 833–4, and in full support of Louis's restoration. By this text Thegan tried to establish, once and for all, that Louis was the legitimate emperor, and that the revolt against him had been the work of evil and godless men. He was a vociferous participant in the debate that raged after 834, when Louis had returned to power, wanting to establish his version of what had happened, in recent years, and why.

Thegan provided a chronologically ordered narrative of the reign of his emperor up to the year 835. Often this consists merely of brief annalistic entries, yet these are interspersed by more extensive chapters, which are more frequent in the second part of the text. Predictably, the chapters where Thegan became most eloquent are also the ones most central to his main concerns. There is a moderately elaborate section at the beginning (cc. 1–5) devoted to the genealogy of Charlemagne and Hildegard, Louis's parents, the latter's superiority over his brothers, his marriage and sons, and the death of his brothers. Then comes the first digression (c. 6), summarised by Walahfrid as 'How the Emperor Charles with the consensus of the Franks committed the leadership of the realm to Louis',[75] followed by those on Charlemagne's death and Louis's

---

[74] Thegan, c. 7, p. 186.

[75] For Walahfrid's prologue and *Capitulatio*, c. 6, see Thegan, p. 170: 'Qualiter Karolus imperator Lodeuuico cum consensu Francorum regni summam commisit.'

compliance with his father's last wishes.[76] Most of the detail of the two imperial coronations of 813 and 816 over which modern historians have argued – did Louis sell out to the papacy or not? – comes from Thegan, who made much of both events to hammer home that this was the legitimate and most Christian emperor. First his own father had made him a co-emperor, ordering his son to take the crown from the altar and place it on his head;[77] then, three years later, the pope himself came to Rheims to confirm Louis as the *imperator christianissimus*.[78] The author lovingly dwelled on every aspect of this ceremony: the emperor prostrating himself thrice in front of the pontiff, the joint prayer in church, completed by Stephen and the Roman clergy, who sang the customary liturgy of praise (*laudes regales*); then, on the next Sunday, the anointing of Louis and his coronation with a crown of wondrous beauty, and the coronation of the Empress Irmingard, who was now called Augusta.

Now that Louis was fully emperor, he deserved an imperial image of the kind that Einhard had drawn of Charlemagne; it was at this point that Thegan inserted the ruler's portrait discussed above.[79] This is then followed by the first of two long chapters (cc. 20 and 44) on a bad custom which Louis 'had not started', according to Thegan, but presumably had continued: to elevate men of humble origins to the episcopate. With a reference to the wicked King Jeroboam, who kept appointing ordinary people to the priesthood and was punished for it, Thegan threw himself into a diatribe against these 'wrathful, quarrelsome, slanderous, stubborn, harmful, wilful, immodest' upstarts, who, once they had gained the desired office, would attempt to raise their entire kin from servitude, through advantageous marriages or 'a little learning' that would enable their entirely unsuitable relatives to enter the priesthood. Although Archbishop Ebo of Rheims, deposed in 835, is not yet mentioned here, he is clearly the target of Thegan's attack. There may have been more personal matters involved, such as Ebo's having curtailed the powers of auxiliary bishops,[80] but more generally, Thegan's anger is about something that angered aristocrats during Louis's reign: clerical learning became a vehicle of upward social mobility. Except for Ebo's lowly origins, his career was quite traditional: he owed his advancement to his proximity to the king – first Charlemagne, then Louis – and to his superior

---

[76] Thegan, cc. 6–7, pp. 180–8.   [77] Ibid., c. 6, p. 182.   [78] Ibid., cc. 16–17, pp. 196–8.
[79] Separated by a brief 'chapter' (c. 18, actually, three sentences) on the death of Pope Stephen and his succession by Paschalis II.
[80] Cf. Tremp, Introduction to Thegan, p. 15; Tremp, *Studien*, pp. 72–4. A shorter echo of the theme of *servi* who should not become *consiliarii* – clearly aimed at Ebo – is found again in Thegan, c. 50, pp. 242–4.

education. As Charles the Bald recalled later, the original candidate for the see of Rheims proved incapable of explaining the Gospels, so Louis, conscious of Ebo's capacity for learning (*capacitas scientiae*), moved his protégé into place.[81] The 'men of the palace' could be of very different social origins; all *nobiles* were powerful, but the reverse did not necessarily hold true.[82] Judging by Thegan's complaint, it was not just royal patronage that had turned the unworthy into high-ranking churchmen who would dole out favours to their kinsmen, but above all royal appreciation of learning. At least four decades of Carolingian *correctio* had turned literacy into a condition for any clerical advancement, and most certainly for bishops who were favoured as royal counsellors. When it came to the hierarchy of the court, the nobility of which Thegan was so proud did not count; others such as Ebo took precedence.

The issue of low-born bishops was not the heart of the matter, however. It was the stick with which Thegan could conveniently beat the scapegoat Ebo, while driving him out of the political arena, laden with the sins of his fellow-bishops. This had happened early in 835, in the church of St Stephen in Metz, where Ebo publicly confessed his sins; but this was not enough, for he was still alive, doing penance. Moreover, there were those who, like the emperor Lothar, wished to shift the blame for the upheaval of 833 on to the bishops collectively. Were they not the ones who had imposed a public penance on Louis?[83] The driving force behind Thegan's *Gesta Hludowici* was the collective shame of loyal bishops, who agonised about the fact that they had become instrumental in the effort to depose the emperor. 'All the bishops harassed him,' wrote Thegan of Louis held captive in Compiègne, 'especially those whom he had lifted up from the vilest servile condition, along with those who had been elevated to this level from barbarian peoples.'[84] It is the 'all the bishops' that rankled most.[85] From their midst, they 'chose one shameless and very cruel man, Ebo, the bishop of Rheims, who descended from generations of serfs, to batter him [Louis] savagely with the fabrications of the others'.[86]

Thegan's subsequent harangue against Ebo and his kind (*invectio in Hebonem et consimiles*), as Walahfrid called it, forms the undisputed centrepiece of the second part of the *Gesta*, which concentrates on the rebellion of 833, its failure, and the humiliation of those Thegan perceived as

---

[81] Airlie, 'Bonds of power', p. 200.   [82] Ibid., pp. 203–4.
[83] Astronomer, c. 51, p. 486.   [84] Thegan, c. 43, p. 230.
[85] Strictly speaking, Louis had some staunch supporters, among bishops too; see Nelson, *Annals of St-Bertin*, p. 27, n. 23; above, chapter 1, n. 184.
[86] Thegan, c. 43, p. 232.

Louis's real enemies: Lothar, his father-in-law Hugh of Tours and, above all, Ebo.[87] The fury of this *invectio* far exceeds the indignation of an aristocratic bishop about an upstart colleague, or any resentment of a more private nature.[88] This was nothing less than a public defamation of Ebo; Thegan's prose was meant to be performative, preventing Ebo's return to his former episcopal see, or any other, for that matter. Above all, Thegan raged about Ebo's lack of fidelity and gratitude towards the emperor, who had liberated him from servitude:

O, how you have repaid him! He made you free, not noble, which is impossible. After your manumission he clothed you with purple and a pallium, but you dressed him as a penitent. He raised you, unworthy and all, to the episcopal dignity, but you wanted to expel him from the throne of his ancestors by a false judgement.[89]

Here was a man who, by his conduct as well as his descent, had been proved not to have a shred of true nobility.[90] Because of Ebo's ineradicable servility, the bishops' judgement in 833, over which he presided, could not be anything but misguided and invalid. For the same reason, Ebo was incapable of the fidelity he owed both his Creator and his emperor: 'You have neither feared God nor honoured the king.'[91] This was said in connection with the command to 'fear God, honour the king' (*Deum timete, regem honorificate*) (I Petr. 2.17),[92] one of many biblical injunctions aimed at Ebo. Apart from biblical ammunition, this chapter also boasts five lines from Virgil's *Aeneid* (VI, 618–22), and the claim that anyone wishing to record all Ebo's crimes would surpass all the ancients, with references to Lucan, Homer, Virgil and Ovid. That all these classical authors suddenly emerge in Thegan's *Gesta* when it matters should be a warning to all those who have doubted his learning. It was not just any plodder who switched effortlessly to the rhetorical genre of the invective. Walahfrid recognised a good *invectio* when he saw one, even if he thought Thegan's prose 'rather too effusive and ardent'.

Which perhaps it was: Thegan's exclamation 'Now may you rot in shame, all the days of your life!',[93] neatly sums up what he had in mind

---

[87] Ibid., c. 35 (the revolt of 830) up to c. 57. (The two younger sons – *iuniores nati* – i.e. Pippin and Louis – have a peaceful encounter with their father in Lyon. Note that Charles is totally ignored; Louis the German is the 'best younger son'.)

[88] Tremp, *Studien*, p. 72: there are indications that Ebo had harmed Thegan and his kinsmen in some way; futhermore, there was the matter of the position of auxiliary bishops.

[89] Thegan, c. 44, p. 232.

[90] On ninth-century aristocratic ethos, see Nelson, 'Ninth-century knighthood'.

[91] Thegan, c. 44, p. 234, lines 2–3.

[92] The subsequent verses, also cited, made it clear that all that Ebo could do was follow the injunction to slaves to submit to their masters: 'Servi, subditi estote in omni timore dominis, non tantum bonis et modestis, sed etiam discolis. Hęc est gratia' (I Petr. 2.18).

[93] Thegan, c. 44, p. 234, lines 21–2: 'corrue nunc in opprobrium omnibus diebus vitę tuę!'.

for Ebo. In 835, at the assembly in Thionville, Louis accused Ebo of having falsely incriminated him, and of having broken every rule in the ecclesiastical book by imposing on him a public penance that excluded him from Christian society.[94] When all was said and done, it was the collective shame of faithful bishops, engendered by Ebo's false judgement, that was the driving force behind Thegan's *Gesta*. The manuscripts were mostly transmitted in the eastern part of the empire, among the loyal folk on the other side of the Rhine called *Germani*.[95] Here, the outrage of bishops at the very notion that they as a group were to blame for the outrageous exploits of their colleagues from Francia and Aquitaine created the furious indignation that was voiced by Thegan. The rebellious bishops' claim that they were the watchmen in the House of Israel, speaking up against sin (Ez. 3.18), was countered by Thegan's passionate argument that they had failed in this duty, and perhaps also by citing this passage from Ezekiel in a very different context: that of the Emperor Louis, restored to his former office, who sent envoys to his son Lothar in 834 to admonish him 'to avert himself from his wicked ways'.[96] For the time being, these bigwig bishops at the court forfeited their right to *admonitio*, Thegan seemed to say; once more, it was the emperor's turn to be the watchman against sin, with full and unimpaired authority.

The corridors of power: the Astronomer

The anonymous *Vita Hludowici imperatoris* is very different from Thegan's *Gesta*. This is indeed a *vita*, in that the author began his narrative with the birth of the kingdom (Charlemagne's conquest of Aquitaine, c. 1) and its future king (Louis, c. 3), and ended with the death of the emperor (c. 65). It is an extensive, learned and eminently readable biography, written by an anonymous cleric who presents himself and his sources as follows:

What I have written, up to the time when he became emperor, I have added to the account (*relatio*) of the most noble and devoted monk Adhemar, who was his contemporary and was raised with him. For later events, since I participated in courtly affairs, I have written down what I saw and what I could find out.[97]

The courtier, who is usually called 'the Astronomer', owes his nickname to the passage where he depicts himself as discussing the meaning of

[94] MGH *Conc.* II/2, p. 697, lines 22–5.
[95] On the manuscript tradition: Tremp (ed.), Introduction to Thegan, pp. 31–40; *Studien*, pp. 99–135; on loyal *Germani*, Astronomer, c. 45, p. 460.
[96] Thegan, c. 53, p. 246, lines 4–5: 'ut averteret se a via sua prava'.
[97] Astronomer, prologue, p. 284.

Halley's comet (837) with the ageing emperor.[98] The author was a learned cleric, that much is clear, but his identity is still a matter of discussion.[99] The most plausible suggestion, in my view, comes from Hugh Doherty, who has argued that the author worked under the patronage of Bishop Drogo of Metz, the emperor's half-brother, who from 835 was also his archchaplain.[100] As Ernst Tremp already noticed, the Astronomer lavished his most exuberant epithets on Drogo, who especially in the last part of the work plays an increasingly prominent role. This was the loyal half-brother who supervised Louis's deathbed, flanked by two other archbishops, Hetti of Trier and Otgar of Mainz, but remaining centre stage all the time in the narrative. The Astronomer asserted that many had told him what had happened there, which suggests that he was in contact with Drogo and the latter's retinue. This does not necessarily contradict Ernst Tremp's suggestion that the author was a follower of Lothar, and started writing at the latter's court, possibly at Lothar's behest. Directly after Louis's death, Lothar presented himself as Louis's legitimate heir, the eldest son who established an altar at his father's grave in Metz.[101] Drogo declared his loyalty to Lothar; he was among those who, at the synod of Ingelheim in August 840, restored Ebo to the see of Rheims.[102] The author of this work may well have been a courtier anxious to find a new patron after Louis's death. Turning to Drogo, with Lothar's might in the background, would have been a judicious move.

As for the date of the *Vita*, if Ernst Tremp is right, the work was written in a surprisingly short time, namely in the winter months of 840/1, when there was still hope that Lothar and Charles the Bald could come to an arrangement. After the battle of Fontenoy on 25 June 841, these hopes were dashed, a context in which some of the Astronomer's positive comments on both Lothar and Charles would make little sense.[103] Doherty,

---

[98] Ernst Tremp's introduction to the edition of the work, pp. 55–66, gives the best survey of the Astronomer's position at the court; see also Tremp, 'Thegan und Astronomus'. On the manuscript transmission of the work see Tremp, *Überlieferung*. On the structure and perspective of the work see Siemes, *Beiträge*; Ernst Tremp, 'Zwischen *stabilitas*'; now also Goetz, 'Perception of "power"'.

[99] Tischler (*Einharts 'Vita Karoli'*, pp. 1109–11) has identified the Astronomer as Bishop Jonas of Orléans, but I remain unconvinced. Ernst Tremp suggested that the author was a palatine cleric, possibly a student of Theodulf of Orléans, whom he calls *vir undecum doctissimus* (Tremp, Introduction to Astronomer, pp. 62). But this expression, used in Einhard's *Vita Karoli* for Alcuin, to my mind does not indicate anything more than that Theodulf was highly respected by the Astronomer.

[100] Doherty, 'Maintenance of royal power', pp. 56–65.

[101] MGH *Poet. Lat.* II, pp. 653–4.   [102] Depreux, *Prosopographie*, pp. 163–7, at 167.

[103] Tremp, Introduction to Astronomer, pp. 67–8; see also Tremp, *Überlieferung*, pp. 138–48, with the suggestion that the Astronomer changed allegiance to Charles the Bald towards the end of writing his text.

on the other hand, thinks the tenor of the *Vita* suits the treaty of Verdun in 843, for all three brothers are portrayed as worthy of succession, including Louis the German, who is shown to be forgiven by his father through Drogo's intervention. The rather favourable portrait of Lothar, Doherty argues, was meant to convince Charles's magnates, many of whom were as averse to Lothar as Nithard was, of the viability of future co-operation.[104] This may be overly optimistic about Louis the German's portrayal, which is less than favourable, to say the least. Furthermore, it should be noted that the manuscript transmission of the *Vita Hludowici* is restricted to the West-Frankish kingdom, and the earliest group of manuscripts is connected with the court of Charles the Bald. This was where the Astronomer's readership was, not in the east, which suggests that Louis the German's role as one of the brothers who needed to be 'repackaged' was negligible.[105] On the other hand, the *Vita* is a long and polished book, the work of a highly skilled author with a clear sense of the balance and construction of his narrative; it is hard to believe that this was the achievement of merely one winter. For all we know, this was a project that had started well before Louis died; there is no reason to think a work that was finished and edited at a certain time was also written then and there. In short, when it comes to the date of writing and the identity of the author of this impressive biography, the jury is still out.

Whatever the case, the Astronomer completed his work in the first few years after Louis's death, and had belonged to the upper echelon of the old emperor's court: the men who he himself called the *proceres palatii*, as opposed to mere *nobiles*.[106] Judging by the regularity with which he cracked down on the *plebs* – the nobles' retainers, rowdy fighting men whose gullibility was the source of much evil – the Astronomer was an aristocrat, with a courtier's standard of behaviour. In his narrative of the rebellions of 830 and 833 the Astronomer turned the easily roused anger of this *plebs* or *vulgus* into the direct cause of Louis's temporary undoing, thus shifting the burden of guilt away from the *populus*, the faithful men.[107] This author detested upward social mobility as much as Thegan did, but rather than denouncing ecclesiastical advancement and literacy as its enabling factors, the Astronomer depicted the low-born as greedy, stupid and therefore easily manipulated; at moments of great injustice, the unruly crowd invariably cheered. The anonymity of the *Life* may also

---

[104] Doherty, 'The maintenance of royal power', pp. 44–8.
[105] Tremp, *Überlieferung*, Tremp Introduction to Astronomer, pp. 115–35.
[106] Le Jan, *Famille et pouvoir*, pp. 136–43; Airlie, 'Bonds of power'.
[107] Astronomer, c. 44, pp. 456, line 1 (*minores*); c. 44, p. 458, line 19 and p. 462, 1. 17 (*vulgus*); c. 48, p. 476, line 19 (*plebs*). See below, n. 127.

indicated the high status of its creator. There was no reason to add a
.e to this text when it was first circulated among the author's peers, for
...., insider would know who was so established in the emperor's good
graces that he was called out to Louis's bedchamber to give his views on
the meaning of a comet. As in Einhard's *Translation of Sts Marcellinus and
Peter*, the author's presence in the text helped to establish its authority and
veracity: the Astronomer wanted his readers to know that he had been in
the habit of discussing comets with Louis himself.[108]

According to the Astronomer, his main source up to 813 was 'the most
noble and devoted monk Adhemar, who was his [= Louis's] contemporary and was raised with him'.[109] From that point on, he claimed to rely on
his own experience, but, as we have seen, for the period from 814 to 829
he followed the chronology and the main narrative structure of the *Royal
Frankish Annals*, freely elaborating on this text and omitting parts if
necessary.[110] As a courtier, the Astronomer must have known Einhard
personally. He greatly respected him, as becomes clear from his frequent
references to the *Vita Karoli*, and from his praise of Einhard as 'the most
prudent of men in his time' (*sui temporis prudentissimus virorum*).[111] Except
in the introductory part of the *Vita* (the prologue and cc. 1–2), where the
Astronomer was directly inspired by Einhard's example, his 'references'
to this text are more resonances than direct imitation – or contestation, for
that matter. This was a confident and learned author who was eminently
capable of fusing the written material at his disposal into a compelling and
even spellbinding narrative of his own.[112] There has been much discussion about his possible reliance on the *Annals of St-Bertin* and Nithard's
Histories, but the present consensus is that possible similarities can be
accounted for by the use of the same sources of information, and also by
the fact that these three authors were discussing the same set of events.[113]
In this last section (cc. 44–64), from 830 onwards to Louis's death a
decade later, the author's own experience and memory played a greater
role in the composition of his narrative. This may be the reason why in this

[108] Astronomer, c. 58, p. 522.
[109] Astronomer, prologue; cf. Tremp, Introduction to Astronomer, pp. 69–74.
[110] Tremp (ed.), Introduction to Astronomer, pp. 81–2. The Astronomer used a class C
manuscript; the Astronomer's copy was closest to C2 (St Petersburg lat. F.v. IV, 4,
probably derived from a special copy made for Charles the Bald) and C3 (St-Omer, Bibl.
Munic. 706, the oldest textual witness to the Annals of St Bertin).
[111] Astronomer, c. 41, p. 442; Tremp, Introduction to Astronomer, pp. 75–81, with a list of
resonances of Einhard's *VK* in the Astronomer's text at p. 78, n. 242.
[112] See the 'Stellenregister' in Tremp's edition, pp. 559–70, which gives a good first
impression of the Astronomer's learning, especially with regard to Cicero, Livy and
Virgil.
[113] See Tremp, Introduction to the Astronomer, pp. 87–8, 92, 96–8.

part of the *Vita* his chronology is now and then confused, especially with regard to assemblies and other meetings; this could happen to anyone recording events from memory.

Central to the Astronomer's narrative are Louis's qualities as a Christian ruler, and particularly the way in which his guardianship of the cult of God and the 'holy church' (*sancta ecclesia*) made him transcend the divide between kingship and priesthood. The spirit of the young king of Aquitaine 'was roused to divine worship and the exaltation of the church so that his works proclaimed that he was not only a king but also a priest'.[114] This image is inspired by the biblical king Melchisedech (Gen. 14.18–19), who was also a priest, and who blessed Abraham after having offered him bread and wine. Louis was by no means the first Christian ruler to be alluded to in this fashion. Melchisedech played a crucial role in Byzantine religious polemics of the mid-seventh century,[115] and in a panegyric poem Venantius Fortunatus had compared the Merovingian King Childebert I (r. 511–58) to this illustrious biblical predecessor; in a similar vein, Gregory of Tours praised King Guntram (r. 561–92) by saying that he was 'like a good bishop'.[116] Significantly, this praise for Guntram was elicited by his care of the Christian cult: the king had ordered Rogations to be held in St-Symphorien as a remedy against a quickly spreading epidemic. In other words, by taking the initiative in this act of atonement the king behaved as if he were a bishop, mediating between God and mankind. This is not to say, of course, that Gregory wished to suggest that Guntram *was* a bishop; such comparisons only stressed the essential divide between the royal and episcopal roles.

This traditional theme resonates in the Astronomer's representation of Louis's care of the *cultus divinus* and the *sancta ecclesia*. The expression *sancta ecclesia* refers not merely to 'the church' in the institutional sense of the word, but to those who mediate between God and mankind, and thereby guarantee God's favour and mercy for the entire polity, provided that He is prayed to in the correct fashion.[117] Precisely because the ruler transcended the distinctions between the various orders within this *sancta ecclesia*, he could be its leader, maintaining an orderly demarcation between the secular and the sacred, and restoring these boundaries, if they had become blurred. In a similar way, the Astronomer elaborated on the conflicting forces of Louis's

---

[114] Astronomer, c. 19, p. 334. On Melchisedech, see Anton, *Fürstenspiegel*, pp. 52–4 and 111–12.

[115] Dagron, *Emperor and Priest*, pp. 6–7, 169–71.

[116] Venantius Fortunatus, *Carmina*, II, 10, 17, p. 40; Gregory of Tours, *Historiae*, IX, c. 21, p. 441. Cf. Reydellet, *La royauté*, pp. 323–7, 421–2; Heinzelmann, *Gregory*, pp. 60–5.

[117] Cf. Staubach, *'Cultus divinus'*; De Jong, 'Carolingian monasticism'.

desire for the contemplative life on the one hand, and his need to remain in the world on the other. Like his great-uncle Carloman, who had become a monk in 747, Louis would have withdrawn from the world, except that his father forbade it. According to God's will, Louis would not merely heed his own salvation, but would exert himself for the salvation of his people.[118] There was another moment in Louis's life when the monastery beckoned: when Queen Irmingard died in October 818, the emperor's faithful men were afraid that he would wish to opt out of government altogether, yet they succeeded in convincing him of the need to remarry.[119] Louis remarried within five months after Irmingard's death, and the Astronomer's depiction of the union had biblical and imperial resonances: like Queen Esther, Judith was chosen from among all the daughters of the magnates of the realm.[120]

Yet Louis's alleged longing for the cloister may have had other, more contemporary connotations. In 833, and possibly already in 830, attempts had been made to force the emperor to make a monastic profession against his will, which he refused to do. By evoking Carloman's voluntary and honourable entry into monastic life and Louis's wish to imitate his illustrious forebear, the Astronomer drew attention to the coerced and therefore perverted conversion his enemies had tried to inflict on the emperor. As for the latter's reluctance to remarry, this may also reflect the Astronomer's ambivalence about the result of this second marriage: Charles. Before mentioning the youngest son's birth in 823, the Astronomer inserted an extensive passage on ominous portents, notably an earthquake affecting the palace in Aachen, strange noises in the night, a girl who fasted for twelve months, lightning, hailstorms, and pestilence among men and animals. All this was based on the narrative of the *Annales regni Francorum*, but their juxtaposition with the birth of Charles was new, and so was Louis's reaction: 'On account of these remarkable occurrences, the most pious emperor ordered through the episcopate that frequent fasts, continuous prayers and generous alms be offered to placate God; he said it was absolutely certain that these signs foretold a great future catastrophe for the human race.'[121] Then follows the passage about Charles's birth, and a section on Counts Eblus and Asinarius, who were ambushed with their armies on their return from Pamplona. Was this a deliberate juxtaposition? It is hard to say. On the one hand, the Astronomer was positive about Charles, and depicted him as a promise

---

[118] Astronomer, c. 19, p. 336. On Carloman's conversion, see Einhard, *VK*, c. 2, pp. 4–5; Krüger, 'Königskonversionen'; Stancliffe, 'Kings who opted out'.
[119] Astronomer, c. 32, p. 392.
[120] Ibid. Cf. De Jong, 'Bride shows' and 'Queens and beauty'.
[121] Astronomer, c. 37, pp. 420–2.

for the future. On the other hand, the arrival of a fourth son in 823 eventually upset carefully laid plans for the succession, and led to the disorder and strife the Astronomer had witnessed. Given the Astronomer's skill in editing his sources and combining them with others, this may indeed have been a meaningful assemblage of apparently disjointed messages.

Whether in 840–1, in 843 or well before this, the Astronomer looked back upon Louis's reign, and on the years of rebellion that stood in the way of a smooth succession by the surviving sons. Familial unity and fraternal solidarity are the central themes that pervade the *Vita*. In spite of all that had happened, the elder sons were still fit to be kings. Above all, Lothar's reputation was in need of restoration. 'At that time [Compiègne, summer 830] he [Lothar] seemed to inflict nothing on his father that was dishonourable.'[122] Of the burning of Chalon-sur-Saône in 834, a vicious measure of reprisal by Lothar well remembered in the early 840s, the Astronomer said that this outrage had not been Lothar's wish.[123] Although such a disclaimer could hardly be made for 833 and the Field of Lies, all the sons were portrayed as behaving with courtesy to their father. When Louis surrendered, the sons refrained from pillaging, and dutifully dismounted from their horses and listened to their father's admonitions.[124] The Astronomer gave Lothar the opportunity to defend himself, having him say that nobody had commiserated more than he did with the calamity that had befallen his father, and shifting the blame to those who deserted his father on the Field of Lies, and to the bishops whose judgement had led to Louis's shameful incarceration.[125]

The Astronomer had other culprits in mind: the devious magnates who incited Lothar and his two brothers to rebel against their father. The prime suspects were Hugh, Matfrid and their allies, who had been conspiring ever since their downfall in February 828. They were the 'cancerous growth' which gradually infested people's minds and roused the rabble, a disease and a pest against which the 'bastion' Bernhard had to be erected.[126] While Louis went off to discipline the Bretons in the spring of 830,

the leaders of the evil faction, able to delay no longer, laid bare their long-concealed wound. First of all the leaders swore a kind of pact among themselves, then they won over some lesser people (*minores*) to themselves, a part of whom was always greedy for change after the fashion of rapacious dogs and birds who seek to increase their own advantage at someone else's loss.[127]

---

[122] Ibid., c. 45, p. 460: 'ipse tamen nihil tunc temporis patri intulisse visus est dedecoris'.
[123] Ibid., c. 52, p. 496; otherwise, Thegan, c. 52, p. 244, and Nithard, I, 5, p. 22.
[124] Ibid., c. 48, p. 478.   [125] Ibid., c. 51, p. 486.
[126] Ibid., c. 43, pp. 452–4.   [127] Ibid., c. 44, pp. 454–6.

These angry sentences were written with the paramount virtue of *fides* in mind, that is, keeping faith with God and one's ruler. This was conduct the Astronomer prized most highly and defined as eminently aristocratic, just as Nithard did and Radbert, albeit from a different perspective. Whereas Nithard angrily blamed the oath-breaking Lothar for the disintegration of the order that had once been, the Astronomer squarely accused the 'leaders of the evil faction', Matfrid and Hugh. They latched on to Pippin in 830, turning him into the leader of their rebellion.[128] By the hatred of the very men who owed their survival to Louis's mercy, the emperor's own life was now threatened.[129] That Matfrid and Hugh had escaped their just deserts in 828 by Louis's pardon and subsequently repaid their lord by successive rebellions is the one axe to grind in a work that is otherwise free of obvious polemics – although a lot of it is going on under the surface. In this context, the Astronomer's qualification of Louis as 'too clement' (*nimis clemens*), announced in his prologue, surfaces once more. *Pace* generations of historians who read royal weakness into this verdict, the Astronomer in fact enhanced his praise by presenting a virtue as a vice.[130] The emperor needed no more forgiveness than St Paul, cited in the prologue, when he scathingly 'apologised' to the Corinthians for having cost them nothing.[131] In a less sophisticated fashion, but according to the same rhetorical principles, Thegan blamed Louis for choosing bad advisers and then excused him because of his assiduous concentration on prayer: signalling the one flaw brought out the virtues all the better.[132]

The Field of Lies was treason magnified: its name, *campus mentitus*, testified to the iniquity of those who, having sworn fidelity to their emperor, revealed themselves as perjurers.[133] Given Lothar's role in this and the Astronomer's condemnation of the rebellion, the notion that Lothar himself commissioned his father's *Vita* seems a bit far-fetched – unless, of course, by 840, the reputation of these men no longer mattered. By then, they had all fallen victim to the epidemic that raged in Italy in 836, with the notable exception of Lothar. Francia was robbed of its nobility (*Francia nobilitate orbata*) said the Astronomer, but he also cited the prophet Jeremiah, to show how the mighty had fallen: 'Thus saith the Lord: Let not the wise man glory in his wisdom, and let not the strong man glory in his strength, and let not the rich man glory in his riches'

---

[128] Ibid., p. 456.   [129] Ibid., p. 458.

[130] Siemes, *Beiträge*, pp. 96–7; Booker, 'Histrionic history'.

[131] Astronomer, prologue, p. 284; cf. II Cor. 12.13. For the Astronomer's claim to write 'without the deceit of adulation' ('absque fuco adulationis'), see ibid., p. 280, line 15.

[132] Thegan, c. 20, p. 204.   [133] Astronomer, c. 48, pp. 474–6.

(Ier. 9.23). Louis's reaction was governed by divine *clementia* and *temperantia*: rather than exulting in the death of his enemies, he beat his breast and asked God to have mercy on them.[134] By 840–1, an author wishing to ingratiate himself with Lothar could blame Matfrid and Hugh with impunity, while exonerating the new emperor. Having Lothar claim that the rebellion of 833 was not his fault, but that of his father's treacherous men, and of the over-zealous bishops who turned Louis into a penitent captive, fits the profile of an Astronomer seeking Lothar's patronage.[135] In the later section of the *Vita*, all Lothar's excuses for not heeding his father's summons and appearing north of the Alps are related sympathetically, as are the Empress Judith's efforts to enlist Lothar's help for the future protection of her son Charles. When as a result of her efficient diplomacy Lothar was asked to be Charles's 'friend and helper, educator and protector' (*dilector et adiutor, tutorque protector*) and offered half of the empire, except Bavaria which was reserved for Louis the German, Lothar thought this was for the common good (*utilis*), and agreed.[136]

All this worked together to evoke the image of royal brothers who, in the end, made their peace with their father – though admittedly Louis the German left it rather late. The Astronomer wrote under the shadow of the rebellions of the early 830s. The revolt of 833, especially, created havoc among the magnates, and yielded countless scores that needed settling in years to come. Only the tip of this daunting iceberg becomes visible in the Astronomer's narrative. The extent of the disorder was revealed when Byzantine legates came to Compiègne and were received by the 'son of the emperor', rather than by Louis himself, and reported back home the 'unheard-of tragedy' that had just occurred.[137] This was the world turned upside down (*permutatio rerum*), an unheard-of crime (*sceler inauditus*).[138] Throughout all this, Lothar remained 'the emperor's son' (*filius imperatoris*), not the *imperator*. Yet in spite of his unshakeable loyalty to Louis, the Astronomer remained equitable to all parties, integrating their apologies and explanations into his narrative. Thus, Lothar's view of the matter was put forth, and Archbishop Ebo is also treated with some sympathy, as the only one of the bishops in Soissons who actually had the courage to face the music, and who, abandoned by his colleagues and worn down, incriminated himself and resigned. Like Thegan, the Astronomer looked for explanations for the years of discord, but instead of Thegan's furious indignation, there is the Astronomer's even-handed apportioning of human fallibility. This also went for Louis himself. There are no direct

---

[134] Ibid., p. 514.   [135] Ibid., c. 51, p. 486, lines 16–21.   [136] Ibid., c. 59, p. 528.
[137] Ibid., c. 49: 'traguediamque reportantem pene inauditam remisit'.
[138] Ibid., p. 48, lines 16–17.

references to Augustine's *De civitate dei*, yet his image of the ideal emperor may well have influenced the Astronomer: a happy emperor (*felix imperator*) was never swayed by flattery. On the contrary, he always remembered that he was human.[139] When the Astronomer said the emperor was *nimis clemens*, he entered a small irregularity in the otherwise blameless catalogue of virtues, particularly that of doing 'nothing in excess' (*ne quid nimis*),[140] which was, according to the Astronomer, Louis's personal motto.[141] Around this one irregularity, excessive clemency, Walter Berschin argued, the entire biography revolves, for it was for this reason that the *Life* changed into a tragedy (*traguedia*).[142] Berschin does not elaborate, but Courtney Booker has taken this pronouncement as his point of departure for a study of the 'emplotment' and memory of the penance of 833, arguing that the loyalist prose of Louis's supporters used a dramatic style that would cast all subsequent understanding of these tragic events in a theatrical mode, down to the present day. That the Astronomer's Louis is at times an almost Christ-like figure, a 'perfect king born in an imperfect age', is an observation worth reflecting on,[143] but I doubt whether the Astronomer's use of the word *traguedia* indicates any conscious 'emplotment' based on a knowledge of antique drama.[144] Legates from Constantinople visited Aachen at a highly uncomfortable time, witnessing the disarray and telling everyone at home that the Franks had become less than imperial. How bad could it get? When Byzantine envoys visited, learned Greek words came to mind. The real tragedy of 833 was that all who had sworn oaths to Louis had deserted him on the Field of Lies. As the Astronomer had Lothar say, let nobody dare to point a finger at him, for all had been implicated in the same crime.[145] It is this joint responsibility that the *Vita Hludowici* tried to come to terms with. Whatever the precise context the *Vita* was written in, it was a bid for a future in which the unity of the family would be once more restored. And wherever the discussion about the identity of the Astronomer may lead us, this theme would have pleased Drogo of Metz and other staunchly loyal

---

[139] Augustine, *De civitate Dei*, V, c. 24, pp. 236–7.

[140] *Regula Benedicti*, c. 64, 12: 'In ipsa autem correptione prudenter agat et ne quid nimis, ne dum nimis eradere cupit aeruginem frangatur vas'; this is the chapter on the way in which the abbot should exercise his discipline.

[141] Astronomer, prologue, p. 282: 'Ita enim ea usus est, ut illud vetustissum proverbium et ad caelum usque celebratum ei fuit familiarissimum, quo dicitur: *Ne quid nimis*.'

[142] Berschin, *Biographie*, III, p. 230: 'Die kleine Unausglichenheit im Tugendkatalog ist Angelpunkt der Biographie; hier liegt die Ursache der Wendung des Lebens zur *traguedia* (c. 49).'

[143] Booker, 'Histrionic history'; see also Innes, 'Politics of humour', pp. 147–53, on Thegan and Notker on the emperor as Christ.

[144] Booker, 'Histrionic history'.   [145] Astronomer, c. 51, p. 486.

men who from May 840 onwards struggled with the legacy of Louis the Pious: two sons very recently (839) reunited, and a third still estranged, albeit forgiven in the nick of time.

Poetic praise: Ermold the Black

A poetic appeal to Louis's *clementia* was made by Ermold the Black (*Ermoldus Nigellus*), a cleric and protégé of Pippin of Aquitaine, who had been exiled from his beloved southern kingdom to the chilly environs of Strasbourg. Sometime between the autumn of 826 and February 828 Ermold wrote an elegiac poem in honour of Louis the Pious in four books, as well as two verse epistles to Pippin of Aquitaine.[146] With his panegyric offerings to both Louis and Pippin, Ermold quite literally tried to write himself back to Aquitaine.[147] It is not clear whether he succeeded or not, and neither is there certainty about his alleged crime, though I suspect it may have had something to do with his politically incorrect views on the veneration of images; his explicit and vociferous protestations that the bodies of the holy fathers should be venerated on earth seem to indicate this, or at least that he had been accused of dogmatic errors.[148] In the past, Ermold has been much disparaged for his factual inaccuracy and his failure to be Virgil, but nowadays his poetical and historical skills receive more appreciation, and rightly so. Apart from having an entire poetic tradition at his fingertips, Ermold is a rich source of information for Carolingian court culture.[149] The cleric had a keen sense of what his patrons would want to hear, and of the hierarchy in Louis's retinue shortly

---

[146] Only two manuscripts: Vienna, ÖNB cod. 614, s. x, fols. 1–66, contains the *Carmen*, with the incipit *In honorem Hludowici christianissimi caesaris augusti Ermoldi Nigelli exulis elegiacum carmen liber incipit primus*; BM Harley 3685, s. xv, with the *Carmen* (fols. 55–92) and the two verse epistles, fols. 30 and 33; see Faral, Ermold, *Poème*, pp. xxxi and 2.

[147] Written after the baptism of the Danish king and queen, in mid-summer 826 at Ingelheim, and before February 828, when Hugh and Matfrid fell into disgrace. Cf. Faral, *Ermold, Poème*, p. viii; Godman, 'Louis "the Pious"', p. 255, argues convincingly that the two panegyric verse epistles for Pippin (also in elegiac distiches) were part of the same plea for clemency; the first letter originated before the *Carmen*, the second one thereafter, for it refers to the *Carmen*. Apart from my own translation and Faral's, I have gratefully used the English working translation by Carey Dolores Fleiner, annotated by Thomas Noble.

[148] Ermold, lines 2595–99: 'What mad idiot could say that the bodies of the holy fathers must not be worshipped on earth? Is not God venerated by these heavenly servants to whom we pray? Peter is not God, but I believe that by praying to Peter, I could be free from the guilt of my crime' (trans. Fleiner). On the crime of which he was accused, see Ermold, lines 2640–3.

[149] Godman, 'Louis "the Pious"', pp. 259–62, and *Poets and Emperors*, pp. 108–25. On the value of the *Carmen* for the history of mentalities and the political ideas of Carolingian intellectuals, see Depreux, 'La *pietas*', pp. 203–4.

before the downfall of Hugh and Matfrid. The *Poem*'s four books respectively feature Louis's kingship in Aquitaine and his victory during the battle of Barcelona in 804 (I), his accession to the throne, his coronations by his father and Pope Stephen, and his first actions as an emperor (II), his valiant campaign against the Bretons in 824 (III), and his apogee as a *christianissimus imperator*, which culminates in the baptism of the Danish King Harald, his wife and his son, with Louis, Judith and Lothar acting as baptismal sponsors (IV).[150] It is a panegyric poem that is inspired by classical verse as well as by Charlemagne's court poetry, especially by the so-called 'Paderborn Epic', written on the occasion of the meeting of Pope Leo III and Charlemagne in Paderborn in 799.[151]

Ermold's aim was to relate the emperor's *gesta*, 'the deeds of the warrior Caesar, which the world rightly recites with pious affection'.[152] Louis was the main target of his praise, along with the 'most beautiful Judith, you who hold the highest authority with him', yet the *Poem* also indirectly addresses a small galaxy of powerful figures at the court. By depicting them in a flattering context, Ermold engaged a wider audience of *homines palatini* who, presumably, were capable of furthering his cause. Possibly his poetic praise was meant for public recitation at the court.[153] If so, the *proceres* might listen to the verses on the valiant Breton campaign of 824, in which Ermold managed to mention Louis himself, his sons Louis and Pippin, as well as Matfrid, Hugh, Helisachar and Lambert, the count of Nantes.[154] Among these great men, Ermold situated himself as being gently mocked by Pippin for his clumsy handling of the unaccustomed sword and shield: 'Pippin laughed when he saw this, marvelled and said, "Put away your weapons, brother! You'd better stick to writing"! (*"Cede armis, frater; litteram amato magis"*).'[155] This is yet another Carolingian author who made sure that his court-connected audience was well aware of his own familiarity with his royal patron.

Such concerted name-dropping occurs regularly in the *Poem*. Its purpose is to flatter those concerned, but not beyond recognition. Those

---

[150] Ermold, lines 2290–313.

[151] *Karolus Magnus et Leo papa*, ed. E. Dümmler, MGH *Poet. Lat.* I, pp. 367–79. See also Hentze, *De Karolo rege*; Godman, *Poets and emperors*, pp. 82–92.

[152] Ermold, lines 40–7: 'Caesaris armigeri conor describere gesta / Quae recitat merito mundus amore pio.' On the difficulties in assigning this text to one particular genre (biography or panagyric epic), see Berschin, *Epochenstil*, pp. 220–2; these *gesta* are set in the mode of an elegy (hence the title *Eligiacum carmen* in the tenth-century ms.), not in the heroic mode of a panegyric epic.

[153] As had been the case with the verse epistles of Angilbert, Alcuin and Theodulf; see Godman, 'Louis "the Pious"', pp. 254–5.

[154] Depreux, *Prosopographie*, no. 184, pp. 288–91; Ermold, lines 1994–2015.

[155] Ermold, lines 2016–19.

mentioned or addressed directly were to be praised to the hilt, but without their glorious role becoming incredible to insiders. Ermold's description of Louis's travel to the assembly in Vannes in 818, prior to confronting the wicked Bretons, has rightly been called a *Stationsgedicht*, by which Ermold pays his respects to great men *en route*.[156] Receiving many gifts, Louis first arrived at St-Denis, where he was received by Abbot Hilduin, the archchancellor, and then at 'the dwellings of Germanus, Stephanus and Geneviève'. From there, he proceeded to the region of Orléans, to Vitry, where Matfrid bade him welcome; in Orléans he asked protection of the Holy Cross and visited the abbey of St-Aignan, enjoying the hospitality of Bishop Jonas and Abbot Durandus; onwards then to Tours and its 'temples' of Martin and the martyr St Maurice, where abbot Fredugisus awaited them with lavish gifts. Then the emperor came to Angers, and prayed to St Aubin, while 'dear Helisachar' came to meet him with much to fill the imperial coffers. Finally he reached Nantes, visiting all the shrines of the saints, and being offered rich gifts by Count Lambert. To be on the safe side, Ermold warned that 'there was also a crowd of counts and powerful men about, but I cannot count either their number or their resources'.[157] In the preceding verses, however, he succeeded in presenting almost all Louis's loyal great men – and his own potential supporters – in their imperially appointed role as guardians of the most powerful relics.

A sacred topography emerges, defined by the presence of powerful martyrs and saints. The fierce competition between Hilduin and Einhard springs to mind: who had the best martyrs? Authority and protection could be derived from the patronage of the saints, and in claiming their share of this, the great men followed the example of their ruler.[158] Louis's voyage to Aachen, after Charlemagne's death, is also depicted as a saint-studded itinerary, along many of the same places but in the opposite direction.[159] Such a royal progress also served as a confirmation of loyalty. All the faithful men, without any exception, offered copious gifts to the emperor. This was part of what Ermold called 'preparing for battle according to ancient custom'.[160] His was a work to be relished by fighting men, Louis included.

The Louis the Pious of Ermold's *Poem* had two faces, which cannot have been too different from the public image of this emperor as contemporaries experienced it. On the one hand, he was the warrior, from

---

[156] Godman, 'Louis "the Pious"', p. 256, *à propos* Ermold, lines 1523–55.
[157] Ermold, lines 1556–8: 'Cetera turba latet comitum necnonque potentum/Quorum nec numerus nec numerantur opes.'
[158] Smith, 'Old saints' and '"Emending evil ways"'.
[159] Faral, *Ermold, Poème*, p. 117, n. 2.   [160] Ermold, line 1559.

beginning to end; on the other, he was represented here as a ruler who provided religious leadership, and defined how pope and emperor should work together: 'You are a holy bishop (*sacer antistes*); I am king of the Christian people: let us protect the people with doctrine, law and faith.'[161] The connection between these two aspects of the ruler, warlike and peace-bringing, is elucidated at the very beginning of the third book, devoted to the Breton campaigns: 'The armies of Caesar grew ever stronger through the gift of the highest God, and through faith, peace was spread to every people. Through great Louis's work, the reputation of the Franks flew across every sea and reached the highest heavens.'[162] The Franks and their honour play an important role in this work, as do the *proceres*, the upper and palace-connected echelon of the Frankish elite, referred to so often by Ermold. This mixed group of high-ranking clerics and laymen seems to be permanently in the background, as the audience for his praise of an emperor characterized by *pietas*, and his essentially peaceable but always victorious Franks.[163] It was the emperor whose clemency could guarantee Ermold's return to Aquitaine, but the counsel of his *proceres* weighed heavily in such decisions, which is why they are addressed and/or mentioned as well – as a group, and individually if they truly belonged to the inner circle. Einhard, for example, 'best loved of Charles, a man wise in intelligence and vibrant in goodness', was depicted as delivering a speech by which he counselled Charlemagne to designate Louis as his successor.[164]

Ermold situated the Franks in the wider context of history, and in doing so, he put not only Louis and his family, but also the magnates (*proceres*) centre stage. For their benefit, Ermold had Charlemagne define the nature of his Frankish and imperial rule:

Francia bore me, but Christ gave me my *honor* and the paternal kingdoms to keep; I have held them, and I have also made them stronger. I was shepherd and

---

[161] Ibid., lines 1030–1, p. 80: 'Tu sacer antistes; ego rex sum christicolarum: / Servemus populum dogmate, lege, fide.' See the much more elaborate statement by Alcuin and Charlemagne in a letter to Pope Leo III: Alcuin, *Epistolae* no. 93, ed. E. Dümmler, MGH *Epp.* IV, p. 136; see also *Karolus Magnus et Leo papa*, lines 487–514, on the meeting of Charles and Leo in Paderborn.

[162] Ermold, lines 1254–7, p. 98; also lines 1402–11, p. 108, Witchar's speech to Murman, praising the Franks.

[163] See Depreux, 'La *pietas*', on the wide semantic field of Louis's 'piety' that far exceeds the sanctimonious associations this term has in modern usage, and on the Franks 'qui partagent la piété de leur chef' (at p. 222).

[164] On Einhard, cf. Ermold, lines 682–97. *Proceres* are mentioned frequently in the *Carmen*. The same group is meant by *turba ... comitum necnonque potentum* (l. 1556 – see above, n. 157). Within this group, there is the inner circle of those who had the king's ear on a more permanent basis, though they did not necessarily live at the court: Einhard is one example of this, Matfrid another.

armament to the Christian flock. I was the first of the Franks to take the name Caesar, and I gave this Romulean name to the Franks to keep.[165]

Throughout his poem, Ermold celebrated the Franks: their origins, customs and bravery, their *Francia* and their Frankish kingdoms (*Francica regna*).[166] When in the autumn of 824 Louis mounted a campaign against the Bretons, 'all Francia joined him, as well as the subjected peoples'.[167] These truly imperial Franks were integrated into a splendid past, emphasised by Ermold's well-known depiction of the decoration of the church and the palace in Ingelheim. As he himself expressed it, 'the illustrious deeds (*gesta*) of God and the memorable ones of generations of men appear magnificent in the *pictura* by which they can be re-read'.[168] Like Ermold's own *gesta* of Louis, these images of the past in Ingelheim could be contemplated time and again, be it in reality or through Ermold's poetic visualisation. On the left hand as one entered the church, the images gave an account (*recensio*) from creation up to the end of the history of Moses, followed by a long procession of prophets and kings and their celebrated actions. On the opposite wall one saw the living deeds of Christ (*Christi vitalia gesta*),[169] who died, rose and now reigned the world.[170] On the walls of this *templum dei*, jointly built by David and Solomon, there was also room for the leaders of the people (*duces populi*) as well as the highest *sacerdotes* and *proceres*; these figures are situated in an Old Testament context, yet the terminology was the contemporary one for the Frankish leadership. Counts, bishops and magnates merited a place in sacred history.[171]

From the church Ermold moved to the palace (*domus regia*), which 'glitters throughout with sculpture, and sings with the genius of the

---

[165] Ermold, lines 715–7719, p. 56: '"Francia me genuit, Christus concessit honorem / Regna paterna mihi Christus habere dedit: / Haec eadem tenui, nec non potiora recepi, / Christicoloque fui pastor et arma gregi. / Caesareum primus Francorum nomen adeptus / Francis Romoleum nomen habere dedi."' This is a clear reference to the imperial dignity; on the *nomen imperatoris*, see Wolfram, 'Legitimationsformel'; Murray, 'Shepherd King'. See also Nelson, 'Kingship and empire', pp. 54–9.

[166] Ermold, lines 115, 131 (arms), 173–5 (customs), 109 (peaceful but disciplined); see Faral's index at p. 256.

[167] Ermold, lines 1999–2000: 'Francia cuncta ruit, veniunt gentes subactae.'

[168] Ibid., lines 2070–1: cf. Lammers, 'Bildprogramm'. On the excavations at Ingelheim, see Lobbedey, 'Carolingian royal palaces', pp. 138–43.

[169] Ermold, line 2100, p. 160; an expression borrowed from Juvencus, *Historia evangelica*, prol., 19, cf. Faral, p. 247.

[170] Ermold, line 2113–4, p. 162. For Ermold, *Deus* and *Christus* seem to have been interchangeable entities.

[171] Ibid., lines 2098–9, p. 160: '[pingitur] Et Davidis opus, Salomonis et acta potentis, / Templaque divino aedificata opere; / Inde duces populi quales quantique fuere / Atque sacerdotum culmina seu procerum.'

greatest deeds of men'.[172] *Gesta* and more *gesta*: we now enter the realm of earthly history, with Cyrus, Phalaris, Romulus, Hannibal and Alexander in one section – powerful rulers, with some evil tyrants added for good measure – and the 'ancestral deeds, closer because of pious faith', on the other. Here Roman exploits join the equally remarkable deeds of the Franks: one sees Constantine constructing Rome, the 'happy (*felix*) Theodosius, Charles Martel, who vanquished the Frisians, his son Pippin, who did likewise for the Aquitanians, and Charles the Wise, radiant and wearing his crown, who subdued the Saxons'.[173] What is highlighted in this poetic visualisation of the past is that the Christian Franks had inherited the Christian Roman empire; this part of history – the 'closer' part, because of proximity by time and faith – adorned the *domus regia*, the part of the palace inhabited by the emperor, whereas sacred history was manifest in the chapel. Through his baptism, the Danish King Harald came to share this glorious past, in which ethnic associations began to fade: the kingdoms that Roman might and Frankish law had failed to retain now sought the rule of 'father Louis', in Christ's name.[174]

Did Ermold succeed in writing himself back into Louis's favour? This remains uncertain, although a celebrated poem by Walahfrid Strabo may yield a clue. Walahfrid wrote his *De imagine Tetrici* in the spring of 829, when he joined Louis and Judith's entourage, probably to serve as young Charles's tutor.[175] The poem is set in the 'humble' genre of a bucolic dialogue between Scintilla, a Muse who speaks the truth, and the poet, who interrogates her.[176] On the one hand, the poet sees the statue of Theoderic, surrounded by a festive crowd, with musicians from everywhere; on the other, there is the strictly hierarchical procession of the royal family and their highest-ranking courtiers, each of them represented by a biblical 'type': Louis/Moses led the procession, followed by Lothar/Joshua, Pippin/Jonathan, Judith and Charles / Rachel and Benjamin,

---

[172] Ibid., lines 2126–7, p. 162: 'Regia namque domus late persculpta nitescet, / Et canit ingenio maxima gesta virum.'

[173] Ibid., lines 2150–63, p. 164. For another historical tableau of Frankish rulers, this time to stress their good record concerning protection of the church, see Ermold's second verse epistle to Pippin, *Ad eundem Pippinum*, lines 147–64, ed. Faral, p. 228.

[174] Ermold, lines 2515–9, p. 190: 'Arma patrum nullo quae non valuere duello, / Sponte sua, capere, te modo regna petunt; / Quod nec Roma potens tenuit nec Francisca jura, / Tu retines Christi nomine cuncta, pater.'

[175] His role as such has been doubted by Fees, 'Walahfrid Strabo'. On Walahfrid's career, see Booker, 'A new prologue', pp. 83–4.

[176] For an in-depth and convincing analysis of the poem, see Smolak, 'Bescheidene Panegyrik'; central in Smolak's argument is the pervasive influence of Prudentius' *Psychomachia*. In a similar vein, see Hoymeier, 'Walahfrid Strabos Gedicht'. For editions of the poem, see E. Dümmler in MGH *Poet. lat.* II, pp. 370–8 (used here), and Walahfrid, '"De imagine Tetrici"', ed. Herren.

Hilduin/Aaron, Einhard/Bezaleel, and finally Walahfrid's master Grimald, somewhat out of step with these biblical alter egos, for he is associated with Homer.[177] The solemn biblical procession is contrasted with the festive and noisy group around the statue, according to the exegetical scheme of type and antitype; what Walahfrid saw, as the opposite of 'stupid Theoderic', was the happy polity where he knew kings to be wise and the wise to rule.[178] As Kurt Smolak has argued convincingly, this debut at the court by the gifted young monk from Reichenau was set in a consciously modest poetical register, as befitted a newcomer who yet had to make his mark.[179] His brief praise poem for Judith, urging her to 'accept all good writing' (*quae bona cuncta precipe scripta*), indicates that he first presented the empress with *De imagine Tetrici*, before daring to approach Louis with such a gift.[180] All the same, the young poet may have allowed himself to take a pot-shot at the competition: Ermold the Black. The negative 'blackness' of the herald holding Theoderic's horse, or of an angry musician figuring in the poem, may have been a veiled reference to Ermold.[181] If Smolak is right, this would mean that Ermold's *Carmen* had made something of an impression on Louis and his retinue, sufficiently so for Walahfrid to see Ermold as a senior colleague to measure himself against. This would argue for Ermold still being a force to reckon with, and against his continued exile. Whatever the case, both Ermold and Walahfrid evoked images of an eminently Frankish political order embedded in biblical and ancient history; both employed the procession as a means to visualise the correct hierarchy that pertained in Louis's palace. Arriving in Aachen in the spring of 829, Walahfrid may have known that open discord threatened within the imperial family. Possibly his appeal to *concordia* was a reference to the various tensions he sensed, yet, as a youngster just sent over from Reichenau, he would have been careful not to give offence.[182] Neither Ermold nor Walahfrid was a clairvoyant, nor a potential prophet of doom. These two poets worked and wrote before the two rebellions against Louis, and could unreservedly depict the palace as the moral hub of the realm, with Louis and Judith at its centre.

---

[177] Walahfrid, *Carmina*, no. 23, pp. 374–6. Cf. Smolak, 'Bescheidene Panegyrik', pp. 99–100.

[178] Walahfrid, *Carmina*, no. 23, p. 378, lines 256–8.

[179] On the careful choice of the poetic genre, see Smolak, 'Bescheidene Panegyrik', pp. 91–2, 107: the young Virgil had praised a peace-bringing Augustus in Ecl. 1.4, and, so it was believed in the ninth century, through the fourth Eclogue also Christ.

[180] Walahfrid, *Carmina*, no. 23a, p. 379.

[181] Smolak, 'Bescheidene Panegyrik', p. 105–7. Other differences, possibly consciously emphasised: Walahfrid distances himself ('I never met you') from Ermold's patron, Pippin, and concentrates on Charles.

[182] Walahfrid, *De imagine Tetrici*, v. 170; Smolak, 'Bescheidene Panegyrik', p. 104.

With hindsight: Nithard on Louis the Pious

Both Ermold and Nithard wrote in order to persuade a ruler to improve their lot.[183] Both Ermold's *Poem* and Nithard's *Histories* had a relatively limited manuscript tradition.[184] Otherwise, these two authors and their works were very different. The first was an exile who glorified Frankish imperial rule, that is, bravery and responsibility shared by Louis and his magnates; the second was an illegitimate member of the ruling family who ended his account of the war among Louis's sons with a bleak vision of the irredeemable failure of Carolingian governance:

At the time there was, on the thirteenth calends of April [20 March 843], an eclipse of the moon; in addition, snow fell abundantly during that night and by the just judgement of God, as said above, all were struck by sorrow. I say this because from then on rapine and evil of all kind spread everywhere, and from then on unseasonable weather dashed the hope of any good to come.[185]

These were the closing sentences of Nithard's fourth and last book. Modern historians have tended to trust the *Histories* implicitly, because its author was a contemporary witness and, to everyone's relief, not a monk or a cleric but a layman, and even a man of action who knew all about war and politics. As the son of Charlemagne's daughter Bertha (d. after 829) and of Angilbert, courtier and lay abbot of St-Riquier (d. Feb. 814), Nithard was also an insider in the Carolingian family. He became the 'bluff soldier telling it straight',[186] whose terse prose suggested distance and secularity.[187] In successive explorations of Nithard's work, however, Janet Nelson has revealed its complexity. Nithard was a man passionately involved in the events he apparently describes so dispassionately, for his own fate and that of the lands he held between Meuse and Scheldt were at stake. He wrote a carefully crafted work, featuring public values while encoding his private history. The first two books were written for Charles the Bald and his entourage, justifying the choices that led to the dismal slaughter at Fontenoy.[188] From the third book onwards, the tone changes. The fighting men began to long for reconciliation, so the core values of fraternity, peace and *christianitas* received more

---

[183] Nelson, 'Public *histories*'.

[184] Nithard's *Historiae* is transmitted in Paris BN lat. 9768, in a manuscript that belonged to St-Médard in Soissons. Paris BN lat 14663 (s. xv) is an incomplete copy of this. See Lauer, *Histoire*, pp. xiv–xv. Title: *Nithard Historiarum Libri IX*. See Löwe (ed.), *Deutschlands Geschichtsquellen*, pp. 353–7. But see Nelson, 'History-writing', p. 440, with evidence for more *Nachleben* of Nithard's *Histories* than is usually assumed.

[185] Nithard, IV, c. 6, p. 144.   [186] Nelson, 'Public *histories*', pp. 196–7.

[187] Wallace-Hadrill, *Frankish Church*, p. 238; Leyser, 'Nithard', p. 19.

[188] Nelson, 'Public *histories*', pp. 196–7.

emphasis.[189] In this context, Nithard famously rendered the text of the oaths of Strasbourg (11 February 842), when Charles and Louis the German and their men swore allegiance to each other, 'for the love of God and the Christian people and our common salvation'.[190] By the time he wrote his fourth book, it was no longer for the king, the court or contemporaries, but for posterity alone, sparing nobody, however influential, and ending with a bitter comparison between the Golden Age of Charlemagne and his own miserable times. His services went unrewarded, and he ended up as lay abbot in his father's abbey, St-Riquier, before being killed in action on 14 June 844, 'fighting again for Charles in another round of Carolingian family conflict'.[191] Nithard's text was not just meant for posterity but addressed a wider audience, namely his Frankish aristocratic contemporaries, whose ethos of fidelity and service to the king he shared.[192] As Nelson has shown, Nithard's perspective as an author was attuned to the political developments of the early 840s; his writing was meant to persuade others to rally to his point of view.[193] Especially in the fourth book of his *Histories*, Nithard voiced the disillusionment of high-minded men who impotently witnessed the disintegration of the world and the values they believed in; his concerns about his own status and lands were pressing, but also, and even more so, was his regret that those who should mind the polity and the common good (*res publica*) thought only of their own gain.[194]

In other words, the traditional view of the gentleman soldier Nithard, an exceptionally secular and therefore trustworthy historian, is rapidly vanishing.[195] Nelson's analysis does justice to Nithard, and so does Stuart Airlie's characterisation of the *Historiae* as a skilfully crafted work, meant to be read in its entirety, that is, including the increasingly gloomy two last books. Nithard lashed out viciously against his two main villains of the piece: Adalhard 'the seneschal', a powerful magnate at Louis's court who became Charles' supporter (in 842 his niece Ermentrude married the king), and, above all, Lothar, who is depicted as the embodiment of treachery: he invariably broke his word, went back on his oaths and made promises without any intention of keeping them. This ruler was the very opposite of all that *fides* entailed, and therefore not worthy of it.[196]

---

[189] Ibid., pp. 207–8. [190] Nithard, III, c. 5, pp. 100–8.
[191] Nelson, 'Public *histories*', p. 225. On the bitter tone of the more 'private' fourth book and Nithard's loss of his lands, see pp. 211–12, 220–5; on the date of Nithard's death, pp. 235–7.
[192] Ibid.; 'History-writing', p. 440. [193] Nelson, 'Public *histories*', pp. 199–216.
[194] Nelson, 'Ninth-century knighthood' and 'Nobility'. On Nithard and *res publica*, see Depreux, 'Nithard et la *res publica*'.
[195] Airlie, 'The world'. I am grateful to the author for sending me his text before publication.
[196] For a critical assessment of Nithard's treatment of Lothar, see Screen, 'Importance of being emperor'.

Nithard aimed to write both these men into the ground, for the benefit of an elite to whom honour and reputation mattered. What about his image of Louis the Pious? Was this as critical as it has been made out to be, highlighting Louis's incompetence and weakness?[197]

This question takes us to Nithard's first book, which covers the reign of Louis, and to its prologue. Here, the author claimed to have considered omitting any narrative about 'the times of your pious father', but to have decided against this, for a factual summary of some key events would clarify 'the truth of your [i.e. the brothers'] altercations' to the reader. Neither could Nithard omit any reference to the venerable memory of Charles's grandfather, which was why the text started with him.[198] As Nithard repeated elsewhere, the contemporary war he wrote about could not be understood without the background of Louis's reign in mind.[199] Against the setting of the flourishing world left behind by Charlemagne – who was *terribilis*, *amabilis*, *admirabilis*, and keeping everyone's nose to the grindstone of the public good – Nithard sketched a portrait of the reign of Louis the Pious that was not exactly hostile, but definitely less than enthusiastic. In the second chapter, the 'heir to all this sublimity' is depicted as the one legitimate son left who did not immediately command loyalty, who restricted the division of his father's riches to himself and his legitimate sisters, who almost immediately had major conflicts with his closest family – Bernard and his half-brothers – and who divided the *universum imperium* among his three sons, before remarrying and begetting a fourth son. Thus, in one chapter the scene is set for the root of all evil: 'Once Charles was born, the father, because he had divided the entire empire among his other sons, did not know what to do for this one.'[200] All this briskly leads up to the rebellions, on which Nithard spilled most of his ink, for it was the faithless behaviour of the emperor's sons and *fideles* that foreshadowed the egotistical disregard for the *res publica* in his own day and age that he wished to expose and indict.

Nithard was not uncritical of Louis, that much is certain. Monks play a rather sinister role in 830, first as those who guard the emperor and try to persuade him to enter monastic life, and then, as the tide turned, as supporters of his restoration. A certain Guntbald, mentioned by no

[197] Depreux, 'Nithard et la *res publica*'; Airlie, 'The world', p. 63: 'Louis's legitimacy, if not his incompetence, is thus secure as it is grounded in Nithard's fundamental starting-point'; p. 75 ('Louis the Pious' weakness').

[198] Nithard, I, prologue, p. 2. On Nithard's narrow and vertical conception of the Carolingian royal family, see Airlie, 'The world'.

[199] See also Nithard, II, prologue, p. 36, where the function of book I for understanding 'the origins of your troubles (dissensionum vestrarum initiis)' is underlined once more.

[200] Nithard, I, c. 3, p. 8.

other author, presumably became Louis's envoy to Pippin and Louis.
Offered bigger shares of the kingdoms, the brothers agreed, 'easily and
greedily' (*facile cupideque*). A few sentences earlier, when the monks and
Louis's other supporters asked him whether, if the *res publica* was restored
to him, he would exert himself to maintain this and above all the *cultus
divinus* upon which all order depended, Louis 'committed himself readily'
(*quod qui facile confessum*).[201] Was this a barely veiled reference to the
somewhat hasty confession of guilt in Compiègne, in the summer of
830? Possibly, but the emphasis of this section is on all those who competed for the position of second in command (*secundus in imperio*).
Incongruously, the monk Guntbald aspired to this status, because he
had been instrumental in Louis's restoration, and so did Bernard, who
had once had this rank; furthermore, Pippin and Louis competed for this
position, yet 'those who then directed the affairs of state, resisted the
ambition of all these men'.[202] Here, Nithard possibly referred to his own
role in counteracting such powers behind the throne.[203] This passage is
typical of Nithard's treatment of Louis throughout the first book: he plays
a relatively passive role. While others act, plot, aspire and scheme, the
emperor is usually on the receiving end of these actions. How Nithard felt
about Louis is difficult to make out, precisely because in the first book,
even though it is about his reign, Louis is not the main character. Instead,
this book serves as the introduction to the unfolding drama of Lothar's
perfidiousness. The very first mention of Lothar concerns his reneging on
his one-time promise under oath to give Charles a part of the realm, and to
be his young half-brother's protector.[204] In the same chapter, which is
crammed with innuendo, Lothar is targeted as the one who incited his
brothers and all the faithful people (*universa plebs*) to restore the *res publica*,
'as if he had any just cause for discontent'.[205] In Nithard's rendering of the
revolts of 830 and 833, Lothar is the driving force behind his father's
plight; he and his supporters, swollen with pride, were after the total
control of imperial rule (*universum imperium*).[206] Lothar's own humiliation at the assembly in Worms in 839, where he prostrated himself before
his father, asking forgiveness, underscored the point that Lothar held his

---

[201] Ibid., pp. 10–12.
[202] Ibid., p. 14: 'at illi, per quos tunc res publica tractabatur, voluntati eorum obsistebant'.
[203] My thanks to Janet Nelson for this suggestion.   [204] Nithard, I, c.3, p. 8.
[205] Ibid., p. 10. *Plebs* can have the meaning of 'common people' (see above, n. 107), but
here, connected with *universum*, the expression denotes Louis's faithful men. See also I,
c. 4, p. 14, on the run-up to 833; malcontents mentioned earlier said the *respublica* was
being led badly, and incited the *populus* to demand just rule.
[206] Nithard, I, c. 5, p. 22.

kingdom thanks to God and his magnanimous and merciful father (*pius et clemens pater*) – and that he swore precious oaths which he then broke, time and again.[207]

In so far as the emperor himself is blamed, it is implicitly and in passing. In Nithard's *Historiae*, Louis's reign is a foil for the emergence of Lothar, who already reveals himself as unworthy of the *res publica* and incapable of its governance. Yet there are others who get their fair share of Nithard's opprobrium, such as the so-called faithful men who had broken their oath and deserted their legitimate emperor for the lures of his treacherous eldest son. Having sacked Chalon in 834, Lothar hoped to seduce the Franks to his side. 'But the Franks, torn with remorse because they had twice deserted the emperor, and now thinking what they perpetrated shameful, disdained to be talked into defection.'[208] This time 'the Franks' recovered from their aberration, yet the virus of infidelity, initiated by Lothar, would not disappear. The rebellions against Louis led directly to the crisis of the early 840s, and from there to the disintegration of the Carolingian empire; Nithard's view of the matter has determined the modern grand narrative of Louis the Pious.[209]

When all was said and done, the moral failure that Nithard observed in his own time was the collective responsibility of royal *fideles* who could not keep *fides*, and thereby betrayed the very code of behaviour that enabled them to take part in governing the state. Fidelity towards God and one's king was the first lesson Nithard's contemporary Dhuoda, the wife of Bernard of Septimania, set out to imprint on the mind of her son William.[210] The fraternal war of 840–3 threw Nithard and others into a moral turmoil. To be faithful to one's lord and king mattered almost as deeply as being faithful to God: these two kinds of *fides* were two sides of the same coin. One's fellow-aristocrats might not always have acted according to the letter of this code of honour, but they shared its basic tenet. Thus, failure in this respect caused shame and a potential loss of reputation, and depicting enemies like Lothar or Adalhard as oath-breakers could be effective. Such political opponents most likely shared Nithard's values, and believed in loyalty as firmly as he did, as is shown by a letter probably addressed by Adalhard to the Empress

---

[207] Nithard, I, c. 7, p. 30. Cf. ibid., p. 32. Cf. Screen, 'Importance of being emperor'.

[208] Nithard, I, c. 5, p. 22.

[209] Halphen, *Charlemagne*, p. 277 ('dans le désarroi où s'âbime l'Empire depuis 833'; T. Schieffer, 'Krise', p. 13 (on self-interest prevailing).

[210] Le Jan, 'Dhuoda'; Nelson, 'Dhuoda'.

Irmingard, Lothar's wife.[211] Nithard's bleak verdict on the *mores* of his day and age can be read as despondent resignation, but also as a reaffirmation of the aristocratic code of conduct he grew up with, and as a clarion call to rally once more under the banner of *fides*.

The final sentences of the *Historiae*, cited at the beginning of this section, express resignation: they were written after Charles's marriage in 842 to the niece of Nithard's enemy Adalhard, and revealed that even this king failed to live up to expectations. As Stuart Airlie expressed it, poetically and accurately, 'Nithard takes care to place Charles's wedding in a harsh and sterile winter landscape from which any prospect of spring is glaringly absent, just as the public order descends into chaotic self-seeking'.[212] This disastrous wedding, at least for Nithard, was followed by ominous eclipses, and preceded by another evocation of Charlemagne's blissful reign, when peace and concord reigned 'because this people walked one and the same straight road, and thereby the public road of the Lord'.[213] Nithard's lament about the loss of unanimity is full of biblical expressions and allusions. It culminates in the angry complaint that, whereas the elements used to be favourable to rulers, they had now become contrary, as Scripture testifies: 'The universe shall fight against the unwise (*Et pugnabit orbis terrarum contra insensatos*' (Sap. 5.21)). Although this looks like a straightforward biblical citation and figures as such in modern editions, Nithard's use of this text is far removed from the original context and meaning. According to the book of Wisdom, from which this phrase was taken, the one who fights is God himself, doing battle on the side of the righteous: 'And he will sharpen his severe wrath for a spear, and the whole world shall fight with him against the mad (*et pugnabit cum illo orbis terrarum contra insensatos*).'[214] When Nithard used this text against Charles, he did so to evoke a natural world that had turned against the king. In other words, Charles was a 'king without justice' (*rex iniquus*), whose inequity affected humans and nature alike: the winter following Charles's marriage to Ermentrude was particularly harsh.[215] To make his lament even more effective, Nithard associated Charlemagne's reign, now well in the past, with the 'right ways of the Lord' in which the just would walk, while

---

[211] MGH *Epp.* III, no. 27, pp. 343–5; Nelson, 'Search for peace', pp. 102–4; Airlie, 'The world', pp. 57–8.

[212] Airlie, 'The world', p.74.

[213] Nithard, IV, c.7, p. 144: 'quoniam hic populus unam eandemque rectam ac per hoc viam Domini publicam incendebat'.

[214] Nithard, IV, c. 6 , p. 142: 'Ipsa elementa tunc cuique rei congrua, nunc autem omnibus ubique contraria, uti Scriptura divino munere prolata testatur: *Et pugnabit orbis terrarum contra insensatos.*'

[215] Nithard, IV, c. 6, p. 142; IV, c. 7, p. 144; on Pseudo-Cyprian's *De abusivis* and the 'rex iniquus', see below, chapter 4, pp. 174–5, 181–2.

transgressors stumbled (Os. 14.10; cf. also Ez. 33.20 and Act. 13.10). But Nithard gave a contemporary twist to these biblical passages: contrary to the self-interest he saw around him, the right way of the Lord in Charlemagne's time had been an eminently public way (*via publica*).[216] This was heavy ammunition indeed, yet it seems likely that Nithard's fourth book was aimed at precisely the same audience as the other three: the court, that is, Charles and his entourage.

Unlike Ermold, Nithard had nothing to gain from flattery or glossing things over. More importantly, unlike Ermold, Nithard was Charlemagne's grandson. So was his royal patron, and even if Charles was a king and his historian a lay abbot who had just lost much prized *honores* because of a deal done with Lothar, he still was a kinsman of his royal patron. Nithard was annoyingly equal to any of the royal protagonists he portrayed in his *Histories*, and not about to mince his words when he was crossed, which is why he did not need to edit what he wrote, or to address his frustrations merely to posterity. Within the exalted upper echelon of the court, well-delivered criticism of the ruler was not just reluctantly allowed, but might also be benevolently accepted and taken in the royal stride.[217] Nithard wrote from the kind of moral high ground on which only the Carolingian great and good operated, while smaller fry aspiring to get there turned their literary efforts in this direction. Throughout his work, Nithard admonished his audience to remember that there had been the age of Charlemagne to which they could return. He used the genre of moral-ising history (*historia*) to admonish his royal and aristocratic contempora-ries, and as a way to hit back at his own enemies, yet he also, and increasingly, adopted the role of the prophet of doom, hurling his unpalat-able truths into the face of the powerful. Towards the end of his *Histories*, Nithard, hitting hard with well-chosen biblical citations, resembles another member of the Carolingian family who gradually turned into a Jeremiah: Wala, as he was remembered by his fellow-monk and successor as abbot of Corbie, Paschasius Radbertus.

Looking back in anger: Radbert on Wala

Born towards the end of the eighth century, Paschasius Radbertus was raised in Notre Dame of Soissons, the convent led by Theodrada, sister to

---

[216] See above, n. 214.
[217] See Nelson, 'History-writing', for a first discussion of the limits and scope of criticising the ruler, and the following chapter of this book, which addresses the genre of the *admonitio*.

Adalhard and Wala.[218] In all possible ways except by blood kinship, Radbert (as I shall call him from now on) belonged to this illustrious family.[219] The kindness of Theodrada and her community earned their charge's undying gratitude, which extended to Theodrada's siblings.[220] We must assume (but do not know) that he had already started his literary formation while he was in Soissons. He left the monastic confines for some years, leading a more worldly life, but by 812 Radbert had become a monk at Corbie, and Abbot Adalhard's pupil. Here he also met Wala. Upon Adalhard's death in 826, the monks sent Radbert to the palace to plead for Wala's succession.[221] Clearly, Radbert's star was rising, as is also apparent from his involvement in the foundation of Corvey in 822.[222] When in 826 Wala succeeded Adalhard as abbot of both Corbie and Corvey, Radbert became Wala's trusted right-hand man. When Wala was at the palace, Radbert was often at his side; when Wala was banished from the palace for his part in the rebellion of 830, Radbert followed him into exile.[223] As Klaus Zechiel-Eckes has argued, Radbert may well have been the monk of Corbie who, once the rebellion of 833 had foundered, compiled the core of 'Pseudo-Isidore', a collection of forged papal letters stressing pontifical authority at the expense of archbishops and rulers.[224] Eventually, in 843, he became abbot of Corbie himself, but he did not hold the abbacy for long. By 851 Radbert was no longer abbot of Corbie. For reasons unknown he had been succeeded by Odo, with whom he was on friendly terms.[225] Radbert retired to St-Riquier, where he may have read Nithard's *Histories*.[226] He died sometime in the late 850s.[227]

Radbert was a deeply learned man and a prolific exegete, whose work included a controversial treatise on the Eucharist, a commentary on Matthew's Gospel and an exposition of Lamentations.[228] Shortly after

---

[218] Radbert was born between c. 785 and 795; Weinrich, *Wala*, pp. 7–10. As an abbess of St Mary's, Theodrada was probably the successor of none other than Rotrud, Charlemagne's daughter (d. 810); Weinrich, *Wala*, p. 14.

[219] Their father Bernard was a son of Charles Martel; Adalhard, who was considerably older than his siblings, was born to a different mother; see Weinrich, *Wala*, pp. 90–2.

[220] Paschasius Radbertus, *Expositio in psalmum XLIV*, pp. v–vi. This commentary was dedicated to Theodrada and her nuns. See De Jong, *In Samuel's Image*, pp. 126–7, 180.

[221] Radbert *EA*, II, c. 11, pp. 38–9; Krüger, 'Nachfolgeregelung'.

[222] Kasten, *Adalhard von Corbie*, pp. 148–54.

[223] Paschasius Radbertus, *De corpore*, p. 3 (dedication to Abbot Warin of Corvey).

[224] Zechiel-Eckes, 'Ein Blick in Pseudoisidors Werkstatt'.

[225] For de more extensive discussion of Radbert's biography, see De Jong, 'Becoming Jeremiah'.

[226] Ganz, 'Opposition', p. 547.

[227] On the conflicting views on Radbert's year of death, see Ganz, 'Opposition', pp. 539–40. On Radbert's abbacy, see Paschasius Radbertus, *Carmina*, p. 39, n. 4.

[228] Paschasius Radbertus, *Expositio in lamentationes Hieremiae libri quinque*; on Radbert's work, see Ganz, *Corbie*, pp. 31–3, 103–20; Chazelle, 'Exegesis'.

Adalhard's death, this loyal pupil wrote a fiercely partisan *Life* of his abbot, in which he blamed Louis for most of Adalhard's trials and tribulations.[229] More difficult to date is Radbert's tribute to Wala, the *Epitaphium Arsenii*.[230] The prevailing opinion is that the first book was written soon after Wala's death (836), and the second only in 850–1.[231] The question is whether Lothar's wife Irmingard, who died on 20 March 851, is portrayed as deceased, or still alive; Radbert related how the empress told him and the monks about Wala's commemoration in Italy, in a past tense that is difficult to interpret ('as she often used to say, in the spirit of pious memory').[232] David Ganz thinks that Radbert may have tinkered with his text until as late as 856.[233] Neither view can be proved, but both are plausible. The death of Bernard of Septimania (844) is mentioned in the second book, so Radbert worked on his text until at least after this date.[234] Although there is an obvious time gap between the two books, there are cross-references which indicate a later phase of redaction. The second book is alluded to in the first, and vice versa; they were intended as a diptych that highlighted different aspects of Wala's greatness.[235] The work was a long-term project, edited as one work by an author who, towards the end, may have made some effort to strengthen the two parts. Did Radbert delay writing his second book until a time when all his main villains had died? There are allusions in the first book to a future time when 'all the torches of the enemies will be extinguished' and the truth can be told to all that will listen.[236] On the other hand, the tension between silence and the duty to speak out is a persistent theme throughout the two books. Yet there is no indication that Radbert was silenced by royal might of any kind. His reference to having been given

---

[229] On Adalhard's biography, see Kasten, *Adalhard von Corbie*, and Depreux, *Prosopographie*, pp. 76–9.

[230] The edition used here by E. Dümmler (Berlin, 1900) is difficult to come by; the only alternative is *PL* 120, cols. 1159D–1650B, which is Dom Jacques Mabillon's text. The references to chapters are from this older edition, and have been retained in the margin by Dümmler. For Radbert's *Vita Adalhardi*, see *PL* 120, cols. 1507–56C. The translation by Cabaniss, *Charlemagne's Cousins*, is not reliable. By far the best introduction to the *Epitaphium Arsenii*, including its literary models, is provided by Ganz, 'Opposition', and *Corbie*, pp. 113–20; see also Berschin, *Biographie und Epochenstil*, III, pp. 318–25.

[231] Weinrich, *Wala*, p. 7. See also Dümmler's introduction to Radbert, *EA*, p. 11.

[232] Radbert, *EA*, II, c. 24, pp. 97: 'Quae quam sepe piae recordationis affectu aiebat ...'

[233] Ganz, 'Opposition', pp. 538–9.

[234] Radbert, *EA*, II, c. 15, p. 83: 'et ad finem usque semper publicus predo vixit' ('and until the end, he [Bernhard] lived as a public brigand as he always had'.

[235] See, for example, the end of book I (*EA*, I, c. 28, p. 58), where the monk Paschasius said, 'Let us now turn our pen to the Gauls, where unspeakable and confusing things (*formodilosa et confusa*) have been happening'; he doubts whether he can write, because of weeping.

[236] Radbert, *EA*, I, c. 21, p. 50 (Severus as the interlocuter, in a passage larded with citations from Terence's *Eunuchus*).

back his 'freedom and quiet of mind' probably expresses public relief at the loss of his abbacy.[237]

Wala's death had left his monks bereft like orphans grieving for a parent. What Radbert produced in response to the loss of their beloved abbot was a moving lament, and a spirited attack on Wala's many enemies. The two chief accusations against him had been that he had not lived a monastic life, and that he had been guilty of infidelity towards Louis. The over-arching aim of the *Epitaphium Arsenii* was to counter this, and to show those whose opinion mattered that Wala had been the most virtuous of monks, and that his fidelity (*fides*) towards the emperor had been impecc-able. Radbert's intended audience belonged to the cloister as well as to the court, which does not mean that their interest in his subject matter was divided accordingly. Monastic regularity was a concern of secular mag-nates and, conversely, what went on at the court deeply interested monks. Because there is only one extant manuscript, produced in Corbie, this has been seen as a text without much impact outside Corbie, yet this is not a conclusive argument against a wider readership. Given the contents and sophistication of the first book, with its frequent references to Terence and other classical authors, I suspect that Radbert intended this for the most accomplished of the monks of Corbie, many of whom he had taught himself; the second book, which largely lacks such learned citations, may well have been written for the great and the good who had been involved in the crisis of the 830s, and whose opinion was well worth swaying. As in Nithard's case, a scant manuscript tradition does not necessarily mean that the author himself was marginal. Whatever his own birth, Radbert had become attached by service to a great family, and wrote with the authority derived from his illustrious connections. Nobody should forget that Wala had been of royal blood, and that he had preferred Radbert as his almost constant companion.[238]

His *Epitaphium*, or funeral oration, for Wala was inspired by Ambrose's *De excessu fratris*, a two-part commemoration and consolation upon the death of Ambrose's brother Satyrus. In the second oration, Ambrose meditated on death as an end to earthly sorrows, and on the promise of resurrection.[239] Another important model, however, was the monastic dialogue, in which a younger monk interrogates an older and more knowledgeable one. This genre was at the heart of late antique and early medieval monastic literature.

---

[237] Ibid., II, p. 60, at the beginning of the second book.

[238] Ibid., I, c. 12, p. 41 (Severus): 'De his ergo nemo ambigit, quoniam ipsi, ut omnes fatentur, ex omni regali prosapie singulares erant in sanctitate et religione, atque in bonitate studiosissimi.'

[239] Ganz, 'Opposition', p. 543; Von Moos, *Consolatio*, I, pp. 140–2, and II, pp. 100–1. Ambrose, *De excessu fratris Satyri*, ed. O. Faller, CSEL 73 (Vienna, 1955), pp. 207–325.

John Cassian's *Collationes* is one well-known example, and the *Dialogues* of Gregory the Great is another.[240] The dialogue could be expanded to a group of interlocutors and thus become a monastic *confabulatio*, a pedagogical conversation within a restricted circle of learned and learning monks. In the *Epitaphium*, the monk Paschasius was the narrator. He represented Radbert himself, the well-informed teacher who sustains the narrative by responding to the sceptical interruptions of the outspoken Severus (his friend Odilman), or to the innocent questions of the young monk Adeodatus; then there was Chremes, a worldly-wise and much-travelled monk, who informed the interlocutors of Wala's exploits in the world outside the cloister,[241] particularly in Italy; and, finally, the illiterate and bald Allabigus.[242] Chremes was a name taken from Terence's *Eunuchus*, a comedy that Radbert knew and frequently cited.[243] Yet these are also familiar figures in monastic life and literature: the interrogating youngster, the patient and learned pedagogue, the cranky and outspoken old monk, not about to mince his words, or the much-travelled monk, regarded with awe and suspicion by those who rarely left the monastic precincts.[244] By the time Radbert wrote the second book, Severus had died and Chremes had left the cloister, so Radbert introduced a new, young and innocent monk, the beardless Theophrastes; by this time Adeodatus, who was also still a discussant, had grown older, and could do his share of remembering the past, together with Paschasius.[245] In the second book, therefore, Radbert makes it clear to his reader that much time had passed since Wala had died, an impression he reinforced by contrasting 'nowadays' (*hodie*) with the past events discussed by the monks.[246] I also suspect that some of these monastic 'types' may have been nicknames of individual monks, and could no longer be used once the actual protagonists had died.

The topic of their discussions was Wala, otherwise known as Arsenius.[247] The historical Arsenius (d. 450) had been a one-time counsellor to the

---

[240] Another possible influence is Sulpicius Severus' *Vita Martini*, with its *confabulatio* about St Martin's death, as David Ganz suggested to me. On the dialogue as a vehicle for biography, see Berschin, *Biographie und Epochenstil*, p. 325.

[241] Chremes figures in several of Terence's plays, in very different roles: *The Self-Tormentor*, *The Woman of Andros*, *Phormio* and *The Eunuch*.

[242] Allebigus makes only a brief appearance, and is characterised by Radbert, *EA*, I, p. 33, as 'glaber iste qui videbatur idiota'. But touched by Wala's spirit, this illiterate monk became a veritable 'philosopher of lamentation', who effortlessly cited Terence.

[243] E.g. Radbert, *EA*, I, cc. 8, 21, pp. 32, 50, 52.

[244] Similar figures can be found in Ekkehard's *Casus sancti Galli*; see De Jong, 'Internal cloisters'.

[245] Radbert, *EA*, II, p. 60.   [246] E.g. Ibid., II, cc. 4, 6, 10, pp. 65, 66, 74, 76–7.

[247] On Wala's biography, see Weinrich, *Wala*; see also Felten, *Äbte und Laienabte*, pp. 265–6; Krüger, 'Nachfolgereglung'; Kasten, *Adalhard von Corbie*, pp. 166–71; Depreux, *Prosopographie*, pp. 390–3.

Emperor Theodosius the Great and tutor of the latter's son Honorius. Arsenius eventually withdrew to the desert as a hermit, which made him a suitable alias for Wala, who had been Lothar's tutor and Louis's counsellor. In 830 Wala was exiled from Louis's court for a second time.[248] He resembled Arsenius in many ways, yet his other alias was equally important: that of the prophet Jeremiah, who had fruitlessly warned his people of the dire consequences of sin, before Israel was exiled to Babylon. Likewise, Wala had operated as a prophet of doom, warning Louis and his court of impending disaster. As Radbert expressed it, in the exegetical terms with which he was familiar, Wala had been the 'type' (*typus*) of Jeremiah.[249] Yet Wala's association with Arsenius and Jeremiah was not just a literary device introduced well after Wala died. Already in 830–3, in a letter to his friend, Corvey's abbot Warin, Radbert spoke of 'our Arsenius' who bore his exile 'like another Jeremiah'.[250]

One of the problems with using the *Epitaphium Arsenii* is that one may run the risk of projecting the concerns of the 850s (or 840s) on to an earlier period. When Radbert countered criticism of Wala for having aspired to worldly riches when he and Adalhard founded Corvey, was this a concern of the 850s, or of 822, when the two brothers created their New Jerusalem?[251] Was Radbert's account of the discussions of the winter assembly in Aachen in 828–9 influenced by the more intransigent views on lay abbots and church property that prevailed two decades later? These are pertinent questions, yet one should not exaggerate the dangers of anachronism. Although some of the key issues of the *Epitaphium* – lay abbots, abbots who did not live as monks proper, and the use of monastic lands for raising the troops of the king and the magnates – were on the agenda of West-Frankish reform synods of the 840s, they were debated equally fervently, if not more so, in the 820s.[252] As for Radbert's misgivings – to say the least – about Louis, these were already fully expressed in his *Life of Adalhard*, where he scathingly referred to

---

[248] Astronomer, c. 45, p. 462; Weinrich, *Wala*, pp. 75–6; *EA*, I, c. 8, p. 33.

[249] Radbert, *EA*, I, p. 19 (introduction of Wala as Jeremiah by Paschasius); p. 20 (Wala with the morals of Arsenius, the *persona* of Benedict and the *officium* of Jeremiah); c. 3, p. 23 (Wala as the *typus* of Jeremiah); p. 24 (as with Jeremiah, Wala's *invectio* stemmed from *amor*, not *odium*; as Jeremiah prayed for Jerusalem, Wala now prays for his brothers of Corbie); *EA*, II, c. 2, p. 62 (Wala is *acsi Hieremias alter*, someone who dares to speak up against rulers); c. 5, p. 66 (because of Wala's *caritas Christi, dilectio patriae et populi, amor ecclesia and fides imperatoris*, he could speak up constantly, like another Jeremiah); c. 8, p. 71 (like Jeremiah, Wala had to turn from *increpatio* to *lamenta*).

[250] Radbert, *De corpore*, prologue for Warin, p. 3: 'quod Arsenius noster quem nostra nunc saecula Hieremiam alterum tulerunt ab illo, in fidei te mihi commiserat ratione.' On Warin and Wala, see Krüger, 'Nachfolgeregelung'.

[251] Radbert, *EA*, I, c. 17, pp. 47–8.

[252] Boshof, *Agobard*, pp. 75–88; Felten, *Äbte und Laienäbte*, pp. 257–79.

Louis's penance in Attigny in 822, contrasting the moral lethargy of Louis and his entourage with the clarity of vision of Adalhard, the 'speaker of truth'.[253] This remarkable passage, written shortly after Adalhard's death in 826, is exceptional in that it is a contemporary comment on Louis, voiced well before the subsequent rebellions.

This critique is not surprising, for the family for which Radbert felt so much admiration and affection had suffered when Louis succeeded his father in 814. Radbert wrote as a monk, but also as an adoptive member of this extremely powerful family of royal blood. Precisely this nurturing adoption had been Theodrada's role at Soissons, which was subsequently complemented by Adalhard's and Wala's at Corbie.[254] Hence Radbert's tenacious loyalty, and his lasting animosity towards Louis. All the same, there was also a constant longing for the palace and a return to the emperor's favour, and the author's vicarious pride in Wala's great influence at Louis's court in the years before 831. Any visit to the court was duly recorded, including a joke which he, Radbert, made to some magnates, who were much amused; Wala, Radbert continued, was sure to have related this to the emperor himself![255] This fits a larger pattern of court-oriented gossip in the cloister, upon which Notker the Stammerer and monastic others drew for their portraits of rulers.[256]

One of the reasons to think of the two books of the *Epitaphium* as one work, rather than as two separate books awkwardly joined at the hip, is that the theme of *fides* is persistent throughout. The notions of faith and fidelity, separate in modern parlance, are treated as one: what one owed God and one's lord was a similar kind of loyalty. In other words, the lord and the Lord were distinguished, but not by what they demanded. Radbert defended his hero against a chorus of anonymous enemies – including, perhaps, the occasional voice of his own conscience – who had said that Wala had not shown due fidelity to Louis (*quasi augusto debitam non servaverit fidem*).[257] Radbert countered this with much reflection on what, to his mind, real *fides* amounted to. It was not just a matter of blindly following a terrestrial ruler, and thus opposing God's precepts. On the contrary, true fidelity should be cemented by love of God and charity (*caritas*) towards one's fellow-men. Without these crucial ingredients, being faithful was no more than adhering to a terrestrial, bestial oath,

---

[253] Radbert, *VA*, c. 51, cols. 1534D–1535A.
[254] De Jong, *In Samuel's Image*, pp. 126–7, 180.
[255] Radbert, *EA*, I, c. 11, p. 39. There are other passages showing Radbert as being closely connected with the court, such as his voyage to Cologne in 830, 'where I was sent on business by Augustus, as you know' (*EA*, I, c. I, c. 8, p. 33).
[256] Innes, 'Memory'; De Jong, 'Internal cloisters'.   [257] Radbert, *EA*, I, c. 3, p. 24.

and to a diabolical obligation.[258] Radbert argued that Wala had tried to be loyal to both his lords, heavenly and terrestrial. The only reason he had forsaken his loyalty to Louis was that he had accorded precedence to the *fides* owed to God. These issues became even more acute during the fraternal wars of 840–3, yet they were already hotly debated during the aftermath of the rebellion of 830. As Radbert claimed in his letter to Warin, Wala 'suffers exile because of *fides*, in the manner of that writer of comedy, because he was full of leaks (*plenus rimarum*), and knowing the truth he did not want to remain silent'. The writer of comedy was Terence, from whose *Eunuchus* Radbert took the expression *plenus rimarum*. Terence's slave says that he leaks like a cracked pot and will be silent only about true secrets.[259] This is exactly the opposite of what Radbert stated about Wala (and, implicitly, himself): knowing the truth, he could not be silent. In other words, Wala's 'leaks' were those of a compulsive truth-teller on a divine mission.

The second book has attracted most interest, first of all as a source on the rebellions against Louis, and secondly, because of its sensational cast of political actors, barely disguised by aliases, drawn from a rather eclectic world of Ambrose. While Wala himself figures as Arsenius or Benedict (of Nursia) and increasingly as Jeremiah, his two arch-enemies, Judith and Bernard, were Justina, wife to the Emperor Valentinian I and relentless enemy of Ambrose, and Naso – presumably Ovid, exiled by Augustus because of his affair with a woman from the imperial house.[260] Louis himself was Justinian, and quite possibly the second emperor of this name, whose reign (681–711) was interrupted by mutilation, deposition and exile, ending miserably with his execution – a truly vicious but suitably ambiguous alias, for it left open the association of Louis with Justinian I, the lawgiver. Lothar featured as Honorius, son of Theodosius I and pupil of Arsenius, a far more honourable alias, and the same held true for his brother Gratian / Louis the German. Why Pippin was called Melanius has remained an enigma. Rather than thinking of St. Melanius, the sixth-century bishop of Rennes, Radbert may have thought of the king who involved Hercules in a contest of archery with his daughter as a prize. This would suit the image of Pippin of Aquitaine, a southern and quite foreign kingdom, with a ruler given to sabre-rattling and strange customs. For the other unsolved alias, Phassur, I suggest Ebo of Rheims. Given that Phassur was the man who incarcerated the prophet

---

[258] Ibid., p. 25 ('terrena obiuratio animalis et diabolica devinctio').
[259] Radbert, *De corpore*, pp. 3–4. The comic is Terence, whose *Eunuchus* (1, 2, 25) is cited.
[260] On Ermold and Ovid's exile, see Depreux, 'La *pietas*', p. 202. See also Smolak, 'Bescheidene Panegyrik', on Walahfrid's references to Ovid.

Jeremiah (Ier. 20.2), and Ebo was instrumental in Wala's banishment from the court in 830, under orders finally to live as a monk should, this seems a likely identification.[261]

Judith died in 843, Bernard in 844: was this the reason Radbert only then finished his second book, when all his main culprits had died? Possibly, but the aliases he used were not intended to disguise the identity of the protagonists. If we can figure them out, so could a contemporary audience that was supposed to see the point of Radbert's judicious and witty choices. Rather than guaranteeing any secrecy, the aliases proclaimed the moral status of those who were typified in this way. By using these 'types' Radbert made clear, from the outset, how he viewed his actors' roles in the drama he described. If Judith was Justina, the reader would know what could be expected of her, and this would then be fulfilled in the course of the text. The *Epitaphium* in fact has multiple layers of role-playing: first, there are the monks who discuss, under Paschasius' guidance, the vicissitudes of Wala's life, and then there is the interaction between this ninth-century cast and those inhabiting the Christian past, such as Justinian and Justina, who were all the more easily recognisable because of their aliases. Radbert's interest in Terence also played a major part here, but so did his vast expertise as a biblical commentator. Typology was what he was best at.

Most modern historians have approached the *Epitaphium Arsenii* as straightforward political polemics, mining the text for salient information on the opposition to Louis the Pious. This is an understandable temptation, but it should be resisted. Infused with the Christian values of its intended audience and the biblical exegesis of which its author was a master, this work laments the loss of a man who transcended the divide between the court and the monastery throughout his life, and the failure of an imperial ideal that was also a religious one.[262] There is a deep concern about the possibility that Wala's alleged crimes might reflect adversely on Jerusalem, that is, the monastic community of Corbie and Corvey. In his first book the shadow of the court is there, but here Radbert concentrated on arguing that Wala was indeed a good monk. In the second book, these concerns have not vanished, yet now the potentially conflicting loyalties to one's earthly and one's heavenly lord move to centre stage, as does the defence of the choices made by Wala.

---

[261] *EA*, II, c. 16, p. 84; Phassur is described as one of Judith's supporters, which strengthens the case for his identification as Ebo.

[262] Ganz, '*Epitaphium Arsenii*', pp. 542 and 548; Ganz, *Corbie*, pp. 119–20; De Jong, 'Becoming Jeremiah'. The latter article is part of my new project on Radbert's biographical work, in the context of his biblical commentary.

Above all, Radbert commemorated his two illustrious patrons 'in whose fellowship I, although unworthy, was the third'. He recalled the brothers vividly as they went about their business, with himself in attendance as an always admiring third party.[263] He grieved for Adalhard and Wala, but also modelled himself, as an author, on these two great men who had refused to be silent, fearlessly speaking up against the mighty of the earth. From the beginning, Radbert positioned himself within his own text as a man who dealt in truth, however unpalatable, not fables. Severus reminded Paschasius – and his audience – of the aim of the operation: to paint an image of morals and character, and to compose history as it had been accomplished. Why did he now tell stories (*fabulae*) instead? The young monk Adeodatus protested: 'Paschasius provided history (*historia*) which you read in your conscience (*conscientia*), which is why you are told not a story, but the truth.'[264] This discussion between two monks is about who can speak up and when, and about the specific claims to veracity made by those who do so with moral authority. To this topic I shall now turn.

---

[263] Radbert, *EA*, I, c.15, p. 43: 'quorum in consortio, etsi indignus, tertius eram'.
[264] Ibid., p. 21: 'Historiam autem huius tua in conscientia legis, unde non fabula tua, sed veritas declaratur.'

Criticising rulers

Radbert's verbal onslaught on Louis the Pious raises some pertinent questions. What was the status of 'criticism of the ruler' at Louis's court? Who could deliver it, and under which circumstances? Was there such a thing as an acceptable mode of expressing criticism to a ruler's face, be it in person or in writing? What were the limits of such opprobrium? When did acceptable criticism turn into a downright offence to the ruler? With regard to Louis the Pious, the implicit assumption has been that this ruler was so weak and indecisive that anyone could tell him off with impunity, particularly reform-minded clerics belonging to the 'party for the unity of the empire' (*Reichseinheitspartei*).[1] The general consensus is that Charlemagne's son was constantly and destructively criticised by his contemporaries; this in turn furnished criteria for dating the key historical narratives produced during his reign. Einhard's *Vita Karoli*, for example, has been understood as an implicit critique of Louis, who, presumably, would instantly recognize his own unworthiness when confronted with Einhard's lucid prose on his father's greatness. This assumption, then, has supported the dating of the *Vita Karoli* to the year 828, on the grounds that this was the time when criticism of the emperor began in earnest.[2] For similar reasons, Ermold's *Carmen* has been dated to 828, rather than to 826; what looks like praise of Louis was in fact an expression of nostalgic longing for the bygone days of Charlemagne's brilliant court.[3] Because of his *De imagine Tetrici*, Walahfrid Strabo has also been perceived as either a prophet of doom who was well aware that Louis had too many sons,[4] or as an outright critic whose depiction of Louis as a New Moses in fact showed him

---

[1] Tischler, *Einharts 'Vita Karoli'*, p. 197; for a critical assessment of the German historiography on *Reichseinheit*, see Patzold, 'Eine "loyale Palastrebellion"'.

[2] Tischler, *Einharts 'Vita Karoli'*, esp. pp. 163–5.

[3] Godman, 'Louis "the Pious"', pp. 256–7, and *Poets and Emperors*, p. 111.

[4] Godman, 'Louis "the Pious"', p. 284.

to be a False Moses.[5] Others have argued that Louis brought criticism upon himself by allowing, or even stimulating, critical writing on Charlemagne.

First he [Louis] had promoted criticism of his father, then he had not only allowed criticism of himself but had publicly confessed his sins, not just once, but twice. He sincerely wanted to do what was right, but he could not discover what it was. And so he opened the door to advice, and reforming, literate, and collectively righteous churchmen – monks and bishops all – were only too happy to step inside.[6]

The criticism of Charlemagne in question is such visionary literature of the 820s as Heito's *Visio Wettini* (824) and Walahfrid's metric version of this text (827), which contain references to Charlemagne being punished in the hereafter for his sexual misconduct. Did Louis indeed 'promote' such texts? A copy of Walahfrid's *Visio* was sent to the palace, and presumably was well received, for the young monk joined Louis's court in 829, only two years later; yet this is not the same thing as actively stimulating a damning critique of Charlemagne. Furthermore, there are two other problematic assumptions: first, that a ruler who is open to (self-) critique orchestrates his own downfall, and secondly, that the criticism offered came exclusively from 'collectively righteous churchmen'.

Louis indeed had vociferous and opinionated clerics as critics, yet these authors operated within a normative frame of reference that overlapped at least in part with the views of lay magnates and, last but not least, with the vision of the ruler himself. This frame of reference was characterised by a sense of responsibility for the common good, and the knowledge that one would be held accountable by God for the way in which one had carried out one's 'ministry'. *Negligentia*, that is, neglecting one's divinely bestowed office (*ministerium*) meant committing a sin; warning others of sinfulness, recalling them to the right path, was the duty of the leadership – first of all of the bishops, but also of others with a 'ministry'. From Charlemagne's reign onwards, such moral warning, or *admonitio*, as it was usually called, pervaded public discourse. 'We admonish you now to re-read your capitularies, to recall the duties with which you have been charged orally and to strive to be so zealous with regard to these that you may receive both reward from God and fitting recompense from that great lord of ours.'[7] Thus wrote a commission of four of Charlemagne's *missi*, clerics and laymen, to the counts within their jurisdiction. In a similar vein, the issues in the political dissension of the late 820s and early 830s were phrased in terms of sin; the most hotly debated questions revolved

---

[5] Ibid.; Herren, 'Walahfrid Strabo's *De imagine Tetrici*', pp. 37–9.
[6] Dutton, *Politics of Dreaming*, p. 111; in a similar vein, Collins, 'Charlemagne and his critics'.
[7] *Capitula a missis dominicis ad comites directa* (a. 806?), MGH *Capit.* I, no. 85, pp. 183–4.

around the question of who had sinned and why, and how the offended deity could be placated.

To approach this world full of fear of God's wrath with modern concepts such as 'reform party' or 'political criticism' is missing the point. As Janet Nelson noted with regard to Charles the Bald, this king tended to accept such critique and use it constructively, in order to learn from his mistakes. Charles 'was clearly willing to tolerate a plurality of views, and the circulation at court of outright criticism of his own politics. He kept his head in the face of criticism, which is why no critic ever lost his.'[8] The same could be said of Louis the Pious. As long as the critical message was voiced as a constructive *admonitio*, based on a duty-bound concern for the ruler's salvation, a lot could be said and accepted. Within this shared discourse, both lofty admonition and self-incrimination defined the moral high ground, as well as the membership of the inner circle of Louis's court. There came a point, however, when positive *admonitio* moved into another register: negative rebuke (*increpatio*). Some of the implications of this particular discourse will be explored in this chapter.

The watchman for the house of Israel

When the rebellious bishops who sided with Lothar imposed a public penance on Louis the Pious in 833, the key biblical text in their formal record of the event was from the prophet Ezekiel:

If, when I say to the wicked, Thou shalt surely die: thou declare it not to him, nor speak to him, that he may be converted from his wicked way, and live: the same wicked man shall die in his iniquity, but I will require his blood at thy hand. But if thou give warning to the wicked, and he be not converted from his wickedness, and from his evil way: he indeed shall die in his iniquity, but thou hast delivered thy soul. (Ez 3.18–19)[9]

The crux of this text is that whoever does not speak up against a sinful fellow-human will be accountable for his sins. The iniquity committed is a sin of omission: not raising your voice while you should have done so. It is clear why the bishops in 833 chose this text to explain their unprecedented action. They collectively assumed the role of Ezekiel's 'watchman for the house of Israel' (Ez. 3.17), and could not but speak out against Louis's

---

[8] Nelson, 'History-writing', pp. 441–2.

[9] 'Si dicente me ad impium morte morieris non adnuntiaveris ei neque locutus fueris ut avertatur a via sua impia et vivat ipse impius in iniquitate sua morietur sanguinem autem eius de manu tua requiram' (Ez. 3.18); *Relatio* (833), MGH Cap. II, no. 197, p. 52: '"Si non annuntiaveris", inquit, "iniquo iniquitatem suam et ipse in impietate sua mortuus fuerit, sanguinem eius de manu tua requiram", et multa his similia ad magisterium pastorale pertinentia, quae in divinis sparsim continentur.'

iniquity, lest God's wrath fall upon the Christian people especially and its bishops in particular. The bishops present during 'Soissons 833' do not enjoy a particularly good reputation. Archbishops Ebo of Rheims and Agobard of Lyons are the only ones we know by name, yet as Thegan feared, the imperial penance reflected badly on the bishops collectively. There is no reason to accuse those involved in Louis's public penance of insincerity, or of covering up 'political reality' when they cited Ezekiel on their obligation to speak out against their ruler's iniquity. By virtue of their episcopal ministry, they were duty bound to do so, and one may assume that it was this particular argument, among others, which swayed those bishops present who did not agree, but tacitly went along with the general decision.[10] The passage from Ezekiel hit at the core of the bishops' pastoral identity: it was their duty to speak up against *iniquitas* and to combat it, lest they incur God's wrath. Their role models were not only the apostles, whose successors they felt themselves to be, but also the prophets who had called Israel's rulers to order. The task of the prophet was to see moral danger and warn the ruler well in time, regardless of whether this truth was agreeable. Nonetheless, steering the people towards salvation was the joint duty – or *ministerium*, in Carolingian terms – of king and prophet.[11]

This sense of joint accountability to God informed much of the so-called criticism of Louis the Pious in the 820s. Such admonition was not uttered haphazardly. It had its own accepted modes of delivery, with an idiom and style derived from Scripture and patristic writing as well as from an early medieval tradition of admonition of kings by bishops and holy men. Bishops who told kings in no uncertain terms what was expected of them as Christian leaders abound in the work of Gregory of Tours and his contemporaries.[12] Monastic texts especially yield a rich harvest of ascetics who combined a close association with the court with regular and fierce admonition of the ruler. The Irishman Columbanus, as portrayed by his hagiographer, Jonas of Bobbio, is one well-known example of an ascetic who stood no nonsense from any powerful ruler, not even from Queen Brunhild.[13] Another foreigner, the West Saxon Boniface, is also worth mentioning in this context, because of his fierce letter of admonition sent in 745–7 to King Aehtelbald of Mercia, denouncing the king's moral shortcomings: he was a fornicator who had never taken

---

[10] Astronomer, c. 49, p. 482.
[11] Apostles: Council of Paris, I, c. 4, MGH *Conc.* II/2, pp. 611–12; prophets: Agobard, *Liber apologeticus*, II.
[12] See above, chapter 2, pp. 83–4.
[13] Jonas, *Vita Columbani*, I, c. 19, pp. 187–93. Diem, 'Monks, kings'; Nelson, 'Queens as Jezebels'.

a legal wife, and was reputed to be committing adultery with nuns and other virgins consecrated to God.[14] This was the letter of a man who adopted the role of the moral watchman, who could therefore speak freely. He was also a monk, whose strict asceticism made him a valued mediator between God and mankind, and a source of sanctity who might empower a ruler. In this context of frank speech on the part of ascetics closely linked to the royal court, one should also situate the visionary literature in which Charlemagne was portrayed as being punished in the hereafter for his sexual sins. Neither Heito nor Walahfrid was engaged in political polemics, and if this was criticism, it was of the mildest kind. These were monks of St-Gall, whose business it was to worry about the souls of rulers. After his penance in the hereafter, Charlemagne would be among the elect who were destined for eternal life, as Heito expressed it, or, in Walahfrid's more courtly terms, 'he will yet attain the *honor* that God has set aside for him'.[15]

Clerics who wished to admonish Louis the Pious had a wealth of literary models to choose from. All the same, there were important differences between their position and that of a Gregory, Columbanus or Boniface. The latter two men had been attractive mediators because they were charismatic outsiders. Gregory of Tours envisaged a total penetration of the *ecclesia* in all domains of secular politics, and a king such as Guntram, who co-operated, was therefore qualified as a 'good bishop'.[16] During the reform synods of the 740s, however, legitimate secular leadership was defined as religious leadership: Pippin could not have become king without assuming the responsibility for the cult of God.[17] With Pippin and Charlemagne, however, the notion of the ruler as the main guardian of the *cultus divinus,* and as the initiator of its 'correction and emendation', became more elaborate and articulate.[18] Old Testament models contributed to this view of kingship, but also, increasingly, to the memory of the Christian emperors.[19] But since the days of Constantine and Theodosius, the position of the emperor had changed. Whereas they had been the protectors of a distinct ecclesiastical domain, Louis's bishops saw their emperor as functioning *within* the church. In the broad sense of the word – as opposed to the restricted meaning of the clergy – this church encompassed the entire polity. Together with the bishops, the ruler constituted the leadership of the *ecclesia.* This in turn meant that *admonitio* was no

[14] Boniface, *Epistolae*, no. 73, ed. Tangl, pp. 146–55.
[15] Heito, *Visio Wettini*, c. 11, p. 271; Walahfrid, *Visio Wettini*, lines 445–74, pp. 318–19.
[16] Gregory of Tours, *Historiae*, IX, c. 21, p. 441.   [17] De Jong, '*Ecclesia*', pp. 126–9.
[18] Ewig, 'Zum christlichen Königsgedanken'; Anton, *Fürstenspiegel*; Staubach, *Rex christianus*; Hen, 'Christianisation'.
[19] Anton, *Fürstenspiegel*, pp. 419–46.

longer a one-way street. The royal responsibility for the salvation of the *populus christianus*, clearly formulated in Charlemagne's *Admonitio generalis*, implied that correcting and admonishing the people were also the business of kings. They also had the duty to 'speak to the wicked', as Ezekiel expressed it, and so did lay magnates such as the *missi* mentioned above, charged by Charlemagne with admonishing the counts to make sure they understood his commands, 'both as regards God and as regards secular matters'.[20]

Admonitio was a key notion in a wide variety of genres, ranging from letters and hagiography to the so-called 'Mirrors of princes'.[21] The authors in question, most often bishops, were at pains to ascertain that their royal recipient would not mistake proper admonition, motivated by pastoral concern, for brazen presumption. As Jonas of Orléans expressed it in his preface to *De institutione regia*, addressed to King Pippin I of Aquitaine: 'I would not dare to write anything for Your Highness with the aim of admonition, were I not buoyed up by your condescending sublimity, and had I not learned from experience that you fervently wish to learn and amply want to hear of all that pertains to the love and fear of God and to the salvation of souls.'[22] This is formal prose, yet Jonas clearly walked something of a tightrope, trying to ensure that his 'tiny gift of admonition' would not offend the mighty Pippin.[23] If the author spoke in his own voice, admonition needed to be embedded in profuse protestations of humility. Meanwhile, biblical texts served as vehicles for potentially less palatable truths. In his preface, Jonas created his own collage of biblical texts to get across what he could not say otherwise: whoever hardens his heart and does not listen to Scripture will fail utterly in his prayer and therefore, by implication, fail as a ruler (*qui obdurat aurem sua, ne audiat lege, oratio eius execrabilis erit*; Prov. 28.9; Deut. 15.7).

This particular use of biblical texts is so familiar that it is easily overlooked: through the authority of Scripture, assuming a biblical voice, those who admonished could speak more freely to their monarch. Old Testament prophets and their fearless dealings with kings provided most of the relevant models for ninth-century authors, yet within this biblically oriented discourse there was also a strand derived from classical rhetoric. When Radbert called Adalhard a 'speaker out of truth' (*assertor veritatis*), this was inspired not just by the image of prophets warning their rulers, but also by the rhetorical tradition of frank speech. For bishops, this was not just a right, but also a duty. Ambrose's confrontation with

---

[20] MGH *Capit.* I, no. 85, c. 4, p. 184: 'sive secundum Deum seu secundum saeculum'.
[21] Anton, *Fürstenspiegel*.   [22] Jonas, *De institutione regia*, p. 150.
[23] Ibid., p. 152, lines 49–50: 'exiguum admonitionis minusculum'.

Theodosius became the most important model for what would become known as the *libertas episcopalis/sacerdotalis*.[24] This principle, debated during councils from 829 onwards, not only referred to the freedom to exercise one's office, but also to the right to address the ruler frankly in everything relating to God's commandments. The ninth-century fusion of prophetical *admonitio* and late antique ideals of *parrhesia* produced a powerful new model for authoritative speech in the presence of the ruler, and for claiming the high moral ground in the presence of kings who were used to doing so themselves as well.

The vocabulary of admonition and sin

With this in mind, the Latin vocabulary of admonition deserves some closer scrutiny. I shall not provide this exhaustively, but merely indicate the biblical context of crucial words such as *admonitio*, *correptio*, *increpatio* and *exhortatio*. No doubt the Carolingian use of such expressions was different from the biblical usage, but it is equally clear that the Latin biblical vocabulary informed all ninth-century notions of what constituted a firm moral warning, be it delivered in writing or in person.

From an initial exploration it becomes clear that the noun *admonitio* figures only once, and then only in an apocryphal book.[25] The verb *admonere* does occur, but not frequently, and mostly in Old Testament books that circulated in the *Vetus Latina* version, translated from the Greek rather than the Hebrew, such as Wisdom or II Maccabees – for the rest, there is one occurrence in Matthew, and the rest are in the Epistles of St Paul.[26] The prominence of *admonitio* within Carolingian religious discourse, in the sense of preaching or admonition, stems less from biblical usage than from a patristic tradition, disseminated in particular by Gregory the Great and his *Regula pastoralis*. With *correptio*, which can also mean admonition, but with more punitive connotations, as in reproach or blame, the situation is different. This is a frequent biblical expression, particularly in the Old Testament, with a marked preference for this noun in *Vetus Latina* translations, especially from Wisdom and

---

[24] See Hürten, "'Libertas'". Usually the ninth-century *libertas episcopalis* referred to the freedom from burdens on one's time and material resources imposed by royal service. See also Garrison, "Les correspondants d'Alcuin', pp. 238–9. Irene van Renswoude's forthcoming Utrecht dissertation 'Licence to Speak: The Rhetoric of Free Speech from Ambrose to Rather' will provide an in-depth analysis of the notion of *parrhesia*, both in Rather's work and also in the writings of earlier authors upon whom he relied, especially Radbert.

[25] III Esdr. 2.22: 'et invenies in admonitionibus scripta de his et scies quoniam civitas ista fuit refuga et reges et civitates concutiens'.

[26] Eccle. 7.3; Matth. 22.2; II Tim. 1.6; Sap. 12.2; II Mach. 8.19; 15.9.

Ecclesiastes.[27] If one adds to this no fewer than forty-eight instances of the verb *corripere*, all in the Old Testament, it is clear that the notion of *correptio* is a prominent one. It is particularly prevalent in the context of the prophets, who warned Israel of its impending doom because of sin and called upon the chosen people to return to their alliance with God,[28] and also in the Psalms, especially the penitential ones that beseech an offended Lord for mercy: 'Thou hast corrected man for iniquity. And thou hast made his soul to waste away like a spider: surely in vain is any man disquieted' (Ps. 38.12).[29] In the Latin Old Testament the verb *corripere* is combined with its synonym *increpatio/increpare*, which is the second most common biblical expression for morally charged rebukes or wrath by those in religious authority. 'For behold the Lord will come with fire, and his chariots are like a whirlwind, to render his wrath in indignation, and his rebuke (*increpatio*) with flames of fire' (Is. 66.15).[30] This is representative of the prophetic use of this word, but as a verb it also occurs in the New Testament, when Jesus drove out a demon: 'And Jesus rebuked (*increpavit*) him, and the devil went out of him, and the child was cured from that hour' (Matth. 17.17). So peoples and demons could be corrected, but so could kings: in his song of thanksgiving David commemorated God's might and the overpowering force of his salvation: 'And the overflowings of the sea appeared, and the foundations of the world were laid open at the rebuke of the Lord, at the blast of the spirit of his wrath' (II Reg. 22.16). When David made sure that Bathsebee's husband Uriah would be killed by ordering him to be placed in the front of the battle against the Ammonites, the prophet Nathan descended upon him, proclaiming 'Thus says the Lord, "Behold, I will raise up evil against you out of your own house; and I will take your wives before your eyes, and give them to your neighbour, and he shall lie with your wives in the sight of this sun. For you did it secretly; but I will do this thing before all Israel, and before the sun"' (II Reg. 12.11–12). Because of David's readiness to repent, God spared his life, but he was to pay for having scorned the Lord by losing the child born from his illicit union with Bathsebee (II Reg. 12.13). The king then tried to move God to mercy by prayer and fasting, but the child died. Because of the king's atonement, David and Bathsebee were granted another son, however: this was Solomon (II Reg. 12.24).

---

[27] Of the thirty-two instances of this noun, twenty-eight occur in the Old Testament.

[28] Os. 10.10: 'iuxta desiderium meum corripiam eos congregabuntur super eos populi cum corripientur propter duas iniquitates suas'.

[29] 'Propter iniquitatem corripuisti hominem et tabescere fecisti sicut araneam animam eius verumtamen vane conturbatur.'

[30] 'Quia ecce Dominus in igne veniet et quasi turbo quadrigae eius reddere in indignatione furorem suum et increpationem suam in flamma ignis.'

This vocabulary of reproach, admonition and correction is part of the Latin biblical idiom, especially in those Old Testament books that deal with God's covenant with Israel, and with Israel's leadership, be they kings, judges or prophets. There is a constant tension between obedience and reward on the one hand, and divine wrath following infidelity on the other. Israel strays, sins and is punished, but if it is penitent, like David, it will live. This social hierarchy dominated by an easily offended deity resembled and reinforced the kind of patrimonial authority exercised by Carolingian kingship and lordship. The Old Testament was particularly peopled with figures who could function as models and 'types' for those exercising legitimate power in Carolingian society: the Old Testament kings for kings and emperors, the prophet for the clerical magnates, and the warrior elite of Israel, as well as judges and patriarchs, for the lay magnates and *fideles*.[31] But there were other correlations as well, such as the close association between the ruler and Christ, with emphasis on their respective roles as king and judge. Such comparisons were not merely in the eye of the clerical beholder. When the Emperor Lothar thanked Hraban Maur for his commentary on the biblical book of 'the most noble *dux* Joshua' who was also the *typus* of Christ, the emperor remarked that, like Joshua, he was a military man, who would merit victory only because of God.[32] Although such explicit identification with a biblical figure on the part of a Carolingian monarch is rare, it cannot have been all that exceptional; after all, Charlemagne's byname was David.[33] From Charlemagne onwards, there was a vested royal interest in biblical commentary, with kings and queens commissioning and receiving exegetical treatises. Some royal recipients expressed a marked preference for particular biblical books, so elective affinities such as Lothar's for Joshua cannot have been all that exceptional.[34]

This is just a brief reminder of the importance of biblical thought and typology for Carolingian court circles. The world of Scripture was an 'imagined community' that was always at the back of the minds of the authors who produced the sources on which we now base our so-called political history. For this very reason, the vocabulary of sin, the object of

[31] Nelson, 'The Lord's anointed', pp. 115–18, on biblical images of authority and their potential use by lay magnates.
[32] Hraban, *Epistolae*, no. 38 (c. 842–6), ed. Dümmler, p. 475; De Jong, 'Old law', p. 166.
[33] Garrison, 'Social world of Alcuin'.
[34] On Hraban Maur's exegesis for kings and queens, and instances of royal preference for specific books, see De Jong, 'Empire as *ecclesia*' and 'Exegesis for an empress'; Gorman, 'Wigbod and biblical studies' and 'Commentary on Genesis'. On Charles the Bald and biblical commentary, see Staubach, *Rex christianus*, pp. 21–104 (and p. 12, n. 45, about biblical commentary for rulers and royal preference for allegory).

all this rebuke, also merits some comment. Apart from the ubiquitous *peccatum*, the preferred expression for sin in Latin Scripture, particularly in the Old Testament, is *iniquitas*. When the collective sins of Israel are at stake, these are denoted as *iniquitas* or its plural, *iniquitates*. In Ezekiel, for example, this iniquity of Israel is combined with 'scandal' into *scandalum iniquitatis*. This concept, derived from the Greek *skandalon* (stumbling block), denoted public sin that was offensive to both God and the people.[35] One of the main goals of *correctio* was the eradication of the kind of 'iniquity' that might cause offence to God and the community. In this sense *iniquitas* often figures in ninth-century texts, but there is another key word that also makes a frequent appearance in the Carolingian discourse on sin: *negligentia*. Like *admonitio*, this was not an expression derived from Latin Scripture. In patristic discourse, *negligentia* had the connotation of 'sin of omission', yet there was nothing venial about it. From around 800 onwards 'negligence' emerged in Charlemagne's capitularies, with regard to dereliction of duty by counts, *missi* and *iudices*.[36] In Carolingian capitularies and conciliar texts *negligentia* could be the equivalent of *iniquitas*, however, or even its cause. As Ezekiel warned, those who do not correct sinners will be guilty themselves (Ez. 3.18). Since *negligentia* was closely associated with the concept of 'ministry' (*ministerium*), the intensity of the sin committed by negligence increased with the importance and impact of the office concerned. Merovingian conciliar records mention this connection only occasionally, with regard to clerical office; by contrast, the acts of the five councils convened by Charlemagne in 813, as part of a massive attempt at empire-wide reform, show a marked increase in the use of *negligentia*. During these gatherings of 813 the negligence of priests, monks and nuns was singled out for correction.[37] As Carolingian reform took shape in the last decades of the eighth century, those who mediated between God and mankind received most attention, for their negligence would undermine the correct worship of God.

The extended application of the notion of ministry progressed during the reign of Louis the Pious, culminating in the conviction that kingship itself was a divinely bestowed *ministerium*, from which all other 'ministries'

---

[35] Ezek. 7.19; 14.3–4; 14.7.

[36] For example: *Capitulare de villis* (800 or before?), cc. 16, 29, MGH *Capit.* I, no. 32, pp. 84–5; *Capitula a missis dominicis ad comites directa* (801–13), c. 4, ibid., no. 85, p. 184; *Capitulare missorum* (802–13), c. 4, ibid., no. 60, p. 147; *Capitulare de latronibus* (804–13), c. 7, ibid., no. 82, p. 181.

[37] Council of Chalon, c. 18, MGH *Conc.* II/1, p. 277 (priests give bribes to bishops and counts *pro quibusdam negligentiis*); c. 40, ibid., p. 281; c. 45, ibid., p. 281; c. 47, ibid., p. 283. Council of Tours, 813, c. 25, ibid., p. 290; c. 26, ibid., p. 290; Council of Mainz, c. 38, ibid., p. 270. Council of Arles, c. 11, ibid., p. 251.

ultimately derived. Accordingly, *negligentia* became a sin of which anyone with an office could be found guilty, above all the ruler himself and his bishops, who bore joint responsibility for the salvation of the *populus christianus*.

Exaltation by admonition: Attigny, 822

In the aftermath of the massacre in Thessaloniki, which occurred in the summer of 390, Bishop Ambrose of Milan urged the Emperor Theodosius to follow the example of an illustrious biblical king:

> David sinned, as kings are wont to, but he did penance, wept and sighed, which kings do not usually do; he confessed his sin, he begged for forgiveness; prostrated, he bewailed his ministry; he fasted, prayed, and transmitted the testimony of his confession to all future generations by making his grief public. What private men blushed to [confess], this king was not ashamed to confess [publicly].[38]

Whether Louis had David in mind when he publicly confessed his sins in 822 is unknown, nor do we know whether he thought of Theodosius, his predecessor who heeded Ambrose's urgent admoniton and came to the basilica of Milan as a penitent, bewailing his sins and asking for the prayers of the faithful.[39] Two decades later, the Astronomer wrote that in Attigny, Louis had 'imitated the example of the Emperor Theodosius and undertook a voluntary penance'.[40] The key words here were *spontanea penitentia*, as opposed to the penance of 833, which had been imposed on the emperor by force. As in the case of Theodosius, humiliation resulted in exaltation, provided the emperor acted of his own volition, for this made his confession a truly imperial gesture of atonement.[41]

All this was added by the Astronomer at a later stage. The basis of his narrative, the *Royal Frankish Annals*, summarised the entire event in a few sentences, with heavy emphasis on Louis's reconciliation with various members of his family:

> After deliberation with his bishops and magnates, the lord emperor reconciled himself with his brothers, whom he had ordered to be tonsured against their will, and he made a public confession and did penance for what he had done to them, as well as for what had been done to Bernhard the son of his brother Pippin, and to Abbot Adalhard and his brother Wala. This he did in the assembly that he held that

---

[38] Ambrose, *Apologia David*, IV, 15, p. 92.
[39] On Theodosius' penance and its political context, see McLynn, *Ambrose of Milan*, pp. 291–8, 315–30; cf. R. Schieffer, 'Von Mailand nach Canossa'.
[40] Astronomer, c. 35, p. 406: 'imitatus Theodosii exemplum, penitentiam spontaneam suscepit'. See Siemes, *Beiträge*, pp. 47–52; Anton, *Fürstenspiegel*, pp. 44–6.
[41] Deschman, 'Exalted servant'.

year in Attigny, in the presence of his entire following; here, with the utmost devotion, he endeavoured to make amends for whatever similar deeds committed by either his father or himself he could find.[42]

The aim of the imperial penance of 822 was publicly to reaffirm Louis's reconciliation with the family members he had removed from the political scene: his half-brothers Drogo, Hugh and Theoderic, who had been involuntarily tonsured in 818, his nephew Bernhard, whose blinding had caused his death in that same year, and his more distant kinsmen Adalhard and Wala, who had been exiled in 814. The preparations for this public manifestation of atonement and reconciliation had already started in October 821, when, during the assembly of Thionville, Louis granted an amnesty to all Bernhard's followers and even restored their property with *magna liberalitas*, as the court annalist expressed it.[43] By the time the assembly of Attigny met in the summer of 822, Adalhard and Wala were back in favour once more. It has been assumed that they were instrumental in Louis's decision to wipe the slate clean by a public confession of guilt, but Radbert's sharp critique of this imperial penance suggests a different scenario: it may well have been Louis himself who took the initiative, and was criticised for it.[44] There was nothing spontaneous about an imperial penance: it took deliberation and planning. In 391, Ambrose's challenge offered the possibility of restoring Theodosius' damaged reputation by transforming a nasty scandal into redeemable sin, but how would his Christian subjects react to the sight of their emperor in the ranks of the professed sinners of the capital?[45] Similar questions must have vexed Louis the Pious and his advisers in 821–2, when the possibility of his 'spontaneous confession' in Attigny was being contemplated. An important difference between Theodosius and Louis, however, was that whereas the former assumed responsibility for his troops having gone on the rampage, the latter's guilt concerned the harm he had done to the members of his family. The endeavour to make amends for 'whatever similar deeds committed by either his father or himself he could find' referred to the sin of harming one's kinsmen. Charlemagne had outlined the dismal possibilities in his *Divisio regnorum* of 806, with the aim of preventing a repetition in the future. His grandsons, born or yet to be born, were not to be put to death, mutilated, blinded, or tonsured against their will without a lawful trial. 'Rather, it is our will that they be honoured

---

[42] *ARF*, s.a. 822, p. 158.   [43] *ARF*, s.a. 821, p. 156.
[44] That Adalhard was behind Louis's penance is assumed by Hartmann, *Konziliengeschichte*, p. 166, citing Kasten, *Adalhard von Corbie*, pp. 142–4.
[45] McLynn, *Ambrose*, p. 327.

by their fathers and uncles and be obedient towards these with all the deference that is fitting for a blood-relationship.'[46]

To treat his younger kinsmen well was what Louis had promised his father on the occasion of his imperial coronation in 813, according to Thegan, but precisely this solemn promise he had undoubtedly broken time and again.[47] A magnificent gesture was indeed called for, a public reconciliation that would enable a new and confident start and silence any criticism of Louis's heavy-handed treatment of his kinsmen, in the presence of the maligned parties themselves and the royal *fideles* present at a well-attended summer assembly. Yet there was more at stake than a public statement that the ruling family was once more reunited. Behind Louis's penance was the conviction that harming one's kinsmen was a grievous sin. The blinding, killing, exile and forced tonsure that had occurred within the ruling family constituted, moreover, the kind of public sin that angered God and might have dire consequences for the people led to salvation by the guilty ruler in question. Public atonement was therefore not just a strategy for reconciliation with Louis's powerful kinsmen. There was also the compelling need to give due satisfaction to the offended deity, whose blessing and approval had been implored by prayer and fasting when, in 817, Louis made solemn arrangements for his succession. Since then, this stable relation to God had been seriously disturbed, and the imperial penance at Attigny sought to redress the balance.

From the late eleventh century onwards, when popes and emperors began to compete for sacred authority, until the modern period with its debates on the opposition between church and state, Theodosius' penance has been often invoked, usually as a model for ecclesiastical authority prevailing over secular might. These are later perceptions and interpretations: at the time, both the emperor and the bishop of Milan made a lot of symbolical capital out of the event.[48] In 822 the full limelight undoubtedly shone upon the emperor. There was no Ambrose who admonished Louis to do penance or delivered a public rebuke (*correptio*). One of the attendant bishops, Agobard of Lyons, related not long afterwards that in Attigny the 'sacred and religious lord emperor' had conducted an inquiry at the very highest level, impressing the need for a stricter orthodoxy upon his bishops and all his great men (*sacerdotibus et cunctis honoratis*), as well as for the eradication of negligence. Louis was in command: 'With divine

---

[46] *Divisio regnorum* (806), c. 18, MGH *Capit.* I, pp. 129–30.
[47] Thegan, c. 6, p. 182. Such a promise is absent from the Astronomer's narrative; see Astronomer, c. 20, pp. 342–4.
[48] McLynn, *Ambrose*, pp. 325–30.

inspiration, he laudably interrogated each order, judiciously found out [what he needed], and faithfully announced [the results] with his own mouth'.[49] Here, one catches another glimpse of the authoritative presence of the king during assemblies, and of the impact of his formal pronouncements on such occasions.[50] Not only did Louis's *admonitio* make a great impression on Agobard, but also the address delivered by the elderly Adalhard of Corbie, who had exclaimed that not since the days of King Pippin had he seen a more glorious ruler furthering the public cause, in so far as he was not humiliated by the negligence of those who had answered his interrogation. Here was a *senex* who had been at the side of kings since the days of Pippin – a real authority, as Agobard implied. On behalf of the entire gathering, Adalhard and other great men (*primores*) exhorted the emperor to avoid sin and moral danger, to apply himself tirelessly to the cult of God, and to doctrine, faith and fidelity, reminding him that sins would lead to disaster and disease among the people.[51] Agobard's depiction of these proceedings were intended as a backdrop to his own radical intervention on church property. The fact that his own speech met with a chilly reception does not make Agobard's vignette of the assembly of Attigny less informative. The archbishop of Lyons wanted to impress upon his readers that he had been among the great and good at the court, listening to lofty addresses by the emperor and Adalhard, and then contributing his own views. What transpires from his report, apart from the obvious fact that Adalhard played a key role, is, first of all, that the assembly of Attigny was the scene of mutual admonition of considerable formality; secondly, that the emperor was the first to investigate and instruct, and finally, that those who 'responded and obeyed' were clerics and laymen who were distinguished from each other as belonging to separate *ordines*, but who nonetheless operated as one group, represented by Adalhard and other *primores*.

All this should be kept in mind when considering the capitulary that resulted from this memorable assembly. This text is known by a modern title, the '*capitula* issued by the bishops at Attigny'. The five decrees concerned look like the outcome of a separate session of the bishops, for they concern the importance of preaching by the learned, the provision of schools for clerics and funding for the education of priests, how to deal with the powerful who would not attend sermons, and the need for priests

---

[49] Agobard, *De dispensatione*, c. 2, p. 121: 'quod utique laudabiliter inspirante Dei gratia quęsivit, ęleganter invenit, fideliter ore suo annuntiavit'; see Boshof, *Agobard*, pp. 84–7.

[50] About a similar interrogation conducted by Charlemagne in 811, Nelson, 'The voice of Charlemagne'; see also *De ordine palatii*, c. VI (29–31), pp. 82–8.

[51] Agobard, *De dispensatione*, c. 3, p. 122.

to refrain from simony.[52] The first sentences of their *capitula*, in response to Louis's initiative, duly acknowledge the emperor's undisputed dominance of the moral high ground. Louis's 'devoted endeavour and salubrious example' had brought the spokesmen to confess to their own negligence, with regard to their conduct, doctrine and office (*ministerium*).[53] Given Adalhard's speech, the 'we' who formulated these *capitula* and confessed their own sins may have included a wider group than merely bishops; lay magnates (*primores*) also had a ministry. One also wonders whether the objects of Louis's self-incrimination played any significant part in the ritual of public penance itself. Adalhard and Wala, Hugh, Drogo and Theuderic were all there, and so were the elder sons Lothar and Pippin. Directly after the assembly, Lothar was sent to Italy with Wala and Gerung as counsellors; Pippin, who had also been present, was married during the gathering in Attigny.[54] In short, everyone who mattered within the family was present there. It is hard to believe their role was merely that of passive onlookers, yet this is what the narrative sources suggest. The episcopal *capitula* as well as Agobard's report imply a more general mood of atonement, however, and a more wide-ranging acknowledgement of guilt and responsibility. Even Charlemagne was included, not in order to shift the blame, but because of filial piety: the sins for which Louis needed to do penance stretched into the past.[55]

At least one spectator was not convinced by the imperial display of humility. For Radbert, writing shortly after Adalhard's death in 826, the embodiment of royal arrogance had indeed now become the humblest of all, but those who expected their wounded eyes to be healed by the royal atonement were disappointed: it was obvious that Louis's self-abasement lacked inner conviction:

What else? The glorious emperor himself undertook a public penance because of his many sins. He who as it were by royal haughtiness had been his own worst tempter was made the humblest of all, so that those whose eyes he had offended by sin would be healed by a royal satisfaction. Doubtless all were particularly intent on his willingness and clearly observed his unwillingness. Had the speaker of truth not returned, it would not at all have become clear how oppressed by lethargy they

---

[52] *Capitula ab episcopis Attiniaci data* (822), MGH *Capit.* I, no. 174, c. 1, pp. 357–8.

[53] Ibid., p. 357: 'Dei igitur omnipotentis inspiratione vestroque piissimo studio admoniti, vestroque etiam saluberrimo exemplo provocati, confitemur...neglegentes extitisse.'

[54] According to *ARF*, s.a. 822, p. 159, directly after the assembly ended Lothar was sent to Italy with Wala and Gerung as counsellors; Pippin, who also had been present, was married in Attigny, and dismissed to Aquitaine.

[55] For the view that Louis stimulated criticism of his father, in Attigny among other places, see Collins, 'Charlemagne and his critics'.

were. Hence ripe old age cured the wound of their blindness, by persuading them to be treated medically with the salubrious antidote of Christ, by means of persuasion.[56]

The prevailing metaphor of this remarkable passage is sight. In Attigny, Louis did penance for the irreparably damaged eyes of Bernard of Italy, but Radbert also evokes the offended eyes of those who had witnessed the emperor's public sins, and who therefore demanded an equally public satisfaction. What their observant gaze saw, however, was an emperor who could not complete the transition from pride to humility, and who showed himself to be a reluctant penitent. Hence, the atonement was not effective and all were struck by lethargy, until Adalhard took the court in hand and applied the medicine of persuasion, curing the wound of blindness by which the emperor and his court were afflicted. Without his help, they were incapable of seeing their own state of lethargy. Whereas Louis was his own worst tempter (*persuasor*), Adalhard persuaded others in their best interests; elsewhere in his *Life*, Radbert called him a 'persuader of virtues' (*persuasor virtutum*). The 'speaker of truth' (*veritatis assertor*) who fearlessly rebuked the mighty, revealing abuses that others could not see or define, was a figure firmly rooted in the tradition of the Old Testament prophetic literature as well as in that of late antique rhetoric. On this persona Radbert modelled not only Adalhard and Wala, but also himself.[57] In this cutting comment on Louis it was only Adalhard who was capable of seeing, and of curing the blindness in which everyone was caught up.

Radbert's *Life of Adalhard* itself shows that the imperial penance in Attigny had not brought about a complete reconciliation with the kinsmen Louis had banished from the court. Wala succeeded his brother as abbot of Corbie in 826, and enjoyed a prominent position at Louis's court, yet at the same time Radbert wrote of Adalhard as bearing the verdict of exile with magnanimity, thanking God that he was found worthy to suffer abuse for defending the truth.[58] No fewer than two archbishops then plainly berated the emperor for dishonouring and exiling Adalhard, for whom this suffering would mean merely heavenly joy and freedom; Louis, 'suffused with shame, regretted having done what shame should have prevented'.[59] Adalhard's greatness of spirit and commitment to the truth are set off by Louis's moral failure. Those who protested that his exile was a crime were comforted by none other than Adalhard himself, who said in parting: 'Meanwhile, spare the ruler granted to us by God, for somehow

---

[56] Radbert, *VA*, c. 51, cols. 1534D–1535A.   [57] See De Jong, 'Becoming Jeremiah'.

[58] Radbert, *VA*, c. 36, col. 1528B: 'Agebat namque gratias quod dignus inventus fuerit pro veritate contumeliam pati.'

[59] Ibid., col. 1528C: 'pudore suffusus, doluit se fecisse quod jam ruboris erat inhibere'.

he is not exercising his own will, but, for the time being, the will of our Lord against whom we have sinned.'[60] In other words, Louis was a scourge sent by God, who was, moreover, incapable of seeing truth and acting upon it. On these grounds, Radbert discredited Louis's penance in 822. The emperor had not displayed true repentance for his sins; only Adalhard could lift the moral fog that enveloped Louis and his court.

The Astronomer's depiction of the penance of 822 was no doubt meant to counteract scathing critics such as Radbert. Here, albeit after Louis's death, we get the imperial view of the matter. The Astronomer elaborated on the tentative suggestion of the *Royal Frankish Annals* that Louis was prepared to carry more guilt than he actually was obliged to do:

> In the next year the lord emperor ordered an assembly to come together at a place called Attigny. He called the bishops to council there, and the abbots and clergy, and also the nobles of his realm, in the first place because he was anxious to be reconciled with his brothers whom he had had tonsured against their will, and then with all those whom he seemed to have harmed. After this he openly confessed that he himself had sinned and, imitating the example of the emperor Theodosius, he spontaneously undertook a penance, both for those things and also for the things he had done to his own nephew Bernard. He also corrected anything he could discover anywhere, whether done by himself or by his father, and took care to placate God by the generous giving of many alms, by incessant prayer by the servants of Christ, and, not least, by his own satisfaction, as if whatever had befallen each one of them, as the consequence of the law, had been caused by his [Louis's] own cruelty.[61]

In 833, it had been claimed that Louis's expiation in Attigny had been insufficient; Bernhard's death and Louis's alleged violence against his *fratres et propinqui* headed the list of charges brought against him. According to the Astronomer, the emperor was thus punished twice for one and the same crime, which was against not only secular but also divine law.[62] His penance in 822 had fully exonerated Louis and, the Astronomer argued, he had in fact assumed a burden of sin for punishments that had been perfectly legal, and within his right as a ruler: Bernhard and the others had brought their mishap upon themselves.[63] Significantly, the Astronomer omitted any mention of Adalhard and Wala as wronged parties. The forcibly tonsured half-brothers also remain unidentified, even though one of them, Drogo of Metz, was possibly the

---

[60] Radbert, *VA*, c. 37, col. 1529A/B: 'Interim vero, quaeso, parcite a Deo collato nobis principi, quod non sua quodammodo, sed Domini nostri cui peccavimus, interdum utitur voluntate.'

[61] Astronomer, c. 35, p. 406.   [62] Ibid., c. 49, p. 482.

[63] See ibid., c. 30, pp. 384–6, on Bernhard's resistance during his blinding as the cause of his death.

Astronomer's patron. The focus was entirely on Bernhard's death, which had been explained away earlier by blaming the victim.

The comparison between Louis and Theodosius obviously served to underline that a public confession was something befitting an emperor, provided it was a voluntary gesture performed with inner commitment – unlike Louis's forced penance in Soissons, eleven years later. Yet there may have been another reason why the Astronomer retrospectively invoked Theodosius as *the* example for Louis's first public atonement, namely to underline that Louis's penance had been imposed according to the ecclesiastical rules. In 833 the rebels simply ignored it, in all likelihood because at Attigny Louis himself had been in charge of the entire ceremony, rather than any bishops who had formally imposed a public penance. By referring to Theodosius, the Astronomer implicitly countered this objection, for the story of Ambrose withstanding Theodosius' protests, keeping him sternly out of church for the duration of his penance, was a familiar one to educated Christians of the ninth century. The most extensive version available to them came from the so-called *Historia tripartita*. This was based on the Greek continuations of Eusebius' *Ecclesiastical History* by three mid-fifth-century historians: Socrates, Sozomen and Theodoret. A century later, as part of Cassiodorus' endeavour to translate Greek Christian works into Latin, Epiphanius took these three authors in hand, using an already amalgamated Greek version of the three histories.[64] The *Historia tripartita* was widely known among Carolingian *litterati*. Its oldest manuscript dates from the early ninth century and comes from Corbie; according to an eleventh-century colophon, it was copied for Adalhard of Corbie when he lived in exile in Noirmoutier.[65] Its vivid narrative makes the most of the dramatic confrontation between the emperor and the intrepid bishop, and concentrates on a key issue of the fifth century: their different spheres of competence. Both the bishop and the emperor shone with virtue, the author concluded,[66] yet when it came to the question of who controlled

---

[64] For a recent *status quaestionis* with reference to older literature, see McKitterick, *History and Memory*, pp. 233–4; on the diffusion of this and other late antique Christian historiography in the Carolingian world, ibid., pp. 235–44; also McKitterick, 'The audience'. On the manuscript transmission of the *Historia tripartita*, see Jacob and Hanslik, *Die handschriftliche Überlieferung*; Siegmund, *Überlieferung*, pp. 56–8.

[65] Leningrad, Lat. F.v.I.11; Jacob, *Die handschriftliche Überlieferung*, pp. 10–11; Ganz, *Corbie*, p. 143. The colophon on fol. a verso reads: 'hic codex hero insula scriptus fuit iubente patre Adalhardo dum exularet ibi' (from 814 to 821). See McKitterick, 'Nuns' scriptoria'. On the *Historia tripartita* in Corbie, see now Zechiel-Eckes, 'Ein Blick in Pseudoisidors Werkstätt'.

[66] *Historia tripartita*, IX, c. 30, p. 546: ' Tali ergo tantaque et praesul et imperator virtute clarebant. Ego namque utriusque opus ammiror, illius fiduciam, huius autem oboedientiam, illius zeli fervorem, huius fidei puritatem.'

sacred space, Theodosius had learned a lesson. As he exclaimed, 'I have just learned what the difference is between an emperor and a bishop, for I have now found a master of truth. Ambrose is the only one I know who is worthy of being called a pontiff.'[67] The chapter ends with a brief conclusion: 'So beneficial is an *increpatio* delivered by a man flourishing with virtue.'[68] All the admonition or rebuke is meted out by Ambrose.[69]

Jonas of Orléans explicitly cited the *Historia tripartita*'s version of Theodosius' penance as an excellent example of the extent to which imperial power depended upon God's favour, and Freculf of Lisieux relied on it in the second book of his *Histories*, offered in 829 to the Empress Judith for the education of her son Charles.[70] In Freculf's adaptation, however, the emperor received all the limelight. Theodosius himself asked to be readmitted to communion; rather than initially refusing, Ambrose immediately granted this wish, provided that the penitent would issue a law that delayed execution for thirty days, an element of the original narrative. Eliminating all detail connected with Constantinople, Freculf shifted the emphasis of the narrative. Whereas the *Historia tripartita* highlights the all-important distinction between the imperial and the sacerdotal roles (*opus*), Freculf was not particularly interested in discussing this division. He did adopt the comment that Theodosius, being well educated, could distinguish between the competences of emperors and bishops, but the main issue then became the emperor's promise to delay the execution of a death sentence for thirty days, and Theodosius' subsequent activity as a lawgiver. Having completed his eight months of tearful retirement in the palace, this emperor 'corrected many laws, added to them and changed them, and issued them under his name'.[71] What mattered to Freculf was that Theodosius was a *sacratissimus imperator* whose voluntary obedience to Ambrose's rebuke made him a worthy model for later emperors. Above all, he corrected existing laws and added new ones in his own name, just as Louis the Pious did, and Charlemagne had done. True, Freculf has the 'most sacred emperor' declare that he was

---

[67] Ibid.

[68] Ibid., p. 546: 'Tantum itaque prode est increpatio a viro virtutibus florente prolata.'

[69] There were other versions known in the West, notably Paulinus' *Life of* Ambrose; see Pellegrini (ed.), pp. 27–30, for a list of the main manuscripts; further, Augustine, *De civitate Dei*, V, c. 24, pp. 236–7: 'et ecclesiastica cohercitus disciplina sic egit paenitentiam, ut imperatoriam celsitudinem pro illo populus orans magis fleret videndo prostratam, quam peccando timeret iratam.'

[70] Jonas, *De institutione laicali*, II, c. 20, *PL* 106, col. 211: 'Hoc qui plenius nosse voluerit, librum historiae tripartitae nonum, sub titulo tricesimo legat.' Freculf of Lisieux, *Historiae*, II, 4, c. 27, ed. M. I. Allen, *Frechulfi Lexoviensis episcopi opera omnia*, CCCM 169A (Turnhout, 2002), pp. 656–60.

[71] Freculf, *Historiae*, II, 4, c. 27, p. 660.

illuminated by Ambrose's reprimands (*correptionibus*) and knew this bishop to excel all others in truthfulness,[72] yet in his version of the story, the sacredness and moral authority of the emperor were no longer contested. Clearly, Freculf wrote with the kingship of his own day and age in mind – that is, with Louis.

Royal admonition

Agobard remembered that Louis announced the outcome of his inquiry on the moral conduct of his bishops and magnates 'faithfully, with his own mouth'.[73] Royal admonition during assemblies and councils seems to have been a normal procedure; in 816, for example, Louis opened a gathering of bishops and abbots in Aachen by admonishing those present to look into the lack of hospitality in religious communities, and into the insufficient learning of canons, an *admonitio* that was allegedly received with enthusiasm by all those present.[74] That the pastoral nature of some capitularies and their similarity to sermons has only recently attracted attention is due to the fact that historians have long viewed these texts as strictly legal documents.[75] The connection between capitularies and sermons is the *admonitio*. This was an integral part of preaching – think of Gregory the Great's *Regula pastoralis* and its thirty-six ways to admonish sinners – and also a striking feature of some important capitularies. The best-known is Charlemagne's *Admonitio generalis* (789), a capitulary with a modern title, but one aptly chosen, for at the heart of this text is a king who reminded his audience that 'we read in the books of Kings [III Reg. 22–3] how the holy Josiah, by visitation, correction and admonition, strove to recall to the worship of the true God the kingdom God had given him'.[76] The corrective activities mentioned here all belong to the traditional set of episcopal duties. Like 'ministry', these originally ecclesiastical notions became integrated into the conceptions of royal rule; in turn, successive royal initiatives of reform of the divine cult helped to revive and reinforce

---

[72] Ibid., pp. 659–60: 'Igitur humiliter veniente imperatore ad Ambrosium deposcendo ut ingredi ecclesiam ei permitteretur, taliter communionem promeruit ab eo, ut legem scriberet atque confirmaret, *quae decreta* furorem evacuaret, et usque triginta dies sententia necis suspensa maneret, *et iudicium rationis* exspectaret ... His et aliis imperator sacratissimus a venerabili episcopo correptionibus inlustratus, eum prae omnibus fatebatur in veritate se agnovisse episcopum' (italics original).

[73] Agobard, *De dispensatione*, c. 2, p. 122.

[74] *Concilium Aquisgranense* a. 816, prologue, p. 312.

[75] Buck, *Admonitio*, pp. 67–155 ('Das Kapitular als Admonitio').

[76] Ibid., p. 83; *Admonitio generalis* (789), prologue, MGH *Capit.* I, no. 22, p. 54: 'Nam legimus in regnorum libris, quomodo sanctus Iosias regnum sibi a Deo datum circumecundo, corrigendo, ammonendo ad cultum veri Dei revocare.'

these ideals in the church. Like Charlemagne's *Admonitio generalis*, the great programmatic capitulary of Louis the Pious, the *Admonitio ad omnes regni ordines* (825), received its name from its modern editor; *ordinatio* has been suggested as an alternative, but this is an equally modern construct, and no improvement.[77] This capitulary was a high-minded statement about the sharing of responsibility within the political leadership, in keeping with the surge of vigorous imperial authority inspired by Louis's public confession at Attigny (822). This capitulary owed its wide dissemination to its having been included in Ansegis' collection, and as such, it had a considerable impact.[78] In the opening statement Louis referred to his father and other ancestors, who, having been chosen by God, had endeavoured to safeguard the honour of the holy Church and the state of the realm (*honor sanctae ecclesiae et status regni*).[79] Following this lofty example, the ruler had taken good care frequently to admonish his addressees – that is, his *fideles*.

Throughout the capitulary, *admonitio* remains the leitmotiv.[80] From the fact that the royal ministry encompassed all other *ministeria*, it followed that the king must be the *admonitor* and the different orders in the realm his helpers; he should therefore admonish everyone according to his own order.[81] This is how the text then proceeds: first, the bishops were admonished (*monemus atque rogamus*),[82] and urged to educate and admonish their priests with great care.[83] In turn, the counts were admonished to give due honour to the holy church, living in peace with the bishops and helping them in their ministry, and to take good care of exercising theirs.[84] They also received an admonition about their fidelity, reminding them of the oath of loyalty they had sworn, and all lay people were admonished to honour the clergy and observe Sunday.[85] Abbots and laymen had to listen to the 'salubrious admonition' of the bishops.[86] Further down in the text, where specific problems are addressed – armies

---

[77] *Admonitio ad omnes regni ordines* (823–5), MHG *Capit.* no. 150, pp. 303–7; cf. Guillot, 'Une *ordinatio* méconnue', who suggests calling this capitulary an *ordinatio*.

[78] Ansegis, p. 65, on the transmission of the *Admonitio ad omni regni ordines*, and pp. 521–41 for the text, divided into twenty-four *capitula* (Boretius' edition gives twenty-six). For Ansegis' biography, see ibid. pp. 4–10. The *Collectio* was completed on 28 January 827; see ibid., p. 12.

[79] Ansegis, II, 2.2, p. 521. Cf. Astronomer, c. 32, p 392, with regard to Louis's legislation of 818/19: 'nichilque intactum reliquit, quicquid ad honorem sanctae Dei ecclesię proficere posse visum sit'.

[80] For the frequency of *admonitio/admonere* in Ansegis' collection, see Ansegis, p. 684 (index); predictably, these words occur most frequently in the *Admonitio generalis* (789) and the *Admonitio ad omnes regni ordines* (825).

[81] Ansegis, II, 2.3, p. 523.   [82] Ibid., 2.4, p. 524, line 2.   [83] Ibid., 2.5, p. 525, line 2.

[84] Ibid., 2.6, p. 526, line 5: 'Vobis vero comitibus dicimus vobisque commonemus.'

[85] Ibid., 2.7, p. 527, line 12.   [86] Ibid., 2.8, p. 528, line 10.

on the rampage, foreign embassies that were robbed, bridges in need of repair – the admonition continues, with references to Louis's earlier *admonitio* with regard to coinage, tolls and tithes.[87] In Ansegis' version of the text, most of these chapters have headings identifying them as admonitions, as in, for example, *De admonitione unius monetae* (c. 17). Again, for this capitulary, *admonitio* is as good a modern title as any, and it was the ruler who did the admonishing.

Although Ansegis listed the *Admonitio* of 825 among Louis's ecclesiastical capitularies, it would be a mistake to think that the contents of this capitulary, or of Charlemagne's *Admonitio generalis*, for that matter, can be classified as 'clerical', or pertaining to the church alone. These two programmatic capitularies were the solemn expression of royal authority and the ruler's ordering of society. This authority was religious by definition, for the correct cult of God was at the very heart of this order. For precisely the same reason, churchmen were closely involved in the drafting of such texts, but it is the 'king's word' (*verbum regis*) that lends authority to a capitulary. Kings addressed their followers, be it in war or in peacetime, by means of direct and often terrifying speech; the assembly was the chosen venue for such a display of royal eloquence. However elusive and difficult to reconstruct, this formal and binding royal speech must have been one of the traditions that sustained written *admonitiones* of the kind discussed here.

Narrative texts of the period are an equally important source for the representation of royal authority by means of *admonitio*.[88] In his *Vita Aegil* Brun Candidus has Louis deliver a veritable sermon to the monks of Fulda, who came to visit and petition the emperor.[89] Obviously the lengthy address on how monastic life should be lived, including citations from the *Vita Pachomii*, was Brun's creation, yet the notion that an emperor could admonish monks on how to avoid sin had to be familiar and credible to Brun's audience. Louis could serve as a literary medium for a highly charged moral message to the community, because the idea that he would say things such as 'Omnes aequaliter, moneo, diligatis in Christo' was perfectly acceptable to his monastic contemporaries. This was how an emperor could be expected to behave; whereas the *claustrum* was an exclusion zone to all others, he was welcome there, and entitled to correct the conduct of those whose prayer was shielded by his protection.[90]

---

[87] Ibid., 2.18, p. 232, line 15; 19, p. 537, line 7; 20, p. 538, line 12.
[88] *Exhortatio* can serve as an equivalent, yet the semantic field is more diffuse than that of *admonitio*. 'To exhort' can refer to various kinds of incitement, including inciting to do evil.
[89] Brun Candidus, *Vita Aegil*, I, c. 8, pp. 8–11 (this is the prose version).
[90] De Jong, 'Internal cloisters', pp. 213–5.

In historiographical texts, one encounters a similar use of Louis's *admonitio* to express royal authority. The Astronomer, for example, gave a highly charged account of the confrontation between the Emperor Louis and his sons on the Field of Lies, when Louis's troops had already deserted. This passage is tightly packed with meaning. Having met each other half way, the sons descended from their horses and came to their father. The emperor then *admonished* his sons to be mindful of the promises they had once made to him, his son [Charles] and his wife. When they had responded in a fitting manner, he kissed them, and trustingly followed them to their camp, where he was immediately separated from Judith and Charles.[91] This narrative addresses various crucial issues, such as the proper hierarchy between father and sons (which was now upset) and the need for promises and oaths to be sincere (which they were not). Yet the central message is that the father did the admonishing, with superior moral authority, compelling his sons to respond 'in a fitting way' (*congrue*), even if their subsequent behaviour fell dismally short of the standards of the Astronomer and his intended readership.

For the Astronomer, the ability to deliver an *admonitio* singles out the ruler, as does his reluctance to mete out sharp rebuke (*increpatio*). In Nijmegen in 830, once the rebellion ran out of steam, Louis verbally corrected his son Lothar, not by *aspera increpatio*, but by *modesta lenitas*.[92] In 839, Louis the German confessed to having done wrong, but the paternal *increpatio* was only a minor one (*paululum*), and the errant son could return to his kingdom.[93] The distinction between admonition and rebuke was a fine one, but it mattered deeply, especially in the Astronomer's portrayal of Louis's chief vice, which was in fact his main virtue: his clemency. In the *Vita Hludowici*, the Emperor Louis was the only one who admonished, directing his *admonitio* at his sons and the people, in the sense of his *fideles*.[94] Significantly, Louis's reinstatement on 1 March 834 in St-Denis is followed by a stern *admonitio* of his sons and the people.[95] With Thegan, this expression especially abounds in the chapter on Louis's coronation in 813. Charlemagne admonished everyone present to accept Louis as his successor,[96] and all thought that the choice of Louis was the result of an admonition by God;[97] Charlemagne

---

[91] Astronomer, c. 48, p. 478, lines 4–12.   [92] Ibid., c. 45, p. 462, lines 15–16.
[93] Ibid., c. 60, p. 534, lines 1–5.
[94] Ibid., c. 40, p. 430, line 12: '… multa quae ecclesia essent utilia ammonuit, statuit ac definivit'; c. 54, p. 504, line 8: '… filiosque et populum admonuit, ut equitatem diligerent…'; c. 54, p. 504, line 11: harsh punishment for those who do not heed this admonition.
[95] Astronomer, c. 54, p. 504.   [96] Thegan, c. 6, p. 180, line 15.
[97] Ibid., p. 182, line 1.

then delivered his famous *admonitio* to his son to honour God and cherish his family members, which yielded promises on Louis's part that Thegan maintained Louis had kept, but others did not.[98] Thegan depicted Louis in the role of authoritative *admonitor* to highlight Lothar's obstinacy in 834: the eldest son refused to heed his father's written warning, delivered by envoys, to remember God and His commandments. Walahfrid Strabo's later heading for this chapter was an eloquent one: *ammonitio patris per legatos directa*.[99]

Clearly, *admonitio* was an integral part of Louis's exercise of authority, as it had been of Charlemagne's, so it belonged to the idiom with which authors could portray legitimate kingship in a way that was recognisable to contemporary readers. The bishops who imposed a public penance on Louis in 833 lived in the same world: their apologetic report, drawn up to defend what had happened to the rest of the Frankish elite, made abundant use of *admonere* and its derivatives, to show that their action was based on legitimate authority.[100] Who admonished whom? That was the question. To be the watchmen on the tower, warning their fellow-men against sin, was part and parcel of the bishops' pastoral ministry, so their *admonitio* needed no defence. The same held true for the Carolingian rulers; admonition had become a hallmark of Charlemagne's public persona, and Louis followed suit.[101] If all was well, ruler and bishops co-operated in a way that allowed for a measure of mutual *admonitio* and acknowledgement of sin or error, with both parties (and their *ministeria*) inhabiting their fair share of the moral high ground.

Admonition from beyond the grave

Behind kings who delivered admonitions stood the divine authority that had chosen them, but this was a God who was easily provoked to anger. Divine warnings could come in different guises, but they meant only one thing:

For what does it matter whether humankind is forewarned of God's impending wrath by a human, by an angel or by a star announcing [it]? Only this is necessary: to understand that the appearance of the star was not without meaning, but admonished (*admonuisse*) mortals so that by doing penance and invoking mercy they may work towards avoiding future danger.[102]

---

[98] Ibid., p. 185, 15; Wendling, 'Die Erhebung Ludwigs'.   [99] Ibid., c. 53, p. 246.

[100] *Relatio* (833): *saluberrimis admonitionibus, salubribus monitis, salutifer admonitio, salubriter admonuerunt*, etc. See below, ch. 6.

[101] Cf. Lauwers, 'Le glaive et la parole'; Lauwers sees much less continuity between Charlemagne and Louis than I do.

[102] Einhard, *Epistolae*, no. 40, p. 130; I only partly follow the translation by Dutton, *CC*, p. 160.

This was what an ageing Einhard wrote to Louis the Pious about the appearance of Halley's comet in the skies over Aachen in June 837. When it came to humans and angels as media of God's messages, Einhard was an expert. He had written a booklet (*libellus*) on the warnings of Gabriel, relayed to him by the cleric Ratleigh; these in turn had been dictated to Ratleigh by a blind man from Aquitaine who sought recovery at Einhard's church in Mulinheim. Einhard corrected the booklet and, as ordered, took this version to Louis, who accepted it and read it, 'but of those things the booklet ordered or admonished him to do, he managed to accomplish precious few'.[103]

For early medieval visions, this type of textual transmission was typical. The visionaries themselves tended to be simpler folk, for example a monk, a blind pilgrim, a 'little woman' (*muliercula*), or a twelve-year-old girl. The authors of visionary texts, however, were most often learned and powerful men, who presented their work as a corrected and improved version of an earlier written record, just as Einhard did in the case of Gabriel's message. All concerned accepted the existence of such a truth; the problem was how to distinguish the true vision from a false one. This is where men like Einhard (specialists) were important – or Abbot Heito of Reichenau and Walahfrid Strabo, or Hincmar, for that matter.[104] Their 'correction' and redaction lent veracity and authority to a story that was by definition recounted clumsily, for truth came from the mouths of babes and sucklings. To some extent, this must have been a literary device, but this functioned only in a world that would find the existence of blind men transmitting a warning from Gabriel to Einhard's secretary entirely plausible. Einhard himself clearly thought that his 'correction' of the angelical message not only was needed, but would also improve its reliability. Only after he rewrote Gabriel's communication would it be fit for the emperor's eyes.

Paul Dutton has argued that such visionary texts were 'a specific tool designed to shift the massive weight of recalcitrant royal power in a new direction'.[105] In other words, if kings would not heed the admonition of their human counsellors, they would be targeted by the heavier artillery of divine displeasure. At times this was certainly the case, yet, in my view, Dutton tends to overestimate the political nature of these dream texts. This is due partly to an influential article by Wilhelm Levison on politics

---

[103] Einhard, *TMP*, III, c. 13, p. 252: 'Sed de his quae per hunc libellum facere iussus vel admonitus fuerat perpauca adimplere curavit.'

[104] On Hincmar as a learned 'corrector' of a visionary text, see Van der Lugt, 'Tradition and revision'.

[105] Dutton, *The Politics of Dreaming*, p. 49.

and visionary literature, first published in 1922, and partly to the traditionally central place of political history in modern scholarship.[106] All this
has contributed to a one-sided concentration on Charlemagne's fate in
hell, to the detriment of an understanding of the entire text. In order to
determine whether visions of rulers being tormented in the hereafter
constituted any kind of critique, and if so, of what kind, these 'political'
passages need to be read within the context of the visionary text as a whole.

A *visio* was a medium through which the sinfulness of humankind could
be addressed, but, as in terrestrial society, the dead who were being
tormented and purged were ordered according to a set hierarchy. Just as
in life kings had headed the different *ordines*, they now presided over the
ranks of the sinners being punished after death. The moral leadership – or,
to put it another way, the religious authority – of the ruler made him more
vulnerable to sin than other humans were; conversely, royal sin, which
also affected the realm and the people, required a more intense penance in
life, and more concerted prayer assistance after death. For this was what
most of such texts were all about: they warned the living about the
intolerable wages of sin in the hereafter, and explained that it was by
prayer, and prayer alone, that those in this world could help those tormented in the hereafter. It was not so much 'recalcitrant royal power'
unwilling to listen to other clerical advice that was addressed by the
authors of visionary texts, but a more complicit kind of royal authority:
kings who viewed themselves as responsible for the correct cult of God
and the salvation of the *populus christianus*. The final reckoning came after
death, so these kings urgently needed purification and prayer to help them
enter the kingdom of heaven. It is no coincidence, therefore, that the first
group of visionary texts featuring Charlemagne in a purgatorial setting
originated in the communities where prayer was a core business: monasteries.[107] The *Visio Wettini* originated in Reichenau around the same
time – *c*. 824 – as the confraternity book which contained the names of
the living and dead members of no fewer than fifty affiliated monasteries
and convents.[108]

The *Visio Wettini* is the most famous representative of this group of
visions from the 820s, and as good an example as any of an *admonitio*
directed at the ruler and a courtly audience by means of a 'dream text'. On

[106] Levison, 'Jenseitsvisionen'; see pp. 237–8 on visions as a means of political propaganda
and manipulation.
[107] The texts in question are the *Visio Rotcharii* (possibly from Fleury); the *Visio cuiusdam
pauperculae* mulieris; Heito, *Visio Wettini*; Walahfrid Strabo, *Visio Wettini*. Cf. Dutton,
The Politics of Dreaming, pp. 50–80, and, on the early medieval precursors of Purgatory,
Gurevitch, 'Cultural traditions'.
[108] De Jong, 'Carolingian monasticism', pp. 649–51; *Das Verbrüderungsbuch de Abtei Reichenau*.

the morning of 3 November, the day before he died, the monk Wetti recounted a vision he had experienced during the night to Abbot Erlebald and three senior monks of Reichenau. One of the latter, the former abbot Heito, recorded this vision in a prose text on which Wetti's pupil Walahfrid based his poetic version. One of Walahfrid's motives was the need to find a new protector after Wetti's death, and for this he turned to Grimald, the future abbot of St-Gall, who was at the time one of Louis's chaplains, and in attendance at the imperial court. In 827, still in Reichenau and barely eighteen years old, Walahfrid completed his *Visio Wettini*, which he sent to Grimald with a letter of dedication.[109] This was a young man intent on making his mark at court, and who succeeded in doing so, for in 829 Walahfrid was summoned to Aachen, to display his many talents.[110]

A brief summary of Walahfrid's text is in order, for this puts the famous section on Charlemagne in perspective. On his journey through the hereafter, Wetti was guided by a beautiful angel, who showed him different categories of sinners and their respective suitable torments, according to a clear hierarchy of the orders of society. First they came upon various members of the clergy: fornicating priests, with the women who had seduced them and monks being punished for avarice. There was an abbot who had been guilty of *negligentia*, and a bishop who did not follow the warning transmitted to him by a vision, namely that he should call upon monasteries for prayer to assist the dead. Admonished (*ammonitus*), the bishop remained incredulous, and now he had to suffer for it.[111] The angel then expounded on the moral of this story, which at the same time is the introduction to the celebrated passage about Charlemagne. Much is won by intercessory prayer, but do not think that this is foolproof, for nobody knows how heavily his deeds will eventually weigh. 'Hence, for my own part', said the angel, 'I maintain that it is effective to atone for my acts beforehand.'[112] Better to be safe than sorry, and with this in mind we move on to the man who once held sway over Ausonia and the Roman people, and whose name (*Carolus imperator*) Walahfrid deftly revealed in the acrostic formed by the first letters of the lines devoted to the emperor. Charles was rooted to the spot while an unspecified animal was tearing at his genitals.[113] Fearfully, Wetti recounted the emperor's great deeds: he

---

[109] Traill, *Visio Wettini*, pp. 2–3, 9–11.

[110] Some doubt has been cast on Walahfrid's role as tutor of Charles the Bald, but that he came to the court as a promising monastic 'intellectual' remains undisputed; cf. Fees, 'Walahfrid Strabo'.

[111] Walahfrid, *Visio Wettini*, line 432, p. 318.

[112] Ibid., lines 444–5, p. 318; Trail, *Visio Wettini*, p. 55.

[113] Walahfrid, *Visio Wettini*, lines 449, p. 318: 'oppositumque animal lacerare virilia stantis'.

had furthered justice and learning for the Lord, he had protected the clergy (*sacra plebs*) and been at the summit of the entire world. Why is he punished so cruelly? The angel answered that this was a king who had sullied his good actions with shameful debauchery, 'thinking his sins would be buried under the great quantity of his virtuous acts, and who chose to end his life in squalor to which he became habituated; yet even so he will attain a blessed life, and joyfully assume the honour that the Lord has set aside for him'. Unlike Heito, Walahfrid added a comment to explain to his audience that the angel admonished (*ammonuit*) them not to spend long years living a good life and then to lose everything by some sin or other. 'Let him who desires to retain his kingdom eternally in heaven take care to moderate himself in all matters on earth.'[114]

After Charlemagne, with logical order, Wetti encountered unjust counts, and the friends of Satan who were guilty of merciless extortion and avarice. He also saw Christ's throne and the saints, who prostrated themselves, beseeching God for a remittance of sins for Wetti himself, who had neglected to be a source of inspiration because of his indolence. Wetti recognized Dionysius, Hilary, Martin and Benedict of Aniane, before they came to the blessed martyrs. Wetti asked how he might save his soul, and a voice from the throne challenged him to recall from their evil path all those he had misled by false doctrine, and to prostrate himself, confessing his guilt in this respect. After a digression on virginity, the sins of the human race, sodomy and concubinage, Wetti declared himself unworthy to transmit the message; but he thereby managed to provoke the angel to great anger: how could Wetti lack the courage to proclaim what divine wisdom had ordained? Then the angel went into full admonition mode, telling Wetti to put his moral life in order, and to allow the rays of blessedness to illuminate it; the angel, who had once aided Samson, would stand guard over Wetti as well.[115] Finally, the angel's *admonitio* returned once more to monastic communities and the 'wound of avarice' (*vulnus avaritiae*); the angel also held forth on excess of food, drink and dress, on men who bow their heads but are haughty in their hearts (*erecto corde*), and on the need for instruction in real poverty.[116]

Only once in this long text did Walahfrid address Louis the Pious directly, berating the pernicious custom of allowing widows to be in charge of nunneries: 'My ruler, it seems that you have created this evil association; give to chaste nuns chaste abbesses; let widows receive some

---

[114] Ibid., lines 473–4, p. 319: 'Omnibus in rebus vitam moderetur in arvis,/Qui cupit in caelis regnum retinere perenne.'
[115] Ibid., lines 675–82.
[116] Ibid., line 699, p. 326: 'Coenobiis etiam monachorum valde monendum est.'

other duty.'[117] The theme comes from Heito's text, but the direct address is Walahfrid's own. For David Traill, this is the most remarkable line in the entire poem: how did an eighteen-year-old monk dare to criticise the emperor himself?[118] The answer is that Walahfrid wrote himself into Louis's court by means of this admonitory and visionary text. The value of such learned and religious men, young as they might be, to a ruler charged with the salvation of his people, lay precisely in their ability to express divine truth in no uncertain terms. So-called 'reform texts' with their criticism of the high and mighty could well express criticism of the ruler, as long as this tallied with what counted as acceptable self-criticism on the part of the ruler and his inner circle. Hence, grievances about widows heading nunneries could be expressed with impunity, and Charlemagne's concubines might be referred to without anyone getting dishonoured in the process. After all, Louis had preceded his bishops in a public confession in 822, loudly proclaiming his sins; to such an emperor, Walahfrid's brand of *admonitio* must have looked less impertinent than it appears to the modern reader. Within limits, such outspokenness was probably highly appreciated; the difference between Heito's prose text and Walahfrid's poetic rendering was that between a hagiographical text for internal use in Reichenau, and an ambitious poem written with a sharp eye for the tastes of the imperial court of which Walahfrid aspired to become a part.

Both Walahfrid's *Visio* and Heito's earlier version emphasized the need to repent while it was still possible. Wetti asked the angel why so many people had recently died of the plague, and got the response that the Last Day was approaching. 'Yes, the day will come,' Walahfrid commented, 'yes, the Lord is coming to assess our actions.' And the angel particularly admonished all to exert themselves in the praise of God, that is, to make sure that prayer was intensified and carried out properly.[119] As a shining example, the angel praised at length Count Gerold, Louis's deceased uncle on his mother's side, who had made lavish donations to Reichenau and was therefore buried in the monastic church.[120] This long digression, based on only a few sentences by Heito, was surely meant to find favour

---

[117] Ibid., line 762, p. 328: 'O princeps, qui tale malum iunxisse videris / Da castis castas, aliud viduata receptet.' Cf. Heito, *Visio Wettini*, c. 22, p. 273.

[118] Traill, *Visio Wettini*, pp. 171–2.

[119] Walahfrid Strabo, *Visio Wettini*, lines 785–95, pp. 328–9: Ecce venit Dominus, nostros ut congreget actus. / Iam vigilare decet, veniens ut quemque coronet. / Praecipue *admonuit* divinis laudibus omnes / Conatu servire bono studioque sagaci.' On the plague of 823, see *ARF*, s.a. 823, pp. 163–4.

[120] Walahfrid Strabo, *Visio Wettini*, lines 802–26, pp. 824–5. Cf. Heito, *Visio Wettini* c. 27, p. 274.

with Louis. Wetti himself, once he had recovered from his vision, made his pupil Walahfrid write countless notes requesting assistance, by prayer, and asking for a hundred masses and a hundred psalms from those likely to give it. By way of vouching for his veracity, Walahfrid inserted the prose model of this request into his poem.

But what about Charlemagne, having his genitals gnawed? As in Einhard's *Vita Karoli*, the old emperor's lack of discipline with regard to women represented the one blemish that soiled a shining reputation. This was also the moral of both Heito's and Walahfrid's rendering of Wetti's vision of Charlemagne in hell: that it took only one 'little obscenity' (*parva obscenitas*) to wipe out all the accumulated credit of an entire life of exemplary rulership. It was no good invoking all your other good deeds to balance this one offence, for that was not how God's judgement worked. Instead, every sin counted, for each was observed by God. If you want to hang on to your *regnum* in heaven, control yourself on earth, said Walahfrid, entirely in accordance with the *mores* of Louis's court. Of course, Charlemagne's punishment was only temporary. He was among the elect who were destined for eternal life, as Heito expressed it; or, in Walahfrid's more courtly terms, he would yet attain the *honor* that God had set aside for him.[121]

Charlemagne's temporary plight in the hereafter was a suitable admonition to his successors that they too should avoid the one blemish that would endanger all they had accomplished. All the same, rulers too needed to be purged of their sins before they could enjoy the company of the saints in heaven. Of Louis the German an annalist wrote that during Lent 874 he had a dream in which he saw 'his father, the Emperor Louis, in dire straits, who addressed him in Latin speech', imploring his son to save him from the torments he suffered, so he might at last attain eternal life. The son then sent letters to all the monasteries in the kingdom to ask for prayer for his father's tormented soul. There is a similar weighing of good and bad deeds here, with the author admitting that Louis had done much that was pleasing to God, yet contending that he had also allowed much that contravened God's law. Had the emperor taken action against married priests and observed the warnings (*admonitio*) of the Archangel Gabriel as recorded by Einhard, he would not have had to suffer such torment.[122] Perhaps this, rather than the *admonitio* itself, was the real criticism: to accuse a ruler of having closed his ears against admonition.

---

[121] Heito, *Visio Wettini*, c. 11, p. 271; Walahfrid, *Visio Wettini*, lines 445–74, pp. 318–9.
[122] *AF*, s.a. 874, p. 82; trans. Reuter, *The Annals of Fulda*, p. 72.

From *admonitio* to *increpatio*

Acceptable *admonitio* had its limits, however. It could develop into an antagonistic recrimination (*increpatio*) or even into a vehement diatribe (*invectio*) of the kind Thegan had written against Ebo, archbishop of Rheims. This development can be observed in the work of Agobard of Lyons. In the 820s he wished to make his mark at the court, gaining the ear of the ruler, and his means to accomplish this was *admonitio*. Initially, he was less than successful. His maiden speech, delivered during the assembly of Attigny (822), did not go down well with the emperor and his counsellors. According to his own report, he behaved impeccably. He, the humblest and lowest of all, began to speak 'carefully, as one does to great men', expounding on the sorry state of ecclesiastical land being in the hands of unsuitable men (*improbi*), by which Agobard meant primarily, but not exclusively, laymen. His original address may have been more outspoken than his written rendering, for in the latter he tried to counter accusations of having sown needless discord among the emperor's lay *fideles*. In writing, he did make allowances, conceding that it was not Louis but his predecessors who were to be blamed for the situation. Furthermore, on practical grounds it would be impossible to amend everything at once. All the same, during this meeting Agobard fearlessly defended the immutability of the canons against the 'new-fangled need' (*nova necessitas*) of rulers who handed out 'sacred goods' as benefices to laymen. He admonished those present concerning the moral danger inherent in such abuse, however unavoidable it may have been once it was introduced.[123] This time-honoured anvil had already been hammered by Carloman's reform councils of 742/3.[124]

As Agobard reported, referring to his speech on church property in Attigny (822), 'When these things had been said by me, the most reverend abbots Adalhard and Helisachar gave a fitting response; whether they relayed what they had heard to the lord emperor, I do not know.'[125] Agobard had been cold-shouldered, as becomes clear from the letter he wrote to Adalhard, Helisachar and Wala, shortly after the assembly:

Recently, when the time to leave the palace had already been granted to us, your sweetest kindness sat down and listened to me, murmuring rather than speaking against those, who support the claims of the Jews. And when these words had been

---

[123] Agobard, *De dispensatione*, c. 4, p. 123; cf. Boshof, *Agobard*, pp. 86–7.
[124] *Karlmanni principis capitulare* (742/3), c. 1, MGH *Capit.* I, no. 10, p. 25; *Karlmanni principis capitulare Liptinense* (743), c. 3, ibid., p. 28.
[125] Agobard, *De dispensatione*, c. 4, p. 123: 'Cum haec igitur a me dicerentur, responderunt pie reverentissimi viri Adalardus et Helisacar abbates. Utrum uero audita retulerunt domno imperatori, nescio.'

heard by you and what had been said from both sides had been modified, you got up, and I did so after you. You entered into the presence of the ruler, I stood behind the door. After a while you signalled that I could enter, but I heard nothing, except for the permission to leave. What you have said about the aforementioned matter to the most clement prince, how he reacted, and what he replied, I have not heard. Afterwards I did not go to you, lamed by embarrassing shame and fatigued by the trouble that assailed me from all sides, not because of the difficulty of the matter but because of lack of nobility of mind.[126]

Agobard was acutely aware of the difference in rank between himself and these great men at the court, claiming that, even if he had wanted to, his modest position did not enable him either to stir up discord or to mediate for peace: unused to high society and shy, he did not dare to raise his voice in such lofty company.[127]

These formal protestations after the event proved fruitless. At Attigny the firebrand archbishop had sealed his political fate for years to come. By bringing up the highly contentious issue of church property amid a general atmosphere of reconciliation and renewed consensus, Agobard made himself unacceptable. Aristocratic feathers were ruffled, and not only those of laymen, but also of bishops, abbots and other clerics whom he had accused of usurping 'sacred matter'. With great difficulty the emperor managed to strike a compromise at the assembly of Compiègne in November 823. Agobard was no longer welcome here. In fact, he remained *persona non grata* at Louis's court, pursuing his pet causes, such as the integrity of ecclesiastical property and the perfidy of the Jews of Lyons.[128] In 828/9 he moved back on to the political scene with a vengeance: one of the four great reform councils of June 829, convened in the previous winter, took place in the archdiocese of Lyons.[129]

Still, if Agobard was indeed so distanced from the corridors of power, the question remains why this outcast and self-professed 'mumbler' kept bombarding the court with letters of admonition. Did Agobard hope to regain royal favour by this course of action? This is what it looks like. Straight after the failure of Attigny, Agobard complained to Adalhard, Helisachar and Wala about Jews who prevented the baptism of their slaves, a matter he broached again in a letter to Wala and Hilduin (826); shortly thereafter followed two elaborate *admonitiones* addressed to Louis himself.[130] Then

---

[126] Agobard, *Epp.* no. 4, p. 164.

[127] Agobard, *De dispensatione*: 'Quippe qui, ut insuetus et timidus, inter tales et tantos viros raro loqui valeam' (p. 121, lines 17–8).

[128] Boshof, *Agobard*, pp. 89–90, 100–1; Heil, 'Agobard', p. 57.

[129] Paris, Lyons, Mainz, Toulouse; Hartmann, *Konziliengeschichte*, pp. 179–81.

[130] The entire corpus of Agobard's anti-Jewish texts is edited in *Agobardi opera*: pp. 115–17 (*De baptismo mancipiorum Iudaeorum* (823), to Adalhard, Wala and Helisachar); pp. 185–221 (*Contra praeceptum impium de baptismo iudaicorum mancipiorum* (826) to Hilduin and

there is a highly suggestive letter to Count Matfrid of Orléans, probably written in 826 or 827, in which the 'little servant' (*servulus*) Agobard admonished this illustrious 'minister of the emperor and empire' to eradicate all corruption at the court. In these abuses the count was deftly depicted as someone who stood 'like a wall' between the emperor and those who should have been corrected by him; in other words, Matfrid condoned corruption by shielding the culprits. Agobard reminded Matfrid that he owed all that precious familiarity with the emperor to the very God who would punish negligent servants, as in the parable where the master said to the servant who merely hid his talents: 'Wicked and slothful servant, thou knewest that I reap where I sow not and gather where I have not strewed' (Matth. 25.26).[131] For good measure, and no doubt by way of self-protection, Agobard wrapped these messages in thick layers of flattery. Towards the end of his letter, he denied that he wanted to accuse anyone of anything, for accusation did not belong to his episcopal office (*officium*). By implication, *admonitio* did.

From 826/7 onwards Agobard addressed his letters to Louis himself, rather than going through prominent members of the court. This was also the time when he intensified his barrage of accusations against the Jews of Lyons, and now directly to the emperor. Slowly but surely, Agobard seems to have regained Louis's confidence. If the admonitory epistle to Matfrid was indeed written late in 827 or early in 828, as Cabaniss has suggested, this was another sign that Agobard's star was rising.[132] Under the cover of earnest admonition, he could now afford to attack one of the most powerful of Louis's *proceres*. Agobard's letter to Matfrid also suggests that the latter's fall from grace in February 828, presumably because of the failure of the Spanish campaign of 827, did not come out of the blue.[133] The ground had been prepared, and Agobard helped to do this.

It would be going too far to say that Agobard merely raised the issues of church property and the position of the Jews in order to gain the emperor's favour.[134] Agobard came from Spain with its Visigothic tradition of anti-Judaism, exemplified by authors such as Archbishop Julian of Toledo. Agobard's sexual imagery with regard to the dangers of Judaism is

---

Wala; *De insolentia Iudaeorum* and *De iudaicis superstitionibus et erroribus* (both 826–7), to Louis); pp. 231–4 (*De cavendo convictu et societate iudaica* (827–8), to Nibridius, bishop of Narbonne). For the dating of these texts, see *Agobardi opera*, pp. xli–xlii.

[131] Agobard, *De iniusticiis*, p. 227.

[132] Cabaniss, 'Agobard', pp. 104–5, a dating followed by *Agobardi opera*, p. xliii.

[133] In 829 Matfrid had to answer charges of corruption; *Capitulare missorum* (829), MGH *Capit.* II, no. 188, pp. 9–10.

[134] Heil, 'Agobard', p. 64, ventures that Agobard's writing on Jews was merely an instrument to avail himself of an audience, after the failure of Attigny and the compromise of 823 on church property.

reminiscent of Julian's choice of metaphors. Whereas the synagogue was a defiled, wrinkled and repudiated whore, the church was an immaculate and smooth-faced virgin chastely wedded to Christ.[135] All the same, after 828 nothing was heard from Agobard about the depravity of Jews or the sacredness of church lands. These two issues had had their uses, and were now dropped.[136] Whereas Ermold the Black used panegyric poetry as the way to ingratiate himself with the ruler and thus to be readmitted into the charmed circle,[137] Agobard chose the *admonitio* as his medium, appealing to Louis in his role as the ultimate corrector of all evil. His letter to Matfrid shows that he was a master of the genre. High-minded admonition, full of praise and flattery, effectively undermined the reputation of this great magnate by suggesting that he prevented the ruler from exercising his duty to correct and amend. Meanwhile, Matfrid's power was already waning, at least to the point that he became vulnerable to Agobard's insidious prose.

Within the category of 'Please listen to my warning, for your own good', falls a remarkable letter to Louis composed towards the end of the year 829 or the beginning of 830. Here Agobard played deftly upon the double meaning of *fides* – faith and fidelity – and called the emperor a 'faithful prelate to whom the republic has been entrusted for governance', wondering aloud how he could be Louis's *fidelis* without pointing out the dangers that threatened him and above all his soul.[138] This was not so much a threat of future infidelity as an allusion to Agobard's duty to act against sin when he saw it, first and foremost when it threatened the emperor's soul. The archbishop appealed to a shared moral high ground, reminding Louis of the solemn way in which he had made Lothar his co-emperor. Agobard himself had witnessed how an assembly in 817 had solemnly assured itself of God's assent by three days of prayer and fasting. Had he only wished it, Agobard claimed, the emperor could have enjoyed a quiet and peaceful life with his sons, just as his father and grandfather had (Agobard conveniently chose to overlook Pippin the Hunchback and other rebellious members of the Carolingian family).[139] His letter was written after the

---

[135] Agobard, *De cavendo*, pp. 232–3, lines 21–32. On Julian of Toledo and his anti-Jewish invective, see De Jong, 'Adding insult to injury'.

[136] Heil, 'Agobard', pp. 58–9. [137] See above, chapter 2, pp. 89–95.

[138] Agobard, *De divisione imperii*, p. 247: 'fideli praelato, cui res publica ad gubernandum conmissa est'. The explicit admonition starts at the beginning of c. 5, p. 249: 'Oro, domne mi, adsit benignissima pietas uestra, ne aspernanter ista accipiatis.' For a discussion of the date of this letter, with reference to older literature, see Boshof, *Agobard*, pp. 204–5, who rightly argues that Agobard referred to the earthquake that shook Aachen at Easter Saturday 829, without making any mention of the revolt that broke out during Lent 830. This is the 'window of time' in which this letter fits.

[139] Agobard, *De divisione*, c. 3, p. 248; c. 4 is about the *Ordinatio imperii*.

assembly of Worms of August 829, where Lothar had been replaced by Bernard of Septimania as the second man of the empire. This very last of Agobard's admonitions to Louis reveals a lot about the 'seeds of discord' that would lead to the revolt of 830. When the Empress Judith had been restored to the throne, Agobard became one of her fiercest critics;[140] in 833, he was one of the leaders of the rebellious bishops. Yet in that late summer or autumn of 829 Agobard's hopes still remained pinned on Louis, his *praelatus fidelis*, as they had all along, from the time when Agobard witnessed the proclamation of the *Ordinatio imperii* of 817.[141]

In the case of that other explicit critic of Judith, Radbert, the transition from *admonitio* to *increpatio* is discernable at different levels. First, there is the development of the *Epitaphium Arsenii* itself, which, however much affected by later redaction, still corresponds to two different phases in time: the late 830s and the late 840s or early 850s. Whereas denunciation of Louis, Judith or Bernard is practically absent in the first book, there is a veritable explosion of it in the second book, together with the full emergence of Wala as the 'type' of Jeremiah, delivering harsh diatribes at every possible occasion. As the monk Adeodatus remarked, 'I see that you deservedly called him another Jeremiah, because of the constancy of his faith and the harshness of his appearance – he who so audaciously rebuked (*invexit*) the emperor.'[142] Radbert's apologetic reassurance that Wala's intransigent *invectio* had in fact been inspired by a spirit of love indicates that according to some, at least, Wala had become far too strident, overstepping the mark.[143] One of the central issues in the *Epitaphium Arsenii* is the question whether Wala transgressed the boundary between acceptable admonition and offensive rebuke, a question which apparently also vexed some monks of Corbie. Radbert hints at different generations, with divergent styles of approaching those in authority: a modern one, full of fatuous adulation, and an older one, among whose exponents he counts himself, whose true fidelity and veracity also implied the willingness to be offensive, if need be. In the *Epitaphium*, Severus is the spokesman who most often voices these sentiments. Nowadays, he grumbles, nobody dares to speak out for the truth, everyone is afraid to offend. We are called rustic, savage and calumniators (*infamatores*). In return for our endeavours, our

---

[140] Ward, 'Agobard of Lyons'.
[141] A point made by Boshof, *Agobard*, p. 206; for the *seminarium discordiae*, see Astronomer, c. 43, p. 454.
[142] Radbert, *EA*, II, c. 2, p. 63: 'Ut sentio, non immerito tu alterum eum Hieremiam dicebas, ob constantiam fidei et frontis duritiam, qui tam audenter augusto invexit.' This is followed by one of Wala's diatribes to Louis on the military use of church property.
[143] Ibid., p. 24; ibid., c. 22, p. 53.

enemies give us hatred (*odium*). They look forward to our death so that we will stop accusing them and not criticise them; if we want to praise Wala, they think it is meant to blame them.[144] This is more than the usual and topical complaint about 'modern times'. Radbert referred to the painful soul-searching that continued long after the conflict of the 830s had subsided, and to a real problem, namely the partial disintegration of what had once been an acceptable style of admonition.

A good *admonitio*, old style, was delivered with eloquence and audacity, based on Scripture and the *patres*, and part of a strategy of *correctio* shared with its recipient(s), whose self-esteem would therefore remain unimpaired. Accordingly, the exalted royal recipient of such a formal admonition could display an impressive magnanimity in the face of unpleasant truths, or exhibit suitable humility of the kind that would enhance his stature. The royal personage might take the message seriously and act upon it, or at least provide a semblance of doing so, out of respect for the status of the admonisher. The ruler could also turn the tables and administer a dose of wholesome admonition to his bishops, his lay *fideles*, or even, on occasion, to the entire Christian people. When an admonition was delivered too sharply or not according to the accepted code, the royal recipient closed his ears and declared his displeasure at the offensive speaker.

In the turbulent years between 828 and 834, admonition turned vicious. One can observe this process in Agobard's letters and treatises, but also in Radbert's reminiscences of Wala in his guise as Jeremiah. Rapidly, *admonitio* developed into *increpatio* or even *invectio* and, finally, into blatant attempts at slander and defamation of the emperor and empress. Meanwhile, amid this deafening chorus, Louis had stopped listening. Yet without the emperor, there could be no orderly strategy of correction, and no effective admonition either, so this time-honoured mode of communication between the ruler and his *proceres* broke down. As we shall see, this was the breakdown in communication that brought matters to a military head in the summer of 833, and was the background to Louis's public penance in the autumn of this year. In 828–9, however, the years that are the subject of the next chapter, the rules of *admonitio* still pertained. Einhard, Wala and Agobard all produced it, with an unprecedented level of sophistication and literary skill. They expected to be listened to. Although Radbert cast Wala in the role of the visionary prophet Jeremiah, he could do so only with hindsight. Those who admonished Louis in 828–9 did so with conviction and hope, and without knowing what was to happen in the years that followed.

---

[144] Ibid., c. 21, p. 52.

4 The wages of sin (828–829)

Scapegoats: Matfrid and Hugh

In his *Poem* in honour of Louis the Pious, Ermold the Black depicted the splendour of a well-ordered imperial court.[1] With hindsight, those in Ermold's spotlight seem to have been dancing on the rim of a volcano. The Danish king Harald's baptism in Ingelheim took place in June 826, but less than two years later, at an assembly in February 828, the two *proceres* who in Ermold's *Carmen* flanked Judith – Matfrid and Hugh – had fallen into disfavour. In the summer of 827, these two men had led the troops of Pippin of Aquitaine, sent to the Spanish March to help those beleaguered by the rebel Aizo. Having allegedly done so 'more slowly than the urgency of the matter required', in February 828 both Hugh and Matfrid were deposed as counts, and deprived of all the *honores* – offices and lands – they held from Louis.[2] An investigation concerning Matfrid's supposed corruption was launched, and Odo, a kinsman of Bernard of Septimania, took his place as count of Orléans.[3] Bernard himself, who had come out of the Spanish debacle as a hero, was on the way up, and would be chamberlain in 829. The *Royal Frankish Annals* show that at the time, Bernard's appointment as *camerarius* was primarily associated with his performance in the Spanish March: he was 'Count Bernard of Barcelona, who earlier presided over the Spanish March'.[4]

The dishonouring punishment of the two most prominent lay magnates in the realm created an upheaval that can hardly be underestimated. Although opinions differ as to whether Matfrid and Hugh deliberately dragged their feet or were falsely accused of doing so, it is agreed that these two men had already been driven into opposition before their downfall in February 828. The machinations of Bernard and his family, allied with Judith and her party at the court, it is believed, had turned the two counts into political opponents of whom Louis wished to be rid at the earliest

---

[1] Ermold, *Carmen*, p. 176, lines. 2290–313.   [2] *ARF*, s.a. 827, p. 173.
[3] *Capitulare missorum* (829), MGH *Capit.* II, no. 188, pp. 9–10.   [4] *ARF*, s.a. 829, p. 177.

148

opportunity.[5] After all, it was Bernard's testimony in Aachen that helped
to condemn Matfrid and Hugh, and Bernard who, as the heroic defender
of Barcelona, came out of the affair looking purer than pure. All the same,
I doubt whether the crackdown of 828 was the result of long-standing
enmity. Except for the occasional glimpse restricted to a particular
moment in time, it is notoriously difficult to be certain about any alliances
at Louis's court, and the temptation to project these backwards in time
should be resisted. Contemporary sources record no sign of bad blood
between Matfrid and Hugh and their emperor until the Spanish defeat. In
the summer of 828 it was Lothar who filled the military breach created by
the disappearance of Matfrid and Hugh, being sent 'with many Frankish
troops' to the Spanish March. According to the court annalist, Lothar
halted in Lyons, where he waited for intelligence of the military movements of the Saracens, and conferred with his brother Pippin. Having
learned that the Saracens were afraid to enter the March, Pippin returned
to Aquitaine, and Lothar to his father in Aachen.[6] Was this foul play on the
part of Lothar and Pippin, in which Agobard had a hand as well, as has
been suggested?[7] Lack of reliable information seems to have been the
main problem, together with an enemy that struck suddenly, plundered
the March and then vanished again. It can only have added to the general
panic in Aachen. As far as I can see, Lothar remained faithful to his father
until August 829 or perhaps even longer, steering a difficult course
between ever more conflicting loyalties. After all, Lothar's father-in-law
was none other than Count Hugh of Tours. In June of 829, Walahfrid
Strabo could still hail the Emperor Lothar as 'the greatest hope of a holy
kingdom, Joshua, the heir with the prophetic name, who lacks nothing in
character, virtue and honour'.[8] The Astronomer, Thegan and Nithard all
pounced on Matfrid and Hugh as the perfidious instigators of all subsequent trouble between Louis and his sons.[9] Along with Ebo, they were the
scapegoats who were blamed for the sins committed collectively in 833.
This was also the main reason for their downfall in 828.

Contemporary authors presented this political fallout as the instanta-
neous reaction to an ignominious military defeat, and their view should be

---

[5] Collins, 'Pippin', pp. 378–81; Depreux, 'Matftrid', pp. 355–360; Brunner, *Oppositionelle Gruppen*, p. 107.
[6] *ARF*, s.a. 828, p. 175.   [7] Collins, 'Pippin', pp. 380–1.
[8] Walahfrid, *Carmina*, pp. 370–8, lines 158–64 on Lothar; '"De imagine Tetrici"', ed. Herren, p. 135.
[9] Thegan, c. 55, p. 250, on 'Hugh the Timid, and Matfrid and all the others who were foremost in that villainy'; Nithard, I, c. 3, p. 8 (in 829 Hugh and Matfrid caused Lothar to renege on his oath to protect his half-brother Charles); ibid., c. 4, p. 16 (Hugh, Matfrid and Lambert, who in 833 were *secundus post Lotharium*, began to quarrel).

taken more seriously.[10] In military terms, 827 was a disastrous year. Not only did the Franks bite the dust in Spain and Pannonia, but Harald, the newly baptised Danish king, was ousted by fellow-Danes.[11] Throughout the succeeding year, and well beyond, these military setbacks remained foremost in Louis's mind, and so did the need to raise an army to combat the 'enemies of God'. All the powerful enemies that had suddenly emerged in 827 were pagans. This held true of the Danes who had attacked the Christian ally of the Franks, but also of the Saracen Abu Marwan, who plundered the Spanish March with impunity, thanks to Aizo's treacherous dealings, and of the Bulgars and local Slavs who had devastated upper Pannonia, without Baldric of Friuli being able to stop them.[12] That the pagans were gaining the upper hand was taken as overwhelming evidence of God's displeasure, and of His punishment for the sins of His people. Matfrid, Hugh and Baldric were scapegoats whose eviction from the palace was one of the first gestures of *satisfactio* to the enraged deity, bearing the sins of the people from the camp.[13]

The embarrassment generated in court circles by the events of 827–8 is clear from the fact that the *Annales regni Francorum* mention Baldric by name, but not Hugh or Matfrid. 'Those who headed the army were found guilty and were deservedly punished by the loss of their *honores*' is all that was said, probably because the annalist was too scandalised by this part of the affair to mention the names of those involved.[14] Apparently, Baldric was in a different category: he was less prominent, and, after all, upper Pannonia was not exactly Spain, where Louis had in his youth won the victories recently celebrated again by Ermold's panegyric verse. The annalist's phrasing of the accusation against Matfrid and Hugh is worth noting: 'This would have been accomplished if the army had not arrived in the March much later than the situation required, due to the negligence of the leaders he [Pippin] had put in command.'[15] The unnamed *duces* of the army that set out for Spain were guilty (*culpabiles*) of *desidia*, or

---

[10] By this I mean the *Royal Frankish Annals* and the royal letters and communications of 828 discussed below.

[11] *ARF*, s.a. 827, p. 173.

[12] As the *ARF*, s.a. 828, p. 174, 'propter eius [Baldric's] ignaviam Bulgarorum excercitus terminos Pannoniae superioris inpune vastassent'. Like *desidia*, *ignavia* is an expression akin to *negligentia*. On Baldric, see Krahwinkel, *Friaul im Frühmittelalter*, pp. 192–7.

[13] The biblical story of the scapegoat can be found in Lev. 16.22; for a by now classic anthropological interpretation of this biblical story, see Douglas, *Purity and Danger*, pp. 41–57.

[14] *ARF*, s.a. 828, p. 174: 'qui excercitui praeerant, culpabiles inventi et iuxta merita sua honorum amissione multati sunt'.

[15] Ibid., p. 173: 'Quod ita factum esset, ni ducum desidia, quos Francorum exercitui praefecerat, tardius, quam rerum necessitas postulabat, is, quem ducebant, ad marcam venisset exercitus.'

slothfulness, an expression which, by the ninth century, had a considerable overlap with *negligentia*: the latter originally designated dereliction of
duty by those in charge of an office, and the former, moral failings; when
office-holding was increasingly defined as a 'ministry', its opposite, negligence, took on the meaning of political sin. Military failure or political
disaster would then be interpreted as God's punishment for such sins of
omission. Thus, it was said that Balderic's inactivity and cowardice had
allowed the Bulgar army to plunder with impunity.[16]

The three humiliating defeats of 827 had a crushing impact on the
palace in Aachen. Those who had watched the heavens could have seen
it coming, according to the annalist. 'As portents of this disaster (*clades*), it
was believed, battle lines were often seen in the sky, and these terrible
movements in the air that accompany lightning in the night.'[17] The key
word in this passage is *clades*, which refers not merely to a military defeat,
but also to a much more serious kind of disaster. In ninth-century texts on
God's anger and its various manifestations, *clades* is a standard expression
that usually designates some kind of a catastrophe caused by the collective
sins of the people, and, in particular, its rulers.[18] That the three major
setbacks against pagan enemies of 827 were seen as a divine punishment,
especially the one in Spain, is clear from the loaded terminology
employed: *culpabilis* had the connotation of sinfulness and justified
blame. Hugh and Matfrid were turned into scapegoats precisely because
they were the greatest lay magnates around. They, more than any other lay
primores at the time, shared the responsibility for the salvation of the
Christian people with their ruler; they, more than anyone except for
Louis himself, were therefore capable of creating the kind of 'scandal'
(*scandalum*) that would offend God.

As in the emperor's case, Matfrid's authority as a count and a *missus* was
perceived as divinely bestowed. This was acknowledged and underlined by
Agobard, who admonished Matfrid, saying that the omnipotent, eternal
and merciful God had elected him, Matfrid, to be the minister of the
emperor and the empire in these dangerous times.[19] The sins of magnates
of Matfrid's calibre, endowed with a ministry, ran a higher risk of scandal-
ising God and thus causing *clades*, a collective catastrophe. The fate of the
scapegoats of 828 was a clear sign of the penitential state going into over-
drive. What was once high-minded *admonitio* became feverish accusation.

---

[16] Ibid., p. 174: 'propter eius ignaviam Bulgarorum exercitus ...impune vastasset'.
[17] Ibid., p. 173: 'Huius cladis praesagia credita sunt viae multoties in caelo acies et ille
terribilis nocturnae coruscationis in aere discursus.'
[18] Blattmann, 'Ein Ungluck für sein Volk'.
[19] Agobard, *De iniustitiis*, p. 225.

The context of this mutual blaming and shaming was the very system of interconnected orders and ministries that depended on the emperor's comprehensive *ministerium*, as it had been formulated in the *Admonitio ad omnes ordines* of 825.[20] This entire order with its structure of interdependent offices (*ministeria*) was perceived as divinely bestowed and inspired, which meant that dereliction of duty counted as a serious sin, and a public sin at that. It was feared and expected that the negligence (*negligentia*) of office-holders would cause 'scandal' (*scandalum*), that is, a notorious offence that would elicit divine retribution. In such a case, an equally public satisfaction was in order. This was the basic principle of Carolingian public penance. Even if the scapegoats of 828 lost their offices and *honores* without any explicit penance being imposed, their downfall was definitely construed and enacted in terms of giving *satisfactio* to an enraged deity. Their negligence had created public disorder and therefore triggered God's wrath. As we shall see, the same perspective inspired the accusations against Louis the Pious in 833. Whereas he should have guaranteed the public peace and order for the people committed to God, he instead proved to be a 'disturber of the peace' (*perturbator pacis*). The discourse on disorder that emerged in 828 is unthinkable without the strong statements about the politico-religious order issued by Louis in the years before. Constant admonition and high expectations reinforced these conceptions of order, of course, and so did the just punishment of a sinful leadership; but there came a point where the singling out of prominent scapegoats by way of royal retribution might backfire. That point came in 828.

For those who later wrote in defence of Louis, Matfrid and Hugh remained the evil geniuses responsible for almost the entire crisis of 830–3.[21] It is interesting to see how the Astronomer used and adapted the crucial passages from the *Royal Frankish Annals* concerning the events of 828. Counts Hugh and Matfrid were now named and shamed, as having 'advanced more slowly and haltingly than was honourable (*serius meticulosiusque quam decuit occurentibus*)', allowing the Moors to devastate the region of Barcelona and Gerona. Just before this catastrophe, the Astronomer added, there appeared in the night sky terrible battle lines reddened with human blood that flashed with the colour of fire. In the Astronomer's version, Louis was not concerned with these terrible portents: 'The emperor learned of these things while he was receiving the annual gifts at Compiègne and he sent auxiliary forces to guard the above-mentioned March and announced that until the onset of winter he was going hunting in the forests around Compiègne and Quierzy.'[22]

---

[20] MGH *Capit.* I, no. 150, pp. 303–7.   [21] *AB*, s.a. 832, p. 18; Thegan, c. 36, pp. 220–2.
[22] Astronomer, c. 41, p. 440.

Hunting as usual – in other words, the situation was well under control. With regard to the crackdown on the scapegoats in February 828, the Astronomer was more explicit, however, damning the memory of Hugh and Matfrid as thoroughly as he could:

In February of the following winter there was a public assembly at Aachen, where, among other things, the business of the Spanish March created a furore, for having been recently conducted so timorously and ignominiously. When these issues were aired and investigated down to the smallest detail, the commanders who had been put in charge by the emperor were discovered to have been the instigators of this sin (*culpa*). Having stripped them of their offices, the emperor ordered them to make amends for their sin of slothfulness. Against Duke Baldric of Friuli it was alleged and proved that on account of his slothfulness and carelessness the Bulgars had devastated our land. He was expelled from his duchy and his power was divided among four of his counts. Even though the most mild spirit of the emperor was always naturally inclined to prefer mercy for sinners, it will soon become clear how those to whom he displayed these qualities abused his mercy by their cruelty; before long it will transpire how they repaid his gift of their life with the greatest disaster (*clades*) they were capable of inflicting on him.[23]

Although contemporary sources give no indication of any death sentence, the Astronomer repeated his allegation that Louis had been merciful beyond the call of royal duty, and that 'they' had repaid Louis's clemency with the worst *clades* they could come up with.[24] That 'they' were in fact Matfrid and Hugh is clear from the context. There is no reticence here because of a possible feeling of embarrassment, or any wish to spare the reputation of these two magnates. Having clarified that the failure of the Spanish campaign had put the entire assembly in a state of righteous anger, the Astronomer then used expressions suggesting that Hugh and Matfrid had committed a scandalous sin for which they needed to do penance. The verb *luere* is part of this penitential vocabulary, and so is the Astronomer's stress on Louis's clemency towards these two sinners (*peccatores*). Unrepentant and ungrateful, however, they then unleashed the greatest disaster of all: Louis's temporary removal from office and his public penance in 833. Well after the emperor's death, the scapegoats of 828 continued to fulfil their original role: by blaming them, as the 'satellites' of Satan, the burden of sin was transferred, and difficult questions did not have to be asked.

Clades: the offended deity

In Adalhard's address to the assembly of Attigny in 822, as recorded by Agobard, the grand old man cited Scripture on the connection between

---

[23] Ibid., c. 42, pp. 442–4.   [24] Ibid., c. 44, p. 458, and c. 45, p. 464.

sin and God's punishment. As Scripture had it, Adalhard declared, sins cause misfortunes, perturbations, disasters, and sterilities in the people (*peccata contrahunt infelicitates, perturbationes, clades et sterilitates in populos*).[25] Except in the more general sense of God's punishing sin by afflictions and plagues, there are no biblical sources for this alleged citation.[26] The closest textual parallel is Charlemagne's capitulary of Thionville (805). This stipulated that in the event of famine, disaster, pestilence, bad weather or any other tribulation (*fames, clades, pestilentia, inaequalitas aeris vel alia qualiscumque tribulatio*), 'men are not to await our decree but are straight away to pray for God's mercy'. It is followed by the instruction that 'in the present year, as regards the lack of food, everyone is to help their people to the best of their capability and is not to sell his corn at an excessively high price; and no foodstuffs are to be sold outside of the empire'.[27] The circulation of this text through Ansegis' *Collectio* and the otherwise wide dissemination of this capitulary explain why this text may have seemed as familiar as Scripture to Agobard, and so does the apparent frequency of instructions for collective atonement suggested by it.[28]

From the late 770s onwards, episodes of collective atonement by fasting, almsgiving and litanies surface in the sources.[29] A remarkable letter by Charlemagne to his wife Fastrada, sent in the autumn of 791, sheds some light on the then current strategies for obtaining divine favour. Charles reported to Fastrada on Pippin of Italy's recent victory against the Avars, and also on his own army's collective prayer and fasting.[30] The penitential aspect of Charlemagne's litanies is evident not only from the fasting and almsgiving, but also from the fact that the clergy who performed the liturgy went barefoot. Furthermore, the letter strongly emphasises the collective nature of the enterprise. Fasting and almsgiving could be reduced in the case of the weak and the poor, but the point was that everybody took part, in however modest a fashion. 'We all applied ourselves and with God's help we completed it,' as Charles wrote to Fastrada.[31] Getting God on one's side before battle was essential, and Charlemagne took preventive action.

---

[25] Agobard, *De dispensatione*, c. 2, p. 122.

[26] There are two instances of *clades* in Scripture: II Mach. 14.14 ('tunc gentes quae de Iudaea fugerant Iudam segregatim se Nicanori miscebant miserias et *clades* Iudaeorum prosperitates rerum suarum existimantes') and II Mach. 14.40 ('putabat enim si illum decepisset se *cladem* maximam Iudaeis inlaturum').

[27] *Capitulare missorum in Theodonis villa datum secundem generale*, c. 4, MGH *Capit.* I, no. 44, pp. 122–3. On Alcuin's letters, see Anton, *Fürstenspiegel*, pp. 67–79.

[28] See Mordek, *Bibliotheca*, pp. 1085–6.   [29] Mordek, 'Zweites Kapitular von Herstal'.

[30] MGH *Epp.* IV, no. 20, ed. E. Dümmler, pp. 528–9. On this letter and Fastrada's influence, see Nelson, 'The siting of the Council at Frankfort'. On intercessory prayer in wartime, see McCormick, 'Liturgy of war'.

[31] MGH *Epp.* IV, no. 20, p. 529.

In the case of such collective gestures of atonement, it was the involvement of the entire community that was the key to success. This becomes clear from a capitulary issued in Herstal in 778/9.[32] This capitulary ordered that each bishop should celebrate three masses and sing three Psalters, 'one for the lord king, the second for the army of the Franks, and the third for the present tribulation'; every priest should contribute three masses; bishops, monks, nuns and canons, as well as those living on their estates, should fast for two days. Almsgiving was allocated according to capacity, with bishops, abbots and abbesses giving one pound of silver, and others half of this, or less; the bishops, abbots and abbesses were also to take in four starving poor and feed them until harvest time – there was a severe famine – or only two or three, if they could do no more. For lay aristocracy, from powerful counts down to more modest vassals and those who had homesteads (*casati*) on their estates, there were also detailed instructions, so that those who had most wealth would give most alms. These laymen also had to feed the poor and to fast, but unlike the clergy, they could buy off their fasting, with rates according to the three categories among which they were divided: powerful counts paid most, 'mediocre counts' less, and minor vassals least. All this had to be performed before the feast of St John (24 June); the atonement was to benefit 'the king, the army of the Franks and the present tribulation'. By involving everyone in this comprehensive atonement, down to the peasants who had a dwelling on the estates, a *populus christianus* was created. Yet there was nothing universal about this particular Christendom. Its membership was determined by one's relation with the ruler, or with the king's *fideles*, regardless of whether these were bishops, abbots or abbesses, or counts or lesser royal vassals. This leadership constituted the 'orders of the realm', as they would come to be called in the *Admonitio ad omnes regni ordines* of 825, and it was the king upon whom the cohesion of these orders depended. Joint prayer was one of the ways in which the different elites integrated in the vast Frankish realm.

One copy of an entire batch of instructions to bishops on how to implore God's mercy, an imperial letter to Bishop Ghaerbald of Liège, survives. After due consultation with his *fideles*, both spiritual and secular, Charlemagne urged his bishops, and probably also his leading laymen, to organise three three-day fasts 'to be observed by all of us, without exception'.[33] According to the letter to Ghaerbald, the emperor had

---

[32] *Capitulare episcoporum*, MGH *Capit.* I, no. 21, pp. 51–2; Mordek, 'Zweites Kapitular von Herstal'.

[33] *Karoli ad Ghaerbaldum episcopum epistola*, MGH *Capit.* I, no. 124, pp. 244–6. For another reference to the famine of 805, prohibiting the sale of grain at usurious prices, see the *Capitulare missorum Niumagae datum* (March 806), c. 18, MGH *Capit.* I, no. 46, p. 132.

learned from his *fideles* that God's displeasure had manifested itself by all kinds of abnormal phenomena across the entire empire: barren soils causing famine, intemperate weather leading to crop failure, pestilence, and incursions of pagan enemies on an unprecedented scale:

> And we can most certainly conclude from these external signs that we who are obliged to suffer such ills outwardly are in every way displeasing inwardly to the Lord. Wherefore it seems to us wholly right that each of us should study to humble his heart in truth, and, on whatever occasion he should discover that he has offended God, whether in deed or in thought, should atone by doing penance, should lament by weeping and in the future should guard and protect himself to the best of his ability against these ills.[34]

As a witness to the penitential state, a polity united by its need to cleanse itself from sin by penance in order to restore its relation to God, this is an impressive statement. All the more surprising, then, that given Charlemagne's record, Louis did not initiate any such large-scale collective act of atonement until the winter of 828. As the imperial penance in Attigny shows, the burden of sin and penance had now shifted towards the ruler and those whose offices were derived from the royal *ministerium*. At the same time, however, the *Royal Frankish Annals* recorded an ever-increasing number of ominous signs and portents. From 820 onwards, every year until 829 (when the *ARF* ended) was marked by eclipses of the sun and moon,[35] earthquakes and tremors affecting Aachen,[36] unseasonable or abnormally destructive bad weather,[37] illness and famine among men and animals,[38] and other miraculous events that were perceived as warnings from God.[39] But in what way? In Thuringia in 822, the annalist informs us, a block of earth 50 feet long and 14 feet wide was mysteriously lifted and ended up 25 feet from its original location. This statement directly precedes the information that Duke Winigis of Spoleto converted to monastic life, and that the Emperor Louis confessed his sins publicly in Attigny.[40] Is this an instance of the narrative technique of parataxis, that is, suggesting meaning by juxtaposition, that is apparently typical of the *Royal Frankish Annals*?[41] This may pertain in some cases, but often one does not get further than detecting a possible stress on the significance of

---

[34] *Karoli ad Ghaerbaldum episcopum epistola*, pp. 245–6.
[35] *ARF*, s.a. 807 (3×), 809, 812, 818, 820, 824, 828 (2×).   [36] Ibid., 803, 817, 823, 829.
[37] Ibid., 801, 814, 820 821, 822, 823, 824, 829.   [38] Ibid., 801, 803, 810, 820, 823, 824.
[39] Ibid., 823, 825 (the fasting girl), 826, 827 (the arrival of martyrs from Rome), 827 (battle lines and shifting lights in the air); 828 (grain from heaven). For an insightful discussion of such portents ('Of Carolingian kings and their stars'), see Dutton, *Charlemagne's Mustache*, pp. 93–127; Collins, 'The "Reviser" revisited' noted a marked increase of portents in the *ARF* from 807 on, and has argued that this reflects a new author taking over.
[40] *ARF*, s.a. 822, pp. 157–8.   [41] See Dutton, *Charlemagne's Mustache*, p. 108.

some particular events. The main contemporary function of annals was to keep a readily accessible record of distant and recent events in the Frankish polity, and for all we know some of these were juxtaposed entirely haphazardly. On the other hand, the cumulative effect of a record like this should not be underestimated. If towards the end of the 820s it transpired from the *Annals* that the shifting earth in Thuringia had been preceded by pestilence among men and beasts, failed harvests and continuing floods in 820 and an extremely severe winter in 821, and followed in the next year by an earthquake in the palace in Aachen, a girl abstaining for ten months from food, twenty-three villages in Saxony burned by lightning, an appearance of the Virgin near Como, along with hailstorms, animals killed by lightning, great pestilence, and mortality, one might well become worried – especially given that the *mirabilia* kept coming relentlessly in the years thereafter. Perceived from Aachen, the world had become an unpredictable place, where divine intervention might strike at any moment, with an ever-increasing frequency. Even the fact that the girl who had fasted for ten months had started eating again merited a mention in the *Annals*, in the entry for 825. Here, it was said that she came from Commercy near Toul, and fasted from 823, 'as noted above in the report on that year', until November 'of the present year'. This suggests that this section was initially kept as a blow-by-blow account, and that the annalist's interest in such miraculous phenomena was becoming more acute. This must have both reflected and influenced the mood at the court, which was jittery, to say the least. This mood – What have we done to offend God? – was at the root of the scapegoating of Matfrid and Hugh. Towards the end of 827 (shifting lights, portents of defeat!), a moral panic had broken out which was to keep Louis's court and those connected with it in its grip for years to come.

The winter assembly of 828–829

During the winter assembly of 828–9, Einhard and Wala used all the authority of long royal service to plead for *correctio* and *emendatio*, using their learning but also their formidable powers of oratory. Both put their admonitions in writing, handing Louis 'booklets' prescribing correction, all bearing the authoritative stamp of divine inspiration: Scripture and the *patres*, angelic and demonic visions. Louis had originally planned to summon a general assembly in the summer of 828, but, as he and Lothar informed his *fideles* that winter, enemy activity had prevented them from doing so.[42] There had been a '*placitum* for a few days' in June

---

[42] *Epistola generalis* (828), p. 599.

in Ingelheim, but this had mainly served to send Lothar, Pippin and their army off to the Spanish March.[43] This was the first time that a proper summer assembly had been omitted during Louis's reign, and it was a bad sign. The big *conventus publicus* of the summer was of vital importance for the exercise of royal power: 'so long as the king could secure attendance, he could refill his coffers, exercise patronage, and maintain consensus at the same time'.[44] The absence of such a gathering in the summer of 828 was a clear sign of disorder. In order to cope with this, a restricted winter meeting of bishops and magnates was called in Aachen, for the winter of 828–9. In fact, this 'meeting of the great' (*conventus procerum*)[45] consisted of a series of shorter gatherings, during which the great and the good debated two related questions: how to raise sufficient military power to combat various enemies, and how to placate God, who was obviously offended.[46] Louis arrived at the palace in Aachen by 11 November 828, St Martin's Mass, to spend the winter, but in the end he remained there until 1 July, so busy with affairs of state (*necessaria regni*) that there was no time for hunting – another sure sign of crisis.[47] Einhard also travelled there, 'in accordance with the custom of wintering in the palace'.[48] Grumbling about being called away from the two Roman martyrs he had only recently installed in Seligenstadt, he made arrangements for his residence in Aachen to be stocked with all the food and drink needed for himself and his entourage. Einhard also hoped to reach Aachen by 11 November, with God's help, and 'if I am still alive'.[49]

By then, Einhard was about sixty years old and suffering from bad health,[50] yet his authority at Louis's court was unparalleled. During this winter meeting he was one of the main spokesmen, admonishing those present orally and by means of 'booklets' (*libelli*). These contained the miraculous visions that had occurred at his new shrine in Seligenstadt, authoritative admonitions from the hereafter. While Einhard attended the winter meeting of 828–9, his martyrs acted as an effective channel of communication with Heaven. He was constantly in touch with his sources of heavenly power, either by messenger or directly, as can be observed in

---

[43] *ARF*, s.a. 828, p. 174.

[44] Nelson, *Charles the Bald*, p. 50. See also Reuter, 'Assembly politics', and Airlie, 'Talking heads'.

[45] The expression is used by Einhard, *TMP*, III, c. 12, p. 252, lines 11–14.

[46] Radbert stressed the one aspect: the emperor gathered his senators and proceres, planning a *placitum* to find out *quid esset in quo Deus offensus esset, vel quibus placari posset operibus* (*EA*, II, p. 61).

[47] *ARF*, s.a. 828, p. 177.

[48] Einhard, *TMP*, III, c. 11, p. 251, lines 34–5; c. 12, p. 252, lines 11–14.

[49] Ibid., c. 12, p. 252, lines 11–14; Einhard, *Epistolae*, no. 5, p. 111.

[50] Stratmann, 'Einhards letzte Lebensjahre'.

his *Translatio*, in which Einhard put his own activities centre stage. Another grand old man held the limelight, and advised the meeting with a written document (*schedula*): Wala, who belonged to Einhard's generation.[51] These were men who had served Charlemagne before they became Louis's courtiers, of an age and experience that commanded respect. No wonder they played a prominent role during what was in fact a crisis meeting; but who else attended, except for the two emperors, Louis and Lothar? It is hard to tell. It was a mixed gathering, where lay magnates defended the merits of the use of ecclesiastical lands for military purposes, and some churchmen, though by no means all, opposed this practice.[52] Presumably Hilduin, Fridugisus and Helisachar were present, but from there on it is a matter of guesswork, especially because the disgrace of Matfrid and Hugh left a vacuum in the highest regions of the lay *proceres*. Was Bernard there, not as the 'second in the empire' he would later become, but as the saviour of Barcelona and an important magnate? We do not know. Ebo most likely attended, and so perhaps did Agobard, but there is no way to be certain.[53] Whatever the case, this was a small gathering that comprised only the leading men of the realm.[54] In the course of the winter, they deliberated with the emperor during a series of meetings; this is how Wala could retire to write his *schedula*, presenting it at the next gathering, and how Einhard could visit his saints in the course of the assembly.[55] Wala resided at the palace, and so did Einhard, in his own well-stocked *mansio*; the winter meeting itself was referred to, with some pride, as 'the *comitatus*'. This was the court as a human configuration: the emperor attended by his eldest son and his *proceres*.[56]

As Einhard was at pains to point out, his presence at this meeting was indispensable. In the very first chapter of the *Translatio* he introduced

---

[51] Radbert, *EA*, II, p. 61. Weinrich, *Wala*, p. 13, situates Wala's birth between 772 and 780, with a preference for a date closer to 772; Depreux, *Prosopographie*, p. 390, follows Weinrich.

[52] Radbert, *EA*, II, c. 2, pp. 63–4.

[53] See Depreux, *Prosopographie*, pp. 21–39, 46–64. Possible lay magnates: Donatus, count of Melun and *missus* to Spain in 827 (Depreux, pp. 160–2); Hildebrand (unknown count and *missus* to Spain in 827); Gerold, count in east Bavaria, possibly present in February 828 and instrumental in Baldric's deposition (Depreux, p. 211); Odo, count of Orléans, Bernard's kinsman who replaced Matfrid.

[54] *De ordine palatii*, c. VI (30), pp. 84–6; cf. Nelson, *Charles the Bald*, pp. 45–50.

[55] Radbert, *EA*, II, p. 60: 'Inde ad comitatum rediens, omnia coram augusto et coram cunctis ecclesiarum praesulibus et senatoribus proposuit singillatim diversorum ordinum officia, excrescentibus malis, et ostendit cuncta esse corrupta vel depravata.' On Einhard returning to the court, see Einhard, *TMP*, I, c. 15, p. 245.

[56] Einhard especially used this expression when he wished to emphasise that he himself was part of this inner and restricted circle; see Einhard, *TMP*, I, c. 1; II, cc. 1, 7, 11; III, cc. 11, 12, 19.

himself as 'still part of the palace and occupied with the business of the world'.[57] By the time he finished the *Translatio*, late in 830, he had retired from active duty at the court, in order to devote himself entirely to his martyrs in Seligenstadt.[58] The *Translatio* reflects on the discussions about *correctio* that had flared up in the winter of 828, and on Einhard's own contribution to the winter meeting; at the time of writing, the text itself was also meant to have an impact on this ongoing debate.[59] But above all, its four books sing the praises of God's omnipotence, which fired the miraculous powers of Einhard's very own martyrs, Peter and Marcellinus.

From the start, the emperor and the court loom large in the *Translatio*. The first of its four books relates how the martyrs were found in Rome, and then transferred, with their express consent and all due honour, to Francia, where they received a new and fitting reliquary. This book ends with Einhard's return to the palace at Aachen, shortly after 18 January, presumably to attend the assembly that deposed Hugh and Matfrid. A royal charter supporting the cult of his saints reached Einhard on the road, so 'he returned to the palace in a highly exultant mood'.[60] The second one opens with Einhard, who, early in the morning in the palace, confronted Hilduin, who admitted that his men had stolen part of the relics Einhard had procured in Rome, and diverted them to his own abbey of St-Médard. It was even worse, for Einhard remembered a rumour spread by 'those of St Sebastian' (Hilduin's Roman martyr), who claimed that already in Rome itself they had stolen the relics in question.[61] The reputation of Einhard and his own martyrs was at stake, which is why this relic theft is so central to the narrative. Einhard demanded the truth, which yielded a *spontanea confessio* on Hilduin's part. Grudgingly, he gave in.[62] Eight days after Easter, when the king was out hunting, Hilduin had the relics

---

[57] Einhard, *TMP*, I, c. 1, p. 239: 'adhuc in palatio positus et negotiis saecularibus occupatus'.

[58] The last miracle described is dated to August 830. According to Dutton, *CC*, p. xxiv, Einhard's attack on Hilduin means that the text was written after the latter's exile in September 830. The letter in which Einhard asked Louis's permission to remain with his saints is Einhard, *Epistolae*, no. 10, ed. Hampe, pp. 11–114; Dutton, *CC*, pp. 163–4. This letter is phrased like an *admonitio* to the emperor, who was urged to fulfil his promises of gifts to the martyrs. See also Tischler, *Einharts Vita Karoli*, pp. 173–81.

[59] Heinzelmann, '"Translatio"'; Smith, '"Emending evil ways"', p. 205: 'Written at the end of 830, the *Translation and Miracles* was thus a renewed call for penance and correction in the aftermath of that spring's revolt against Louis the Pious.'

[60] Einhard, *TMP*, I, c. 15 , p. 245: 'ad palatium sumus cum magna exultatione regressi'. Does the plural indicate that his wife Imma accompanied him? This possibility cannot be excluded. For a detailed and enlightening analysis of this first book, see Heinzelmann, '"Translation"', pp. 277–84.

[61] Geary, *Furta Sacra*, pp. 45–9, 118–20.

[62] Einhard, *TMP*, II, c. 1, pp. 245–6, with the truth of the theft and the return of the relics set out in cc. 2–3.

transferred from St-Médard to the altar of St Mary's at Aachen. From here, Einhard took them to a ready-made chapel in his own house in Aachen, where big crowds gathered from Aachen and its vicinity.[63] When Hilduin told Louis about this, the emperor wanted to come to Einhard's improvised chapel, but Hilduin suggested that Louis would have the relics installed in St Mary's once more. This happened, and Louis prayed humbly to them, presenting them with a small estate, while Judith gave them a belt made of gold and jewels weighing 3 pounds. Then the relics returned to Einhard's own chapel, where they remained for forty days. The emperor went hunting, and Einhard returned to Seligenstadt with his relics.[64] This became a triumphant journey full of miracles, but Marcellinus made it clear that he was not best pleased at his body being divided between two receptacles, even if these were in the same church at Seligenstadt. By November 828, when Einhard readied himself to travel as usual to the palace in Aachen, one of the guards had a scary vision that made it patently clear that Einhard could not do so until he had joined each portion of Marcellinus' relics to the rest of his body.[65]

The winter meeting of 828–9 is discussed in the middle of the third book of the *Translatio*, and so are the two *libelli* with visionary advice offered by Einhard to the emperor and the attendant great men.[66] Both of the visions recorded in these 'booklets' had occurred in Seligenstadt, because of Peter and Marcellinus. Once the deliberations in Aachen had started, Einhard's cleric Ratleigh turned up, bearing a *libellus* with *capitula* issued by the archangel Gabriel himself. In the guise of the martyr Marcellinus, the archangel had appeared to the blind man Alberic, exhorting him to remember everything that Gabriel was about to tell him: 'For I want these things to be written down and shown by your lord [Einhard] to the emperor Louis who is to read them. But they are not just for him to know, for these things are extremely important to that ruler into whose kingdom these martyrs have come by divine command.'[67] Having dictated 'twelve *capitula* or more', and four additional ones, Gabriel/ Marcellinus ordered Alberic to turn this into a book and to take it to his lord, who was at that time resident at the palace. This was divine authority being transmitted through a very precise chain of command, with the verb *praecipere* as the key word. Gabriel ordered (*praecepit*) Alberic to relate the *capitula* and have them turned into a booklet; he was then to command

[63] Ibid., cc. 3–5, pp. 246–7. On the rivalry over Roman relics betweeen Hilduin and Einhard, see Smith, 'Emending evil ways'.

[64] Einhard, *TMP*, II, c. 6, p. 247.   [65] Ibid., c. 9, p. 247.

[66] Ibid., III, cc. 12–14, pp. 252–4.

[67] Dutton, *CC*, p. 2; Einhard, *TMP*, III, c. 13, pp. 252–3.

(*praecipias*) Einhard, on the authority of the martyrs, to take the booklet as quickly as he could to the emperor. 'Who do you think I am who commands (*praecipio*) you to do this?' Gabriel asked. The angel had ordered (*praecepi*) these commands to be written down because it was God's will that, through the authority of the martyrs (*ex auctoritate martyrum*) these would be conveyed without delay to the emperor. This vision revealed nothing less than precepts and mandates (*praecepta et mandata*) to be obeyed by the Frankish leadership.

As consultations at the palace proceeded, another *libellus* was brought from Seligenstadt by Ratleigh, for Einhard to polish and present to the gathering. This time there was no question of precepts and mandates. Instead, these were the pronouncements and arguments (*verba et ratiocinationem*) of a certain demon who called himself Wiggo. He had spoken through the mouth of a sixteen-year-old girl, who was mad and had therefore come to the shrine of the martyrs to seek a cure. When the priest had recited the exorcism and questioned her in Germanic, the only language she knew, the demon answered with her voice, in Latin, that he was an assistant and disciple of Satan. With eleven companions, he had wreaked havoc in the kingdom of the Franks for some years, destroying crops, killing cattle and unleashing plagues and pestilence.[68] Responsibility for all the adversity and evil that the people had deservedly suffered was claimed by this Wiggo and his band. Asked by the priest why he had been granted such power, the demon answered: 'Because of the wickedness of the people and the various sins of those who are set over them, who love gifts and not justice.'[69] Then followed a long list of all the sins committed by the people and their *rectores* daily, headed by perjury, drunkenness, adultery, murder, theft and rapine – but this was only the beginning. There were also greed, pride and vainglory, mutual hatred and distrust, a reluctance to pay tithes or give alms, the use of false weights and other frauds, and a stubborn refusal to observe Sunday and the feast days. Because of their disobedience to God's commands and the utter neglect of what the faithful had promised in baptism, Wiggo and his companions had been given the liberty to make them pay, the demon declared – still in fluent Latin through the mouth of the girl. Yet the demon was unable to withstand the might of the martyrs; he was forced to leave the girl, who suddenly could speak Latin no more. 'Oh grief!', exclaimed Einhard; 'upon what misery our times have fallen, that not good men but evil demons are the *doctores*, and the instigators of vice and the persuaders of crimes are the ones who admonish us about our correction.'[70]

---

[68] Ibid., c. 14, p. 253.   [69] Ibid.   [70] Ibid., p. 254.

These perilous times had turned a demon into a *doctor*, someone who instructed the people and their leadership concerning God's truth. Wiggo did so in the language of sacred truth, Latin; he was no independent power, but acted, with his companions, 'as we were ordered', and because they were granted the liberty to do so. In other words, this demon was an emissary of an offended deity who had lost all patience with the multifarious sins of the Franks. Significantly, it was the *regnum Francorum* that was identified as deserving demonic punishment. The kingdom of the Franks was defined as a community of sinners; by implication, its ruler bore a grievous responsibility, yet he did not do so alone. These were still collective sins (*iniquitates*), committed by the people and its divinely constituted leadership. The list of portents and calamities mentioned by Einhard is a familiar one, recorded in the *Royal Frankish Annals* in the first three decades of the ninth century. The two *libelli* offered by Einhard to Louis contain visions that work like mirror images: the first was transmitted by an angel, and the second by a demon. The first was phrased in the mandatory idiom of royal capitularies, the other in the exhortative language of the *admonitio*, yet both conveyed the same message: repent before it is too late![71] The notion that Wiggo represented Louis, because of their similarity of names (*Hludovicus*), can safely be discarded.[72] To write fervent pleas for correction with Louis as a central member of the intended audience, and then to portray him as a demon at the same time, makes no sense. As for the *libellus* with Gabriel's precepts, Einhard indeed remarked that Louis accepted it and read it, 'but of those things the booklet ordered or admonished him to do, he managed to accomplish precious few'.[73] This is not Einhard writing off Louis as a failure, but the grand old courtier in his admonitory mode, as he also was in early 830 when he wrote a letter to Lothar that has been described as 'rude'.[74] Feeling duty bound to admonish Lothar about his salvation, Einhard warned the king against forsaking the obedience he owed his father and allowing himself to be persuaded by men who had their own interests

---

[71] The vision of Wiggo contains the two key elements of the so-called Letters from Heaven: repentance and the observance of Sunday. Condemned by Charlemagne (*Admonitio generalis*, c. 78, p. 60), these letters had a long history in the medieval and modern West. See Delahaye, 'Note sur la légende'; Priebsch, *Letters from Heaven*.

[72] Differently, Dutton, *Politics of Dreaming*, p. 97.

[73] Einhard, *TMP*, III, c. 13, p. 252: 'Et ille quidem suscepit atque perlegit. Sed de his quae per hunc libellum facere iussus vel admonitus fuerat perpauca adimplere curavit.' The story of the *Annals of Fulda* (874) on Louis in purgatory, asking his son of the same name for assistance by prayer, may well be based on the information provided by Einhard's *TMP*; see *AF*, s.a. 874, pp. 81–2.

[74] Wickham, *The Inheritance of Rome*, ch. 17.

at heart.[75] Here we have the 'persuaders' inciting others to crimes mentioned in the *Translatio*. In Einhard's letter to Lothar, their crimes were
clearly defined: 'For I believe that it is not hidden from your Prudence
how great an abomination it is in God's eyes for a son to be rebellious,
since God commanded through Moses that such a man should be stoned
to death by all the people, as you can read in Deuteronomy [21.20–1].'[76]
Far from being a rude letter to Lothar, however, this was Einhard warning
the eldest son and his entire circle that rebellion would mean God's anger
and peril for their souls: 'I love you, God knows, and therefore I admonish you so faithfully; you should not take into account the low status of the
person who admonishes, but rather the salvific nature of his advice.'[77] In
doing so, Einhard resorted to a shared discourse of admonition current at
Louis's court, which I discussed in the previous chapter. This discourse
had its key biblical texts: with regard to Lothar and the sin of filial
disobedience, not only Einhard but also Thegan and Hraban Maur
cited this forceful passage from Deuteronomy, expecting to convince
their readers.[78] In this context of moral alertness and dire warning, the
martyrs had their own role to play: 'In the fourteenth year of the Emperor
Louis's reign, with Christ's favour, the Lord deigned, because of the relics
of the saints, to reveal miracles and wonders in the very palace of the king
in order to strengthen the faith of his Christian people, just as he had at
the birth of the church.'[79] Through Einhard's very own martyrs, the
Frankish court was connected to the early church.[80] It was in this context
that Einhard's two *libelli* entered the discussion, counselling repentance
and revealing his martyrs' efficacy as mediators between God and mankind. Thus, together with Wala, Einhard took centre stage in the debates
of that winter.

With Wala, we are back with Radbert's intriguing *Epitaphium Arsenii*. Most of
this author's commentary on the turbulent period that started in 828 is
contained in the second book, which may have been completed as late as
the 850s.[81] Unlike Einhard, Radbert had the benefit of hindsight, which in
his case was more like a curse. In his second book, his cast of confabulating
monks had partly changed, and those who stayed had become older, sadder

---

[75] Einhard, *Epp.*, no. 11, pp. 114–15; trans. Dutton, *CC*, pp. 147–8.
[76] Dutton, *CC*, p. 146; Einhard, *Epp.*, no. 11, pp. 115.   [77] Ibid.
[78] Thegan, c. 53, p. 246; Hrabanus Maurus, *De reverentia filiorum erga patres et subditorum erga reges*, ed. E. Dümmler, MGH *Epp.* V, pp. 404–15.
[79] Einhard, *TMP*, IV, c. 10, p. 259; trans, Dutton, *CC*, p. 117.
[80] On the *Historia tripartita* as a connection with the early church, see above, chapter 3, pp. 129–30.
[81] See above, chapter 2, pp. 103–4.

and wiser. Apart from the narrator, Radbert's alter ego Paschasius, and Adeodatus, the young interrogator of the first book who was now a grown man, a third monk became part of the *confabulatio*: the beardless Theofrastus, who took over from Adeodatus as the junior interlocutor.[82] Having announced the overarching theme of the book, that is, the lament for Wala and the uncovering of truth,[83] the narrator Paschasius was prompted by Adeodatus, no longer young, but still asking good questions – such as, How had this great crisis started? Nobody with his wits about him, Adeodatus said, would believe that such things could have happened without God having been offended.[84] This elicited a diatribe on Paschasius' part. Well before it had become apparent that the entire empire was beset by evil, he explained, God's just judgement had already castigated the people with daily calamities and scourges. Hence the emperor with his senators and *proceres* had wondered why it was that the offended divine majesty had cautioned his people so intensively and for so long, according to Scripture's testimony that 'vexation alone shall make you understand what you hear' (Is. 28.19).[85] Before the next assembly (Worms 829) was to take place, all were to investigate wherein God was offended, and how he could be placated.[86] This was the cue for 'our Arsenius' to respond to this imperial order, searching both Scripture and the *patres* to ascertain in which respects Christ's *ecclesia* had become depraved, and by which carnal acts the entire people (*universus populus*) had become corrupted.[87]

To this end, and to aid his own memory, he edited a small booklet (*schedula*) in which he recorded all the vices of this kingdom, and so circumspectly, that none of his adversaries could deny all this. Returning to the meeting, in the presence of the emperor and all the prelates and magnates, he expounded on all the duties of the various orders. He showed how evil was encroaching and all was corrupt and depraved.[88]

In Radbert's confabulation, it was young Theofrastus who formulated how God had shown his anger: by disaster (*clades*), pestilence, famine,

---

[82] Radbert, *EA*, II, p. 60: 'Nolo mirari, frater, si te glabrum ad hoc Adeodatus elegit'; *glabrum* means 'hairless' and can therefore also mean 'tonsured', but this would not distinguish this young monk from his fellows. Radbert's alter ego Paschasius calls himself *decrepitus* in this passage, which also suggests that book II was written at a much later stage than its predecessor.

[83] Ibid.: 'threnos et veritatem'.

[84] Ibid., p. 61: 'qui credat haec sine offensa Dei in populo contigisse'.

[85] Is. 28.19 (*sola vexatio intellectum dabit auditui*) is cited in the longer version of the *Epistola generalis* of December 828: MGH *Capit.* II, no. 185, p. 5; on this letter see below, 'Letters from the palace'.

[86] For a clear and convincing analysis of this chronology, see Ganshof, 'Am Vorabend'. Weinrich, *Wala*, pp. 92–3, presents a different and, to my mind, mistaken view.

[87] Radbert, *EA*, II, c. 1, p. 61.   [88] Ibid.

intemperate weather and terrifying visions. These were the sins of the realm (*peccata regni*), but never before had so many saints pervaded the realm to such an extent, nor had their signs reached so many people, believers and unbelievers.[89] This is the same theme one encounters in Einhard's *Translatio*, and probably a reference to Einhard's message to the winter assembly: terrifying disasters and dazzling miracles were to awaken the people, and above all its leaders. Radbert, who had been present himself, was the narrator of Wala's thoughts and actions during the gathering of 828–9. Like another Jeremiah, with divine authority on his side, Wala made it clear to his distinguished audience wherein they had offended God. The root of the problem, Wala argued, was the imbalance between the two orders within God's *ecclesia*. A disciplined order and a stable *respublica* depended on distinct offices that were fulfilled by each of the two *ordines*. First, there was the 'inner' and divine one, then the 'outer' and human one; without any doubt, it was by these two orders that the stability of the entire *ecclesia* was governed. The ruler should not stray beyond the competence of his office and thereby neglect this, for he would be accountable to God at the last judgement. Bishops and other clerics charged with the cult of God should do the same and concentrate on divine affairs. The king should appoint *rectores* who were capable of ruling God's sacred people, not according to their own wishes and urges, but according to their love of God and justice. He then admonished Louis to heed his warning:

Unless you follow this command, king, a worse punishment will hit you, and if God is ignored, all will perish, for they are one in you. Do not neglect the care of anything, for it is in you alone, as Solomon says, that the entire stability of the realm is anchored; do not, however, interfere with divine affairs any more than is needed.[90]

The interference in question was royal infringement on ecclesiastical property. This was one of the central points put on the agenda by Wala in the winter of 828–9. The ruler's use of ecclesiastical lands to reward his followers with benefices or *honores*, thus maintaining his military forces, had been standard practice since at least Charles Martel.[91] In the reigns of Pippin and Charlemagne, no protest was heard on the part of wealthy ecclesiastical institutions whose lands served to maintain armies. In spite of a capitulary permitting the free election of abbots in 818/19, Louis continued the practice of granting ecclesiastical lands to his followers.

---

[89] Ibid., pp. 61–2.   [90] Ibid., p. 63.
[91] Reuter, '"Kirchenreform"'; De Jong, 'Carolingian monasticism', pp. 664–6; more generally, S. Wood, *Proprietary Church*.

Some attempt at regulation was made, which led to the emergence of the *abbas laicus* as a separate category, and a division between the lands of the abbot and those destined for the upkeep of the community. Nonetheless, laymen in control of ecclesiastical property remained a familiar phenomenon.[92] After Agobard had delivered his criticism of this practice at Attigny in 822, Louis had a hard time smoothing the ruffled feathers of the lay magnates who saw their benefices endangered. With some difficulty, a compromise was struck in 823, but now it was Wala who argued along lines similar to those of Agobard six years before.[93] He asked Louis why he gave away the *honores ecclesiarum* that had been legitimately consecrated to God to serve the poor. Ecclesiastical property should not be seized without due consultation of the *clerus et plebs Dei*. The king had his *respublica* in order to sustain his army, and the same held true for Christ and that 'other republic' (*altera respublica*).

These two republics were meant to be complementary: in order to work together, they should be distinct from each other. The gist of this section of the *Epitaphium* is that this balance had been disturbed, and needed to be redressed. The two orders, ecclesiastical and secular, shared an equal burden of sin; both had to atone for having offended God. The king or emperor should be 'bound to his office', and would be called to account by God at the last judgement for having maintained the balance of and distinction between the divine and human spheres.[94] The monk Theofrastus daringly interjected that without divine providence no ruler could be saved, for there was nothing sweeter to the powers of this world than booty stolen from churches, but Paschasius corrected the young man. Indeed, God's wrath had struck our princes because worldlings (*saeculares*) got their hands on His domain, yet bishops and other priests were also to blame. They had shamelessly and greedily transferred what should be internal and divine, namely the cult of God, to the sphere of the external, although it had been written that no man who was a servant of God should entangle himself with secular business (II Tim. 2.4).[95] All this had led to presumption and confusion, with churchmen anxiously

---

[92] The granting of ecclesiastical property as a benifice to laymen was an issue different from that of lay abbots. These certainly were discussed in 828, but the really sharp critique started only in the 840s; Wala was not a fierce critic of lay abbots. See Felten, *Äbte und Laienäbte*, pp. 288–304.

[93] See Agobard, *De dispensatione*; Boshof, *Agobard*, pp. 86–90.

[94] Radbert, *EA*, II, c. 2, p. 62: the *ordo disciplinae* and *status respublicae* reflect the distinction between the various *officia* (read: ministries): *intus divina, exterius humana* .... *Ut sit imperator et rex suo manicpatus officio*. He needs to be vigilant, *qui pro his omnibus adducet eum Dominus in iudicio*.

[95] Radbert, *EA*, II, c. 2, pp. 63–4; II Tim. 2.4: 'nemo militans inplicat se negotiis saecularibus ut ei placeat cuise probavit'.

defending property that was being despoiled by laymen who claimed the support of royal authority.

This was how Wala argued in the presence of the king, said Paschasius, and there was nobody who could deny it. One can hear the chorus of detractors in the background, but one also gets a glimpse of how these men actually talked when they were formally in session. A discussion had broken out, especially among the clerics present, on how to guarantee the 'dignity and honour of the churches' (*dignitas et honor ecclesiarum*) – as if they had never read the decrees of the holy fathers, Paschasius added with disdain. Against Wala's counsel to be guided by the *auctoritas divina* at all times, and to correct what diverged from Scripture and the fathers, the lay magnates objected that ecclesiastical property was needed to sustain the armies. Wala countered that the king often used the *facultates ecclesiarum* for himself and his men, but according to the fathers this was anathema; to take away gifts consecrated to the altar was a sacrilege.[96] If it is true, Wala told Louis, that the *respublica* cannot survive without recourse to the wealth of churches, it should be used in an orderly fashion, according to Christian principles: for example, when it was needed for defence, rather than because of robbery (*ob defensionem magis, quam ad rapinam*). Whoever committed such robbery ran the risk of being cursed by the maledictions of the fathers. It was up to the bishops to apportion land for military use in a reasonable fashion, and not to allow themselves to get involved too much in secular pomp.[97]

Radbert wanted to eradicate the notion that Wala/Jeremiah had been one of these radicals who maintained that churches should retain merely the landed wealth needed for the upkeep of the clergy, leaving the rest to the *militia saecularis*. This misrepresentation was voiced by the youth Theofrastus, and immediately refuted by Paschasius, who exclaimed that Wala would never have done anything so rash. All 'our Arsenius' had wanted was that nobody should sin against God.[98] The theft of church property was not the only offence he discussed in the presence of the emperor; there were other matters, such as lay abbots, uncanonically granted bishoprics, and, above all, the incongruous position of the palace chaplains (*capellani*). Wala chastised this *militia clericorum in palatio* for their worldly ambition and gain, and especially because they were not a proper ecclesiastical order. These chaplains lived neither under a monastic rule, nor canonically, under a bishop.[99] These clerics, who belonged,

---

[96] Jonas's compilation of 836 supports the same position; cf. *Epistola concilii Aquisgranensis*, MGH *Conc.* II/2, pp. 725–67. Wala's *scedula* of 828 must have looked quite similar: biblical and patristic ammunition to be fired at one's political opponents.

[97] Radbert, *EA*, II, c. 3, pp. 64–5.   [98] Ibid., p. 64.

[99] Ibid., c. 5, p. 66; Fleckenstein, *Die Hofkapelle*, p. 35.

first and foremost, to the palace, represented an anomaly that spelled dangerous *confusio*. These objections, by the way, could well have been those of Radbert himself, who had to cede his abbacy to one of these privileged palatine clerics.[100] In between exiles, Wala did not lack the access to the ruler that inspired so much envy in other clerics. On the other hand, the ecclesiastical reforms Louis initiated from 816 onwards inevitably made the position of palatine clerics an ambiguous one. At least theoretically, there was no longer any legitimate place for a religious community that did not live under the authority of either an abbot or a bishop. The palatine clerics continued to exist, but they were open to criticism from their less fortunate brethren.[101]

At this point, Radbert made it clear that Jeremiah's mission of that winter remained unaccomplished, so he inserted a *confabulatio* about Wala's motives and those of his opponents. Adeodatus opened this discourse. How was it possible that someone who was so humble could speak so constantly in the presence of the emperor, amid so many prelates and magnates? This gave Paschasius the opportunity to enlarge upon Wala's position. No authority could divert him from the love of Christ, his fatherland and people, the church, and his loyalty to the emperor (*caritas Christi, dilectio patriae et populi, amor ecclesia, fides imperatoris*). He anticipated the future, so he never hesitated to speak his mind on issues that his opponents, by implication, had utterly neglected: the well-being of the realm, the salvation of the people, the stability of the religious communities and the safeguarding of the peace.[102] Adeodatus then embarked upon a diatribe against a leadership who had behaved like bandits, up to the present day; the sinfulness and foolhardiness of these people had made it impossible for any ruler to explain the ways of the state regarding justice.[103] Paschasius joined in with a lament about the general loss of authority and integrity that afflicted the *respublica* of his day and age. Since nobody had listened to Arsenius or the voice of God, their prosperity had turned into adversity, and their strength had been broken; the most eloquent had become mute, for those speaking and acting did so without moral virtue; good counsel had eluded them, and all wisdom had been devoured.[104] In the winter of 828–9, Wala saw it all coming, but, laid low by a fierce bout of diarrhoea, he kept silent from then on until God's

---

[100] Ganz, *Corbie*, p. 22; Nelson, *Charles the Bald*, p. 179.
[101] De Jong, 'Carolingian monasticism', pp. 629–34, with reference to older literature.
[102] Radbert, *EA*, II, c. 5, p. 66: 'Propter quae nunquam, quia futura praeviderat, dubitavit sententiam pro statu regni, pro salute populi, pro stabilitate ecclesiarum, et religione pacis dignam dicere etsi quibuslibet displicuisset.'
[103] Ibid.; Nelson, 'Kings without justice'.   [104] Radbert, *EA*, II, c. 6, p. 66.

judgement struck and the extent of the divine punishment became evident.[105]

Despite Radbert's gloomy hindsight, during that winter in Aachen there still existed a consensus that the offended deity should and could be placated by an energetic correction of the sins that had upset the order in the realm. With this in mind, *missi* were sent into the empire and councils were convened. It is to the letters and instructions issued from the palace during the early months of 829 that I now turn.

Letters from the palace

Decision-making got under way quickly. From December 828 onwards, a series of letters and instructions were issued from Aachen, which shed further light on these consultations and their outcome.[106] The first was the summons to organize councils (*conventus episcoporum*) in Mainz, Paris, Lyons and Toulouse. Otgar of Mainz, Ebo of Rheims, Agobard of Lyons and Noto of Toulouse were to preside over these gatherings; altogether sixteen archbishops were explicitly named and ordered to attend, together with their suffragans.[107] For Radbert, these reform councils were merely an empty gesture to please the emperor,[108] yet their brief reads like a summary of Wala's agenda: the bishops should investigate how and why the two orders had strayed from the right path (*a recto tramite*). On the one hand, the conduct of the rulers and the rest of the *populus* should be scrutinised, and on the other that of the *pastores*. The councils should meet on the Octave of Pentecost (23 May); on the Octave of Easter (4 April) a group of *missi* should start their inquiries, gathering information that would presumably also benefit the bishops who had by then gathered. The outcome of all this hectic activity was apparently awaited with some anxiety, for on no account should the findings of the councils be made public before the appointed time. The bishops should elect a secretary (*notarius*) from their midst to record their decisions, who was to

---

[105] Ibid., p. 67.

[106] The list, established and commented on by Ganshof, 'Am Vorabend', pp. 47–51, is as follows: 1. The *Constitutio de synodis anno 829 in regno Francorum habendis* (Dec. 828; MGH *Capit.* II, no. 184). 2. *Hludowici et Hlotharii epistola generalis* (Dec. 828; MGH *Capit.* II, no. 185). 3. *Capitula ab episcopis in placito tractanda* (beginning of 829; MGH *Capit.* II, no. 186); *Capitula de missis instruendis* (beginning of 829; MGH *Capit.* II, no. 187); *Capitulare missorum* (beginning of 829, MGH *Capit.* II, no. 188); *Tractoria de coniectu missis dando* (beginning of 829; MGH *Capit.* II, no. 189). To this should be added the prologue to the *Episcoporum ad Hludowicum imperatorem relatio* (summer 829; MGH *Capit.* II, no. 196).

[107] *Constitutio de synodis*, MGH *Capit.* II, no. 184, p. 2.   [108] Radbert, *EA*, II, c. 4, p. 65.

be sworn to silence.[109] It was Jonas of Orléans who was chosen for this important function. He not only drafted and edited the decisions of the council of Paris, but probably also prepared the report (*relatio*) that recapitulated the findings of all four ecclesiastical gatherings.[110] As for the appointed time (*tempus constitutus*), it is generally assumed that this was the assembly in Worms in August 829, but, given the urgency and secrecy of the matter, an immediate report to the emperor while he was still residing in Aachen seems more likely. This would also explain what the 'diverse business' was that kept Louis in Aachen until 1 July.[111] The various reports had to be gathered, digested and turned into recommendations for the *conventus generalis* in Worms.

There was another letter, also sent in December 828 by the August Emperors Louis and Lothar, to 'all those faithful to God's holy church and to us', reminding these *fideles* that earlier in that year, on the advice of the bishops, an empire-wide fast had been ordered, along with prayer, in the hope that God would deign to reveal how He had been offended, and grant a period of peace and tranquillity so that the much-needed *correctio* could be implemented. Since the initial plan to organize a general assembly in 828 had been thwarted by enemy incursions, the emperors had decided to have a *placitum* with only some of their faithful men, in order to attend to the most pressing affairs.[112] This letter informed all the *fideles* who would normally have attended the plenary assembly, but who had been excluded from the winter meeting, of its main decisions: having synods and sending out *missi*.[113] 'Because of the common salvation, the honour of the kingdom and the well-being of the people', the recipients of the letter were to assist the *missi* in all respects; they should also know that one day a week the emperors were accessible for legal appeal, to further this operation. Starting on the Monday after the Octave of Pentecost (24 May), when the councils were to meet, a general three-day fast was to be observed, and all those obliged to do military service were to prepare themselves with horses, weapons, clothing, carts and food, so that they would be ready to depart whenever they received their marching orders, and able to go on campaigning as long as needed.

This letter aimed to inform and involve all *fideles* of both emperors, so many copies of it must have circulated at the time; yet all that remains of it

---

[109] *De ordine palatii*, c. VI (31), p. 88.
[110] *Relatio episcoporum* (829), MGH *Capit.* II, no. 196, pp. 27–51. Since most of this text is taken from the *acta* of Paris (829), it is difficult to see how Jonas could not have composed it.
[111] *ARF*, s.a. 829, p. 177.
[112] *Epistola generalis* (828), MGH *Capit.* II, no. 185, pp. 4–6, at p. 4.
[113] *De ordine palatii*, c. VI (30), pp. 84–6.

is one copy in an eleventh-century manuscript.[114] A more extensive version of this letter has had a much better survival rate. It was even included in the two most important ninth-century manuscripts of the council of Paris (829), one from Northern France and the other from St-Martin in Tours.[115] These contain the following section:

Who does not realise that God has been offended by our depraved acts and provoked to fury, when he sees His anger savage the realm committed to us by him for so many years with manifold scourges, for example by constant hunger, by the death of animals, by plagues among men, by the sterility of almost all fruit trees? And *as I have said earlier*, by the fact that the people of this realm are miserably vexed and afflicted by the most diverse sicknesses and disasters and by such a gripping poverty that all the abundance of things has somehow vanished? And let us not doubt that this happens because of a just judgement, because scandals have often sprung up in this kingdom because of tyrants, who attempt to destroy the peace of the people of God and the unity of the people. For this also should be ascribed to our sins, that the enemies of Christ's name, who entered this kingdom, have committed robberies, set fire to churches, captured Christians and killed the servants of God, boldly and with impunity – indeed, most cruelly. It is therefore through a just judgement of God that we, who have sinned in all respects, are scourged inside and outside. We are obviously ungrateful for God's kindnesses, for we are found to use these not for God's will, but for our carnal pleasure. And therefore the creatures of God, divinely committed to us, rightly fight for God against us ungrateful ones, as it is written: 'The whole world will fight with him against the unwise' (Sap. 5.21). Truly, because we are vexed and persecuted in so many ways, it is fitting and necessary that we return with our whole heart to Him, by whom we are persecuted, in order that this prophecy is fulfilled in us, as it says: 'Vexation alone shall make you understand what you hear' [Is. 28.19].[116]

The passage from Wisdom on fighting the unwise was also cited by Nithard, with some adaptation, in order to signal that in his view,

---

[114] Barcelona Ripoll 40, first half of eleventh century, fol. 5r a–b; cf. Mordek, *Bibliotheca*, p. 21. The current editions by Boretius (MGH *Capit.* II, no. 185, pp. 3–6) and Werminghoff (MGH *Conc.* II, pp. 599–601) are based on earlier editions by Sirmond and Baluze. The best survey of the manuscript tradition is given by Werminghoff, MGH *Conc.* II, p. 598.

[115] Vat. Lat. 3827, end of ninth century, N-France, 74v–75r, followed by the *acta* of Paris 829, 75v–111r; BnF lat. 5516, St Martin of Tours, end of ninth century?, 116v–117r, also as a preface to Paris 829; Vat. Chigi III 239, sixteenth century, 101v–104r; Vat. Reg lat 1041, seventeenth century, 59–60; these last two early modern manuscripts are dependent on Vat. Lat. 3827. On this manuscript, see Mordek, *Bibliotheca*, pp. 858–63. In Vat. Lat. 3827, on fol. 74v, the letter immediately follows after Theodulf's *Capitula episcoporum* (ed. Brommer, MGH *Capit.* Episc., I, pp. 103–42) with *Incipit epistola caesarea* in a rubricated capitalis rusticus, followed by *in nomine domini dei et salvatoris nostri iesu christi hludouuicus et lotharius – diligenter fideliterque conservet.* On fol. 75r, in the same hand, also in rubricated capitalis rusticus: *Incipit praefatio sinodi apud Parisiorum urbem iussu gloriossimorum imperatorum Hludowici filii que eius Hlotharii habitae.*

[116] *Epistola generalis* (828), MGH *Conc.* II/2, pp. 599–601, italics added.

Charles the Bald had become *rex iniquus*, a king without justice.[117] In both manuscripts that contain the longer version of this imperial *epistola generalis*, this figures as an introduction to the text of the Parisian council, with an identical layout and written by the same hand. Obviously the early medieval compilers of these manuscripts considered this longer version to be Louis's and Lothar's official imperial summons to this council. The modern editors of the *Monumenta Germaniae Historica* had a different view, however. They thought that the shorter letter was the original one, which they therefore called the A-version; the longer text was thought to be an interpolated version of this 'original' letter, which was presented as the B-version.[118] Historians followed this line, with some even regarding the longer version as a falsification by some anonymous cleric intent on damaging the emperor's reputation.[119] The most likely candidate to have concocted this forgery was supposedly one of the bishops who attended the council of Paris in 829.[120] My view of these two imperial letters, the short and the long, is that neither can be described as a falsification.[121] These are two different versions of the same imperial summons, intended for specific audiences. Both versions retain the *intitulatio*, the address to all *fideles* and the information that four church councils had been convened. Both texts refer to the year 828 as 'this year' (*hoc anno*). What is left out in the long version is everything that was of interest for ordinary counts and bishops not present during the winter meeting: the impending legation of the *missi*, the regular administration of justice in the palace, and the preparations for military action. Instead, the longer version ends with detailed instructions about the four synods to be held. What one can say, at least, is that the long version was made to fit the needs of bishops and other clerics involved in the synods, rather than those of all the *fideles* who had to prepare for fighting. Instead of setting it aside as a falsification, the longer text should be treated as one of the many written communications that were issued from Aachen during the winter of 828. As the debate evolved, so did the flurry of 'booklets', summonses and letters, each more urgent than the last. The so-called 'B-version' belongs in this context.

In a summons by two emperors, the expression 'as I said earlier' (*ut ita dixerim*) is obviously out of place, yet this in itself is no reason to think of this text as a forgery. Another memorandum may have been copied into

---

[117] Nithard, IV, 6 , p. 142; Nelson, 'Kings without justice'.
[118] See the introductions by Boretius, MGH *Capit.* II, pp. 3–4, and Werminghoff, MGH *Conc.* II, pp. 597–9.
[119] Ganshof, 'Am Vorabend', p. 45, n. 30; Morrison, *The Two Kingdoms*, pp. 45–54.
[120] Dutton, *Politics of Dreaming*, pp. 98–9.   [121] Patzold, 'Eine "Loyale Palastrebellion"'.

this text.[122] In general, the tenor of the 'long version' is very close to the arguments of Wala and Einhard, as I have tried to reconstruct them. On top of this, the biblical phrase *sola vexatio intellectum dabat auditui* (Is. 28.19) was also central to Wala's stance during the winter of 828–9. In other words, if you do not want to hear it, you will have to feel it![123] It looks as if the incongruous *ut ita dixerim* slipped in as a citation from one of the many oral and written pronouncements with which the palace in Aachen resounded at the time. For the nineteenth-century editors of this text, the very idea that an official and imperial letter would speak of 'the scandals caused by tyrants who attempt to destroy the peace of the people of God' seemed suspicious. Why would Louis and Lothar speak of themselves in this way? So the long version must be a forgery. Yet the two emperors did not say 'We are tyrants', neither did the letter have them say that those who rebelled against them had the right to make this accusation.[124] That God's creatures would withstand tyrants, just as, according to the book of Wisdom, the entire universe would fight against the mad (*insensati*), was a certainty shared by the main spokesmen of the Aachen winter meeting. That sinful rulers would be punished by anomalies in the natural world, such as crop failure, plagues, famine and other calamities, was not an entirely novel idea either. It was a notion that pervaded most of the Old Testament.[125]

Alcuin's letters, as well as the tract *De duodecim abusivis saeculi*, which originated in Ireland in the first quarter of the eighth century, helped to articulate already existing notions of God's punishment of evil in society.[126] By the time the *Twelve Abuses of the World* surfaced in continental manuscripts, and in the acts of the council of Paris (829), the text was ascribed to Cyprian, the third-century bishop and martyr of Carthage.[127] The 'degrees of abuse' (*gradus abusionis*), as they were called in the text itself, were represented by 'types', such as the preacher without virtue, the old man without religion, the youth without obedience, the woman

---

[122] There is the familiar enumeration of disasters which also figures in Einhard's tale of Wiggo, and in Radbert's assessment of the situation in 828: *EA*, II, c. 1, p. 61: 'licet audeat detegere peccata populi longe diu accumulata, clades, pestilentias, fames, inaequalitates aerum, terroresque etiam visionum'.

[123] As noted by Dümmler: Radbert, *EA*, II, p. 61, n. 1. The second biblical text cited in the long version of the letter, *pugnabit pro eo orbis terrarum contra insensatos* (Sap. 5.21), is cited by Nithard in his sombre conclusion to his *Histories*, but with *pro eo* omitted, so the text gets the meaning: 'all the universe shall fight against the unwise'.

[124] See Einhard, *VK*, c. 2, p. 4, where Charles Martel is described as a suppressor of tyrants, and below, chapter 5, on Bernard of Septimania as a tyrant. Tyranny meant illegitimate rule.

[125] Blattmann, 'Ein Ungluck für sein Volk'; de Jong, '*Sacrum palatium*', pp. 1262–3.

[126] Anton, 'Pseudo-Cyprian', pp. 572–6.   [127] Meens, 'Politics'.

without modesty, the bishop who neglected his ministry, or the people without law. Scholarly attention has mostly concentrated on the *rex iniquus*, who was the ninth type of this series.[128] The rule of an unjust, or, better, sinful king, who was incapable of correcting his own iniquities, had consequences for his entire realm, on a truly cosmic scale. His people would lack peace and would be afflicted by crop failure or carried off into slavery, children would die, enemy armies would prevail, herds would perish, storms would make the soil and seas infertile, depriving mankind of fruit and fish.[129] In his record of the council of Paris in 829, Jonas of Orléans cited the section on the *rex iniquus* chapter and verse; it was also well known to those who gathered with Louis and Lothar the winter before.[130] Those involved had no idea that this was an Irish tract. In the ninth century, Pseudo-Cyprian was thought of as a work of Cyprian, with the tremendous authority of pristine Christianity.

Taking all this into account, as well as Louis's earlier readiness to shoulder blame as part of his royal office, the long version of the letter is not at all incredible as an imperial communication. On the contrary, it reflects much of the 828–9 agenda for discussion as we know it from other sources. The thrust of these communications is the same: the key words are *iniquitas* ('our sins') and the ensuing *clades*.[131] The idiom and tenor of the long version of the imperial letter belong to this atmosphere of self-examination and soul-searching, imposed by Louis (and in 828 also by Lothar) on the entire realm. If they did not say it, they should have said it. This is more than a flippant remark. The so-called falsified letter stayed well within the limits of the contemporary discourse on royal religious authority, of which humbly confessing one's sins had become an integral part. In a court anxiously looking for moral guidance, Louis and Lothar had become the epicentre upon which all *admonitio* and even *increpatio* was focussed, but it should not be forgotten that they also embodied the hopes of all concerned, including the author of the 'B-version', for a return to order and peace. In this text a penitent Louis and Lothar presented themselves, declaring that they had 'sinned all the more because we should have been the embodiment of salvation (*forma salutis*)

---

[128] Ps.-Cyprian, *De duodecim abusivis saeculi*, pp. 32–60; for the *rex iniquus*, see ibid., pp. 51–3; on the *femina sine pudicitia*, see Smith, 'Gender and ideology'.

[129] *De duodecim abusivis saeculi*, p. 52. On these cosmological disasters and their context, see Meens, 'Politics', pp. 355–7.

[130] Council of Paris (829), II, c. 1, MGH *Conc.* II/2, pp. 649–51; Jonas, *De institutione regia*, c. 3, ed. Dubreucq, pp. 184–96; Meens, 'Politics', p. 353, with reference to earlier literature and some of the relevant manuscripts.

[131] *Relatio episcoporum* (829), MGH *Capit.* II, no. 196, p. 27. This is also referred to in the first section that the long and short version of the *Epistola generalis* have in common: MGH *Capit.* II, no. 85, p. 3.

for all and should have had the care [for the salvation] of all (*cura omnium*) because of our imperial authority'. If this was a forgery produced by 'a bishop', it was also an eloquent statement about royal religious authority.

A penitential council: Paris, 829

Of the four councils that met on the Octave of Pentecost 829, only the one that gathered in Paris has left a written record. Nothing is known of what went on in Lyon and Toulouse. In Mainz almost the entire East-Frankish and Lotharingian episcopate was present, yet it remains unclear how this well-attended meeting dealt with the instructions from the court.[132] The same imbalance characterises the joint report of the bishops presented to the emperor in Worms in August 829. The bulk of this is derived from the acts of the council of Paris, probably because here too it was Bishop Jonas of Orléans who served as the 'secretary' stipulated by the emperors.[133] The council of Paris is considered a landmark in the history of political theory, for it cites Pope Gelasius' letter to the Emperor Anastasius. This gained tremendous influence from the late eleventh century onwards, when it became the key text for Gregory VII and other popes who claimed the superiority of sacerdotal *auctoritas* over imperial *potestas*.[134] In traditional historical scholarship, which had its roots in the German *Kulturkampf* and related movements, the sudden appearance of Gelasius' doctrine of the two swords in 829 was taken to be the first clear manifestation of bishops who tried to elevate the *sacerdotium* above the *imperium*.[135] This was not the aim of Pope Gelasius, however, when he wrote his letter in 494,[136] nor was this what those gathered in Paris in 829

---

[132] Hartmann, *Konziliengeschichte*, pp. 179–81; the Council of Mainz judged the dispute between the Saxon monk Gottschalk, who argued that his oblation as a child had been invalid, and his abbot Hrabanus Maurus. See De Jong, *Samuel's Image*, pp. 77–91.

[133] *Relatio episcoporum* (829), MGH *Capit.* II, no. 196, pp. 27–51; on its manuscript transmission, see Mordek, *Bibliotheca*, p. 103. See also Lukas, 'Neues aus einer Salzburger Handschrift', on the adaptation of various manuscripts to different audiences. One version is transmitted as the last section of the decrees of the council of Paris: MGH *Conc.* II/2, pp. 667–82. See Hartmann, *Konziliengeschichte*, p. 186, n. 18. It should be noted that, unlike all the other documents of 828 and the acts of the council of Paris itself, this *Relatio* was directed to Louis alone, rather than to Louis and Lothar.

[134] Gelasius, *Epistolae*, 12, 2, p. 351: 'Duo quippe sunt, imperator auguste, quibus principaliter mundus hic regitur: auctoritas sacrata pontificum et regalis potestas, in quibus tanto gravius est pondus sacerdotum, quanto etiam pro ipsis regibus hominum in divino reddituri sunt examine rationem.' The letter was written in the course of a theological controversy, and addressed the question of who had juridical competence in these matters, the emperor or the pope; Gelasius had Ambrose and Theodosius' penance in mind. See Ensslin, 'Auctoritas', pp. 661–8.

[135] Ullmann, *Carolingian Renaissance*, pp. 56–7; Morrison, *The Two Kingdoms*, pp. 41–51.

[136] Ensslin, 'Auctoritas'.

had in mind. When they quoted Gelasius' famous letter to the Emperor Anastasius on sacerdotal authority and royal power, they had no intention of proclaiming a doctrine of the two swords, or of undermining the position of Louis the Pious; on the contrary, these bishops dealt with an extremely powerful ruler, and tried to reaffirm their own authority (*pondus sacerdotum*) by projecting themselves as the only valid mediators between an enraged deity and a penitent Carolingian leadership – royal, ecclesiastical and secular.[137] In this complementary order of the world, the ruler transcended the divide between the sacred and secular, while he was at the same time responsible for maintaining the distinction between the various 'orders' (*ordines*). Reform was the royal reaction when these essential boundaries became too blurred, in a gesture of supreme authority that, at the same time, highlighted the synergy between the different orders.

The bishops in Paris in 829 did not claim any real ascendancy over the emperor, nor did they consciously develop a '*Staatstheologie*' of any sort.[138] They had other things on their minds, such as carrying out the imperial order to identify the offences committed against God (*offensa Dei*) and to act upon them. The synod of Paris addressed the issues that had been raised during the winter meeting in Aachen. To say that decisions of the council are presented like a diptych that treats first the priesthood (*persona sacerdotalis*) and then kingship (the *persona regalis*) is not untrue, but somewhat misleading, for the crux of the matter was the question: How have we offended God? Just like Wala, the bishops thought the answer lay in the 'confusion' between the two orders: the priesthood, led by the episcopate, and the *populus*, headed by the ruler. First and foremost, this was a text that charted sin and recommended atonement. The bishops in Paris were well aware that they had to report back to two emperors, and not one: whatever they had discussed or decided, according to the *admonitio* of the two rulers (*principes*), they had taken care to write down briefly, divided into *capitula*.[139]

Brevity was not the bishops' (or Jonas's) strong suit. It is impossible to do full justice here to the considerations of the bishops gathered in Paris in 829, and to the wealth of biblical and patristic knowledge they brought to bear upon the questions at hand. Yet their introductory chapter deserves some extra scrutiny, for it sets the tone for the rest of this text. It starts with

---

[137] Toubert, 'La doctrine gélasienne'. On the context of the council of Paris (829), see De Jong, '*Ecclesia*', pp. 129–31.

[138] Hartmann, *Konziliengeschichte*, p. 182 (Staatstheologie); for an effective critique of anachronistic interpretations of the Carolingian councils of the 820s, see Anton, 'Zum politischen Konzept'.

[139] Council of Paris (829), prologue, MGH *Conc.* II/2, pp. 608–9: 'in subsequentibus breviter capitulatim adnotare curavimus'.

a reminder of human infirmity, and with the Pauline warning that he who thinks that he stands should take heed lest he fall (I Cor. 10.12), followed by the penitential psalm *De profundis clamavi ad te, Domine* (Ps. 129.1). In the tribulations of the world, we humbly seek God's help, said the bishops, moving on to the penitent Ninevites, who atoned, together with their king, in sackcloth and ashes (Ion. 3.5–6). Ahab and Manasseh, although they were idolatrous kings, nonetheless succeeded in averting God's wrath by doing penance (III Reg. 21.29; II Par. 33.12–13); somewhat incongruously, in order to bring in the New Testament and stress the power of penance, the *meretrix* Mary Magdalen was also cited as an example. God is often offended and provoked to anger, but a worthy penance (*dignus satisfactio*) will always lead to forgiveness. Men must bear the scourges for their sins without complaint, and humbly bear the tribulations they deserve. God wants sinners to better their lives and live, not die.[140]

This entire first section is an affirmation of the efficacy of penance as a means to avert God's wrath, and of the bishops' indispensable role in this process. What follows is a further elaboration of this theme. The *ecclesia* committed by Christ to his orthodox servants, the August Emperors Louis and Lothar, to rule and to protect (*ad regendam tuendamque*), is now afflicted by various kinds of plagues and many disasters (*multifaria clades*) of the kind sent by God to those who do not obey his demands. Nevertheless, there are many 'princes inspired by Heaven' who heeded this and converted. Then follows a long list of biblical examples, headed by the previously mentioned penitential king of the Ninevites. God will be angered by sin, but He will also be placated by penance. After due consultation with the bishops, the *optimates* and the rest of their *fideles*, this was what the rulers had decided to do: to placate God's rage (*furor domini*) by penance. It was to the *sacerdotes* they now had to turn, for they could reconcile the sinner to God by penance, just as the leper was purified from his sordidness by the priest (Lev. 13.7; 14.2). In a rather free rendering of Matth. 16.19,[141] the bishops declared that whatever they established (*statuta*) on earth would also be established in heaven, and whatever they would loose on earth would be loosed in heaven; the sins of whoever they would forgive would be forgiven. The *sacerdotes* were the vicars of the apostles and the leading lights of the world, and through them and their instruction, therefore, the most pious rulers had believed they

---

[140] Ez. 18.23: 'numquid voluntatis meae est mors impii dicit Dominus Deus et non ut convertatur a viis suis et vivat'.

[141] Matth. 16.19: 'et tibi dabo claves regni caelorum et quodcumque ligaveris super terram erit ligatum in caelis et quodcumque solveris super terram erit solutum in caelis'.

could beg for God's mercy.[142] Rightly so, for as Jerome had commented
on the prophetic text *Interroga sacerdotes legem* (Agg. 2.12): 'If you are a
sacerdos, you know the law, and if you do not, you are not a *sacerdos*.'
Their knowledge of the *lex* (Scripture) defined the *sacerdotes*. Hence, the
rulers, well instructed in the 'legal and prophetic institutions', resolved
to consult the *sacerdotes*, who knew the law on their and their people's
sins. After some sentences about the four synods, which are mostly
taken from the imperial summonses,[143] comes an interesting turn of
phrase, with legal inflections: 'whatever shall be found, they [the bish-
ops] will clearly denounce, in the interest of correction and according to
the ministry imposed on them'.[144] Jerome's exegesis of Mal. 2.7 as well
as this text itself are cited to emphasise once more the sacerdotal knowledge of the law: like an angel of the Lord, the *sacerdos* was a messenger of
the truth. So, obedient to the summons of the glorious and orthodox
principes, the bishops were eager to confer about the salvation of the
people, according to their ministry; they reported that the council had
gone into session on 6 June.

Until now, I have avoided translating *sacerdotes*, for this expression
requires some explanation. In a more general sense, this meant 'priests',
as in the passage from Jerome cited in this introduction, and in this sense
the expression also figures in the decrees of 829, for example when
sacerdotes (priests) are distinguished from bishops (*pontifices*).[145] Yet in
many other instances in this text, the priesthood, referred to collectively as
sacerdotes, were the bishops themselves, who jealously guarded their liturgical prerogatives against priestly encroachment, such as reconciling public penitents (c. 46) or dispensing confirmation after baptism (c. 33). It
was only towards the end of the first section on the priesthood that priests
in the strict sense of the word (*presbyteri*) enter upon the scene, mostly in
terms of what they could *not* do: imposing the veil on virgins without
consulting their bishop (cc. 40–1), allowing such women to play a leading
role in their churches (c. 42), celebrating mass in private houses (c. 47) or

---

[142] Council of Paris (829), prologue, p. 608: 'quibus et in evangelio a Domino tanto
confertur potestas, ut quae statuerint in terra statuta sint et in caelo et quae solverint in
terra soluta sunt et in caelis et quorum remiserint peccata remittantur eis. Hos quippe
constat vicarios esse apostolorum et luminaria mundi. Per hos igitur eorumque doctri-
nam tales tanti piissimi principes sibi suisque fideliter crediderunt misericordia propitiari
posse divinam.'

[143] *Constitutio synodum*, MGH *Capit.* II, no. 184, pp. 2–3.

[144] Council of Paris (829), prologue, p. 608, line 29: 'correctionis gratia iuxta ministerium
sibi iniunctum patenter denuntiarent'.

[145] Council of Paris (829), I, c. 33, p. 634; more frequent is the distinction between *episcopi*
and *presbyteri*, as in c. 16, p. 623 (bishops and priests must not allow ecclesiastical
property to be used by their kinsmen).

by themselves (c. 48), or serving at more than one church, for reasons of avarice (c. 49). These *presbyteri* seem to have been local priests of the sort much in need of discipline and education, rather than full members of the group referred to as *sacerdotes*.[146] Along with a rhetoric that reinforced the episcopal group ethos, social distinctions must also have played a role in this terminology. It is no coincidence that the bishops also referred to ordained monks and canons as *sacerdotes*; like the bishops themselves, these 'institutionalised clergy' usually came from the higher echelons of society.[147] Clearly, some priests were more sacerdotal than others. Yet high rank also had its drawbacks, in that the sins of bishops angered God more than any others.

The later power of the church should not be projected back on to this one council in Paris, however articulate these bishops in 829 may have been. They belonged to an episcopate that, as a cohesive and corporate body, had asserted itself in new ways, acquiring a new sense of identity, since the Carolingian dynasty took power. The bishops proclaimed that they were the successors of the apostles and the exclusive mediators between God and mankind, not because they fulfilled this role, but because their actual status fell short of these aspirations. The *libertas episcopalis* for which they clamoured was in fact a rather modest bid for independence in the face of overwhelming royal might, inspired by a better knowledge of late antique canonical writings.[148] Many such texts, gathered by Charlemagne and his circle, began to make a greater impact on episcopal self-perceptions only by the 820s. Bishops and other learned men read and pondered the patristic heritage that was becoming available, and took these authoritative models of imperial Christianity to heart. Jonas's erudite record of the Paris council allows a revealing glimpse into this process, for this was also a didactic text, in which biblical and canonical passages were gathered so they might become more widely known. This was how the brief and garbled quotation of Gelasius' letter was presented, which claimed that 'two august empresses' ruled this world.[149] Many a bishop reading this must have been surprised, but the astute reader must have realised that all this chapter wanted to get across

---

[146] Relevant here is a genre of texts now known as *capitula episcoporum*: MGH *Capit.* Episc. I/III, ed. P. Brommer and R. Pokorny (1964–2005); cf. Van Rhijn, *Shepherds*.

[147] De Jong, '*Imitatio morum*'.

[148] Council of Paris (829), III, c. 94 (27), MGH *Conc.* II/2, p. 680; *Relatio episcoporum* (829), MGH *Capit.* II, no. 197, p. 51.

[149] Council of Paris (829), I, c. 3, p. 610: 'Duae sunt quippe, inquit, imperatrices augustae, quibus principaliter mundus hic regitur.' The two empresses, a corruption of 'imperator auguste', figure in the two ninth-century manuscripts of the decrees of Paris (829), as well as in Jonas's *De institutione regia*, so this was, presumably, the authoritative tradition Jonas wished to transmit.

was that within God's church there were two 'lofty persons', the sacerdotal and the royal.

The acts of the council were organised according to this principle, like a diptych. After a first big section on *religio christiana* and the *cura pastorum* – that is, the cult of God and pastoral care, the domain of the bishops and their clerics – came a second one on 'kings and princes and the general population'.[150] This was followed by recapitulation of both books addressed to Louis and Lothar, the orthodox and invincible *augusti*.[151] What was at stake in 828–9 was that both 'persons' perceived themselves to be negligent of their God-given *ministerium* and in need of correction.[152] Not only the rulers were to blame, but also the bishops; those whose duty it was to criticise others had to be capable of self-correction. This held true for Louis, but even more for the bishops. Thus, the first and by far the largest section of the synodal *acta* deals with the many ways in which the bishops themselves felt they had failed. It consists of a long litany of episcopal sins: simony, avarice, cupidity, vanity, lack of hospitality, using church property for their own glory, oppressing the faithful, leading less than chaste lives. If the lives of bishops did not conform to the precepts of the church (*doctrina*), this would engender *scandala*, that is, offence to God. It was better to have no bishops than negligent ones.[153] Episcopal *negligentia* was dangerous, for bishops were the ones to ensure that the irate God was satisfied by a *digna paenitentia*, and they were responsible for the prayers for the imperial family – in short, the burden of mediating between God and the ruler was theirs.[154] After all, they were the successors of the apostles.[155] The second section of the conciliar acts famously includes Pseudo-Cyprian's chapter on the unjust or sinful king (*rex iniquus*), a text that has been viewed as episcopal ammunition directed against Louis.[156] This was not how Jonas saw Pseudo-Cyprian, however, and it helps to remember that one of the

---

[150] Council of Paris (829), II, prologue, p. 649: 'specialiter de regibus et principibus et generaliter de omnibus fidelibus'. Some years later, Jonas incorporated the second section of the Paris acts, on royal conduct, in his *De institutione regia*, a tract presented to Pippin of Aquitaine; see Dubreucq, *Le métier du roi*, pp. 35–49, with reference to older literature. Dubreucq (at pp. 48–9) opts for 831 on not entirely convincing grounds. The traditional date is 834. See Anton, *Fürstenspiegel*, pp. 213–23.

[151] Council of Paris (829), III, pp. 667–80; separately edited as *Relatio episcoporum* (829), MGH *Capit.* II, no. 196, pp. 27–51.

[152] See, above all, Anton, 'Zum politischen Konzept'; also De Jong, '*Sacrum palatium*'.

[153] Council of Paris (829), I, c. 4, pp. 611–2.   [154] Ibid., c. 5, pp. 612–4.

[155] Ibid., c. 4, p. 611, line 7.

[156] Council of Paris (829), II, c. 55(1), pp. 650–1; Ps.-Cyprian, *De duodecim abusivis*, c. 9, pp. 51–3; Moore, 'La monarchie Carolingienne'; but see Blattmann, 'Ein Unglück für sein Volk', and Meens, 'Politics'.

other 'reprehensible persons of this world' was the negligent bishop (*episcopus negligens*), who was the other major concern of the council of Paris.[157] Whatever the case, Pseudo-Cyprian pales into insignificance compared to many other authoritative texts cited, particularly biblical ones: Scripture contained all that kings needed to know about fulfilling their ministry.[158]

Above all, the acts of the council of Paris are a statement about the joint need of the two 'persons' to identify their sins and do penance for the scandal they had caused in the *sancta ecclesia*. The concept of 'scandal' is crucial here, for it denotes the kind of sin that disrupts a divinely sanctioned social order. To restore this order meant, first of all, clarifying and reimposing distinctions between *ordines*. Unlike the *Admonitio generalis* issued in 825, which presented all the offices (*ministeria*) as derived from the ruler's all-encompassing ministry, the council of Paris envisaged a dualist order of two complementary 'persons', one sacerdotal, the other royal. Both these 'persons' were inside an all-embracing *ecclesia*, an expression that denoted the Christian people as well as the Christian polity.[159]

Bishops were the ones who managed communication with God, mediating between the offended deity and sinful humankind; their negligence would have dire consequences. The council was therefore much concerned with the bishops' mediating function in general, and with penance in particular, which, along with prayer, was the primary instrument of their mediation between God and mankind. The well-known decree that the 'booklets written against canonical authority, that are called *paenitentiales*', should be found and burned by the bishop, should be interpreted in this context.[160] The background of this precept was the attempt on the part of bishops to assert their authority over many other clerics, including monks in orders, who administered penance with the aid of books of penance of doubtful provenance.[161] In 829 these *codicelli* were fiercely denounced, with dire warnings derived from Ezekiel (13.8–10); yet the manuscript evidence suggests that in great ecclesiastical centres such as St Gall, Lorsch, Rheims and Salzburg, these penitentials were not burned, but copied and read.[162] That the bishops should 'also' instruct their

---

[157] *De duodecim abusivis*, c. 10, pp. 53–6.
[158] Council of Paris (829), II, cc. 62–3 [8–9], pp. 659–61.
[159] Ibid., III, c. 93 [26], p. 679; Anton, 'Zum politischen Konzept'.
[160] Hamilton, *Practice of Penance*, p. 6; Council of Paris (829), I, c. 33, p. 633 ('codicelli contra canonicam auctoritatem scripti quos paenitentiales vocant').
[161] See Meens, 'Frequency', with a list of manuscripts containing tripartite penitentials; more generally, Hamilton, *Practice of Penance*, pp. 2–8.
[162] For a discussion of their use, see Meens, 'Frequency', pp. 40–5.

presbyteri in the correct and canonical penance comes as an afterthought, followed by the wistful remark that until now the carelessness and ignorance of such men has led to the ruin of many souls.[163] In other words, while the *presbyteri* were still considered a fairly hopeless category, to be episcopally instructed but without too many expectations of improvement, the *sacerdotes*, who were targeted by the decree on books of penance were of a different type. I suspect that many of this priestly cadre were members of religious communities – monks and canons who used these manuscripts for a variety of reasons, including pastoral care, and who did not automatically submit to episcopal authority.[164]

The bishops did not spare themselves.[165] It was their vanity, arrogance and cupidity that could engender 'scandal', which in turn would endanger the 'status of the holy church of God' – or, in other words, the Frankish polity.[166] As rumour had it, and as appeared from plain evidence, the bishops' *ministri*, and archdeacons in particular, were as avaricious as Eli's sons, victimising both the *presbyteri* and the faithful. Thus, many of the faithful were scandalised, the sacerdotal ministry came into ill repute, and the *sacerdotes* neglected their duties.[167] Once more, there is the distinction between the higher strata of the clergy, referred to as *sacerdotes* on the one hand and the *presbyteri* on the other. All the same, there is evidence that some bishops implemented the decisions of the synods of 829 in their own bishoprics, through synods organised in their dioceses.[168] This was the short-term effect of these reform synods. For the long-term impact, one has to look ahead, beyond the troubles of 830–3, to the time when Louis had reasserted his authority and held another corrective council in Aachen (836). Most of the acts of Paris 829 were then recapitulated, and adapted to new circumstances. The original format of the two complementary orders, divine and human, had become less tight in 836, with the laymen manifesting themselves as a separate group with a moral voice of their own.[169] Yet regardless of this adaptation, and the rebellions of the

---

[163] Council of Paris (829), I, c. 33, p. 633: 'Presbyteri etiam imperiti sollerti studio ab episcopis suis instruendi sunt.'

[164] The various uses of tripartite penitential signalled by Meens, 'Frequency', supports the idea that many of these texts were copied in great ecclesiastical centres, especially monasteries. For a discussion of the 'institutionalised clergy' as a separate category, see De Jong, '*Imitatio morum*'.

[165] Chapters concentrating on the sins of bishops: cc. 5, 11–31. Chapters concerned with penance: cc. 5, 32, 46, 54.

[166] Council of Paris (829), c. 19, p. 625.

[167] Ibid., c. 25, p. 628: 'multi scandalizantur et ministerium sacerdotale vituperantur et in ecclesiis a sacerdotibus multa propter eos negleguntur'.

[168] Hartmann, 'Neue Texte'.

[169] Council of Aachen (836), MGH *Conc.* II/2, pp. 705–24.

recent past, the basic programme remained the same. How can we make sure we placate an easily offended God? Unbeknown to those who discussed this issue in Paris in June 829, this very question would be hotly debated only a few months later. This time the imperial palace, referred to by the bishops as Louis's 'sacred house' (*domus sacra*), would be enveloped by a scandal that, some argued, was sure to have offended God in unprecedented ways. It is to the slander against Judith and Bernard, and to the rebellion of 830, that we now turn.

5   Purity and danger (830–831)

The reputation of the palace

In his *Gesta Karoli*, composed for Charles's great-grandson Charles the Fat, Notker 'the Stammerer' praised the palace at Aachen: its church, the royal residence, and the houses (*mansiones*) of the men of different rank attached to the palace. The very clever Charles had them built in such a way that the king himself, through the railings of his *solarium*, could observe all the secret activities of everyone who came and went, without anyone being aware of the royal gaze.[1] This image is reminiscent of the watchful abbot and his *decani*, with which, as a monk, Notker was no doubt familiar, yet the ever-vigilant ruler was not merely a figment of the monastic imagination. In Einhard's *Life*, Charlemagne not only woke four or five times at night, but would even get up to solve disputes. Surely in the eyes of ninth-century educated readers, this was a better activity to fill one's watchful royal nights with than sending for storytellers. This was what Suetonius' Augustus did, one of the main models for Einhard's *Vita Karoli*.[2]

As for the comparison between Carolingian monasteries and palaces, contemporaries surely knew the difference. Whereas monasteries had a duty to protect the sanctity and inaccessibility of their inner space, the *claustrum*, palaces had more fluid boundaries, and many outsiders came and went without the strict surveillance to which abbots and abbesses subjected their visitors. All the same, as Matthew Innes has argued, outsiders and insiders perceived the royal household with the monastery at the back of their minds: as a place where the young were educated and a superior way of discipline was maintained. It was a place where aristocratic youngsters and others intent on upward social mobility learned how to behave themselves.[3] As the monk and schoolmaster Hildemar of Corbie/Civate (c. 845) expressed it, the king's household was 'the school

---

[1] Notker, I, c. 30, p. 41. On this passage, see De Jong, 'Charlemagne's balcony'; Nelson, 'Aachen', pp. 223–4; Airlie, 'The Palace of memory', p. 5.
[2] Einhard, *VK*, c. 24, p. 29; Suetonius, *The Lives of the Twelve Caesars* II, 78.
[3] Innes, 'Place of discipline'.

of human service' (*scola humani servitii*), as opposed to the monastic 'school of the service of the Lord' (*scola dominici servitii*).[4]

For courtiers (*aulici*) it was customary to rise early. This is what Einhard said of Louis's court in Aachen as it was in 828. The old courtier explained how at dawn he went in search for the Archchaplain Hilduin and found the great man sitting outside the royal bedchamber, waiting for the emperor to get up. Einhard had some differences to settle with Hilduin. Standing side by side at 'a certain window, from which one could look into the lower parts of the palace', they discussed their bone of contention, the relics of Peter and Marcellinus that Einhard had imported from Rome and that had been stolen by Hilduin and diverted to his monastery of St-Médard in Soissons.[5] In this narrative, Einhard emphatically situated himself at the heart of the court, as someone who knew its most intimate habits. He also revealed a frighteningly transparent world in which all who belonged to this court were permanently observing and being observed. There was no chance of escaping the ever-watchful eyes. What is he or she doing there? Where is the emperor, and who is in attendance? Most of all, this eternal watchfulness was focussed on the king and queen themselves, and the place where they were together: the royal bedchamber. Perhaps there were limits to the courtiers' permanent observance: Hilduin had to wait outside the royal bedchamber until Louis had woken up and summoned him. But this temporarily restricted access did not make royal lives any less transparent.

Like religious communities, the royal household was vulnerable to *mala fama*, destructive gossip that could spread like wildfire. Monasteries and especially nunneries anxiously protected themselves against too much outside knowledge of the affairs of the community. Any communication between *claustrum* and *saeculum* was therefore closely guarded.[6] Obviously the palace community was not cloistered. It was an 'institution with fluid contours',[7] as it travelled between royal residences, *palatia* as well as *villae*, waxing in the summer for assemblies and waning in the winter, when the ruler was surrounded only by his inner circle.[8] Still, the court was a strictly hierarchical and exclusive community. Insiders proudly announced themselves as 'men of the palace' (*homines palatini* or *aulici*) who knew the palace inside out and enjoyed royal favour and 'familiarity'. Agobard,

---

[4] Hildemar, *Expositio*, prologue, p. 66.
[5] Einhard, *TMP*, II, c. 1, p. 243; trans. Dutton, *CC*, p. 83.
[6] On monasteries and *fama*, see Diem, *Das monastische Experiment*, pp. 312–21; also De Jong, 'Internal cloisters'.
[7] Depreux, *Prosopographie*, p. 9: 'Le palais, un institution au contours flous', which opens an excellent discussion of the palace of Louis the Pious (pp. 9–39).
[8] For a more extensive discussion of the Carolingian court, see Innes, 'A place of discipline', and Nelson, 'Was Charlemagne's court a courtly society?'

ferociously envious of Count Matfrid's constant access to Louis, reminded the count that he owed it all to God's benevolence, not to his own merits.[9] To fall out of favour usually led to a total collapse of a courtier's reputation and self-respect. Some of Radbert's loudest laments were about Wala's and his own undeserved loss of that precious *familiaritas* after the revolt of 830. To have been part of the charmed inner circle and then to be ousted amounted to shameful exile. This was one of the reasons why Wala was typecast as Jeremiah: after 830, he had become the outsider, the *peregrinus*, the man banished to and imprisoned in the most distant cave.[10] Radbert's complaint about this exclusion was interspersed with claims that, given half a chance, the emperor wanted nothing better than to restore Wala to his former illustrious position as the imperial right-hand man. But the chance did not arise, partly because Wala would not admit sins he had not committed – in other words, the moral high ground remained a hotly contested territory.[11]

All relatively closed communities with high moral aspirations are vulnerable to gossip and scandal, and the court of Louis the Pious was no exception. In this fiercely competitive society, in-fighting spilling out into the outside world was the first danger to the reputation of the palace. In an extensive precept on the need for charity (*caritas*) in both the clerical and the lay order, the council of Paris (829) focussed on those 'adorned with the honours of the palace'. Be they clerics or laymen, they should be mutually bound in *caritas*, rather than plotting each other's harm and dishonour. This decree ends with another eloquent denunciation of those consumed with mutual envy. Eager to see their companions ruined and dishonoured, they lacked loyalty towards the ruler whose familiarity they enjoyed, and whose helpers (*adiutores*) they should be, according to God's command. As the bishops warned, courtiers who lacked *caritas* 'defiled the honour of the palace, giving a bad example to others, and, what is even more unbecoming, they give much joy to the enemies of the name of Christ', namely, pagans.[12] This *honor palatinus* had an impact on the entire Frankish polity: outside knowledge of dissension in the palace meant a collective loss of face and authority.[13] Against the background

---

[9] Agobard, *De iniusticiis*, p. 227.

[10] Radbert, *EA*, II, c. 10, p. 74: 'Retruditur autem et elevatur in quadam longissimo terrarum spatio altissima et artissima specu.'

[11] Ibid., p. 75.

[12] Council of Paris (829), II, c. 6 (60), MGH *Conc.* II/2, p. 656; Jonas, *De institutione laicali*, c. 9, pp. 226–30; at p. 230: 'et honorem palatinum, malum exemplum aliis dantes, commaculant et, quod his indecentius est, ad inimicos nominis Christi magnum tripudium transmittunt'.

[13] See Agobard, *Liber apologeticum*, I, c. 2, p. 309; *Relatio* (833), p. 52, lines 43–5 (with the key expressions *ignominia*, *vilitas* and *derisio*).

of the deposition of Matfrid and Hugh in February 828, and the 'hotbed of discord' (*seminarium discordiae*) that had expanded like a cancerous growth ever since, as the Astronomer expressed it,[14] the worries of the bishops meeting in Paris are understandable. In 829 the issue of disreputable dissension in the palace was on the agenda. In the interest of the honour and stability of the realm and the well-being of the people, the bishops said, the emperor was to choose good *ministri* who would display mutual affection:

for it is fitting that your sacred house should appear admirable to all, that it be there to be imitated, and that the renown of its reputation should pervade most abundantly among the subjects of your imperial rule as well as foreign nations.[15]

Less than one year later, this 'sacred house' (*domus sacra*) was rocked by a major scandal. According to Agobard of Lyons, the imperial bed had been defiled, the palace soiled, the realm thrown into confusion and the once illustrious name of the Franks obscured.[16] Discord and competition among courtiers were certainly important factors in the scandal that erupted in the spring of 830, but to this dangerous cocktail another and equally potent ingredient was added: male fear of female power and sexuality. The first signs of this were already visible during the later part of Charlemagne's reign.[17] Yet it was in 830 that, for the first time in the history of the post-Roman West, the imperial bedchamber became the centre of the political arena. The Empress Judith's alleged lasciviousness was presented as fatally undermining the order and integrity of the Frankish state.

The one and only queen

Whereas in Charlemagne's court many women shared the spotlight – wives, concubines and daughters – in his son's palace there was only the queen, on whom all eyes were fixed. Panegyrists, eager to depict the palace hierarchy in a way that would please their patrons, had a keen eye for the different positions of royal women. The author of the narrative verse *Karolus Magnus et Leo papa* of 799 depicted Queen Liutgard emerging from the 'proud bedchamber' with her entourage. Liutgard was

---

[14] Astronomer, c. 43, pp. 452–4.
[15] Council of Paris (829), III, c. 24, MGH *Conc.* II/2, p. 678; *Relatio episcoporum* (829), c. 59, MGH *Capit.* II, p. 49: 'Decet quippe, ut sacra domus vestra cunctis spectabilis appareat et imitabilis existat et fama suae opinionis sive alios imperii vestri subiectos sive exteras nationes habundantissime perfundat.' On the Carolingian concept of the sacred palace, see De Jong, '*Sacrum palatium*'.
[16] Agobard, *Liber apologeticum*, I, c. 2, p. 309.   [17] Nelson, 'Women at the court'.

resplendent in royal attire, with glittering jewels and clothes shimmering with purple and gold. But unlike Judith, she had competition from 'an orderly file of virgins' led by Charles's daughter Rotrud on horseback. Upon each of the six daughters the author lavished as much praise as on Queen Liutgard, and each of these daughters entered on to the public stage with a female retinue.[18] By contrast, on the occasion of the baptism of the Danish king in 826, Ermold the Black portrayed Judith exclusively in male company.[19] On public occasions such as the royal hunt and the baptism at Ingelheim, the empress was escorted by counts Matfrid and Hugh,[20] or surrounded by *proceres* and *potentes*,[21] joining the emperor at the head of the dinner table[22] or watching anxiously over her son Charles, together with his tutor.[23] This was a queen who was mercilessly the centre of attention. This constant observation was mitigated only by the ceremonial presence of the ruler himself, the princes and the chief courtiers. Likewise, the royal procession envisaged by Walahfrid Strabo in 829 consisted entirely of men, starting with Louis and ending with Walahfrid's teacher Grimald – except for Judith, who is compared to lovely Rachel, who led 'Benjamin, the solace of grandfathers' (six-year-old Charles), by the hand.[24] This was not merely a matter of poetic fancy or flattery. When Ermold addressed his empress as the worthy wife and beautiful Judith, who, with her husband, rightly wielded the highest imperial authority, this was fulsome praise, but of a kind that was meant to please the emperor and a courtly audience, to whom the queen/empress had become much more important to the governance of the polity, in practice as well as on ceremonial occasions when the court presented itself to the outside world.[25] To sum up, if one is to go by the evidence of panegyrics, and I think one can, a change had occurred since the days of Charlemagne in the way in which the queen presented herself during ceremonial occasions: instead of being surrounded by a flock of girls, she was now portrayed in the company of powerful men. Between the court of Charlemagne and that of Louis, the gender dynamics underwent a fundamental change.

---

[18] *Karolus Magnus et Leo Papa*, pp. 370–2, lines 177–267. See also Theodulf's poem on the court, which also puts the daughters in the limelight: Godman, *Poetry*, p. 154. Cf. Nelson, 'La cour impériale', pp. 186–9.

[19] On Ermold's dependence on *Karolus Magnus et Leo papa*, see Godman, *Poets and Emperors*, p. 111.

[20] Ermold, p. 176, lines 2302–6.   [21] Ibid., p. 182, lines 2377–80.

[22] Ibid., p. 180, lines 2354–5; p. 184, lines 2418–20.   [23] Ibid., p. 182, lines 2394–400.

[24] Walahfrid, *De imagine Tetrici*, pp. 374–7, lines 147–239. Cf. Godman, *Poets and Emperors*, pp. 133–45.

[25] Ermold, p. 200, lines 2645–6: 'Tu quoque, digna sibi conjux, pulcherrima Judith, / Quae secum imperii culmina jure tenes.'

The contrast between Charlemagne's supposedly immoral court and Louis's more virtuous successor has been much exaggerated, usually with reference to the Astronomer's depiction of Louis's takeover of Aachen.[26] Even before his accession to the throne, Louis had long been angered about 'what his sisters had been getting up to in his father's household, by which stain alone his father's house was soiled'.[27] Louis wanted to remedy this abuse, said the Astronomer, while preventing that a new scandal would arise like the one that once happened on account of Odilo and Hiltrude. Once Louis had taken possession of Aachen, 'the emperor ordered the entire troop of women, which was huge (*qui permaximus erat*), to be excluded from the palace, except for a very few whom he deemed suitable for royal service'.[28] The sisters' shameful conduct was situated *in contubernio paterno*, that is, in their father's company and in his household; this had caused a moral contamination of the 'paternal house' (*domus paterna*) that affected the entire palace community. The Astronomer deftly contrasted the royal quarters with the palace at large, suggesting that this female depravity spread outwards from the centre like a stain that affected the entire royal household.

It is not surprising that later generations have read illicit relations between the father and his daughters into this highly charged prose.[29] Yet this interpretation does not fit the Astronomer's otherwise deferential treatment of Charlemagne, or the utter taboo of incest even among distant kinsmen, let alone close ones, that prevailed within early medieval aristocracies.[30] Furthermore, the Astronomer's innuendo is clearly directed against the dominant role of women in the palace, and on the fact that their choice of partners had been beyond male control. For this reason, he brought up the notorious case of Hildtrude, Charles Martel's daughter by his Bavarian wife Swanahild, who had eloped with the Bavarian Duke Odilo, against her brothers' express wish. From this union Charlemagne's adversary Tassilo was born.[31] The Astronomer's message is unambiguous: undisciplined behaviour on the part of the women of the palace would not only damage royal authority and the ruler's reputation, but would also yield dangerous political opponents of the kind of Tassilo, that is, men of royal blood who might pose a challenge to the throne. One lead player in the Astronomer's narrative about 814, Wala, was portrayed as such a potentially dangerous

---

[26] See the discussion of this text by Nelson, 'Women at the court'.
[27] Astronomer, c. 21, p. 348: 'Moverat autem eius animum iamdudum, quamquam natura mitissimum, illud quod a sororibus illius in contubernio exercebatur paterno, quo solo domus paterna inurebatur nevo.'
[28] Astronomer, c. 213, p. 352.
[29] On the ambiguity of the innuendo against Charlemagne's daughters, see Nelson, 'Women at the court', pp. 239–40.
[30] De Jong, 'An unsolved riddle'.   [31] Fredegar, *Chronicae, Continuationes*, c. 25, p. 180.

opponent: 'Above all Wala was feared, who occupied the highest rank with Emperor Charles, in case he might be organising something sinister against the emperor.'[32] In this powerful depiction of a regime change, fraught with anxiety, Wala and Louis's sisters represented the old regime; yet Wala was also the one who had to prove his loyalty by cleaning up the palace at Aachen, and expelling the 'troop of women' and their associates. It was he who headed a small advance expedition that was to bring back order to the palace, locking up the worst offenders for Louis himself to deal with, once he had made his solemn entry into the palace.[33] What better way to emphasise Wala's total submission to the new ruler than to make him the instrument of the old guard's undoing? Once more, the Astronomer's choice of words indicates that unspeakable debauchery (*stuprum*) had been going on in Aachen, along with the kind of arrogance (*superbia*) that amounted to treason. The message was that under Charlemagne, what should have been a place of discipline had become disordered by women.

Was this a straightforward denunciation of Charlemagne's sexual morals – to wit, he had too many concubines? I very much doubt it. All this was about the fear of powerful royal women who were seen as creating disorder in the palace, expressed in terms of pollution. The daughters and other female relatives (nieces from Italy, for example) who wielded political influence were the focus of this literary onslaught – not Charlemagne's alleged womanizing, serial monogamy or whatever else one makes of it.[34] Charlemagne's unmarried daughters were much more important than the universally cited concubines to anyone at the time, including the Astronomer. It should also be remembered that this author wrote in the early 840s, with first-hand experience of the scandal of 830. This, in turn, he may have projected on to the transition of 814. The Astronomer said openly what Einhard had only hinted at: that Charlemagne did not control his daughters, to his peril. According to Einhard, the emperor had kept his daughters unmarried because he could not do without their company (*contubernium earum*). The ensuing gossip about the daughters' conduct was Charlemagne's only misfortune. As Einhard expressed it, 'because of this, though he [Charles] was otherwise fortunate, he encountered the mishap of bad fortune. This, however, he ignored, as if on their account no suspicion of any immoral conduct arose or no scandal (*fama*) was spread.'[35] This may well be a rhetorical strategy. Real praise was all the more effective if perfection was mitigated by one flaw, and not a very serious flaw, for that matter. Indulging one's daughters and overlooking

[32] Astronomer, c. 21, p. 346. Cf. Nelson, 'Women at the court', p. 240.
[33] Astronomer, c. 21, p. 348.   [34] Cf. Nelson, 'Women at the court'.
[35] Einhard, *VK*, c. 19, p. 25.

their peccadilloes could count as such.[36] Still, Einhard wrote his *Vita Karoli* in Louis's court, and his oblique remark about the daughters creating scandal may well have been a public acknowledgement that *mores* at the court had changed since the old emperor's death.

From their different use of the expression *contubernium*, it is clear that the Astronomer built upon and reinforced Einhard's discreet innuendo. *Contubernium* was not an everyday word, so biblical commentators needed to explain it, and did so by giving examples their audience would understand.[37] Most often, the illustrations they chose have something to do with people who live together and are related by familiarity, kinship, love or friendship. Hraban Maur, for example, citing Alcuin, compared Wisdom's proximity to God to the companionship of friends (*contubernium amicorum*). What Hraban had in mind was *amicitia* in the sense of male loyalty and solidarity: the mutual comfort of friends, he maintained, made domestic worries bearable and ensured a good night's sleep.[38] In an entirely different context, but with a similar meaning, Agobard warned against the dangers of Christians and Jews living in the same household (*habitandi contubernium*).[39] At times this 'household' could be expanded to the entire community of Christians (*contubernium Christianorum*), from which the excommunicated were excluded, yet there was also the intimate meaning of the companionship between man and wife. Thus, Einhard referred to his deceased wife Imma as his *contubernalis carissima* (dearest spouse).[40] Writing of Charlemagne's daughters, he said the old emperor could not do without 'their company' (*contubernio earum*), without any negative inflections. Equally lacking in moral indignation is Nithard's reference to the 'palace clean-up' of 814. His own mother Bertha was one of Louis's (half-)sisters banished 'to monasteries', as Nithard expressed it. For him the most important thing was, however, that Louis had endowed his legitimate sisters (including Bertha) with their rightful inheritance.[41] As far as one can see, there was no particular resentment on

---

[36] On the use of this ironic style in the Astronomer, see Siemes, *Beiträge*, pp. 96–7.

[37] In the first of two biblical instances, one also finds the military connotation: when Christ ordered the people to divide themselves into groups of fifty or a hundred, they did so *secundum contubernia* (Marc. 6.39). In the second biblical passage, Wisdom is said to be 'living with God' (*contubernium habens Dei*) or to have, more literally, 'God's company', who therefore loves her above all others (Sap. 8.3).

[38] Hraban Maur, *Expositio in Ecclesiasticum*, PL 109, VII, c. 10, col. 998A.

[39] Agobard, *De cavendo convictu et societate Iudaica*, p. 232, lines 59–60.

[40] Lupus, *Epistolae*, no. 3, p. 16.

[41] Nithard, I, c. 2, p. 6: 'quas et instanter a palatio ad sua monasteria abire praecepit'. Presumably, those expelled from the palace were Hildegard's daughters Bertha, Gisela, Hiltrud, and Fastrada's daughter Theodrada. Nithard implied that there were also non-legitimate sisters in Aachen, who had no right to any inheritance. Cf. Nelson, 'Women at the court'.

the son's part about his mother's exile from the palace. Nithard had to accept this brave new world.

The Astronomer's dark intimations about what Louis's sisters had been getting up to 'in their father's household' (*in … contubernio paterno*), a reason for Louis's anger and decisive action, was of a different order altogether.[42] This narrative has come to dominate modern views on Charlemagne's daughters. Enhancing Einhard's subtle hints, and appealing to collective memory, the Astronomer successfully hammered home that upon his succession Louis had imposed a new moral order in Aachen as well as on the entire Frankish realm. The regime change of 814 was defined in terms of purification, and the dangerous contamination as this 'enormous troop' of unruly women that needed to be expelled. There is no doubt that Louis did banish his sisters and their retinue from Aachen; what is not at all certain, however, is whether the new emperor did so because he was shocked by the lewd conduct of his female relatives. This was the Astronomer's compelling narrative, written well after the scandal that engulfed Judith in 830. He did not have to invent the many women that inhabited Charlemagne's palace, but he certainly made the most of any hint of their sexual misconduct that he could find in his sources – written and otherwise. The denunciation of sexual misconduct was invariably linked to the Astronomer's aversion to women with political clout. Female authority was a contradiction in terms that spelled disorder, in the royal bedroom as well as in the public domain of the palace and the kingdom.

The actual creation of a new moral order within the palace itself was a matter of time, and of successive generations, as is shown by the treatise *De ordine palatii*.[43] The so-called *Capitulary about the discipline of the palace in Aachen* (a modern title), a text usually dated to c. 820, represents a stage in this process.[44] This precept was aimed at the court in the broadest sense of the word, and was intended to identify and drive out all those whose behaviour might contaminate the moral order of the palace. A system of constant investigation and observation was devised. The household officers (*ministeriales*) of the king, the queen and their children should ascertain whether anyone in their own retinue or that of others was hiding prostitutes, murderers, adulterers or other criminals. The investigation left no stone unturned:

---

[42] Astronomer, c. 21, p. 348; see above, n. 27.   [43] See above, chapter 2, pp. 60–1.
[44] *Capitulare de disciplina palatii Aquisgranesis* (?820), MGH *Capit.* I, no. 146, pp. 297–8, from MS Paris BnF lat 4788, fol. 114r–117r; for a translation, see Nelson, 'Aachen', pp. 238–9. Louis's seneschal Gunzo is mentioned (Depreux, *Prosopographie*, pp. 227–8), and so is Peter, his main chef (ibid., p. 349). See Mordek, *Bibliotheca*, pp. 546–9, for a description of the manuscript (third quarter of the ninth century, probably France), now illegible in many places.

Ratbert the estate-manager (*actor*) is to have a similar inquiry made in his area of office (*per suum ministerium*) as is in the houses (*mansiones*) of our servants both in Aachen and in the nearby estates belonging to Aachen. Peter and Gunzo must make a similar inquiry throughout the personal rooms (*scruae*) and houses of all our estate managers, and Ernald through the houses of all traders whether they trade in the market (*in mercato*) or elsewhere, and whether they are Christians or Jews. The deputy seneschal (*mansionarius*) is likewise to make inquiry with his junior officers through the houses of bishops and abbots and counts, those who are not themselves estate managers, and our vassals (*vassi*), at a time when those lords (*seniores*) are not there in those houses.[45]

The net was cast wide: the houses and dwellings of anyone of any importance, in Aachen itself and in the nearby estates, were to be scrutinised. One is reminded of Notker's notion that Charlemagne could see everywhere, into the deepest nooks and crannies of the residences of his courtiers, and of Einhard, gazing down with Hilduin from their vantage point high up, near the imperial bedchamber, into a palace that was waking up at the crack of dawn.[46] On this bedchamber the watchful eyes of courtiers had always been trained, but more so on the queen now that no other royal women diverted their attention. In 816 when Pope Stephen crowned Empress Irmingard, he blessed her, saying, 'Hail, woman beloved by God! May you have a long, healthy life that lasts through the years; loved one, may you, the beloved of your husband, always watch over the marriage bed!'[47] Bearing children and ensuring the purity of their descent – those were the two most important duties of an early medieval queen, or of any aristocratic woman for that matter. Yet when the scandal broke in 830, the expectations of Judith were higher, among her adversaries as well as her defenders. A good queen was also the king's helpmate in the governance of the palace and the kingdom (*adiutrix in regimine et gubernacione palacii et regni*).[48] In the public arena, she was a force to be reckoned with, not just during ceremonial banquets and hunting parties, but also as a royal personage who could be approached if one needed to beg for pardon or favour, and with a moral authority of her own.[49] In other words, she shared the 'pinnacles of imperial rule' (*imperii culmina*) with her husband.[50] A rhetorical question asked by Agobard, one of the empress's most intransigent critics, fully expresses the importance of Judith's public role: 'If the queen is incapable of governing herself, how

---

[45] Nelson, 'Aachen', p. 238.   [46] De Jong, 'Charlemagne's balcony'.
[47] Ermold, p. 86, lines 1101–7.   [48] Agobard, *Liber apologeticus*, II, c. 2, p. 316.
[49] See Nelson, 'Gendering courts in the early medieval West', pp. 194–5, on Judith and female agency at the palace.
[50] Ermold, p. 200, lines 2645–6.

then can she guard the honour (*honestas*) of the palace, or how can she effectively handle the reins of the realm?'[51]

Sexual slander

In the spring of 830, or possibly even earlier, rumours began to fly. Thegan darkly hinted at accusations that were too blasphemous (*impius*) to repeat or even to be believed. 'They' said that Queen Judith had been violated by 'a certain Duke Bernard', a royal kinsman and the emperor's godson. These were all lies, Thegan countered.[52] So there was more at stake than Judith's alleged adultery with her chamberlain. According to the then current definition of incest, the fact that Bernard was Louis's godson made the relation an incestuous one. Judith was accused of having had sexual relations with a spiritual kinsman, a much more serious transgression than mere adultery. Incest would become one of the recurrent elements in slander levelled at early medieval queens. One of the more spectacular instances was Queen Theutberga, the wife of Lothar II; in the 850s she was accused of having had sodomitic intercourse with her brother.[53]

Thegan's reluctance to repeat the allegations once Judith had returned to power was understandably shared by many. The only contemporary verbal onslaught on Judith still extant is Agobard's first *Apology* for the elder sons of Louis, a fiery exhortation that may have been preached as a sermon in the camp of the rebellious sons, on the Field of Lies in 833.[54] The archbishop made the most of inverting the two interconnected qualities praised by Judith's supporters: her beauty and virtue, which upheld the honourable order (*honestas*) of the palace. The beauty that had only shortly before been the hallmark of the empress's royal dignity now became the visible sign of her moral depravity, polluting the palace and dishonouring the Franks; it was no longer associated with inner virtue and regal *gravitas*, but instead with the irresponsibility and levity of youth. All peoples to the end of the earth should know, Agobard exclaimed, that Louis's sons had justly risen against their father, in order to expurgate the

---

[51] Agobard, *Liber apologeticus*, I, c. 4, p. 311: 'si qua regina semetipsam regere non novit, quomodo de honestate palatii curam habebit? aut quomodo gubernacula regni diligenter exercet?'
[52] Thegan, c. 36, p. 222.
[53] Airlie, 'Private bodies', p. 19; on incest legislation and its early medieval ramifications, see de Jong, 'An unsolved riddle'. On the accusations of adultery against Judith and subsequent queens, see Bührer-Thierry, 'La reine adultère'; further, Ward, 'Agobard of Lyons'; Koch, *Kaiserin Judith*, pp. 107–15.
[54] Boshof, *Agobard*, pp. 228–9; Agobard, *Liber apologeticus*, I.

palace of sordid crimes and the factions perpetrating them. In this palace
Louis had reigned peacefully, duly performing his marital duties to his
still-young wife; but then his age had made him tepid and frigid, allowing
the queen to become lascivious and wanton, first secretly, but then
openly.[55] Agobard's resentment and anger were concentrated on
Judith's 'apostasy', for in his view this was the crime the empress had
committed when she took off her veil and returned to the palace, rather
than remaining in Ste-Croix and performing the penance imposed on her.
Having exchanged her royal gown for the habit of a nun (*mutato habitu
regali, induto habitu sanctimonialis*), she should have remained in monastic
custody, but now she was back again, and her husband preferred her
advice over that of other counsellors.[56] Agobard did not even bother to
mention Bernard. His target was Judith herself, who had caused a wound
of iniquity that should be cleansed and covered by a scar of health, without
any effusion of blood.[57] This implicit call for penance, expressed by the
usual medical metaphors and defined as an alternative to bloodshed, is
one of the reasons why this text is best dated to the months prior to the
Field of Lies in 833, rather than to the aftermath of Judith's restoration in
831, as I formerly thought.[58]

Radbert, who wrote roughly two decades after these events, was fero-
cious about Judith, whom he called Justina after the empress who had
persecuted Ambrose. Yet Bernard/Naso, the evil adulterer, was Radbert's
real *bête noire*. Nothing happened without Naso's will, he claimed, and the
king and queen were totally under his domination.[59] He painted the day in
August 829 in Worms, when Bernard was appointed chamberlain, in
apocalyptic hues: 'Oh that day (*dies illa*) on which a near-permanent
darkness reached this earth, and the danger that tore apart and divided a
peaceful and united rule, that violated brotherhood, separated kinsmen,
and created enmity everywhere ...'[60] The catalogue of all that Thegan
thought too terrible to repeat can be found in the *Epitaphium Arsenii*:
Bernard, who had designs on the throne and wished to marry Judith,
their joint efforts to poison Louis while making it look like illness, and
Bernard's plans to kill off the elder sons, beginning with Pippin, and then

---

[55] Ibid., c. 2, p. 309.   [56] Ibid.
[57] Ibid., p. 312: 'ut exprimatur vulnus iniquitatus et obducatur cicatrix sanitatis, absque sanguinis effusione'.
[58] De Jong, 'Bride shows', p. 269.   [59] Radbert, *EA*, II, c. 9, p. 71.
[60] Ibid., c. 7, p. 67: 'O dies illa, quae pene aeternas huic orbi tenebras attulit et discrimina, quae pacatum imperium et unitum conscidit particulatim ac divisit, germanitates violavit, consanguineous dirempsit, inimicitias ubique procreavit' See also ibid., p. 68: 'O dies illa, dies tenebrarum et caliginis! O dies exsecranda, quando tale coeptum est consilium!' (cf. Ioel 2.2).

the chief courtiers (*optimates*), by whatever possible ruse.[61] But Wala was not fooled. Nobody had any doubts about the adultery – that was out in the open – but from him, Wala, the elder sons learned how many sooth-sayers and diviners had flocked to the palace, from the entire world, as if the Antichrist had appeared with all his *maleficia*. Wala finally revealed the odious plans for Louis's death, and for the overthrow of the imperial order, at which all this malign craft was aimed. The sons and magnates then decided they would rather die than allow this to continue; the abominable and infamous Bernard was the cause of all this.[62]

Radbert may not have been a good character witness for Judith, but he is an important source of information for the kind of slander that circulated at the time. The 'palace of memory' he reflected on in the early 850s was a once well-ordered moral universe that had been contaminated by the unspeakable pollution of sin. Accordingly, Wala's remedies were charac-terised in terms of purification. The adultery that had already become public should no longer be 'concealed in confusion'. Given that there was already a scandal, let it come out in the open, like a boil bursting, and be dealt with in the proper way, by a public penance. All the diviners and dream-interpreters who had bewitched the emperor, so that he no longer took advice from the right kind of counsellors, should be driven from the palace. Adultery, incest, poison, witchcraft, designs of the second-in-command to murder the ruler and marry the queen – all these accusa-tions belong to the standard repertoire of palace intrigues throughout Western history, yet Judith was the first queen whose alleged adultery developed into such a full-blown scandal.[63]

As has been noted, one of the reasons why this scandal could develop was the daily co-operation between the empress and the chamberlain. Both of them had a key role in the royal household, which threw them together and laid them open to suspicion. Both had formal access to the treasure and handed out gifts to royal followers and foreign visitors.[64] *De ordine palatii* gives a good idea of how Judith and Bernard may have operated together in the public space of the court, in a section that, following Janet Nelson's arguments, I regard as part of the original core of the work written by Adalhard:[65]

The honourable order (*honestas*) of the palace and especially the royal treasure, as well as the annual gifts to the king's household retinue (apart from food, drink and

---

[61] Radbert, *EA*, II, c. 9, p. 72.   [62] Ibid.: 'scelestus, flagitiosus, et auctor totius malitiae'.
[63] Bührer-Thierry, 'La reine adultère'; De Jong, 'Bride shows' and 'Queens and beauty'.
[64] Ward, 'Caesar's wife', pp. 206–7; on early medieval queenship, see Stafford, *Queens, Concubines and Dowagers*.
[65] Nelson, 'Aachen', pp. 228–32.

horses), pertained primarily to the queen, and under her, to the chamberlain. Depending on the nature of the occasion they made sure to foresee future needs at the right time, so that nothing would be lacking at the time when it was required. The chamberlain took care of the gifts for various legates, unless this concerned something that, at the orders of the king, was more fitting for the queen to handle together with himself. All this and similar things were meant to ensure that the Lord King, without any domestic or palatial cares and in so far as was reasonable and right, had, with constant trust in the everlasting God, his mind permanently ready for the ordering and safeguarding of the well-being of the entire kingdom (*status omni regni*).[66]

Jointly, the queen and the chamberlain occupied themselves with the ceremonial and practical aspects of life at the court, and particularly with visiting *fideles* and legates. Generally, the chamberlain took care of the latter, but if foreign visitors were sufficiently eminent, the royal couple would oversee their reception in person. The queen outranked the chamberlain, but ideally they operated as a team that enabled the king to concentrate on the stability of the realm. The queen and chamberlain were also responsible for the *honestas* of the palace, an expression that I translated above as 'honourable order', for want of a better phrase. 'Dignity' is much too weak a term, for it is all about the reputation of the palace, of which the bishops in 829 said that it was a 'sacred house' that should be admirable (*spectabilis*), worthy of imitation and with an impeccable reputation (*fama*).[67] For foreign embassies and important visitors, the queen and chamberlain were the public face of the royal household, the portal through which guests passed before they were admitted to the ruler himself. Only the most illustrious visitors merited an immediate reception by the king and queen.

Not all queens and chamberlains working together were accused of adultery, however. The case of Judith and Bernard was special, in that both were perceived as monopolising access to Louis, and barring others from gaining the emperor's ear. This was not just a slanderous allegation; it was a fear that was not unfounded. Well before 830 Judith was already a go-between (*ambasciator*) between Louis and those asking for favours from him, and a patroness in her own right.[68] Her enemies all sang the same refrain: Louis, bewitched by Judith's beauty, would listen only to her, and no longer to his trusted counsellors, who felt excluded and

[66] *De ordine palatii*, c. V (22), pp. 72–4. My translation differs from the one offered by Gross and Schieffer: 'ornamentum' should not be translated as 'Schmuck' or jewelry but as 'royal attire', that is, the king's treasure; also, it was not the *milites* who gave gifts; rather, they received them, otherwise the addition about food, drink and horses makes no sense. Or are we to believe that the king's retainers presented him with these commodities?
[67] Council of Paris (829), III, c. 24, MGH *Conc.* II/2, p. 678.
[68] Depreux, *Prosopographie*, pp. 284–6.

mightily offended. The deposition of Matfrid and Hugh at the beginning of 828 disrupted the usual channels of patronage, adding to the general feeling of insecurity. Some turned instead to Judith, who to some extent seems to have filled the gap. And then there was Bernard, made chamberlain with extraordinary powers. He was Louis's support (*supplementum*), Nithard said; the emperor commended Charles to Bernard's protection, and made him second in the empire, after himself.[69] The Astronomer called Bernard a bastion (*propugnaculum*), erected against the relentless plotting of Matfrid and Hugh, but he also noted that this did not clear the hotbed of discord. On the contrary, it grew out of control.[70] Once he entered Aachen, Bernard rode roughshod over established positions at the palace. As Radbert explained, the 'most sacred emperor' (*sacratissimus augustus*) was deluded by wiles of the devil into repelling those whom he himself or his great father had raised and educated at the court. Ties that had been forged from adolescence onwards were now threatened with dissolution, and men of the palace with a long record of service were deprived of the private audiences, intimate conversations, familiarity and counsel, and the oaths of loyalty and *honores* – in short, of all the proximity to the ruler they had enjoyed for so long.[71]

In Radbert's view, Bernard had been Wala's greatest adversary, yet he also reminded his interlocutors and readers that old ties of kinship and friendship existed between these two great men. Both belonged to the top echelon of the Frankish elite; they were magnates (*proceres*) from illustrious families with a considerable history of friendship, kinship and inter-marriage.[72] Bernard's father Count William of Toulouse and Wala were cousins, both descended from Charles Martel. William and Wala had long been on friendly terms. As a young man Wala had married William's daughter; to the young Bernard, Wala had been like a father.[73] Of course Wala reminded Bernard of this shared past, said Radbert, but the monster was drunk with desire and would not listen.[74] The tide of fury that rose up against the chamberlain owes at least some of its intensity to the fact that this was a family fight. The leading protagonists were members of the ruling family, be it close or distant, whose lives had also been intertwined

---

[69] Nithard, I, c. 3, p. 10.   [70] Astronomer, c. 43, p. 454.

[71] Radbert, *EA*, II, c. 9, p. 71: 'ut omnes repelleret, quos aut ipse aut magnus pater eius imperator nutrierat, secreto, a colloquio, a familiaritate et consilio, a fidei fide, ab honoribus, et ab omni consortio prioris vitae'.

[72] Weinrich, *Wala*, pp. 17–18.

[73] Radbert, *EA*, II, c. 8, p. 69. Weinrich, *Wala*, p. 18, n. 16, thinks her name was Rothlindis; nothing else is known of her.

[74] Radbert, *EA*, II, c. 8, p. 69: Arsenius talked to the emperor and the *proceres*: 'praemonuit, in his quae fiebant, quod senserat'.

for generations with royal service. Charlemagne had conquered Italy in 774 together with Bernard, Wala's father.[75] From Wala's point of view, Bernard of Septimania belonged to a younger generation that had once been dependent on his patronage, but now threatened to become a wall between himself and the emperor. Both Wala and Bernard rose to a level of power where they seemed like a viable alternative to the legitimate ruler, and were accused of scheming for the throne; yet in the final confrontation in 830 both men lost their positions. Judith, in the end, turned out to be more of a winner than most.

Purity and danger

'The palace became a brothel (*prostibulum*) where adultery governs and the adulterer reigns, crimes are amassed, and abominations and divinations of all kinds of sorcerers are found, so many that I had never believed they still existed in this world, and of all these evils, none was left out, and it was all reported everywhere, to everyone.'[76] Radbert cast Wala in the heroic role of the purifier of the palace, who sent religious men there to mingle with the others and investigate, like so many undercover agents.[77] He is the only author to dwell at length on witchcraft (*maleficia*) in all shapes and sizes: soothsayers, diviners, fortune-tellers and dream-explainers. Bernard was depicted as the 'instigator of all this evil'.[78] By resorting to malign arts of all kind, the chamberlain had predetermined Louis's death and the subversion of imperial rule.[79] The rebellion of the spring of 830, Radbert claimed, was not to deprive Augustus of his *imperium* or to treat him dishonourably (in so far as the situation allowed), but to expel the enemy and all his accomplices from the palace.[80] Radbert's rhetoric brings to mind Christ's expulsion of the money-changers from the Temple, but also the Astronomer's narrative about Wala's cleansing of the palace of 814. Gaining control of the palace and, by proxy, the polity, required an act of purification, and Wala was thought capable of effecting this.

That accusations of witchcraft were not merely part of Radbert's repertoire of slander is revealed by the fate of Bernard's sister, the nun Gerberga, in the summer of 834. When Lothar had captured Chalon-sur-Saône and destroyed the city in a frenzy of revenge, Gerberga was

---

[75] Weinrich, *Wala*, pp. 11–2.   [76] Radbert, *EA*, II, c. 8, p. 69.
[77] Ibid., pp. 69–70.   [78] See above, n. 62.
[79] Radbert, *EA*, II, c. 9, p. 72: 'Ad ultimum vero de nece patris et de totius imperii edixit subversione, qualiter auspiciis, auguriis, consiliis, atque insidiis, necnon et omnibus malignis artibus esset praefixit.'
[80] Ibid.

drowned in the river Saône, 'in the manner of sorcerers', as Nithard expressed it.[81] Deeply disapproving, Thegan added the information that Lothar thus tortured her until she died, according to the judgement of the wives of his wicked counsellors. By implication, this was about as bad a judgement as one could get.[82] Even Radbert seems to have had his doubts, for he had Adeodatus voice the objection that all this adultery, sorcery and other offences existed only in the minds of the common people (*vulgi aestimatione*).[83] Yet clearly accusations of witchcraft also played a crucial role in the mutual strategies of defamation of the political elite, with dire consequences for some of the accused.[84] Gerberga's cruel execution shows that one cannot treat the charges against Judith as mere literary polemics on the part of enemies intent on misleading their audience by consciously spreading lies. According to the Astronomer, Judith feared for her life in April 830, and I see no reason to disbelieve him. He wrote disapprovingly and anxiously about the aggressive crowd that was easily roused to fury. This *vulgus*, the rank and file of the army and their hangers-on, always lurked in the background of royal and aristocratic conflict, ready to turn on new scapegoats created by the changing allegiances of their leaders.[85]

Such crowds were dangerous, precisely because they could be easily manipulated by accusations of adultery and witchcraft. Yet they were not the only ones to perceive the dark arts as a real threat. So did the wives of the wicked counsellors who condemned Gerberga, and Radbert himself, for that matter. The witchcraft charges of the early 830s were part and parcel of the infighting within the highest echelon of society, the membership of the imperial court. Those who were excluded by Bernard attacked him by claiming he had filled the palace with practitioners of the dark arts. One of those Radbert had in mind was probably Gerberga; it stands to reason that during Bernard's brief tenure in Aachen, his sister gained a prominent place at the court. Bernard's siblings suffered grievously from his stellar career: his brother Heribert was blinded, and Gerberga ended up at the bottom of the river. This latter revenge was a gendered one. While blinding was the most extreme measure (except for execution) to eliminate a man from the political competition, accusations of witchcraft and adultery were aimed against – and in Gerberga's case, deployed by – powerful women. They operated in places beyond the public

---

[81] Nithard, I, c. 5, p. 22 ('more maleficorum'); see also Astronomer, c. 52, p. 496 ('veneficia'); *AB*, s.a. 834, p. 14 ('in cupa positam').
[82] Thegan, c. 52, p. 244.   [83] Radbert, *EA*, II, c. 9, p. 73.
[84] Cf. Riché, 'La magie à l'époque Carolingienne'.
[85] Astronomer, c. 45, p. 462.

gaze, raising male suspicion about all that went on in the secret reaches of the *domus*.

In more respects than one, Louis's court of the early 830s fits Mary Douglas's typology of societies prone to witchcraft beliefs. These are part of a larger category of societies with a strong sense of hierarchy and an insistence on clearly delineated group boundaries; sin or evil manifests itself as a contamination, comparable to a malignant disease that will spread and then corrupt the entire social and cosmic order. In the case of witchcraft-prone societies, an already present anxiety about potential disorder and the resulting contamination can become much stronger when members of the group become less secure about their place in the hierarchy, and about their ability to guard its boundaries. This then results in a pervasive fear of evil, usually perceived as coming from outside, but insiders as well are suspected of being, and revealed to be, secret evildoers that need to be expelled or destroyed. Precisely because order and integrity are so precarious, much energy is devoted to internal social control and the guarding of external boundaries. Since the lines of authority are unclear, as is the precise social ranking of those involved, the identification of a polluting invader is difficult; confusion and fear mean that the enemy is perceived everywhere. Evil is perceived as a form of pollution; accordingly the eradication of this internal enemy takes the shape of a purification.[86]

All this brings to mind Louis's court in the years preceding the rebellion of 830, in which the hierarchy in the palace had been askew ever since February 828, when Matfrid and Hugh fell from grace. The resulting power gap created a confusion that led to firm measures, such as putting Bernard in charge, and then to yet more scapegoats. Underneath it all, there was the shrill insistence on the need for a restoration of order, both inside the palace and in the realm at large, and a fear of disorder that was expressed in terms of polluting sin. Its contaminating power would ultimately lead to the disintegration of the polity, through God's punishment of his people, for its own sins and, above all, that of its leadership. As I discussed in the previous chapter, these anxieties were voiced in the winter of 828–9, especially by Einhard and Wala, but they were by no means dispelled by the remedies that were proposed. Less illustrious authors jumped on to the bandwagon, with less civility towards the queen than the great men who had basked in her company. The visionary text that came closest to a harsh critique of queenship is the brief and curious *Vision of the Poor Woman of Laon*, a text with a manuscript tradition that, like so many

---

[86] Douglas, *Natural Symbols*, pp. 88–9, 136–42, 169–70.

of these writings, originated in Reichenau. It has been ascribed to Heito, and to the late 820s, but this seems unlikely;[87] this was a much less skilled author at work, and he conflated Louis's two queens, Irmingard and Judith. Supposedly, Irmingard was deposed at a time of crisis, but this fits Judith in 830 and 833, not her predecessor. Guided by a man dressed like a monk, the poor woman saw the 'ruler of Italy' (Charlemagne) in a torment that could be ended only if his son Louis would make a substantial donation on his behalf.[88] Then the woman met the avaricious Bego, Louis's son-in-law and the former count of Paris, who was fed liquid gold, and Queen Irmingard, Louis's deceased wife, who pushed millstones up a hill and implored her visitors to ask her husband to help her.[89] Louis would know that they were her truthful messengers, Irmingard said, when they mentioned the orchard, where she had a secret conversation with him 'at the stormy time of my deposition'.[90] Then her guide showed her a wall where the name of Bernard of Italy glowed in golden letters, while that of Louis was so faded that it was hardly legible any more. Before he perpetrated the murder of Bernard, explained the woman's guide, there was nobody whose name had been quite so illustrious as the emperor's, but 'the killing of the one had meant the obliteration of the other'.[91] Here, no angels eloquently admonish their charges about the best means of atonement and the value of prayer. Louis should have done his duty by his father and his deceased wife, but he had obviously omitted to do so; that Bernard of Italy died because Louis authorised his murder (*homicidium*) could not be put more bluntly.

The charges levelled against the empress and her chamberlain in 830 are highly revealing articulations of ninth-century ideals of politico-religious order. It is the very notion of order itself that is constantly hammered home, by defining and attacking the evils of its opposite: *perturbatio, confusio, conturbatio, turbulentia*. Agobard's prose is a case in point, with its interconnected metaphors of illness, pollution and disorder. The healing knife of penance should expose and cure the wound of

---

[87] Houben, 'Visio', pp. 32–40, thinks the text stems from the late 820s. The oldest manuscript witness (Cod. Aug. Perg. 111) contains the *Visio Wettini* in a hand of the late 830s (92r–97r); on 91v this short text has been squeezed in.

[88] Houben, 'Visio', p. 41: 'quendam principem Italiae'. Cf. Heito, *Visio Wettini*, c. 11, p. 271, where Charlemagne is referred to as 'quendam principem, qui Italiae et populi Romana sceptra quondam rexerat'. There is some obvious dependence on the *Visio Wettini*, but the different styles of these two references to Charlemagne are representative of the unequal literary skills of their respective authors.

[89] On Bego, see Depreux, *Prosopographie*, pp. 120–2.

[90] Houben, 'Visio', p. 41: 'et da ei signum, ut sciat a me missam te fore, istud quod meę depositionis tempestate sola cum ipso loquabar in uno pomerio'.

[91] Ibid., p. 42: 'Illius interfectio istius obliteratio fuit.'

iniquity, without deadly carnage, without bitter disputes, and without the 'disorderly and foetid fusion of the spirits of the polluted' (*absque turbu-lenta et fetida comixtione spirituum immundorum*). Such imagery was the stock-in-trade of penitential literature, which presented the priest as the 'good doctor' ready to cure his patient of the illness caused by sin; yet the healing knife to which Agobard referred was not just any act of atonement, but a public penance of the sort imposed for public and scandalous sins. There was nothing private about Judith's adultery or about the discord among courtiers that had impaired the 'honour of the palace'. This notion of *honor* or *honestas palatii* denoted the integrity and order of the royal household, and the beneficial effect of this internal order on the polity at large. Sin in the palace was by nature public sin, and once it became known in the outside world, the scandal caused did inestimable damage, offending God and sending shockwaves of disorder through the kingdom. This causal chain, with pollution spreading outwards from the palace, was made explicit by Agobard when he explained why the elder sons had taken action against their stepmother in 830: the paternal bed had been contaminated, the palace soiled, the realm confused, and the name of the Franks, which until then had been renowned in the entire world, had been obscured.[92]

If one inverts all these anxious polemics revolving around disorder and impurity, one ends up with the positive counter-image: the palace as it should be, the epitome of divinely approved order at the centre of a peaceful polity. In this context, the key words were *pax* and *concordia*, *tranquillitas* and *quietas*, *fides* and *caritas*. All these notions and their synonyms denoted the right order in which Christians lived in harmony, with one another and with God; according to this conception of political order, God's people were guided towards salvation by their ruler. These were the fundamental notions that informed the discourse on public order, hierarchy and authority; to relegate them to the domain of imprac-tical religious idealism is missing the point. *Fides*, the loyalty to one's lord, was a paramount virtue in Carolingian aristocratic society, secular and ecclesiastical. The obligations and practice of earthly fidelity also reson-ated in the *fides* due to God. To translate *fides* as faith in this context means introducing modern and anachronistic notions of 'belief'. For Radbert, *fides* to God should always prevail over loyalty to earthly lords, yet for Wala and his supporters this was by no means an easy decision. There was nothing abstractly spiritual about Carolingian *fides*; to accuse someone of

---

[92] Agobard, *Liber apologeticus*, I, c. 1, p. 311: 'videntes maculatum stratum paternum, sordidatum palatium, confusum regnum, et obscuratum nomen Francorum, quod hac-tenus clarum fuerat in totum orbe.'

infidelity hit where it hurt. Likewise, that other central ninth-century concept, *ministerium*, was full of concrete imagery. The ruler, the magnates and the clergy belonged as limbs to a single body, the 'Church-Commonwealth', as Philippe Buc aptly called it.[93] This conceptualising of the polity in terms of physical integrity, with the head (the ruler) and the limbs ideally functioning in unison, created a minimal tolerance for public conflict and disorder. It also meant that conduct of the ruler and those sharing his ministry could endanger the integrity of the body politic and its salvation. Combating this very danger was what Carolingian 'reform' was all about.

The polemics against Judith reveal that by 830, the same held true for the ruler's wife: the empress. The question posed earlier about kings – how can they govern their people if they cannot govern themselves? – was now asked about Judith, whose youth and playfulness were emphasised in order to show that she was incapable of good government: rather than a *domina legitima*, she was a *domina ludens*.[94] The image of Pseudo-Cyprian's fifth 'aberration of this world', the woman without modesty, must have come to mind.[95] Those rushing to the empress's aid, such as Hraban Maur in his commentaries on the biblical books of Judith and Esther, underlined the gravity and legitimacy of the empress, and the fact that she had a ministry divinely bestowed upon her.[96] In an acrostic poem, Hraban incorporated the image of Judith as a ruler blessed by the hand of God.[97] In his prose preface Hraban further underlined the empress's legitimacy, this time by calling himself 'a tiny particle of the people committed to you by God'.[98] From opposite ends of the political spectrum, these churchmen expected their empress to be a model of dignity, embodying, together with the ruler, a palace without discord or scandal, at the centre of a realm that was truly at peace.

Rebellion and restoration

As soon as the rebellion broke out, after Easter 830, Judith had sought refuge in the nunnery of St Mary in Laon, but she was not safe there.

[93] Buc, 'Political rituals', p. 194. Cf. Airlie, 'Private bodies'.
[94] Agobard, *Liber apologeticus*, I, c. 5, p. 311.
[95] Ps-Cyprian, *De duodecim abusivis*, pp. 40–3, on the *femina sine pudicitia*; see Smith, 'Gender and ideology', pp. 59–60.
[96] De Jong, 'Exegesis' and 'Bride shows'.
[97] Geneva, Bibliothèque Publique et Universitaire, MS lat. 22. Cf. Sears, 'Louis the Pious as *miles Christi*', p. 620 and fig. 54.
[98] Hraban, *Epistolae*, no. 17a, p. 420, lines 28–9: 'nos etiam quantulacumque pars plebis a Deo vobis commissae sub pietate vestra degentes'.

Pippin sent armed men to take his stepmother from the church of the convent, and had her brought to Verberie for interrogation. According to the succinct version of the *Annals of St-Bertin*, Pippin took away his father's royal power (*regia potestas*) as well as his wife, dispatching her to the convent of Ste-Croix, Radegund's foundation at Poitiers, while Judith's brothers Rudolf and Conrad were also tonsured and shut up in monasteries.[99] The Astronomer's narrative is more elaborate, and more damning of Judith's captor. After submitting the empress to severe duress, including torture and death threats, Pippin and his men got the empress to promise that, provided she was given ample time to talk to Louis, she would persuade the emperor to lay down his arms, receive tonsure and commit himself to a monastery; she herself would then take the veil and convert to monastic life as well. When Judith did get to meet Louis, he gave her permission to take the veil, to save her life; as for his own tonsure, the emperor demanded time for further deliberation. When the queen returned, her captors gave in to the demands of the rabble and ordered her to be exiled and locked up in St Radegund's nunnery.[100] The Astronomer's choice of words ('*et in monasterio sanctae Radegundis iusserunt retrudi*') is meaningful, for the expression *retrudere* indicated that force had been used; this was not a voluntary entry into monastic life.[101]

In early medieval political conflict, monasteries played an important role. Religious communities, mostly male but occasionally, as here, also female ones, served as places where the powerful might find a temporary or more enduring refuge, and the hope – but not the certainty – that their adversaries would respect the sacredness of the inner precinct of the religious community.[102] The high born who were allowed to leave the political arena unscathed, retreating into monastic space, were never meant to become monks immediately, or, for that matter, monastic prisoners. Both parties kept their options open; this was the aim of the operation. For men, such monastic exile amounted to something one might refer to as 'political tonsure'. During Louis's reign it occurred on quite an unprecedented scale, as an integral part of the emperor's clemency with his major opponents. In 818, in the aftermath of Bernard of Italy's revolt against Louis the Pious, the initial death sentence for Bernard and other ringleaders was converted into blinding, a punishment which cost Bernard his life. Yet most of Bernard's followers were treated more leniently. According to the *Royal Frankish Annals*, all the bishops

---

[99] *AB*, s.a. 830, pp. 2–3.   [100] Astronomer, c. 44, pp. 456–8.
[101] On this terminology, see De Jong, 'Monastic prisoners', pp. 326–7.
[102] See De Jong, 'Monastic prisoners', and the literature referred to there; also, recently, Meens, 'Sanctuary'.

involved were deposed, and committed to monasteries as a matter of course; as for the laity, those most guilty were exiled, while those deemed to be more innocent were to be 'tonsured, to live in monasteries'.[103] Only three years later the tide had turned. At the assembly of Thionville in 821 the emperor declared a general amnesty, allowing all insurgents to leave their monasteries as well as their involuntary clerical state. Probably most of the former rebels availed themselves of this opportunity, although Radbert noted that some chose to stay, now giving freely to God the tonsure that had been forced upon them ignominiously and against their will.[104] The rebellion of 830 elicited a similar response. According to the Astronomer, Louis the Pious displayed a truly imperial leniency towards his opponents: 'He ordered the laymen to be tonsured in appropriate places, the clerics to be locked up in suitable monasteries.'[105] Only three months later, however, Louis decided to become even more lenient, returning their property to the insurgents and giving those already tonsured a choice between remaining clerics or returning to the lay state.[106]

Some were offended by the frequency with which Louis sent his adversaries into monastic exile, only to recall them when it suited him. In the early 840s, when Archbishop Ebo of Rheims fought for his rehabilitation, he scathingly wrote of the 'modern authority of the palace', which had compelled lay men and women to assume the monastic habit of the penitent, only to allow them to return to their former secular status as soon as peace had returned.[107] By contrast, he, Ebo, who had completed the full seven years of monastic penance imposed on him, could not return to his episcopal see.[108] Apart from Ebo's understandable anger about this arbitrariness, his remark reveals the close association between monastic exile and public penance. This connection emerges in eighth-century sources and remains an important element in ninth-century representations of political tonsure or veiling: the rebels were defined as serious sinners who were sent to the monastery to do penance for their iniquities. By implication, once they had completed their atonement to the emperor's satisfaction, they could once more return to the world, resuming their former status. This was what Ebo called the 'modern' and therefore unfounded authority of the palace; bishops should be the ones to determine whether a penance had been properly performed, and to absolve the sinners accordingly.[109]

---

[103] *ARF*, s.a. 818, p. 148; Astronomer, c. 30, p. 386.   [104] Radbert, *VA*, c. 50, col. 1534.
[105] Astronomer, c. 45, p. 464.   [106] Ibid., c. 46, p. 466.
[107] Ebo, *Liber apologeticum, forma prioris*, MGH *Conc.* II/2, p. 799.
[108] See below, chapter 7, pp. 000.   [109] See De Jong, '*Paenitentia publica*', pp. 885–6.

This implicit debate about the authority to impose and lift penance, and to determine its duration, had an impact on the way Judith's monastic exile was depicted and interpreted, and so did the prevailing notion that in order to be binding, a conversion to monastic life – including a profession – should be voluntary. The empress's supporters argued loudly and clearly that duress had invalidated her assumption of the veil, as well as her enduring commitment to do penance in Ste-Croix. No valid vows had been broken. Conversely, the other party maintained that Judith had become a nun (*sanctimonialis*), with all the ensuing obligations of permanence. There was room for argument, for royal women who were removed from the political arena by means of monastic exile were relatively rare.[110] Whether in 830 Louis himself was also pressurised into making a monastic profession is hard to determine. The Astronomer maintained that this was what Pippin had in mind, in 830: that Judith would be veiled permanently, and that she would persuade Louis 'to commit himself to the monastery' (*sese monasterio conferret*).[111] Nithard, who blamed Lothar, was even more explicit: the monks who, at Lothar's orders, guarded the emperor tried to get him to accept the monastic life.[112] Possibly. But I suspect this was a projection of the events of the rebellion of 833 on to the earlier revolt. All other sources indicate that in 830 Louis played along and compromised, to the extent that the rebels could say that the emperor had the right to avenge his adulterous wife, yet he spared her, declaring that she should take the veil and do penance. Also, there was real hope that Louis would restore Lothar and all the others who had fallen from grace to their former position. This is suggested by Radbert in a remarkable little speech attributed to Louis, delivered during the assembly of Compiègne in June 830, when Lothar had arrived, taking charge of the rebellion. Even though he hid something different in his heart, as Radbert darkly intimated, the emperor thanked his followers, and admitted to having sinned as no king before him had done. Louis then solemnly vowed to do nothing without their counsel. 'I decide and wish that imperial rule, as it has been ordered in the past and instituted together with you in the past, will remain as it is', that is, a return to the situation when Lothar was co-emperor. According to Radbert, it was the emperor himself who had granted the adulterous empress her life, ordering her to take the veil and do penance.[113] After these promises,

---

[110] Queen Balthild, who in 664–5 withdrew to Chelles, is one example; although she probably did not relinquish the political arena voluntarily, this was the way her hagiographer carefully presented this case of monastic exile. See De Jong, 'Monastic prisoners', pp. 316–7; *Vita Balthildis*, c. 10, p. 495. Another case in point is Adalhard's sister Gundrada (Radbert, *VA*, c. 35, col. 1528A), who was also exiled from the court to Ste-Croix in Poitiers.

[111] Astronomer, c. 45, p. 458.   [112] Nithard, I, c. 3, p. 10.

[113] Radbert, *EA*, II, c. 10, p. 73.

Louis was restored to the throne, raised up with *laudes*, and became the recipient of a loyalty from his faithful men that was even more loyal than before, if this were possible.[114]

Then comes another of Radbert's many assurances that Wala/Arsenius was not disloyal but acted from the noblest of motives, accompanied by the usual enumeration of all that Wala stood for: 'the love of Caesar, imperial rule, the fatherland, all the elder sons, his zealous faith in God, Christian religion and the salvation of the citizens (*cives*) of the realm'.[115] As Radbert stressed, at this assembly Wala was praised as a liberator, especially when Lothar/Honorius came upon the scene and was restored to his co-emperorship in Compiègne.[116] The point is not who really said what in June 830, but that those who genuinely saw themselves as the loyal saviours of their emperor were convinced, there and then, that the old order had been restored. They trusted Louis's declaration to this extent, and much of their subsequent fury was due to their feeling that their loyalty, their *fides*, had been ill-founded and misused by their emperor. It is not at all unlikely that Louis struck a compromise in the summer of 830, paying lip-service to the aims of the loyal rebels and biding his time. An indication of this is the total absence of young Charles in any of the narratives concerning the rebellion of 830.[117] Whereas in 833 his movements were carefully recorded, there is no way of telling where he was during that first revolt; given his tender age, he was most likely with his mother in Poitiers. It did not matter, because the central issue at the time was Lothar's restoration as co-emperor and Pippin's support for his brother's cause, not seven-year-old Charles and his potential claims to the inheritance. *Pace* Nithard, the little prince was still under his eldest brother's tutelage, and no threat to anybody. This would change in the succeeding years, when Louis privileged his youngest son in order to discipline and punish the elder ones, in a series of rearrangements of the succession – but this was another matter altogether.

Louis managed to retrieve his authority largely by his truly imperial humility in Compiègne, building on his earlier atonement in Attigny in 822, in combination with excellent diplomacy. To divert the second general assembly of 830 to Nijmegen, well within the reach of loyal *Germani* but less so for disloyal *Franci*, was nothing short of a brilliant move.[118] The same holds true of the Astronomer's portrayal of Louis during this crucial assembly: it shows a legitimate monarch radiating authority and order, as opposed to Lothar and his allies, who only

---

[114] Ibid.   [115] Ibid., pp. 73–4.
[116] Ibid., p. 74 ('consors imperii et successor totius monarchiae').
[117] Signalled by Nelson, *Charles the Bald*, p. 89.   [118] Astronomer, c. 45, p. 460.

managed to produce chaos. Careful not to be outnumbered, his biographer said, the emperor ordered that every participant should bring only one retainer. Hilduin, who brought a small army, was banished to Paderborn, to spend the winter there in a tent; Wala was exiled to Corbie, to live there like a monk, instead of as the courtier-abbot he had been before. All this was recounted by the Astronomer, who then went on to describe something like a war of nerves. Lothar's followers urged him either to fight or to retreat just a little, even without the emperor's permission. In other words, all the son's movements were subject to his father's authority. Thus they deliberated all night; in the morning Louis sought a rapprochement and invited Lothar to come to him like a son, ignoring their common enemies. Reluctantly, Lothar 'came to his father' (*ad patrem venit*), a turn of phrase that signalled the restoration of the proper hierarchy.[119] Louis did not lash out at him with bitter rebuke (*aspera increpatio*) but corrected him calmly and with moderation. Throughout this passage, the emperor's full control is contrasted with his son's lack thereof; by implication, Lothar was not worthy to take his father's place:

> When he [Lothar] had entered a little way into the royal residence the crowd began to rage against him by diabolical instigation, and the fury might have led to mutual slaughter had not the emperor's prudence intervened. For while they were rushing about against each other in an almost insane fury, the emperor walked into full view of everyone with his son. After he did this, that whole animal-like commotion quietened down, and after they had heard the emperor's speech, that tumult of the whole people dissipated.[120]

True imperial governance and prudence thus prevailed over the animal-like forces of rebellion. The other main theme in the Astronomer's depiction of Louis's return to power was his clemency, which was much too great in the eyes of many; although all were legally found guilty of *lèse-majesté*, none was actually executed.[121] A significant detail was that their death sentence was also pronounced by the 'sons of the emperor'. In other words, once they had been forgiven, Lothar and Pippin had to judge their former allies – a subtle but effective form of humiliation. For this reason, the emperor kept Lothar firmly at his side; with the other sons, presumably including Charles, Lothar had to witness Judith's purification on 2 February, the day of the Purification of the Blessed Virgin. Only then did Louis give his sons permission to leave, said the Astronomer – Lothar to Italy, Pippin to Aquitaine and Louis to

---

[119] Pössel, 'Symbolic communication', pp. 108–16.
[120] Astronomer, c. 45, pp. 462–4.   [121] Ibid., p. 464.

Bavaria.[122] This was another clear statement signalling a full restoration of the old order. The sons were once more at their father's beck and call.

Judith's restoration, as I said, was contentious from the very beginning. Once the assembly in Nijmegen of October 830 had been concluded, she was recalled from her nunnery in Poitiers to the palace at Aachen; the emperor himself returned there before Christmas 830. This much is clear, but then the questions begin. According to Thegan, Judith's name had been fully cleared in Nijmegen; ecclesiastical authority had discharged her from her obligation as a penitent, releasing her from her monastic obligations. As Thegan had it, 'The lord emperor went to his seat [at Aachen] and his wife came there to meet him. He received her honourably on the orders of the Roman pontiff Gregory and because of the just judgement of other bishops.'[123] Another author favourable to Judith also stressed that she had already been cleared by an ecclesiastical verdict – in Nijmegen – and evoked a vivid image of the empress's triumphant *adventus* towards Aachen. First, a drove of magnates rode out to fetch Judith from Poitiers; as she approached the palace, her son Charles was sent to meet her with Archbishop Drogo of Metz and other great men. After Judith's triumphant entry into the palace at Aachen – the place from which she had been driven (and note that it was Aachen, not any other palace) – Louis himself returned Judith to her 'pristine honour'.[124] The Astronomer's view of Judith's restoration was more ambivalent, however, and more in keeping with that of the court annalist, who also made it clear that the empress's restoration did not happen of its own accord. Judith was recalled to the palace, but she was 'not judged worthy of conjugal honour until she had purified herself in the prescribed legal manner from the accusations'. If this *domina* was to be legitimate once more, she first had to be cleansed. The court annalist explained what happened on 2 February, the day of the Purification of the Virgin, during an assembly gathered in the palace in Aachen:

Standing there, in the sight of the Lord Emperor and his sons, she declared her willingness to purge herself of all the charges levelled against her. Then the whole assembled people were solemnly asked if anyone wanted to charge her with any crime. When no one was found who wanted to bring any wrongdoing whatsoever against her, she purged herself according to the judgement of the Franks of all the things of which she had been accused.[125]

---

[122] Ibid., c. 46, p. 464.   [123] Thegan, c. 37, p. 224.
[124] *AMP*, s.a. 830, pp. 97–8. Whereas Thegan suggested that Judith went to meet Louis – preparing him an *adventus* – this version of events has Judith returning first, triumphantly. On Judith's triumphant return to Aachen in 834, see Thegan, c. 51, p. 244.
[125] *AB*, s.a. 831, p. 4; trans. Nelson, *Annals of St-Bertin*, p. 23.

With the full might of Louis's restored imperial power behind the empress, it was not surprising that no accuser dared to come forward. Yet this entire rehabilitation rankled. At the instigation of the Old Enemy, the queen, who should have persisted in the habit of a nun, had been taken back to the palace, where she behaved as if she was the legitimate wife, which was impossible. Because she was indecently and scandalously positioned at the pinnacle of royal might, the former evil once more grew and multiplied. What should good sons do: take this quietly and look the other way?[126] Thus wrote Agobard, defending the sons after they had risen against their father again in the summer of 833.

Although the two rebellions should not be conflated, the revolt of 830 to some extent prepared the ground for its successor. The resentment and frustration of those who thought they had loyally assisted Louis by expelling Judith and Bernard from the palace were intense. According to Radbert, Louis was driven not by *fides* and justice, but by the inspiration of a woman (*femineo instinctu*), which said he could not rule well unless he took his wife back. Lothar, long a *consors* and proclaimed emperor by all, was expelled; the oaths sworn to him were violated on his father's authority; and good and illustrious men who had fought *pro fide*, driven out the tyrant, cleansed the palace, saved the people and the fatherland, and restored the emperor to the throne, together and in fidelity with his son – all these once most beloved men, the first of the palace (*primi palatii*), were now damned and sent into exile.[127] That those who lost out in the revolt felt resentful was nothing out of the ordinary, yet Radbert voiced the aggrieved reaction of men who were convinced that they had only seemed to fight against their emperor. In fact they had fought *for* him (*pro principe contra principem*)[128] and for all the ideals of reform they had shared with him throughout the 820s. More generally, they saw themselves as the champions of royal service, the embodiment of the fidelity to the earthly lord that did not clash with the overriding *fides* due to God. This was indeed a 'loyal palace rebellion', but the unity of the empire was not the issue. The main bone of contention, in 830, was loyalty itself. There was a common ground defined by *fides* from which Louis had retreated, leaving his *fideles* in the lurch, after all they had done for him. This problem of wounded and repudiated fidelity was exacerbated by Louis's punishment of his rebel sons by a series of new succession arrangements, starting with the one of February 831, which left Lothar with only the kingdom of Italy. In a world acutely conscious of perjury as a public sin that would offend God, the resulting tangle of conflicting oaths

---

[126] Agobard, *Liber apologeticus*, II, c. 3, p. 316.
[127] Radbert, *EA*, II, c. 10, p. 74.   [128] Ibid., c. 9, p. 73.

of fidelity increased the general sense of insecurity, fuelling both fear and the urge to resort to atonement as a remedy for all these evils. All this created the volatile dynamics of the next major confrontation: the penitential state was spinning further out of control. In 833 one of the main accusations against Louis was that he had forced his sons and faithful men to perjure themselves, and therefore endangered their souls. It was the rebellion of 830 and the ensuing restoration that had necessitated these conflicting oaths, setting the scene for the major revolt of 833 and the emperor's infamous public penance.

6   Scandal and satisfaction (832–834)

An unexpected visitor

In the three main narratives about Louis's reign (*AB*, Thegan and the Astronomer), the scene for the rebellion of 833 was set by tell-tale signs of encroaching disorder. This was partly due to the strategies of authors writing with hindsight, but the significant behaviour of the protagonists in the story was not just a matter of literary fancy. The authors appealed to an audience which shared assumptions about what constituted order and regularity, and could spot a deviation from normal practice when they saw it. This, presumably, included the protagonists themselves, who viewed disorder and abnormal behaviour along similar lines. For example, in the Astronomer's *Life of Louis*, the royal hunt serves as an indicator of political stability. If Louis could not depart regularly to the Ardennes or Nijmegen to chase game 'according to the custom of the Franks', this was a sure sign of disturbance; when he resumed hunting, it meant that order was restored. Like assemblies, hunting forays with the ruler helped to build solidarity and co-operation among the elite, which was why ninth-century authors could use the resumption of the royal hunt as shorthand to convey that a dangerous conflict had now subsided.[1] The Astronomer ended his narrative about the rebellion of 830 on this note. After Easter 831, in the palace in Ingelheim, Louis had recalled all the rebels he had sent into exile the autumn before. He restored their property and, if they had been tonsured, gave them a choice between remaining in the clerical state or returning to the secular one. 'From there the emperor crossed over to the region of Remiremont through the Vosges and there he gave himself over to fishing and hunting as long as he liked and he sent his son Lothar to Italy.'[2]

Yet the restoration symbolised by customary hunting was a short-lived one. That trouble was brewing was signalled by another kind

---

[1] Nelson, 'The last years', p. 154, n. 44.   [2] Astronomer, c. 46, p. 462.

of narrative, featuring disobedience or even defiance on the part of Louis's
sons.[3] In a world in which filial obedience was an exacting and inflexible
norm, sons who would not come when summoned by their father stood
for a shocking breach of order. By emphasising Pippin's wayward behaviour, both the court annalist and the Astronomer made it clear to their
readers that this was a son who was morally unsound: he was the son
'who would not come'. Pippin did not bother to attend the assembly
at Thionville in 831. He arrived in Aachen only a few days before
Christmas of that year, where his father, displeased with his son's behaviour, 'received him less favourably than he had been used to doing
before'.[4] This in turn provoked Pippin, who left a few days later and
returned to Aquitaine, before daybreak and without his father's permission. 'At this, the Lord Emperor was deeply upset and angered: he had
never thought that such things could happen where his son was concerned
or that he could actually flee from his father's presence.'[5] A showdown
was called for, but these plans were obstructed by Louis the German's
attempt to annex Alemannia at the end of March 832.[6] If Louis indeed
had plans to make Lothar and Charles his sole heirs, and these plans had
already matured in the preceding winter, it is easy to understand why the
two other sons felt threatened and rebelled.[7] Yet the Astronomer situated
this latest plan for succession in the summer of 832, and presented it as the
just deserts for two sons who had disobeyed their father.

With hindsight the rebellion of 833 was foreshadowed by the elder sons'
previous behaviour, and especially by Pippin's recalcitrance. Summoned
to Orléans by 1 September 832, Pippin received a stern paternal rebuke
(increpatio) concerning his flight without permission, as well as a sentence
of monastic custody so that his conduct might be 'emended' and his father
pacified.[8] Elaborating on the confrontation between father and son in
Aquitaine, the Astronomer made the most of Pippin's bad morals, and
of his fleeing in the dark when he was taken to Trier for corrective custody,
roaming through Aquitaine as it pleased him.[9] This emphasis on Pippin,
who wandered where he could and would, reflected the contemporary
suspicions of 'wandering' (vagare), which was the exact opposite of

---

[3] On ninth-century norms of conduct for royal sons, see Kasten, *Königssöhne*, pp. 199–271;
   also R. Schieffer, 'Väter und Söhne', pp. 149–64.
[4] *AB*, s.a. 831, p. 5: 'Quem domnus imperator propter inoboedientiam illius non tam
   benigne suscepit, quam antea solitus fuerat'; Nelson, *Annals of St-Bertin*, p. 24.
[5] *AB*, s.a. 832, p. 5; trans. Nelson, *Annals of St-Bertin*, 24.
[6] Goldberg, *Struggle*, pp. 64–7.   [7] Astronomer, c. 47, p. 470.
[8] This is the version of *AB*, s.a. 832, p. 8; cf. Astronomer, c. 47, p. 470.
[9] Astronomer, c. 47, p. 470.

orderly conduct. St Benedict's sharp condemnation of wandering monks (*monachi gyrovagi*) springs to mind.[10]

In her illuminating analysis of ninth-century narratives and symbolic communication, Christina Pössel has shown that the way in which people approached the emperor constituted a particularly sensitive area. Due deference signalled order and authority, while the lack thereof revealed those who attempted to undermine the stability of the state. For this very reason, authors fully exploited stories about 'approaching' (*ad ... venire*) to communicate moral judgements to their readership. Almost always such judgements were implicit, delivered in the course of a narrative that concentrated on action rather than on reflection. This presupposes audiences with a shared code of conduct as to what was the right kind of behaviour when 'coming towards' the ruler.[11] Ninth-century narratives highlight the formality of the approach (*adventus*) of the ruler, and of the reciprocal and deferential 'coming towards' the illustrious guest, usually referred to as *occursus*. Praying and visiting at the major monasteries on his way to Brittany, Louis received the *occursus* and the gifts of the abbots in charge; Ermold called Louis's visit to Tours the *adventus Caesaris*.[12] Apart from the more elaborate reception ceremonies in religious communities, with special hymns and prayers composed for the visiting ruler, there were non-liturgical but equally strictly ordered ways of receiving royal persons. Another example is the portrayal of the Empress Judith's triumphant return to the palace in Aachen in the autumn of 830 as a proper royal *adventus*, with the *occursus* being performed in two stages. First, Louis sent his magnates to meet her and bring her to him in a way briefly characterised as 'honourably' (*honorifice*); during the last part of her journey she was accompanied by her son Charles, Bishop Drogo of Metz, and more magnates.[13] The author of this text, a supporter of Judith, wanted to make clear to his audience that the empress had indeed been restored to her former position with all the ceremony that was her due.

That Pippin 'would not come' was therefore a serious challenge to Louis's authority. By contrast, that Louis 'let his son, who had so much been led astray, come to him' – that is, Louis the German on the Lechfeld in May 832 – signified that order had been restored.[14] Because his readership knew full well how sons should approach their father, Thegan could summarise the beginning of open hostilities in 833 in one terse sentence:

---

[10] *Regula Benedicti*, c. 1.10–11; Astronomer, c. 47, p. 470.
[11] Pössel, 'Symbolic communication', pp. 108–16.
[12] Ermold, lines 1542–4, 1548–50; Willmes, *Der Herrscher-'Adventus'*, p. 79.
[13] *AMP*, s.a. 830.
[14] *AB*, s.a. 832, p. 7. The annalist blamed Matfrid for having incited Louis to rebel.

'After Easter he [Louis] learned that his sons again did not want to come to him in a way that was peaceful.'[15] This meant that they wanted to come only with troops in tow. In response, Thegan continued, Louis gathered an army and went to meet them on the Field of Lies, 'where the fidelity of many vanished'.[16] In fact, already shortly after Christmas, in Aachen, Louis had received word that his three elder sons were now united against him. He went to Worms, where he remained from the beginning of Lent (26 February) until mid-June, summoning an army and working out a strategy.[17] In the course of May, Lothar travelled north from Italy to take over the leadership of the revolt. With him he brought an unexpected visitor. The arrival of Pope Gregory IV north of the Alps created confusion that bordered on panic.

The presence of the pontiff in the rebellious sons' camp put the Frankish bishops on the spot. Whichever way they turned, they would have to be disloyal. Although the pope was officially on a mission of arbitration between the imperial father and his elder sons, the rumour was that he planned to excommunicate Louis and his bishops if they resisted the rebellious sons. In reaction, the bishops loyal to Louis threatened to excommunicate the pope if he dared to carry out this plan.[18] Contemporary narratives express the political tensions produced by the papal visit in terms of a breach of protocol: Pope Gregory had 'come in the wrong way'. The Astronomer presented an entirely reasonable Louis, who justly blamed the pontiff for not coming to him with customary ceremony: 'To the pope of the Roman see he [Louis] put the question why, if he had come in the way of his predecessors, he was dreaming up so many delays in view of not coming to him (*non sibi occurendo*).'[19] Predictably, the other party accused Louis of having received the pope without due deference and ceremony, which elicited the response that the sons had prevented the emperor from doing so. Rather than a quibble about superficial ceremony, this was a debate about legitimate authority. Who conducted himself according to a divinely sanctioned tradition, Louis or Gregory?

The protocol of a meeting between pope and emperor was carefully recorded and well remembered, so if such rituals were contested afterwards and represented as 'good' or 'bad', it was against a background of

---

[15] Thegan, c. 42, p. 228: 'Post pascha audivit, ut iterum filii sui ad eum venire voluissent non pacifice.'

[16] Ibid.: 'qui usque hodie nominatur Campus-Mendacii, ubi plurimorum fidelitas extincta est.'

[17] *AB*, s.a. 833, p. 8; according to the Astronomer, c. 48, p. 472, Louis went to Worms only in May.

[18] Astronomer, c. 48, p. 472.   [19] Ibid., p. 474.

precise expectations.[20] In 800, when Charlemagne visited Rome, the pope had come towards him over a distance of 12 miles from the city boundary; the next day, Charles proceeded towards Rome through groups of citizens and pilgrims chanting hymns of praise, while Pope Leo and his clergy waited on the steps of St Peter's.[21] This reception 'with the highest honour' stuck in Frankish memory, and so did the visit of the last pope before Gregory to venture north. When in 816 Stephen IV came to crown Louis and Irmingard in Rheims, this had been a joyous and solemn occasion. The court annalist stressed that Louis expected the papal *adventus*, and could therefore receive Stephen with 'great honour'.[22] Building on the *Royal Frankish Annals*, the Astronomer specified that Louis proceeded a mile outside Rheims to greet his illustrious visitor; then he helped him dismount and led him into the church, where appropriate praises were sung.[23] According to Thegan, Louis performed a threefold prostration at the feet of the bishop of Rome.[24] The way in which these two authors lovingly dwelled upon this highly successful papal visit, handled by Louis in a truly imperial fashion, was perhaps also a reaction to the more recent and confusingly unceremonious appearance of Gregory IV in 833. The Astronomer portrayed an unduly meddling pope, who, in consequence, got nowhere, a view that has come to dominate modern historiography.[25] Thegan, however, could not bring himself to say anything against either Louis or the pope, so his version of Gregory's visit was as a proper *adventus* in which everybody played their role. The elder sons and the pope 'went towards' Louis (*obviam eum*), as they should; the pope and emperor then had a conversation; the pope was the first to honour Louis with huge and countless gifts, and the emperor reciprocated in kind.[26]

There is no reason to doubt that Pope Gregory intended to mediate between Louis and his elder sons. From a letter written by Agobard of Lyon to Louis while the pope was on his way, it transpires that around Easter Gregory had asked Agobard to procure peace and concord by prayer and fasting.[27] Agobard did his utmost to reassure Louis that the pontiff came with good intentions, and not 'irrationally, to fight', as the emperor seemed to think. If the latter were the case, Agobard argued,

---

[20] Buc, *Dangers of Ritual*; specifically on Rome and *adventus* ceremonies, Buc, 'Text and ritual'.
[21] *ARF*, s.a. 800, pp. 110–12; Buc, 'Text and ritual', p. 135.   [22] *ARF*, s.a. 816, p. 144.
[23] Astronomer, c. 26, p. 366.   [24] Thegan, c. 16, p. 196.
[25] With the exception of Fried, 'Ludwig der Fromme', pp. 266–5, who goes overboard in the other direction, viewing Gregory's presence on the Field of Lies as the prelude to the future world-historical struggle between pope and emperor. For a more sensible approach, to Louis and the papacy, see Noble, *Republic of St Peter*, pp. 308–22, and *Louis the Pious*.
[26] Thegan, c. 42, p. 228.   [27] Agobard, *De privilegio apostolicae sedis*, c. 5, p. 305.

the pontiff should be driven away, but in fact his coming (*adventus*) was well considered and timely.[28]

Even though the pope's attempt at mediation failed, this contemporary letter shows that the unexpected papal visit hit both the emperor and the Frankish clergy like a bombshell. Their shock at the time still reverberated in the writings of the 840s. The Astronomer's portrait of a pope who made huge but ineffectual threats was completely redrawn by Radbert. He depicted Wala/Arsenius and Pope Gregory IV as close allies, who had worked together for all that was good and orderly: peace, the reconciliation of the father and the sons, of magnates and seniors, for the well-being of churches, the unity of the people and the salvation of the entire empire. Wala's authority was incomparable: in both rebellions he was constantly in demand as a mediator and leader. In Radbert's view, Gregory's *adventus* was not humanly orchestrated but divinely inspired. As by a miracle, a closed route in the Pennine Alps opened up to the 'sacrosanct apostolicus', so that he could travel north.[29] Wala and Radbert made a dangerous journey, for Justina was back at the court. In the end, they were graciously received in the camp of the rebellious sons, first by these kings themselves and their retinues, and then 'with plenty of veneration and great eagerness' by the most holy pontiff. There they found a flustered Pope Gregory, who had been terrified by the resolve of Louis and his followers to resist 'the royal sons, the magnates and the loyal men'. Above all, Gregory was upset by those who had said he should be deposed 'because he had come without being called'.[30] Radbert's alter ego, Paschasius, related how he and Wala had supported the pope by supplying him with appropriate canon law for the occasion:

We also gave him some propositions confirmed by the authority of the holy fathers, his predecessors, whom nobody can contradict, which said that his was the power – actually that of God and St Peter the Apostle – to go where he pleased and to send [missionaries] to all the *gentes*, for the faith and the peace of the churches, for the preaching of the gospel and the proclamation of the truth. In him was all the elevated authority and living power of St Peter, by which all should be judged, to the extent that he himself should be judged by nobody. The pope accepted these writings gratefully and was much comforted.[31]

It is difficult to say whether this unshakeable belief in papal authority had been equally outspoken in 833. Although Agobard was an early example, the intensity of these pro-papal feelings probably owes a lot to the resentment of clerics who suffered from Louis's restoration in 834, and whose

---

[28] Ibid., c. 4, p. 305.   [29] Radbert, *EA*, II, c. 14, p. 81; Weinreich, *Wala*, pp. 79–80.
[30] Radbert, *EA*, II, c. 16, p. 84.   [31] Ibid.

pro-papal sentiments became more radical over time.[32] With the founder-
ing of their ideals, these men began to see the papacy as a moral haven in a
ruthless world. For Radbert, Louis's refusal to receive Gregory 'in the
manner of the kings of old, with hymns and *laudes*', signalled not only the
failure of the pope's mission of peace and concord, but also the withdrawal
of God's support from the emperor, which in turn provoked the divine
judgement that led to Louis's downfall. The very night after the pope's
departure, Louis's men went over to the other side in droves.[33]

The issues just indicated, such as the threats of excommunication and
the anger about the pope's uninvited and unceremonious voyage north,
also surface in a text which surely belongs to the year 833, even though its
authorship remains contested. This is a letter purporting to be Pope
Gregory's response to the accusation that he had come to excommunicate
the Frankish bishops, undermine their authority and dishonour imperial
power.[34] The text survives only partially, without an exordium or conclusion, in a late ninth- or early tenth-century manuscript (BnF lat. 2853)
which contains most of Agobard's work. Here it figures as part of a small
dossier of documents pertaining to the year 833.[35] The authenticity of this
letter has long been disputed; to those who believe it to be a forgery, its
presence among Agobard's writings has made the latter the main suspect.[36] There is one element in the papal letter that suggests that Agobard
may have had a hand in it: the unusual expression *ecclesia Gallicana* for the
Frankish church is also used in one of Agobard's anti-Jewish treatises.[37]
Other evidence points in a different direction, however. For one thing, the
level of verbal aggression exceeds anything Agobard ever produced, even
when he was at his most furious. As Egon Boshof pointed out, the tone of
Gregory's epistle and the sources used differ markedly from the two
genuine letters Agobard wrote only shortly before.[38] The archbishop's
attempt to convince Louis of Gregory's good intentions, for example, is

---

[32] Zechiel-Eckes, 'Ein Blick in Pseudoisidors Werkstatt' and 'Auf Pseudoisidors Spur'.

[33] Radbert, *EA*, II, c. 17, p. 88.

[34] Edited by Ernst Dümmler among Agobard's letters: Agobard, *Epistolae*, no. 17, pp. 228–32,
but omitted in the now standard edition of Agobard's work: cf. Van den Acker, Introduction
to Agobard's *Opera omnia*, pp. xxi–xxii.

[35] BN lat. 2853 (s. ix/x); on this manuscript, cf. Van den Acker (ed.), 'Introduction', pp. li–
lii. The papal letter is on fols. 192–196v; it is followed by the first *Liber apologeticus* (fols.
197r–200r), and preceded by nos. 15 (fols. 187–90) and 16 (fols. 190–2). Letter 16 has
been edited by Van den Acker, pp. 303–6, as *De privilegio apostolicae sedis*, which is the
editor's title, not that of the manuscript.

[36] For a helpful summary, see Boshof, *Agobard*, pp. 225–8.

[37] Agobard, *De iudaicis superstitionibus*, c. 3, p. 201: 'omnes Ecclesiarum Gallicanarum
reverentissimi gubernatores'; Gregory, *Epistola*, MGH, *Epp.* V, p. 231, line 21: 'ut
noveritis non vos posse dividere ecclesiam Gallicanam et Germanicam ab unitate tunice'.

[38] Boshof, *Agobard*, pp. 226–7.

bolstered by relevant papal pronouncements and canonical texts, yet these are absent in the letter said to be by Gregory IV, which draws its ammunition mostly from Scripture. This argues against Agobard as the forger, but also against Gregory as the author, unless one assumes that this pope had no access to the papacy's authoritative written tradition. On the other hand, the pope was on the move, presumably without his archives.

This is not the place to solve such problems, one way or another. If this document circulated in 833, one can see how it may have ended up among Agobard's papers as part of a dossier pertaining to this year, without necessarily being a forgery.[39] Precisely because of its rudeness, 'Gregory's letter' strikes me as part of a fierce internal debate among Frankish churchmen about the scope and limits of papal influence, rather than as the view from Rome. For all we know, the text may have been drafted by a Frankish cleric, to be sent off in the pope's name. There is at least one other instance of Frankish clerics operating as ghost writers for a pope, trying to move papal authority in a favourable direction.[40] If this letter was written by Gregory himself, this was also the first papal reference to the 'Gelasian' thesis of papal/imperial dualism. Did Gregory know that this text had been cited and discussed by the Frankish bishops in Paris in 829? Or was this complementarity of secular and ecclesiastical authority an issue that was hotly debated in Aachen, rather than in Rome, and which would, once more, point to a Frankish authorship of this letter?[41] These are questions yet to be answered.

Whoever he was, the author of the letter came down heavily and none too subtly on the side of papal authority. The arguments used are sufficiently interesting to consider in some detail; in keeping with convention I shall continue to refer to the author as 'Pope Gregory'. To begin with, the pope declared his displeasure about the way the bishops had addressed him in *their* letter, as brother and pope, rather than with due reverence. Scathingly, Gregory repeated the bishops' contention that of course they would not have denied their pontiff a proper *occursus*, 'had not the sacred imperial command taken precedence'.[42] Gregory countered that the command of the Apostolic See was no less imperative. On the contrary, the bishops should have realised that 'the governance of souls (*regimen*

---

[39] Van den Acker (ed.), Introduction to Agobard, *Opera omnia*, p. xxii.

[40] As Tom Noble pointed out to me, there is a parallel in the massive Paris dossier of 825 on images, where Franks 'helpfully' wrote letters for Pope Eugenius II to send to Constantinople.

[41] These reflections were prompted by Tom Noble's comments on an earlier version of this chapter. I hope we can resolve them together, in due course.

[42] Agobard, *Epistolae*, no. 17, p. 228: 'occursum vestrum nobis non negandum, nisi sacra iussio imperialis prevenieret'.

animarum) is greater than imperial rule, for the former is pontifical, whereas the latter is temporal'.[43] The pope then pointed out that the blessed Gregory of Nazianzen had not been afraid to preach in church in the presence of emperors, citing a garbled version of one of his namesake's sermons, which stressed that *intra sacra altaria*, rulers were subjected to bishops. The other non-biblical authority cited was St Augustine on the 'happy emperor' (*felix imperator*), in support of the contention that such emperors should never forget to offer a sacrifice of humility and prayer to the true God, in order to atone for their sins.[44]

This discussion of precedence and authority is followed by a scathing passage on the psychology of the Frankish bishops. First, they said they were overjoyed by Gregory's visit, and then they maintained they were deeply saddened by it, which surely revealed their instability of mind (*instabilitas mentis*). In their letter the bishops had also claimed that the pope had come 'to impose some presumptuous excommunication devoid of any just cause'.[45] Confused in word and mind, they had admonished the pope to refrain from this, lest the imperial *potestas* be dishonoured and the episcopal *auctoritas* impaired. Tell me, Gregory asked: what is the meaning of these words? And what does more damage to the emperor's honour, an excommunication or the acts worthy of excommunication? And did you think you could depose me without dishonouring the *cathedra Petri*? Caiaphas was impious, but his see was sacred (Ioh. 22.51). The discussion then turned to the thorny issue of oaths, and to the fidelity Gregory had sworn to Louis upon his accession to papal office.[46] The pope countered that if he did not confront Louis with all the sins that the emperor had committed against the unity of the church and the kingdom, he would be a perjurer like the bishops, even if he had sworn an oath. You bishops swear and counter-swear, promising him [Louis] fidelity, but now that you see him acting contrary to *fides*, and hurtling towards damnation, you do not attempt to save him; this makes you perjurers, for you do not work for the emperor's salvation.

This was heavy ammunition indeed, for it hit the bishops where it hurt hardest, namely their ministry and their possible negligence (*negligentia*) in its exercise. As we shall see, the rebellious bishops in Soissons justified

---

[43] Agobard, *Epistolae*, no. 17, p. 228: 'Neque ignorare debueratis maius esse regimen animarum, quod est pontificale, quam imperiale, quod est temporale.'

[44] Augustine, *De civitate Dei*, V, c. 24, pp. 236–7.

[45] Agobard, *Epistolae*, no. 17, p. 229; 'dicentes nos venire propter quandam presumptiosam et omni racione carentem excommunicationem faciendam'; cf. Astronomer, c. 48, p. 474: 'parum quid subrupuit episcopis imperatoris praesumptionis audatiae'.

[46] See *Constitutio Romana*, MGH *Capit.* I, no. 161, p. 324; Noble, *Republic of St Peter*, pp. 313–22.

Louis's penance by Ezekiel's prophetic words: whoever failed to warn a sinner of his iniquity was accountable for his death (Ez. 3.18). The Frankish bishops' assertion that they would have received the pope 'venerably' if only he had come to the emperor, as the latter wanted, was met with the indignant rebuke that the bishops should read, not just in Scripture but also in their consciences, that they had pursued only earthly rewards, and that they were reeds shaken by the wind (Matth. 11.7). As for the earlier division of the realm, the *Ordinatio imperii* of 817, their contention that this arrangement could be changed according to the new situation (*rerum opportunitas*) was doubly misguided. As Gregory pointed out, this was a matter not of opportunity but of importunity. Changing the solemn succession arrangement of 817 had caused upheaval, dissension, commotion, plunder and other evils. Furthermore, this reversal was contrary to the will of God and therefore had engendered many sins. As Gregory asked rhetorically, what was opportune about this new *divisio*?[47] Then, with a barrage of biblical texts, he countered the bishops' argument that the pope had no right to excommunicate in their dioceses unless invited. It was at this point that the 'Gallican and German church' (*ecclesia Galicia et Germanica*) was mentioned, which should on no account be separated from the unity of the church of which Rome was the head.

Towards the end of the letter, Gregory summarises the key issues involved. To threaten the pope with deposition was absurd, inappropriate and downright stupid. Moreover, the Frankish bishops had done so not 'because of a crime such as homicide, sacrilege, theft or something of this sort, but [merely] because I have not come in the way you yourselves wanted'. In other words, the bishops' refusal to perform an *occursus*, as well as their preoccupation with correct protocol, was ridiculed. The other central area of dispute was fidelity. The bishops should have been ashamed of themselves, Gregory fumed, for having accused him of breaking his oath to the emperor. Did they not know that perjurers cannot depose another perjurer? You know fully well that I have not perjured myself, Gregory retorted, yet is there none of you who wonders whether he himself is a perjurer? The bishops should remember that the more one shakes a sewer, the more shit comes out of it. As for their position being irrevocable, as they had claimed, did they really want to say that their present malicious judgement could not be retracted in the face of a judgement of God? As for their threat, never had anything like it been done since the beginning of the church. Even if he were a perjurer, the pope said, which was of course not the case, the same applied to the bishops.

---

[47] Agobard, *Epistolae*, no. 17, p. 230.

Ultimately, the questions of protocol and perjury were driven by larger issues. The Frankish leadership, especially its clerical part, felt duty bound publicly and properly to recognise the two greatest authorities on earth, the emperor and the pope, and to be loyal to them; but what could one do if these two divinely sanctioned authorities were suddenly at cross-purposes? By debating who should come to whom, and how, a divinely sanctioned political order was articulated. Underneath it all lurked the fear of the sin that would inevitably be committed if one made a choice between Lothar, whose authority was now suddenly boosted by the presence of the pope, and Louis, who was still the legitimate emperor. Regardless of who wrote the letter ascribed to Pope Gregory IV, it tells us much about the anxieties that assailed the Frankish clergy in 833, when this pope paid an unexpected visit.

Debates on the Field of Lies

Was the massive defection of Louis's faithful men, which gave its name to the 'Field of Lies', in fact a divine judgement which showed that Louis should undertake a public penance for his sins? The Astronomer's answer to this question was a resounding negative, yet one can see why many at the time thought they had been delivered from an impending disaster of the first magnitude: the shedding of the blood of men to whom one was or had been bound by ties of kinship, fidelity and friendship. This calamity could no longer be averted in 841 in Fontenoy, but it was staved off in 833 in Alsace because most of Louis's men walked over to the other side. Whereas in Radbert's narrative the failure of the pope's mediation and his departure triggered an immediate desertion that took only one night, the Astronomer paced his story differently. He situated the first confrontation between Louis and Gregory on the battlefield, right before the armies were to come to blows.

When on both sides the battle lines were arrayed, not far from each other, and it was thought that the battle was imminent, it was announced to the emperor that the Roman pope was about to arrive. As he approached, the emperor received him as he was lined up for combat, albeit less honourably than was fitting, telling [the pope] that he had prepared this kind of reception for himself, since he had come towards [the emperor] in such an unaccustomed way.[48]

Welcomed and led off to Louis's tent, the Astronomer's Gregory then turned into a visitor highly supportive of the emperor, claiming that he would never have come had he not heard that Louis worked unremittingly

---

[48] Astronomer, c. 48, pp. 474–6.

against the discord of his sons and wanted to bring peace, nothing but peace. Listening attentively to the emperor's views, Gregory remained with him for some days. Just as Louis sent the pope back to broker a mutual peace, the defection started. By a mixture of bribery and threats, the emperor's men and their followers went over to the camp of the sons, flowing like a river. The pope himself was not allowed to return to Louis, as he had been ordered to do (*ut fuerat iussus*). In the Astronomer's account, Louis's domination of Gregory is palpable: the pope had become the emperor's emissary to his sons.

As for Louis's troops going over to Lothar, the Astronomer pointed out that this went on for days, until the Feast of St Paul's (30 June). By implication, this was not a divine judgement, otherwise it would never have taken so much time.[49] The ones to effect this 'judgement' were the *plebs*, that is, the non-aristocratic retainers, who were also referred to as the *vulgus*.[50] During both rebellions, these rowdy fighting men figured as the Astronomer's chosen instrument of evil; on the Field of Lies they were ready to attack the emperor, just to please his sons. Louis now had his back to the wall, yet, as the Astronomer made clear, the emperor retained all his authority. The sons came to him and even performed a proper *occursus*; Louis duly admonished them, telling them to get off their horses and come towards him (*sibi occurentes*); he reminded them of the loyalty they had sworn to himself, Judith and Charles only recently, in 831.[51] The sons agreed, Louis kissed them, and he trustingly followed them to their camp. Yet when Louis arrived, Judith was separated from him and taken to the encampment of Louis the German, while the emperor himself, with only a modest retinue, was taken into custody by Lothar, together with young Charles. In the Astronomer's version of events Louis represented the forces of order, while his sons and other opponents had to rely on the *plebs* to exert their questionable authority. Their disorder prevailed, so with great sadness Pope Gregory returned to Rome, his mission unaccomplished.[52] No divine judgement had occurred.

Predictably, Radbert propagated the opposite view, also by means of a dramatic confrontation between the father and his rebellious sons. In his narrative leading up to the defection of Louis's troops, Radbert inserted a curious altercation between Louis and Lothar, with the latter in the guise of his brothers' spokesman. It is construed as a *querela*, a judicial complaint in

---

[49] Ibid., pp. 476–8. According to Thegan and Radbert, this took only one night; Thegan, c. 42, p. 228; Radbert, *EA*, II, c. 18, p. 88.
[50] Astronomer, c. 45, p. 462, line 17; cf. ibid., p. 305, n. 107.
[51] Astronomer, c. 48, p. 478; Thegan, c. 42, p. 230.
[52] Astronomer, c. 48, p. 478; Nithard, I, c. 4, p. 16.

which each accusation was followed by a refutation. Radbert specified that during the negotiations that went on between the different camps, Louis presented his sons with *capitula*, written accusations to which the sons then answered, presumably also in writing.[53] Although Radbert used this as a literary device by which he could fully articulate the arguments of the opposition, an exchange of documents was most likely part of the negotiations on the Rothfeld. Furthermore, this kind of formal dispute, with the accused publicly answering charges, whether orally or in writing, belonged to contemporary judicial practice.[54]

As presented by Radbert, Louis's *querela* against his sons is a strangely imbalanced altercation. To a series of tersely worded written accusations formulated by Louis (the *propositio paterna*), the sons responded elegantly and extensively, with their *responsio filiorum*. Louis's blunt accusations concentrated on filial obedience (remember that you are my sons), fidelity (remember that you are my vassals), the protection of the Apostolic See (my prerogative, but Lothar has usurped it), Gregory's visit (why did you prevent the pope from coming to me?), Lothar as the chief insurgent (you are inciting your brothers to rebel and forced them to stay with you), and, finally, again, on fidelity: 'You [Lothar] have wrongfully received our vassals and kept them with you.'[55] By contrast, the sons' responses are elaborate and well structured, aimed at convincing Radbert's audience. Their core argument was that they had acted out of filial love and reverence, trying to save their father from his insidious enemies. Whereas the latter were trying to change Louis's natural clemency and mercy into bitterness and hostility, the sons wished only to restore their father's glory, honour and prosperity. Hence they were not only dutiful sons but also loyal *fideles*.

This argument resembles Radbert's defence of Wala: Louis turned those who were his real friends into enemies. A second line of defence was that the sons had come to meet their father in Alsace as supplicants, begging for his pardon and mercy. Because the insidious enemies of glorious imperial rule were out to kill them, they had not dared to come *simpliciter*, that is, without troops.[56] In other words, the impending

---

[53] Radbert, *EA*, II, c. 17, p. 85: 'Tamen ut eluscant quae proposui, commemoranda sunt capitula, quae augustus pater quasi pro querela filiis direxit, ut enuntiaret quid contra requiret'; ibid., p. 88: 'Haec siquidem est alterna altercatio, hac querele ad invicem, haec propositio paterna et responsio filiorum.'

[54] See Niermeyer, *Mediae Latinitatis Lexicon Minus*, s.v. *querela*, p. 876, for 'law suit' and a wealth of related meanings, mostly drawn from Carolingian sources.

[55] Radbert, *EA*, II, c. 17, p. 87: 'Vasallos quoque, inquit, nostros indebite recepisti, et eos tecum retines.'

[56] As Hilduin and other rebels were ordered to come to the Nijmegen assembly in 830: Astronomer, c. 45, pp. 460–2.

military confrontation was entirely of their father's making. As for Lothar's supposed usurpation of the protection of Rome, had it not been Louis himself who made his eldest son first a co-emperor, and then the defender of this city (as could be seen on every charter and coin), and who had intended Lothar to be crowned emperor at the altar of St Peter's? Speaking for his brothers in an impassioned speech presented as delivered orally, Lothar hotly denied having forbidden Gregory to go to the emperor. On the contrary, Lothar himself had taken the pope to his father, in order to effect a reconciliation. Moreover, the other sons and Louis's faithful men had fled to Lothar, begging him to intercede on their behalf. In his plea, Lothar – called Honorius throughout – appealed to all that he had learned at his father's court:

> This I have always learned in your sacred assembly, and in your senate of illus-trious men; this I have observed in your deeds; this I have heard from you; this we have read in the deeds of the Ancients: that one should honour strong and eminent men of great merit, rather than expel them. With providence, they have thwarted the attacks and attempts of evil men; with authority, fidelity, constancy, magna-nimity and good counsel they have resisted insidious audacity, namely that of those men whose levity and destructiveness have fouled your imperial rule with every possible depravity.[57]

This is the mirror image of the Astronomer's confrontation between father and sons. Instead of a saddened Louis, temporarily rendered powerless by the mob, but still fully in control of himself, his sons and the situation, here one encounters Lothar as the embodiment of tradi-tional values – above all, *fides* – who had to remind his confused father of all that the latter had once stood for and taught his offspring. Honorius came out of this *querela* as the moral victor. At this point in Radbert's narrative Gregory appeared, in an entirely pontifical and appropriate way, blessing those present and announcing his intention to mediate in the conflict.[58] Louis, however, refused the pope a worthy reception with hymns and *laudes*, claiming that he had not come like his predecessors. The way in which Louis voiced this hoary old objection, for so it was presented, is entirely in keeping with his role in the preceding *querela*. The emperor acted as a moral simpleton and was unworthy of true authority. Of course sons had to honour fathers and faithful men had to be faithful, yet, as Honorius pointed out, there were other and better ways to comply with these moral imperatives. Pope Gregory, meanwhile, declared that he had merely come to bring peace and concord. 'So, emperor, if you receive us and the peace of Christ in a worthy way, His peace will be with you and

---

[57] Radbert, *EA*, II, c. 17, p. 87.   [58] Ibid., p. 88.

also with your realm; if not, the peace of Christ will return to us, as you read in the Gospel, and be with us.'[59] This rather free adaptation of Luc. 10.6 ('and if the son of peace be there, your peace shall rest upon him: but if not, it shall return to you') functions as a dire warning, and perhaps even as a malediction. Louis was oblivious, due to his 'obstinacy of mind and hardness of heart, and the womanly seduction which deceived the father of mankind'. In the final analysis, the cause of all evil was Eve, in the guise of Justina/Judith. To drive this point home Radbert inserted a digression in which the young monk Theofrastus lamented Louis's inability to see the truth. 'Daily he seemed to ponder God's law, and yet with a hardened heart he moved so far away from the law of true love.'[60] Of this *vera dilectio*, and of the people and the church of Christ committed to him, Louis had lost sight because of the will (*voluntas*) and wiles (*persuasiones*) of one woman.[61] Radbert's choice of words was deliberate and precise: *voluntas* denoted the unrestrained human will of someone incapable of self-control and self-governance, and therefore of ruling others. As we have seen, this was one of the main themes of the polemics against Judith.

Once the emperor had refused to heed the pope's warning, his fate was sealed. In one night, all Louis's men went over to the other side. Wala and Radbert, present in Lothar's camp, must have seen them coming. Radbert had his alias Paschasius give a spirited account to the spellbound monks, relating how he and Arsenius/Wala witnessed this miracle and went to tell Pope Gregory what had happened. One of the Romans from the papal retinue began to chant, 'The right hand of the Lord hath wrought strength' (*dextera Domini fecit virtutem*; Ps. 117.16). Gregory and all others present perceived this as a judgement of God; the verdict was (*adiucatum est*) that the glorious and mighty imperial rule (*imperium*) had now fallen from the hands of the father, for the son who was his heir and co-emperor to take up and accept.[62] This interpretation of the defection of Louis's men prevailed during the assembly in Compiègne, when the emperor was judged guilty of sins so grave that they could redeemed only by a public penance.

Public sin and public penance

Louis summoned his *fideles* to meet at Compiègne by 1 October 833, yet by the time the assembly began, Lothar had taken his father's place,

[59] Ibid.
[60] Ibid.: 'Que cotidie visus est meditari in lege Dei, et tam longe a lege vere dilectionis indurato corde recessit.'
[61] Ibid.   [62] Ibid., c. 18, p. 89.

receiving the astounded Byzantine legates and their gifts. This general assembly was to decide on Louis's fate, and therefore debated the various options. Agobard's second *Apology* for the rebellious sons gives some insight into the arguments in favour of a public penance. The references to the 'one-time emperor' who had lost his *regnum* because of divine justice and had yet to atone for his offences, firmly situate Agobard's treatise in the period between the Field of Lies and Louis's public penance in Soissons; it was this kind of theoretical ammunition that the archbishop of Lyons must have aimed at those present in Compiègne. With a comprehensive biblical dossier on kings who had atoned for their sins, Agobard tried to sway the faint-hearted. Behind most of these kings there had been a faithless woman; in Louis's case, this was Judith. For Agobard as well, she was the cause of all evil (*tocius mali causa*). Instead of being Louis's helpmate in the governance of the palace and the kingdom, she had created disorder and upheaval (*commotio et conturbatio*).[63] Agobard recalled how only recently the sons had intervened and restored their father to his former honour and glory.[64] But Judith, who should have done life-long penance for her sins, now brazenly and indecently inhabited the palace as if she were the legitimate queen.[65] He who watches over Israel was displeased, and the sons became worried that what had befallen King Achab would happen to their father: Jezabel had incited Achab to commit evil in the face of the Lord, and 'he was made abominable' (*et abominabilis factus est*; cf. III Reg. 21.26).[66] Confronting an obvious objection on the part of his audience, namely that Achab's abomination specifically concerned the veneration of the idols of the Amorites, Agobard explained that the idol-worship of the 'old people' in the time of the Law was entirely comparable with the sins committed by the new people of God (*novus populus*) in the time of Grace, such as coveting riches, glory and the honours of this world.[67] For the murder of Naboth the Israelite, committed at his wife's insistence, Achab was rebuked (*correptus*) by Elijah, and corrected by his penance, postponing divine wrath, but not averting it. Eventually, God destroyed Achab's house, just as He destroyed the house of Jeroboam (IV Reg. 9.7–10).[68] All this, Agobard explained, showed how much bad wives could harm their husbands. Priests, on the other hand, like the priest Joiada who purged Jerusalem from foulness and

---

[63] Agobard, *Liber apologeticus*, II, c. 2, p. 316 lines 1, 4–5, cf. Ward, 'Agobard of Lyons'.
[64] Agobard, *Liber apologeticus*, II, c. 2, p. 316 lines 23–34.
[65] Ibid., c. 3, p. 316, lines 5–8.
[66] Ibid., c. 3, p. 317 line 16.
[67] Agobard, *Liber apologeticus*, II, c. 4, p. 317, lines 3–9.
[68] Ibid., c. 5, p. 318, line 13, 'concessum est ei, ut filii eius usque ad quartam generacionem regnarent post eum'.

pollution – that is, a treacherous woman – were to be rewarded with earthly and eternal recompense (IV Reg. 11.13–16); others, like Jehu, with only earthly remuneration.

Casting himself in the role of Joiada, Agobard admonished Louis not to lose his heavenly kingdom, now that, deceived by a woman, he had already forfeited his earthly realm. Blaming Judith remained at the core of Agobard's argumentation, yet in this second *Apology* Louis was moved to centre stage. Referring to the Field of Lies, Agobard proclaimed that Louis should heed God's judgement, for nothing happens on earth without cause. He then wove together a string of citations from Job, the man who withstood the wiles of a woman, leading up to a biblical citation highly appropriate to Louis's public penance 'He looseth the belt of kings, and girdeth their loins with a cord' (*balteum regnum dissolvit, et praecingit fune renes eorum*) (Iob 12.18)[69]. The other key text cited by Agobard was also from Job: 'He changeth the heart of the princes of the people of the earth, and deceiveth them that they walk in vain where there is no way' (*qui immutat cor principum populi terrae et decepit eos ut frustra incedant per invium*) (Iob 12.24). God is terrifying, even to the rulers of this earth. One haughty ruler, humiliated and forced to confess, was King Nabuchodonosor, who praised God after having lost his mind.[70] This is not to say, Agobard innocuously remarked, that we should compare our one-time emperor to these impious and unfaithful kings, yet on whomever allows himself to be deceived by a sinful woman shall fall what is written: 'He that troubleth his own house, shall inherit the winds' (Prov. 11.29). A storm had blown through the palace, with the empress at the centre, resulting in *conturbatio*: innumerable false oaths and a tremendous amount of plunder, along with homicide, adultery and incest. All these sins made it necessary, said Agobard, for 'our most religious one-time emperor' to look into his heart and do penance, humbled under God's hand.[71] Louis could still reach the happiness of eternal life, but the elevation (*exaltatio*) of temporal life was not suitable for someone who was so perturbed (*conturbatus*) in his mind and house, and who, by divine dispensation and justice, had ceded his place to someone else. This someone was not an enemy and stranger, but his own beloved son. Therefore Louis should render incessant thanks to God for being succeeded by a loving son, instead of by an aggressive enemy.[72]

---

[69] The association may have been Ps. 118.61: 'funes peccatorum circumplexi sunt me', in which the *peccatores* could be taken as 'sinners'.

[70] Agobard, *Liber apologeticus*, II, c. 6, p. 318, line 24: 'rex superbus, et humiliatus, confitetur coactus'.

[71] Ibid., c. 7, p. 319, lines 7–10: 'pro quibus omnibus peccatis necessarium est religiosissimo quondam imperatori, ut redeat ad cor suum, agat penitentiam humiliatus sub manu Dei'.

[72] Ibid., p. 319, line 17: 'non successit illi in regnum inimicus expugnator, sed filius amator'.

In short, Louis's sins, committed at Judith's behest, had angered God so much that He had withdrawn His favour. All the one-time emperor could do now was save his own soul. Given Lothar's involvement in his father's deposition, this argument in favour of public penance has generally been interpreted as a cynical effort to dress up a political takeover as a religious ritual. Ensuring that Louis's loss of imperial power would be permanent was certainly part of the operation, but there is also another and more important side to Agobard's arguments. With complete conviction, and being deeply worried about the consequences of royal sin, he appealed to a gathering of bishops and magnates for whom public sin and divine anger were political problems of the first magnitude. Agobard confronted his fellow-bishops with their duty to warn sinners, steering them towards salvation by means of a public penance.

Stripping Louis's penance of its religious content and meaning in order to expose its 'actual' aim, namely deposition, does not get us closer to contemporary perceptions of what happened in Compiègne. What contemporaries would have looked for was the distinction, not between religious and secular strategies of self-abasement, but between humiliation that was voluntary and therefore honourable, and humiliation imposed as an involuntary punishment.[73] Whereas in the first case the person begging for pardon and mercy kept the initiative and therefore his honour, in the second the culprit tended to be the passive object of a dishonourable retribution. Early medieval authors were extremely sensitive to this distinction, and those writing about Louis's penance were no exception.[74] Louis's spontaneous confession at Attigny (822) fell into the first category, and so did his public declaration of guilt at Compiègne in 830. Both these imperial gestures of humility enhanced his authority and prestige, helping him to regain his political balance; in both cases Louis was accused of insincerity and duplicity by those who sought to undermine this strategy.[75] In 833 he may well have hoped to win the assembly over by another demonstration of exemplary humility. Fearing Louis's ability to sway public opinion by yet another dramatic gesture of atonement, however, the rebels did not give him a chance to do so.[76] While his fate was discussed in Compiègne, the emperor was kept secluded in the monastery of St-Médard in Soissons, visited by delegations of bishops who bombarded him with their 'most salubrious admonition'.

---

[73] Reuter, 'Contextualising Canossa', pp. 160–2.   [74] De Jong, 'Monastic prisoners'.
[75] Radbert, *VA*, c. 51, cols. 1534D–1535A; Radbert, *EA*, II, c. 10, p. 73; *Relatio* (833), p. 53, lines 40–1.
[76] *Relatio* (833), p. 53, lines 40–1.

In the end, Louis gave in and decided to submit to what the rebellious bishops defined as an 'ecclesiastical and public penance'.[77] Although learned bishops such as Jonas of Orléans presented this as a venerable custom dating back to 'pristine Christianity', the Carolingian revival of *paenitentia publica* was an invention of tradition. Late antique penance had included public self-incrimination as well as a highly public entry into the *ordo paenitentium* to which sinners were admitted by bishops. Such a penance was a once in a lifetime affair, with lasting consequences: for the rest of their lives, former penitents were barred from military service or any public office, including membership of the clergy.[78] Late antique penance did not know of the sharp contrast between public and secret sins, or of the corresponding public or secret atonement that was so characteristic of its ninth-century successor. This connection emerged in the early medieval West, and can first be glimpsed in the monastic exile imposed on prominent political players – first clerics, then laymen – in the Merovingian kingdoms of the sixth and seventh century.[79] The next step, taken in eighth-century sources, was that such political crimes were classified as sins affecting the entire community, to be atoned for by a penance performed in a monastery. In this context, *scandalum* became the key expression denoting 'public sin', in the sense of an offence that had undermined a divinely sanctioned order of society.[80] Whoever had been publicly apprehended for committing rebellion, sedition, robbery, perjury, theft, fornication or other grave crimes should atone publicly after laying down their arms; they should be excluded from communion, for they had offended God and scandalised the holy church – that is, God's people. Members of the elite, especially, whose sins tended to be notorious by definition because of their leading position and the code of conduct defined by their ministry, were liable to be punished by public penance.[81] Its counterpart was 'secret' penance, or *paenitentia occulta*, which in principle covered the same grave sins, in so far as these had not become public, offending both divine and human sensibilities. Unlike public penance, which was an episcopal prerogative, a secret penance could also be imposed by an ordinary priest. As Hraban Maur explained,

[77] Ibid., lines 5–6. Cf. *AB*, s.a. 833, p. 10; Astronomer, c. 49, p. 480.
[78] Jonas, *De institutione laicali*, I, c. 10, col. 138B/C; cf. De Jong, 'Transformations of penance', pp. 190–202. For an informative recent study of late antique penance, see Uhalde, *Expectations of Justice*, esp. pp. 103–34.
[79] De Jong, 'Transformations of penance', pp. 202–17.
[80] De Jong, 'Monastic prisoners'; see also De Jong, 'What was *public?*'
[81] See Council of Mainz (851), 11b (MGH *Conc.* III, pp. 248–9) regarding Albgis, who carried off a woman publicly (*publice auferens*), thus defaming the church (*ecclesiam diffamavit*) – he was banished, to do penance. See Kottje, 'Buße oder Strafe?', pp. 455–7; Leyser, 'Canon law', p. 63.

those who confessed their crimes secretly, accusing themselves of having sinned gravely, could be redeemed, if they showed real remorse and atoned by fasting, alms, vigils and tearful prayer.[82] Of course there was nothing particularly secret about someone who suddenly undertook such penitential actions. The distinction between 'public' and 'occult' penance lay in the degree of publicity that surrounded the sin itself, the confession, the ritual of imposition and the subsequent atonement. In the case of a *paenitentia publica*, all these four stages were fully in the public eye, while the self-abasement and shame of the sinner contributed to his or her redemption. For ordained clerics a public penance was therefore to be avoided, not only because the canons of the ancient church forbade it, but especially because the scandalous publicity harmed ecclesiastical authority. If priests and bishops had sinned publicly, they were to be deposed; if this was not the case, grave clerical sinners could submit to a so-called 'canonical' penance and redeem themselves.[83]

Paenitentia publica, Carolingian style, owed little to the tradition of penance as a voluntary redemption of sin, but much to the longstanding practice of monastic exile. Initially the prerogative of bishops, by the early ninth century this had become a royal punishment of those who had upset the public order by rebellion or other flagrant crimes. Louis used this monastic exile on a much greater scale than his father. The rebels made amends in a monastery, initially not as monks but as tonsured clerics. As an instrument of royal discipline, this punishment could not be anything but open-ended. In tune with the changes in royal wrath or favour, it could amount to a life-long monastic conversion, or be suspended when the ruler decided it was time to recall the exiles.[84] The bishops who reinvented *paenitentia publica* were less flexible, however. Having assiduously studied the canonical texts from late antiquity, they were well aware of the fact that in an age much closer to Christ, undertaking a penance had life-long consequences. Those who had been in the 'order of penitents' were eventually readmitted to communion, but they were expected to lead semi-ascetic lives ever after. Translated into ninth-century practice, this meant that public penitents remained in the religious communities where they had been sent to perform their penance. This was the fate intended for Judith after she had been veiled in 830, but Louis, who treated his wife's alleged penitential conversion as a straightforward case of monastic exile, decided otherwise. Hence a furious Agobard claimed that Judith

---

[82] Hraban Maur, *Paenitentiale ad Heribaldum*, c. 10, *PL* 110, col. 475A.
[83] Council of Paris (829), c. 35, MGH *Conc.* II/2, p. 635; cf. Council of Chalon, c. 7, a. 813, MGH *Conc.* II/1, p. 275.
[84] Kottje, 'Buße oder Strafe?'; De Jong, 'What was *public*?', and 'Monastic prisoners'.

had broken her vows and had no right to lead a married life. This is not to say that the binding nature of a 'public and ecclesiastical penance' was uncontested, either then or in 833 when this formal way of atonement was imposed on Louis the Pious. On the contrary, the question whether public penitents could resume their functions in public life remained a matter for debate throughout the next decades.

In 833 nothing much was certain in the domain of public penance except that the ruler and his bishops saw this as a means to curtail the unruly conduct of aristocrats, hitting them where it hurt: in their ability to fight. Rather than being a self-evident act of deposition by means of an already established ecclesiastical discipline, Louis's public penance was an audacious experiment. A penitential practice that had become an instrument of royal discipline, recently infused with the authority of the ancient church, was now turned against the ruler himself. That the bishops who did so were not entirely sure of the lasting effect of a formal *paenitentia publica* becomes clear from their subsequent efforts to make Louis commit himself to monastic life by a binding profession.[85] The emperor flatly refused to take this last step, however, and nobody could force him to do so, for this would invalidate the entire commitment. The road back to reconciliation and the throne remained wide open.

The bishops argue their case

Given that the assembly in Compiègne had been summoned well before-hand, there must have been a considerable group of magnates and bishops in attendance. Ebo was there, of course, in whose province the palace of Compiègne and the monastery of St-Médard in Soissons were situated, and Agobard, whose personal attestation to Louis's penance has been preserved. Otherwise, those present can only be guessed at. After all, once Louis had been restored, bishops were not exactly eager to boast that they had participated in his downfall. Even Radbert was completely silent on the topic, either because Wala did not witness the imperial penance, or because he found it too embarrassing for words.[86] Judging by those who fled or were punished in 834, those also implicated were Bartholomew of Narbonne, Herebold of Auxerre, Jesse of Amiens and Burchard of Vienne, but there must have been many others, most of whom claimed

---

[85] *AB*, s.a. 834, p. 11; Thegan, c. 43, p. 230. Both Nithard (I, c. 3, p. 12) and the Astronomer (c. 44, p. 458) situate the episode of Louis being pressured into a monastic profession in the rebellion of 830.

[86] Cf. Radbert, *EA*, II, cc. 18–19, pp. 89–90; the narrative moves directly from the divine judgement on the Field of Lies to Lothar's takeover and its dubious consequences.

afterwards that they had been forced to co-operate.[87] All the bishops present in Compiègne had to draw up a record of what had happened and sign it, and all these signed documents (*cartulae*) had to be given to Lothar 'as a reminder of what had been done'.[88] Finally, the gathering decided to summarise all these individual attestations, creating a joint declaration that was signed by all the bishops present. On top of all these documents, there was also Louis's own confession.

This veritable explosion of writing served several purposes. First, the signatories committed themselves irrevocably to this 'weighty affair' (*tantum negotium*), namely their joint judgement that Louis's sins should be atoned for by a public penance.[89] Second, according to ecclesiastical custom, the documents aimed to establish one interpretation of what had happened, and to publicise this as the authoritative and irrefutable reading of events.[90] Third, the entire documentation was to be kept in Lothar's archives, proving once and for all that his father was no longer the rightful emperor. And last but not least, the many written attestations helped to raise the levels of publicity even further. As the written record of Louis's sins spread, the 'scandal' grew, and a public atonement became even more necessary. This was also the function of the written confession Louis handed over to the bishops, prior to his deposition of arms. These documents were performative ones. On that fateful day in October 833, the church of St-Médard could hold only a limited amount of people; many more heard of what had happened there through word of mouth and, above all, by reading about it. In the vast Carolingian polity with its widely dispersed imperial aristocracy, such written representations of rituals were indispensable to ensure effective publicity. Often, the ultimate effect of political rituals depended as much on their description after the event as on their actual performance; Louis's public penance in 833 is a case in point.[91] But apart from this, writing magnified the scandal and thereby the irrevocable consequences of the emperor's penance.

Of the personal attestations, only Agobard's survives, along with the communal *Relatio* of the bishops, alas without any of the original subscriptions. In their joint statement the bishops were at pains to make it clear that Louis had already been deprived of his imperial power by the sudden and just divine judgement in June that had made his faithful men turn

---

[87] Zechiel-Eckes, 'Ein Blick in Pseudoisidor's Werkstatt', p. 55; Boshof, *Ludwig*, pp. 211–12; Kottje, *Bussbücher*, pp. 234–40.

[88] *Relatio* (833), p. 55, lines 31–3.   [89] Ibid., line 34.

[90] Ibid., p. 52, lines 18–20: 'id iuxta morem ecclesiasticum scriptis committant: videlicet ut posteris omnem ambiguitatem et occasionem iuste detrahendi vel reprehendi penitus amputent'.

[91] Buc, 'Political rituals', p. 196.

away from him on the battlefield.[92] They proclaimed themselves to be under the rule (*sub imperio*) of the glorious Emperor Lothar, in the first year of his reign.[93] As Agobard specified, the assembly in Compiègne met in the fourth month of Lothar's imperial reign, for the divine judgement had struck Louis in June of 833.[94] Hence, Louis was termed 'the venerable man', or 'the venerable lord, the one-time emperor'.[95] The bishops' first aim was to establish the authority whereby they had imposed an irrevocable penance on their one-time emperor. In their opening sentence they called themselves the 'vicars of Christ and holders of the keys to the kingdom of heaven', a claim which is not such an outrageous bid for episcopal superiority as it seems at first glance.[96] The contemporary context was that the bishops had both the right and the duty to excommunicate sinners and impose a binding public penance, and to effect a reconciliation with the church once proper 'satisfaction' had been given. This power of the keys they derived from Christ himself, who had conferred it on his disciples: 'Amen I say to you, whatsoever you shall bind upon earth shall be bound also in heaven: and whatsoever you shall loose upon earth shall be loosed also in heaven' (Matth. 18.18).[97] Moreover, the duty to save souls by imposing penance was at the very core of the episcopal ministry, as the bishops made clear by citing the key text from Ezekiel (8.18), which explained that if bishops did not attempt to correct sinners, these sins would rebound on themselves: 'If you do not warn the sinner about his sins, says [the prophet], and he dies in his sinfulness, I shall require his blood from your hands.'[98] In other words, what was at stake was not merely the emperor's manifold sins, but also the bishops' own fear of negligence.

---

[92] *Relatio* (833), p. 53, lines 2–3: 'et ab eo divino iustoque iudicio subito imperialis sit subtracta potestas'.

[93] Werminghoff's MGH edition (p. 52, line 22) has the reading *super imperio*, but as Georg Pertz already suspected (cf. *Relatio* (833), p. 54, n.a) and Courtney Booker has now shown conclusively, the correct reading is *sub imperio*; see Booker, 'A new prologue', pp. 91–4.

[94] Agobard, *Cartula*, p. 56, lines 17–8.

[95] *Relatio* (833), p. 53, line 12: 'ad eundem venerabilem virum perrexit'; Agobard, *Cartula*, p. 56, lines 20–1: 'per negligentiam et, ut verius dicam, per ignaviam domni Hludovici venerandi quondam imperatoris'.

[96] *Relatio* (833), p. 51, line 3: 'vicarios Christi et clavigeros regni caelorum'.

[97] Matth. 18.18: 'Amen dico vobis quaecumque alligaveritis super terram erunt ligata et in caelo et quaecumque solveritis super terram erunt soluta et in caelo'; *Relatio* (833), pp. 51–2: 'Quibus a Christo tanta collata est potestas, ut quodcumque ligaverint super terram sit ligatum in caelo, et quodcumque solverint super terram sit solutum in caelo.'

[98] Ibid., p. 52, lines 4–6: '"Si non annuntiaveris", inquit, "iniquo iniquitatem suam et ipse in impietate sua mortuus fuerit, sanguinem eius de manu tuam requiram.' The reference is not a literal one but it sums up the essence of the biblical passage.

The precariousness of their position is evident from the *Relatio*. Almost every sentence is geared towards convincing the reader that everything had been done by the book. The full vocabulary of authoritative *admonitio* was harnessed to this cause. When a delegation of bishops travelled from Compiègne to Soissons in order to admonish Louis, the latter expressed of his own accord (*libenter*) his assent to their counsel and their most wholesome admonitions (*saluberrimis admonitionibus*), yet he asked for a few days' respite, so that he could give a well-considered response to their salubrious warnings (*salubribus monitis*).[99] In a similar vein, Louis, glad of such a *salubris admonitio*, begged his son Lothar to come quickly, so that they could be reconciled and he, Louis, could submit in the presence of all to the episcopal judgement, in the manner of a penitent.[100] This relentless bombardment of *admonitio* was kept up in the portrayal of the actual imposition of penance. In the packed church of St-Médard, in the presence of Lothar, his magnates and all his faithful men, Louis confessed, prostrate on a hair shirt in front of the main altar,[101] to have executed his ministry in an unworthy way, to have offended God in manifold ways, to have scandalised the holy church and, by his negligence, to have led the people into disorder (*perturbatio*). To expiate these sins, he asked for a 'public and ecclesiastical penance'. Louis was then admonished not to be deceitful in the face of God, as he had been during that other synod in the palace of Compiègne (830) where he had been rebuked (*correptus*).[102] Beyond any doubt, it was the bishops who now established their authority by means of their *admonitio*.

Another central purpose of the *Relatio* was to drive home the point that Louis's sin was of a public nature, and so he deserved a formal 'public and ecclesiastical penance'. The three pivotal and overlapping concepts to denote sins that were in the public domain were *negligentia*, *scandalum* and *perturbatio*. Negligence, as I explained earlier, was the neglect of a divinely bestowed 'ministry' by those holding office, be they kings, bishops or others.[103] *Scandalum* literally meant 'stumbling block'. A central biblical text comes from Isaiah: 'And he shall be a sanctification to you, but for a stone of stumbling, and for a rock of offence to the two houses of Israel, for a snare and a ruin to the inhabitants of Jerusalem.'[104]

---

[99] *Relatio* (833), p. 53, lines 5–12.   [100] Ibid., lines 17–23.
[101] There is no other way of translating the *super cilicium* of *Relatio* (833), p. 53, line 29; apparently a *cilicium* could be penitential garb, to be worn (see below, n. 157) and a rough mat on to which one could prostrate oneself, or possibly both.
[102] Ibid., lines 38–40.   [103] See above, chapter 3, pp. 121–2.
[104] Is. 8.14: 'et erit vobis in sanctificationem in lapidem autem offensionis et in petram scandali duabus domibus Israhel inlaqueum et in ruinam habitantibus Hierusalem'. See also I Petr. 2.8.

Imprinting the fear of God on to the people of Israel, the prophet warned that He would become their stumbling block if they did not obey. In the prophetic book of Ezekiel, which was close to the bishops' mind in 833, 'scandal' is an inducement or temptation to sin (*scandalum iniquitatis*), for instance gold and silver (Ez. 7.14) or idols (Ez. 14.3 – 4.7). Accordingly, the noun could also refer to a 'scandal' in the modern sense of the word, namely something that offended moral sensibilities. As a verb, *scandalisare* often denoted the action of leading people into sin or confusion; as such it was akin to *perturbatio*, the creation of disorder, but with the more specific meaning of such actions being 'scandalous'. An instance of this was the public misconduct of priests against which the council of Paris (829) had fulminated. Instead of guiding the faithful to salvation, the leadership of the church induced them to sin by their blatantly bad example. Bishops who did not live according to God's precepts caused *scandala*; it was better to have no bishops than negligent ones.[105] Public sin of this kind offended God and scandalised the church, a dual consequence that was repeated mantra-like throughout the *Relatio*. An eminently public confession was the only adequate reaction and 'satisfaction'. Prostrate, for all to see, Louis proclaimed that he had 'very unworthily handled the ministry that had been entrusted to him; that in so doing he had offended God in many ways and had scandalised the church of Christ, and that his neglect had led the people entrusted to him into multifarious disorder'.[106] This passage was the direct prelude to Louis's request for a public penance and for the help of the bishops to whom God had given the power to bind and to loose.

The list of eight accusations handed to Louis emphasised even further that his sins were of a public nature.[107] (1) Contrary to his father's *admonitio* and his own promises at his coronation in 813, Louis had harmed his relatives, notably his nephew Bernard. (2) He was a creator

---

[105] Council of Paris (829), I , c. 4, MGH *Conc.* II/2, p. 12; see also ibid., c. 16, p. 623 (scandalous misuse of ecclesiastical property); c. 19, p. 625 (the vanity of bishops: they offend God, cause scandal to their flock and endanger the church of God); c. 22, p. 627 (laymen wishing to become clerics should be duly examined, lest they cause scandal); c. 25, p. 628 (avaricious bishops scandalise many people); III, c. 10, p. 674 (hasty accusations against bishops cause scandal). On the various meanings of *scandalum*, secular and religious, see De Jong, 'Power and humility', pp. 36–9, and 'Sacrum palatium', pp. 1265–9.

[106] *Relatio* (833), p. 53, lines 29–33: 'et prostratus in terram super cilicium ante sacrosanctum altare confessus est coram omnibus ministerium sibi commissum satis indigne tractasse, et in eo multis modis Deum offendisse, et ecclesiam Christi scandalizasse, populumque per suam negligentiam multifarie in perturbationem induxisse. Et ideo ob tantorum reatuum expiationem publicam et ecclesiasticam se expetere velle dixit poenitentiam'; see also ibid., p. 52, lines 32–4; p. 52, line 44, to p. 53, line 1; p. 53, lines 13–15.

[107] Ibid., pp. 54–5.

of scandal (*auctor scandali*) and disturber of the peace (*perturbator pacis*); he had infringed the *Ordinatio imperii of* 817, and the oaths which upheld it. (3) He gave orders for a superfluous military campaign, conducted during Lent (830). (4) In the course of his restoration in 831, he violated the rights of those who had warned him of the designs of his enemies, dispossessing them, thwarting justice, and doing injustice to bishops and monks, judging them in their absence. (5) At the same time, Louis incited his sons and the *populus* to commit themselves to unreasonable and contradictory oaths, and allowed Judith's oath of purgation. (6) He subsequently conducted unnecessary militarily campaigns which led to murder and perjury, adultery, robbery and arson, in God's churches and elsewhere. (7) In his divisions of imperial rule after 830 he acted against the general peace and the salvation of the polity (*imperium*), and he made his men swear an oath against his sons, treating them as enemies.

This was a mixture of old grievances and more recent ones, but they all supported one central tenet: that these were eminently public crimes that had created *scandalum* and offended God, and therefore merited a *paenitentia publica*. This conclusion was reiterated in the last and most general charge:

That so many evils and disgraceful acts perpetrated in the kingdom entrusted to him, because of his negligence and lack of foresight, were not enough for him – sins too many to enumerate, from which doubtless sprang the endangering of the kingdom and the dishonouring of its king. On top of these miseries he dragged all the people in his power to a common destruction, even though he should have been, to this same people, the leader of salvation and peace, and even though God's mercy had decided to take pity on his people, in an unheard-of and invisible way, to be proclaimed to our age.[108]

The *populus* referred to here are Louis's *fideles*, the fighting men whom he took to the Field of Lies, as well as the Christian people committed to him in a more general sense of the word; the very last of his public sins had been the military showdown with his sons. All of the accusations have to do with public order and the political arena, in keeping with the upper echelon of Frankish society, which was especially targeted by public ways of amendment (*satisfactio*). In their joint report the bishops specified beyond any doubt that Louis's amendment was an *ecclesiastical* public

---

[108] Ibid., p. 55, lines 14–20: 'Quod non suffecerint ei tot mala et flagitia per suam negligentiam et improvidentiam in regno sibi commisso perpetrata, quae enumerari non possent, pro quibus et regni periclitatio et regis dehonestatio evidenter provenerat: sed insuper ad cumulum miseriarum novissime omnem populum suae potestatis ad communem interitum traxerit, cum debuisset esse eidem populo dux salutis et pacis, cum divina pietas inaudito et invisibili modo ac nostris saeculis praedicando populo suo misereri decrevisset.'

penance of the kind that was incompatible with the royal office, and to be imposed and lifted only by 'episcopal hands'.

Yet the bishops' front was not united. Quite apart from the later claim that many churchmen in Compiègne had consented only because they were afraid, a comparison between the *Relatio* and Agobard's individual report reveals some fundamental differences. Whereas the *Relatio* characterised Louis's sins as *negligentia* or *flagitia*, and only once as *crimina*, the latter was Agobard's preferred expression.[109] On the other hand, the rhetoric about Louis having offended God and scandalised the *sancta ecclesia*, which is so typical of the joint episcopal report, is absent in Agobard's *cartula*.[110] Two distinct views of public penance emerge. On the one hand, there was Agobard's legalistic interpretation of excommunication as a punishment for grave crimes, as it had functioned for centuries in the churches of Gaul and Spain.[111] His assertion that everything leading up to Louis's penance had been 'sincerely investigated, established faithfully, [and] executed in an orderly fashion' evokes a legal tradition in which Agobard was an expert, and which he summarised as the 'law and order of public penance'.[112] He stressed Louis's role as an individual sinner in need of salvation, repeating that the 'one-time emperor' had committed the kind of serious crimes (*crimina*) which could be atoned for only by a public penance. This was underpinned by three citations from the penitential psalms of David, in the Old Latin version which was no doubt used in the liturgy for public penance in Lyons. First of all, however, Agobard's *cartula* was a legal testimony to the fact that he had participated in the collective judgement of the bishops: 'I have agreed with those who judged, and, agreeing, I myself have judged.'[113] As we have seen, the legitimacy of the *iudicium sacerdotale* was also a key issue in the joint *Relatio*, yet here the overall emphasis was on the 'political' sins by which he had offended God, scandalised the church and thrown his people into a state of confusion. Here Louis is treated not just as an individual sinner, but as someone who had sinned as

---

[109] Agobard, *Cartula*, p. 56, lines 33–9; p. 57, lines 5–8.

[110] *Relatio* (833), p. 52, line 33 ('quae ad scandalum ecclesiae, et ruinam populi, vel regni interitum manifestis indiciis pertinebant'); p. 52, line 47, to p. 53, line 1 ('in multis nefandis consiliis Deum irritaverit et sanctam ecclesiam scandalizaverit'); p. 53, lines 13–14 ('Deum offenderat et sanctam ecclesiam scandalizaverat'), p. 53, line 30–1 ('et in eo multis modis Deum offendisse, et ecclesiam Christi scandalizasse'); p. 53, line 38 ('ut aperte confiteretur errata sua in quibus maxime se Deum offendisse profitebatur'); p. 54, line 10 ('auctor scandali et perturbator pacis'); p. 55, line 2 ('quantum Deum offenderit ipse novit').

[111] Cf. Kottje, 'Buße oder Strafe?'; De Jong, 'Transformations of penance'.

[112] Agobard, *Cartula*, p. 56, line 28; p. 57, line 9.

[113] Agobard, *Cartula*, p. 56, lines 23–5; p. 57, lines 17–18.

a ruler, *ex officio*, and now needed to give satisfaction to the human community as well as to the offended deity. Behind this, there was a broader concept of public penance as an act of contrition embedded in a variety of more or less voluntary gestures of self-abasement, all of which qualified as honourable means of making amends to the Lord – or the human lord – one had offended.[114] This was the view of penance that Louis had shared with his leadership and that had informed his earlier acts of humiliation. In its very strictness, the 'law and order of penance' that prevailed in 833 in Compiègne and Soissons was a strange element in this familiar world of begging for pardon and favour. Different concepts of law underpinned these two potentially overlapping but by no means identical interpretations of offence and satisfaction. Whereas the first depended on a grand and sweeping gesture of humility that turned the ruler into God's readily forgiven and exalted servant,[115] the second was predicated on episcopal mediation, and on a precise measure of penance, carefully set in relation to the sin in question.

The case against the bishops

The bishops' strenuous attempt to control the interpretation of Louis's penance by means of the written word failed as soon as the old emperor regained power. Subsequently, the episcopal narrative was furiously contested. The court annalist, Thegan and the Astronomer all maintained that a penance had been imposed on Louis in entirely the wrong way, and for the wrong reasons. The accusations levelled at the emperor had been false, and so was the judgement pronounced by the bishops. As we have seen, this false judgement was at the heart of Thegan's invective against Ebo. The bishops were attacked through their Achilles' heel, namely their contention that Louis had 'asked' for a penance. On this weakest link in their argumentation the opposition immediately homed in, protesting that the emperor had been an unwilling victim of bullying and coercion on the part of his son and the rebellious bishops.[116] This had continued during subsequent efforts to force him to make a 'voluntary' monastic profession, which everyone knew was a contradiction in terms.[117] As the court annalist phrased it, Louis 'kept saying that he would never make any such commitment as long as he had no real power over his actions'.[118]

---

[114] Koziol, *Begging Pardon*; Moeglin, 'Pénitence publique'.
[115] Deschman, 'The exalted servant'.
[116] *AB*, s.a. 833, p. 10: 'Et tam diu illum vexaverunt, quousque arma deponere habitum mutare cogentes, liminibus ecclesiae pepulerunt'; Thegan, c. 43, p. 230; Astronomer, c. 49, p. 480.
[117] *AB*, s.a. 834, p. 11.   [118] *AB*, s.a. 833, p. 20; trans. Nelson, *Annals of St-Bertin*, p. 28.

The Astronomer argued that the entire penance had been illegal. The plotters of this unheard-of outrage had wanted to make sure that, now that Louis had lost his power, the clock could no longer be turned back. Together with 'some bishops' their verdict was that for 'those [sins] for which the emperor had already done penance he should once more perform a public penance, so that, having deposed his arms, he would somehow irrevocably give satisfaction to the church. Yet even foreign laws do not punish one transgression twice, and our law holds that God does not pass judgement twice for the same offence (*non iudicare Deum bis in idipsum*).'[119] In this context, 'our law' (*nostra lex*) was the prophetic book of Nahum (1.9); the phrase 'foreign laws' (*leges forenses*) presumably referred to the Roman legal tradition. By his penance in 822, the emperor had fully atoned for the sins committed against Bernard of Italy and other relatives, so these should not have been included in the list of accusations of 833. The crux of the matter is, however, that for the Astronomer, Louis's earlier and voluntary acts of penance were as efficacious as the formal *paenitentia publica* imposed on him at Soissons. Whereas the bishops had argued that Louis could not save his soul without their mediation, in the Astronomer's view his emperor's magnificent gestures of penance in the manner of Theodosius had earned him divine mercy.

This perspective was shared by Hraban Maur, who had been the imperial couple's loyal supporter in these years of trouble.[120] In his commentary on Kings, Hraban stressed the efficacy of royal atonement: 'Thus this David sinned grievously and scandalously, a sin that God was to chastise by means of the prophet [Nathan] and he himself [David] was to wash off by penance.'[121] In the course of 834 Fulda's learned abbot sent Louis 'a little work in twelve chapters' with a dedicatory poem explaining that he had gathered the 'divine doctrine of the Law' on the duty of sons to be obedient to their father.[122] Assembling an extensive and appropriate biblical dossier, Hraban confirmed that the rebellion of Louis's sons had been unjustified and sinful, yet he also urged the royal father to be lenient towards his wayward sons. Since he was held in high esteem as one of the great legal experts of his time, Hraban's opinion counted. In his view, those who had imposed a public penance on Louis had contravened divine law, that is, Scripture. As he pointed out, there was no biblical precedent to be found, 'be it in the time of the Law, or under the grace of

---

[119] Astronomer, c. 49, pp. 480–2: 'non iudicare Deum bis in idipsum' (Nah. 1.9, cited according to the Vetus Latina); cf. Landau, 'Ursprünge'.

[120] De Jong, 'Old law', 'The empire as *ecclesia*', and 'Exegesis for an empress'.

[121] Hraban, *Commentaria in libros IV regum*, PL 109, col. 98D.

[122] Hraban, *De reverentia*; the poem is on p. 403. The edition is based on BN lat. 2443 fols. 13v–29, s. IX. 2/4, from Mainz.

the New Testament', for emperors, kings or judges who had been condemned by a synodal decree or an episcopal judgement.[123] Furthermore, he posed a pertinent question: should someone who had publicly confessed his sins be excommunicated if there was no proof that the transgressions in question should indeed be defined as public?[124] Hraban's answer was a resounding negative, supported by a great number of major biblical figures who had all publicly confessed their sins for all to hear, trusting God's forgiveness. These precedents ranged from Moses and the Psalmist to Job, Isaiah and Jeremiah. Whenever these prophets had made a public confession together with their people, proclaiming their iniquities, they had received divine mercy all the sooner.

Once more, an alternative scenario emerges in which Louis, having loudly and tearfully confessed his manifold sins, might have turned the mood of the assembly around, creating room to make his peace with God and his opponents. Instead, this strategy was thwarted by those bishops who argued that a public confession in itself created the kind of 'scandal' that could be expiated only by an excommunication and a formal *paenitentia publica*. By this approach they prevented Louis from claiming the moral high ground, both during his penance and afterwards. There was no way in which Louis's humiliation in 833 could be rewritten afterwards in Theodosian terms, as a manifestation of imperial humility that enhanced the emperor's prestige. The recent and painful memory of Louis's dishonouring captivity could not simply be glossed over. This had shocked contemporaries much more than the emperor's public penance itself: even annalists who made only the briefest of references to the 833 upheaval singled out the fact that Louis had been in the custody of his eldest son.[125] Clearly the nature of the *custodia* in St-Médard mattered. It was specified as 'public',[126] or, by the Astronomer, as strict (*arta*), major (*magna*) or an incarceration (*carceralis*), as opposed to the less dishonouring *libera custodia*.[127] To some extent, Louis's stalwart refusal to enter a monastery helped to counterbalance the image of his impotence during the rebellions, but more often the coercion involved was highlighted to

---

[123] Ibid., c. 8, p. 412, lines 14–7.   [124] Ibid., c. 9, p. 412, lines 25–9.
[125] *AF*, s.a. 834, p. 27; *Annales Xantenses*, s.a. 834, p. 8.
[126] *Annales Xantenses*, s.a. 834, p. 8.
[127] Astronomer, c. 48, p. 480, line 4; c. 49, p. 482, line 10; c. 51, p. 486, line 20. What the Astronomer refers to as *custodia privata* (c. 45, p. 464, and c. 47, p. 470) is more commonly known as *libera custodia*, a partly voluntary 'house arrest', usually in a religious community. Cf. Nithard, I, c. 2, p. 8, on Louis's half-brothers, who in 818 were tonsured, to live *sub libera custodia* in various monasteries; De Jong, 'Monastic prisoners', pp. 298–9.

invalidate both the public penance and its supposedly enduring consequences, inevitably impairing Louis's authority.

That this argument counted is obvious from the *Relatio*'s claim that
Louis had 'asked' for his penance. Given the long and still-flourishing
enforced political tonsure, this was open to debate, yet in the Carolingian
revival of the penance of 'pristine Christianity', voluntariness was reintro-
duced as an important and even constituent element of the ritual. As
Bishop Jonas of Orléans asked, rhetorically, 'Who nowadays performs a
penance according to the example of the Fathers and sanctioned by
canonical authority? Which grave sinner liable to be punished by a public
penance puts down his military belt and comes to church in the presence
of all the faithful to be separated from Christ's body? Who, in sackcloth
and ashes, raises the remorseful lament of the penitents of yore?'[128] If such
a penance were to be effective, the sinner had to undertake this of his own
volition, motivated by contrition.

In 833 the bishops presented Louis's penance as the perfect example of
a penance according to the ancient model, for everything depended on the
ritual being executed in a correct and canonical fashion. Yet the bishops'
insistence on the voluntary character of imperial penance may also have
been intended to save some of Louis's face and honour. After all, he was to
remain alive, albeit as a penitent in a monastery; to offend him to the point
of perennial enmity and utter shame would not have served the purpose of
regime change. Lothar and his allies must have wondered what to do with
the 'one-time emperor'; the idea seems to have been that, as he was getting
older, he should engage in a suitably penitential anticipation of death. The
Relatio contains a tell-tale reference to Louis's advanced age: in the last
years of his life (*in extremis positis*) he should do penance in order not to
lose his soul.[129] In 855 Lothar himself would become a monk in Prüm in
order to prepare for death. Twenty-two years before, his father's public
penance followed by monastic conversion may have offered all concerned
an honourable way out of a insoluble deadlock. In seventh-century Spain
the honourable way out for a king was to adopt the status of a public
penitent. Chindasuinth (653), Wamba (680) and Erwig (687) all gave up
royal office by becoming penitents, thus avoiding a bloody conflict and
making room for their successors.[130] Possibly, with his back to the wall,
Louis himself at some point agreed to co-operate, biding his time and

---

[128] Jonas, *De institutione laicali*, I, c. 10, cols. 138B/C; De Jong, 'Transformations of
penance', pp. 189–90.
[129] *Relatio* (833), p. 53, line 9.
[130] Fredegar, *Chronicae*, IV, c. 82, p. 186; Twelfth Council of Toledo (681), ed. Vives,
Concilios visigóticos e hispano-romanos, p. 386. *Laterculus Visigothorum*, nos. 46–7, p. 468.
See De Jong, 'Monastic prisoners', p. 315.

keeping his options open as much as possible. Extensive negotiations went on during the assembly of Compiègne, with envoys scuttling back and forth between Lothar over there and Louis in Soissons. An offer from Lothar for his father to end his life peacefully and honourably in a monastery may have been one of the topics of these preliminary exchanges.[131]

Penance and public humiliation

One thing is certain: the spectacle of Louis's penance in 833 did not lack thorough preparation; by stage-managing this the bishops did their utmost to convey an unambiguous message, both to those present and to those who would read the episcopal narrative at a later stage. Gerd Althoff has drawn attention to the apparent paradox of rituals of submission that were presented as spontaneous and voluntary, but only after careful negotiations of the terms. Such public demonstrations of humility towards rulers or other figures of authority needed to be staged (*inzeniert*), for far too much depended on the outcome in order to leave matters to chance.[132] In Louis's case, it was crucial to supporters and opponents alike that the emperor's tears and gestures of contrition were genuine, and *not* stage-managed. A public confession should be open and transparent, without any ulterior purposes remaining hidden 'inside'; dissemblers and crafty men would provoke God's wrath (Iob 36.13).[133] This sincerity was what the *Relatio* attempted to impress on its audience, along with the efficacy and irrevocability of the penance imposed. The bishops did their utmost to stage-manage all this, yet their massive *Inszenierung* misfired. Or was it soon overtaken by another attempt to consolidate political consensus by means of ritual communication? In Althoff's view, Louis's penance of 833 set in motion a series of rituals of inversion by which a volatile political situation was 'fixed' and visibly portrayed, time and again, expressing the new consensus that had been negotiated behind the scenes.[134] To some extent, this was indeed the case, but the concept of *Inszenierung* is only a partial help to understand the rituals of the 830s and the way these were presented in texts. More than anything else, the dossier on Louis's penance shows that control over the understanding of a ritual like this, both in the present and in the future, could only be limited.

Even though it is difficult to make out, one should assume that the audience of 833 – spectators and readers – interpreted the imperial penance according to a grid of familiar gestures of self-abasement, with

---

[131] *Relatio* (833), p. 53, lines 7–9. [132] Althoff, 'Demonstration und Inszenierung'.
[133] *Relatio* (833), p. 53, lines 40–4; cf. Radbert, *VA*, c. 51, cols. 1534D–1535A.
[134] Althoff, *Macht der Rituale*, pp. 57–64.

greater or lesser religious connotations. For tenth- and eleventh-century France, Geoffrey Koziol has shown that public penance was part of a much wider spectrum of rituals of begging for pardon and mercy, from human lords as wells as the Lord of lords.[135] Two important rituals by which a supplicant could throw himself at the mercy of his lord were usually referred to as *deditio* and *harmiscara*. The main elements of *deditio* were a highly public and previously negotiated prostration at the feet of one's lord, as well as a confession or self-accusation, which was then followed by an equally public act of forgiveness and reconciliation. Lothar's submission to his father in Blois (834) was a good example of this.[136] As for *harmiscara*, the element of shaming was stronger here, with culprits usually having to carry an object such as a saddle to show their unworthiness; at the palace in Aachen in around 820, those who harboured criminals were made to carry them to jail on their shoulders.[137] Among the spectators in Soissons must have been at least some who witnessed such secular strategies of humiliation, at the court and elsewhere.

For contemporaries reflecting on Louis's penance of 833, an important distinction to make was the one between a voluntary and therefore honourable gesture of self-abasement on the one hand, and an involuntary and therefore shameful humiliation on the other. As we have seen, this produced something of a double bind: in order to be valid, the penance needed to appear as Louis's initiative, but in order to be retrospectively invalidated, the element of coercion should be stressed. Along these lines, the bishops and their opponents argued their case, attempting to turn their interpretation into the dominant one. The other major question for contemporaries confronted with Louis's penance was whether this had been a manifestation of God's will, or just a human action without any divinely favoured authority. There is a lot to be said against putting religious and secular gestures of self-abasement into strictly separate categories, when those enacting and witnessing these rituals in fact drew upon a common symbolic language. As Timothy Reuter argued, whether Henry IV in Canossa in 1077 performed a *deditio* or a penance was a moot point, for this was in the eye of the beholder. If a secular ritual of submission had religious overtones, these were usually intended: the king who received and pardoned penitent rebels wielded a religious kind of authority.[138] No doubt there was much transfer between these apparently different

---

[135] Koziol, *Begging Pardon*, pp. 100–1, 181–213; De Jong, 'Power and humility'.
[136] Althoff, 'Das Privileg der deditio', p. 118.
[137] *Capitulare de disciplina palatii Aquisgranensis* (?820) c. 3, MGH *Capit.* I, no. 146; Moeglin, 'Harmiscara'; de Jong, 'Power and humility', pp. 46–7.
[138] Reuter, 'Contextualising Canossa', p. 162.

spheres: in order to understand public penance, one had to know about monastic conversion and exile, but also about *harmiscara* and *deditio*.[139] Jean-Marie Moeglin's insights with regard to late medieval penance and 'amende honorable' are also pertinent to our understanding of how Carolingian public penance and related forms of self-abasement may have been perceived. Discussing the ways in which the notion of making honourable amends was transferred from the world of human action to the sphere of the divine, and then back again, Moeglin points out that the relation between a public sinner and the offended deity was theoretically so asymmetrical that there were no terms for negotiation of the type practised prior to a public *deditio*. In practice, however, there was the concept of God's anger, which demanded 'satisfaction' (*satisfactio*), which in later medieval texts even becomes defined as God's wounded honour.[140] Moeglin argues that, in the long term, it was this tension between divine mercy and human agency that made public penance such a powerful source of inspiration for more 'secular' (read 'intra-human') rituals of reconciliation, provided these were enacted between two parties of unequal status. In other words, *paenitentia publica*, with its implicit acceptance of divine agency and sacerdotal mediation, had a powerful impact upon the way in which secular acts of public submission were shaped and understood. Ninth-century 'offence of God' was not yet understood in terms of 'wounded honour', as if God were a party in the conflict, but God's anger at the disruption of a divinely sanctioned social order played a major part in the development of public penitence and other gestures of self-abasement. Those who took Louis to task in 833 constituted themselves as the guardians of that order, and the ones who performed the inexorable duty of pacifying an angry deity. Louis himself had assumed this responsibility, both towards God and towards those who begged him for pardon and mercy. The emperor's perennial forgiveness of his enemies, for which he was praised and blamed, was based on a contemporary understanding of how divine mercy functioned, and on the perceived similarities between divine and royal authority.

This being said, one should keep in mind that those whom Louis governed, be they clerics or laymen, could and did distinguish between the presence and absence of divine agency when they witnessed what we now call a political ritual. This crucial point was made recently and forcefully by Philippe Buc, with reference to the way in which Lothar had become co-emperor in 817. In 833, Agobard reminded Louis of the fasts, prayers and masses which had made it abundantly clear that Louis's

---

[139] De Jong, 'Power and humility', pp. 43–7.   [140] Moeglin, 'Pénitence public', pp. 230–6.

decision to favour his elder son had been divinely inspired. Agobard had agreed, at the time, and was deeply worried about God's anger about any deviance from this divinely approved scheme. As Buc expressed it, 'the liturgical techniques employed to secure inspiration from God were simultaneously the means used to convince the public that this inspiration verily came from God'.[141] Similarly, in 833 the entire apparatus of authoritative public penance was mustered for this dual purpose, securing divine endorsement of Louis's penance and impressing it on all and sundry that God was on the side of Lothar and his bishops. By a massive production of authoritative documentation, the bishops tried to establish the holiness and efficacy of Louis's penance, and, furthermore, to heighten the level of publicity, which would mean an even greater justification for this *public* penance. The performative nature of the momentous event in Soissons, witnessed by many, was extended by an avalanche of episcopal attestations. All this went well beyond the public expression of previously agreed political consensus. If there was ever a ritual that was hotly contested after the event, in the way discussed by Philippe Buc,[142] it was Louis's public penance in 833. The key issue in this particular contention was the question of whether the imposition of the imperial *paenitentia publica* had been a matter of divine inspiration or of human error. Once Louis regained power, those who claimed that it had all happened with divine approbation were drowned out by a chorus of authors claiming that these proceedings had lacked any shred of legitimacy. Their contestation was such that, with a few exceptions, the rebels' version of the imperial penance and their motives became submerged, remaining hidden in manuscripts with a very limited circulation, until these voices were discovered much later.[143]

From a modern point of view, the interpretation offered by the bishops in 833 looks like clerical propaganda, that is, a barely veiled religious legitimation for what was in fact the cynical deposition of a monarch. By contrast, the robust denial, by ninth-century authors supportive of Louis, of the sacrality of Louis's penance seems to be the more commonsensical and therefore trustworthy version of what had happened. This contrast between scheming bishops and level-headed historiographers is misleading, for it obscures the fact that all those who were involved in this

---

[141] Buc, 'The monster and the critics', p. 445.

[142] On the 'struggle for meaning' after the ritual event, see Buc, *Dangers of Ritual*, pp. 1–12, 67–87, 'Ritual and interpretation', and 'Text and interpretation'.

[143] On the manuscript tradition of the *Relatio* (833), see Booker, 'A new prologue'; on the mansucripts of Agobard's work, see Van den Acker, *Agobardi opera omnia*, pp. xlvii–lv; on the manuscripts of Radbert's *Vita Adalhardi* and *Epitaphium Arsenii*, see Ganz, *Corbie*, p. 145.

struggle for interpretation were familiar with the phenomenon of 'good ritual' that managed to harness God's favour and support. All the contestants involved, including Louis himself, were convinced that the ruler of the Franks was accountable to God for the salvation of his people, that kingship was a 'ministry' to be executed faithfully, and that if God's anger was aroused, it was the ruler and his leadership who should be the first to make amends. The question was: how did this royal religious authority work out in practice, in relation both to a demanding deity and to the king's partners in mediation between God and humankind, the bishops? Least of all was Louis's penance in Soissons a confrontation between the ruler and his bishops. All those involved in this conflict aspired to the same lofty goal, namely the exercise of authority with the clear hallmark of divine approval. This was the yardstick by which Louis's *paenitentia* was measured, by those who imposed it and by those who attacked it. The key aspects of imperial sin defined by the bishops in 833, *negligentia*, *scandalum* and *perturbatio*, represented the exact opposite of what had become the ideals of order typical of Louis's reign. These were most explicitly expressed in his great programmatic capitulary of 825, the *Admonitio* to all orders of the realm, with its Pauline metaphor of the ruler as the head, being assisted in his ministry by the 'limbs' that were the various *ordines*.[144] Having raised hopes and expectations regarding the harmonious co-operation of all the limbs that made up the body politic, Louis had to answer for it when he fell short of these ideals; yet one should keep in mind that those who rebelled in 833 did so from the same ideological position as the emperor whom they badgered into accepting an ecclesiastical public penance. In the crisis years of 828–34, political adversaries kept their eyes trained on signs of divine anger or approbation, convincing others of the virtue or sin they had observed, and of the need for atonement. In this volatile situation, *Inzenierung* was surely attempted, but with little chance of success. Overheating, the machinery of the penitential state spun out of control.[145] It took two years for it to cool down, with major rituals of inversion in 834 and 835, and Louis increasingly regaining control of a situation that had got completely out of hand – for all concerned.

Turning the tables

Once Lothar had fled on 28 February, the bishops 'who had been present there came and reconciled the Lord Emperor in the church of St-Denis,

---

[144] See above, chapter 3, pp. 132–3.
[145] These automobile metaphors I gratefully borrowed from Stuart Airlie's comments on the penultimate version of this chapter.

and clad him in his royal robes and his weapons'.[146] In other words, the bishops present decided to switch allegiance there and then, facilitating Louis's restoration by putting their liturgical stamp on the changed situation. In doing so, they enacted the exact reversal of the ritual performed in Soissons, which should make it crystal clear that Louis was once more fit to rule. However much contemporaries may have contested the bishops' imposition of an 'ecclesiastical' public penance on their emperor, they did take the effects of this ritual seriously, and so did Louis himself. The excommunication as well as the implicit deposition needed to be undone, as quickly as possible – that is, on the first Sunday after Louis's liberation in St-Denis. As in the case of the imperial penance of four months before, the written word helped to publicise the emperor's reconciliation and enhanced its efficacy. The elements themselves conspired with the emperor's absolution, for floods and storms subsided once the emperor had been reconciled.[147] Contemporary readers must have understood the significance of nature's favourable reaction: the reign of a *rex iniquus*, namely Lothar, was now over, and the legitimate ruler was restored.[148] The Astronomer, who noted all this, also signalled that the worst was now over by highlighting Louis's gratitude for the complete loyalty of his sons Louis and Pippin, and also the resumption of normal life at the court and the restoration of order. In other words, the emperor, restored to power, went to the Ardennes to hunt and fish.[149]

The second important symbolic moment came in the end of August 834 in Blois, when Lothar had decided to stop fighting the superior force of his father's combined troops. With regard to Lothar's position, there are subtle differences between the Astronomer's narrative and that of the court annalist. Whereas the Astronomer depicted the eldest son as a humble supplicant, begging for his father's mercy in a suitable way, the *Annals of St-Bertin* presented Lothar as someone who kept kicking, even though he was beaten.[150] The underlying moral of both versions is the same: begging for pardon and mercy was what Lothar should do. So the Astronomer showed a Lothar who 'came as a supplicant to his father' (*supplex ad patrem venit*). Louis responded in kind. Father and son had mastered the same idiom of humility, with the difference that for the rightful emperor, there was nobody to beg mercy from but God. Lothar, meanwhile, should turn to his father. For Thegan the confrontation

---

[146] *AB*, s.a. 834, p. 12; trans. Nelson, *Annals of St-Bertin*, p. 29. See also Astronomer, c. 51, p. 488.

[147] Astronomer, c. 51, p. 490: 'sed illius absolutione ita quodammodo coniurasse visa sunt elementi'.

[148] Ps.-Cyprian, *De duodecim abusivis*, pp. 51–2; see above, chapter 4, pp. 210–11.

[149] Astronomer, c. 52, p. 492.   [150] Ibid., p. 498; *AB*, s.a. 834, pp. 14–15.

between father and son in Blois was a supreme occasion to put the knife in, and he did not hesitate to do so. In an introductory chapter that Walahfrid entitled 'The father's admonition sent to Lothar by envoys', Thegan explained that Louis exhorted his elder son by letter to depart from his wicked ways. This was a direct reference to the prophetic text (Ez. 3.18) which had had such a central position in the bishops' defence of Louis's public penance, making clear that the boot was now on the other foot: once more, it was Louis who was the one to admonish others, warning them against their sinful ways.[151] This was followed by the precept 'not issued by prophets or by apostles, but by God himself', to honour one's parents, culminating in the proclamation: 'that you may take away the evil out of the midst of you, and all Israel hearing it may be afraid' (Deut. 21.21).[152] But Lothar still would not heed his father's exhortations; instead, he slunk away in the night, like a fugitive.[153] A delegation headed by Bishop Badurad of Paderborn then ordered (*praecepit*) the rebellious eldest son to distance himself from his impious seducers, so it would become clear whether God wished this discord to continue or not. An indecisive Lothar asked the envoys for advice, and finally allowed himself to be convinced that he and his seducers should throw themselves on the emperor's mercy. The envoys returned to report to Louis. As befitted a rueful son, Lothar then went to this father. His submission was shown by 'coming towards' his father, expressed by the repeated use of the verb *venire*, and by the lofty height, moral and otherwise, from which Louis received him:

After them [the envoys], Lothar came to where his father was sitting in his tent, which was erected in a very high place in a great field, where the entire army could see him, and his sons and faithful men stood beside him. Then Lothar, approaching (*veniens*), fell at his father's feet, and after him his father-in-law, Hugh the Coward, and then Matfrid and all the others who had been the leaders in that outrage. After they rose from the ground they confessed that they had sinned badly. Then Lothar swore fidelity to his father, said that he wished to obey all his commands, and agreed to go to Italy and to stay there and not to leave except on his father's orders. Then the others swore as well. Then the most pious prince gave them his pardon, provided they would keep this oath. He let them keep their patrimonies and everything else they had except whatever he himself had given them with his own hand. They parted there and Lothar travelled to Italy with his most malicious sympathisers. Immediately Matfrid, who was the instigator of all

---

[151] Thegan, c. 53, p. 246: 'ut averteret se a via sua prava'; Ezech. 3, 18: 'si dicente me ad impium morte morieris non adnuntiaveris ei neque locutus fueris ut avertatur a via sua impia'.

[152] Thegan, c. 53, p. 246: 'ut auferatis malum de medio vestri, et universis Israel audiens pertimescat'.

[153] Thegan, c. 54, p. 248: 'sed quadam nocte elongavit se ab eo, quasi fugiendo'.

their evil deeds *par excellence*, died, as did many of the others. Those who survived were struck by a fever.[154]

Thegan presented the epidemic of 836 and its death toll among Lothar's supporters as occurring directly after their arrival in Italy, as a divine punishment for their wickedness. Hugh especially came in for more than his fair share of slander, with Thegan claiming that the count of Tours had been so cowardly during the Spanish campaign that his *domestici* chanted (*cecinerunt*) that he did not dare to come out of his own doorway. Whereas Ernst Tremp saw this as evidence of oral tradition, such mocking songs roared by one's retainers and servants strike me as a Carolingian aristocrat's worst nightmare. This was why Thegan integrated it into his strategies of defamation.[155]

These strategies were primarily aimed at Ebo, archbishop of Rheims, whom Thegan blamed for the emperor's humiliation in 833: 'He invested you with purple and the *pallium*; you clothed him in a hair shirt' (*tu induisti eum cilicio*).[156] Immediately after Louis regained control, the mutual blaming and shaming started. Whereas Pippin of Aquitaine and Louis the German were hardly mentioned in this respect, Lothar and his allies, notably Matfrid, caught part of the fallout, yet this was nothing compared to what Ebo had to contend with. Lothar and his supporters shifted the responsibility to the bishops who had imposed a penance on his father; the bishops, collectively, blamed Ebo and let him carry the burden of guilt. Like the proverbial scapegoat, he carried the episcopal sins outside the church.[157] As the Astronomer recounted, when Ebo protested that he was the only one to be judged, the other bishops exculpated themselves by claiming that they had witnessed the imperial penance as unwilling spectators.[158]

In a letter of 867 to Pope Nicholas I, Charles the Bald begged to differ. Here, the king set out his views on the endless complications that had followed Ebo's ordination of a number of clerics in 840–1, when he had been briefly restored to the see of Rheims. The events of 833 and their aftermath formed the background to Charles's argument. He chose his words carefully, stating with deliberate ambiguity that 'the said Ebo, together with almost all the bishops, some willing, some unwilling, had removed the aforesaid emperor from the communion of the church, while

---

[154] Thegan, c. 55, p. 250.
[155] Thegan, c. 28, p. 216; Tremp, *Studien*, p. 44. On the seriousness of such jokes, see Innes, 'Politics of humour', and Kershaw, 'Laughter after Babel's fall'.
[156] Thegan, c. 44, p. 232, lines 9–10.   [157] Boshof, *Agobard*, p. 256.
[158] Astronomer, c. 54, p. 500; to these belonged Hildemann of Beauvais; Boshof, *Agobard*, p. 256. Thegan's message was subsequently spread by Walahfrid Strabo; see Booker, 'A new prologue'.

he had not confessed or been convicted by anyone, and robbed him of his wife, his son and his dignity amid all his faithful men'.[159] In Charles's eyes, the bishops were by no means exonerated, but neither was Ebo himself, sixteen years after his death in 851. In this truly remarkable letter, Charles began at the beginning, for only recounting the story from Ebo's birth onwards would clarify matters for the pope.[160] As the king explained, Ebo was born to parents who belonged to the *familia* of the royal fisc. It had been Charlemagne himself who had taken the talented young boy under his wing, giving him responsible tasks in the palace and then granting him his liberty. Ebo was even promoted to the 'nobility of the priesthood', and, as such, was sent to serve Louis the Pious in Aquitaine. Soon, his zeal and intellect led to his appointment as Louis's librarian (*bibliothecarius*). Ebo's star continued to rise, for he was present when the new emperor received Stephen IV in Rheims in 816, though not yet as archbishop of Rheims. This dazzling appointment came later in that year, when the elected candidate, a certain Gislemar, had proven incapable of reading from the Gospels, let alone understanding the text. A bright young palace trainee was preferred over the obvious but unworthy candidate.[161] Meanwhile, there are gaps in Ebo's biography. Was he really Louis's 'milk-brother', as Flodoard of Rheims claimed, or was this a romantic tale spun about an unfortunate archbishop who was twice deposed, and ended his life as bishop of Hildesheim, in the far east of the Carolingian world?[162] Whatever the case, it was Charlemagne who gave Ebo a chance in life, and Charlemagne's grandson who reflected on what a chance this was, and how it might have affected Ebo's judgement. During the rebellion of 830, Ebo remained staunchly loyal, Charles recounted, all the way to Louis's restoration, 'as was right' (*ut recte erat*).[163] The charter evidence indeed indicates that during the second rebellion, Ebo remained at Louis's side until the armies gathered on the Rothfeld.[164] Radbert gave him the alias 'Phassur', Jeremiah's jailor (Ier. 20.2), and mentioned him as one of Judith's allies who were with Louis in Worms in 833.[165] All this suggests that Ebo joined Lothar's camp only on the Field of Lies. Did he do so in the wake of others, believing their defection to be a divine judgement, or in exchange for the abbey of St-Vaast, allowing himself to be bought, as Flodoard claimed? Even if the latter allegation was part of the

[159] Council of Troyes (867), MGH, *Conc.* IV, p. 240, lines 15–18.
[160] For Charles's concise summary of Ebo's life, see ibid., pp. 239–40.
[161] Airlie, 'Bonds of power', pp. 202–3; Goetting, *Das Bistum Hildesheim*, pp. 59–61.
[162] Flodoard, *Historia*, II, c. 19, p. 467; Goetting, *Das Bistum Hildesheim*, pp. 57–9.
[163] Council of Troyes (867), MGH *Conc.* IV, p. 240, lines 7–10.
[164] Depreux, *Prosopographie*, p. 173; cf. BM 922 (893), and BM 925 (896) a.
[165] Radbert, *EA*, II, p. 84.

campaign of slander waged against Ebo after his downfall, as it would seem, the sudden defection of his loyal archbishop must have come as a tremendous shock to Louis.

Of Ebo's flight after Louis's restoration there are many versions, each more dishonouring than the last. The man fled, therefore he was guilty. Charles's view of the matter was that the archbishop sought refuge with a recluse in the diocese of Paris, where he was captured. He was then taken to a 'general council of nearly all the bishops and abbots, both canonical and regular, of his whole empire', which Louis had summoned to Thionville on 1 February 835, on the Feast of the Purification of the Virgin. As I signalled earlier, this was a date heavy with significance. This was when Louis had called his very first assembly and began his reign, in 814, and also the date on which an assembly confirmed his restoration to power in 831.[166] For the bishops who been implicated in the imperial penance, the hour of reckoning had now come. According to the court annalist, everyone present signed a joint declaration as well as their own *cartula* to confirm that the emperor had been undeservedly deposed, and was now restored to his ancestral honour. Just as Louis's deposition of arms had been reversed in St-Denis in March 834, so now the authoritative documentation of 833 was undone by similar measures.[167] On 28 February the entire assembly gathered at the church of St Stephen in Metz to celebrate mass. Here the revised version of what had happened in Soissons was read out 'publicly, to all who were present', and the 'holy and venerable bishops' lifted the crown from the altar to restore it to Louis's head. Not so Ebo, however, who was identified as the standard-bearer (*signifer*) of the faction that had opposed the emperor. As the court annalist recounted,

Ebo ascended to a high place in that same church and declared in the presence of all, in a loud and free voice, that Augustus had been unjustly deposed; that everything done against him had been committed sinfully and plotted against every norm of equity; and that afterwards he [Louis] had been deservedly, justly and worthily re-established again on his own imperial throne.[168]

The next stage was that the entire assemblage returned to Thionville, where Ebo, once more according to the court annalist, 'confessed a capital crime in the plenary synod, proclaiming himself unworthy of the episcopal ministry and confirming with his own subscription that he resigned from that office by the consent and verdict of everyone'.[169]

---

[166] Astronomer, c. 20, p. 344, lines 21–4.

[167] *AB*, s.a. 835, p. 16; trans. Nelson, *Annals of St-Bertin*, p. 32.

[168] Ibid., pp. 16–7; trans. Nelson, *Annals of St-Bertin*, p. 33, with some adaptations by the present author.

[169] *AB*, s.a. 835, p. 17; in a similar vein, Astronomer, c. 54, pp. 500–1.

With deadly symmetry, all that had been done against Louis was reversed. He had been formally reconciled to the church and invested with his arms by the bishops, who had then recalled and countermanded their own collective testimony to the public penance and publicly restored the crown to their emperor; Ebo's public proclamation of guilt in St Stephen's and his signed confession of a capital crime also completely mirrored and negated what Louis had done at Soissons. Yet symmetry between the two confessions is less clear than it seems at first glance. The capital crime to which Ebo confessed in Thionville has remained a matter for speculation. Did he perhaps own up to some sexual misdemeanour?[170] The key to this enigma lies in the ninth-century distinction between a public and a secret confession, which should be followed by a corresponding atonement. High-ranking clerics knew their own version of public penance, which was usually referred to as a *paenitentia canonica*; generally, this amounted to a deposition from office. Episcopal transgressions creating scandal were a sensitive issue. At the council of Paris (829) the bishops complained about overly hasty accusations and rough royal justice that had led to the kind of slander (*mala fama*) that destroyed episcopal reputations and endangered the souls of the faithful.[171] Obviously, the bishops did not want to be declared guilty before they were properly tried, but behind this, there was also the justified fear that the publicity generated by slander would turn their sins from secret ones into scandalous *crimina*, which would require their deposition. The vastly preferable alternative was a secret confession, followed by a so-called secret or 'occult' penance that would still enable the priestly or episcopal sinner to regain his rank and return to his former office.[172] As long as the confession remained secret, there was no 'scandal', and the cleric concerned had a right to be tried by clerics only, without the presence of the emperor or laymen. Thus argued Hraban Maur, the abbot of Fulda, to whose monastery Ebo was sent after his trial in 835.[173]

As Charles's letter to Pope Nicholas shows, Ebo's trial in Thionville was dominated by a tug-of-war between those who tried to get the proceedings against the archbishop defined as 'secret', thus enabling his eventual return to the see of Rheims, and those who did their utmost to prevent this by heightening the publicity involved. The result was an equivocal verdict, which was to haunt Ebo himself and, from his appointment in 845 onwards, his successor Hincmar. With the latter, King Charles had his share of conflict, so the letter of 867 can hardly be qualified as impartial; yet with regard to Ebo's trial, this royal epistle reveals the struggle that

---

[170] Nelson, *Annals of St-Bertin*, p. 33, n. 3.   [171] Council of Paris (829), III, c. 10, p. 674.
[172] Kottje, *Bussbücher*, p. 217.   [173] Ibid., pp. 217–39; De Jong, 'Old law'.

went on in the 830s between his supporters and those aiming for his permanent deposition. Predictably, Louis belonged to the latter group. As Charles related, his father had been 'crowned and reinstated in his former imperial rule by all the bishops, clergy and people', after Ebo's public confession in Metz.[174] Once the assembly reconvened in Thionville, Louis ordered Ebo to reiterate the public confession he had made in the cathedral of Metz, but this time in the presence of the entire assembly, including his lay magnates and Louis himself. It was the maximum amount of publicity, and the irrevocable consequences thereof, that Louis had in mind. The bishops were caught in the middle. According to Thegan, they dithered in deposing 'the foulest peasant' (*turpissimus rusticus*) Ebo, because they feared he would reveal their own complicity in Louis's penance.[175] Apart from this very real consideration, there were other concerns. On the one hand, they wanted to give the emperor the satisfaction he demanded, but on the other, they were concerned to uphold the dignity of the episcopal office. In the end, they persuaded Louis to accept a less public procedure. Ebo would confess not in the presence of the laity (*coram laicis*) but in a place reserved for those in sacred orders (*in sacrario*).[176]

This was how Ebo's trial proceeded. The secrecy of Ebo's confession was further ensured by the fact that only three bishops had heard it; their hearing of Ebo's confession was observed by three other bishops, who could testify that Ebo had confessed, yet did not hear what had been said.[177] In principle, only three bishops, sworn to secrecy, actually knew of Ebo's sins, but in the course of the trial, those working for more publicity did get their way. Under pressure, as he later claimed,[178] Ebo signed a document in which he declared that he had confessed his sins secretly and deemed himself unworthy of the episcopal ministry and office.[179] With hindsight, Ebo protested that there was nothing prejudicial in a public written declaration (*publica inscriptio*) of having made a

---

[174] Council of Troyes (867), MGH *Conc.* IV, p. 240, lines 32–3: 'Ibi etiam idem piissimus imperator ab omnibus episcopis, clero et populo est honorabiliter coronatus et pristino restitutus imperio.'

[175] Thegan, c. 56, p. 252.

[176] Ibid., lines 33–8. *Sacrarium* is used metaphorically here; literally, it was a sacristy or robing room.

[177] Ibid., p. 241, lines 18–24. The three confessors were Aiulf of Bourges, Modoin of Autun and Badurad of Paderborn; the three others were Noto of Arles, Theoderic of Cambrai and Aicharius of Noyon.

[178] Ebo, *Apologeticum forma prior*, MGH *Conc.* II/2, pp. 796–7. On the manuscript transmission of the older and more recent versions of the *Apologeticum*, see Goetting, *Das Bistum Hildesheim*, pp. 69–70, n. 103. See also Hartmann, *Karolingerzeit*, p. 198.

[179] MGH *Conc.* II/2, p. 702.

confession. On the contrary, his compliance had furthered the remission of his sins,[180] and had managed to calm the fury of his persecutors.[181] Meanwhile, the contents of his confession remained secret. But what actually happened was that Ebo's adversaries had tried to corner him with the fact of having signed this document, claiming that he had gone 'public' in declaring himself to be unworthy of the episcopal office. Such scandalous publicity would require an irrevocable deposition. A secret procedure would enable Ebo to return to his see, after due penance, but this secrecy was being rapidly undermined.

At this point, the Empress Judith intervened, effecting a compromise which would satisfy both her husband and the divine law. As her son explained to the pope, when he, Charles, was born, Judith had sent a ring to Ebo so that he would pray for her son. If anything untoward happened, Ebo could send it back to her with a request for help, and this he did now, lacking worldly support and human solace.[182] Invoking the dignity of the episcopal ministry, Judith got Louis to agree that he would no longer work towards Ebo's deposition. 'According to the moderate counsel of our glorious mother', as Charles expressed it, referring to the bishops who were trying Ebo, 'they would satisfy the most pious emperor and proclaim no other judgement on Ebo than [the one] he had himself publicised in writing'.[183] Ebo's written declaration of sinfulness and unworthiness could not be undone, but since he still had not confessed any specific sin in public, either orally or in writing, theoretically a return to office remained possible.

After the trial, this precarious secrecy was undermined even further. Charles maintained that he had never seen an authentic copy of Ebo's confession that had been signed by all the bishops gathered in 835; his sins had remained secret, and were known only to his three confessors. Yet Ebo's declaration of guilt did circulate in a version with a joint and signed declaration of forty-three bishops appended, in which the three confessors had become six, who had testified *viva voce* that Ebo's sin (*peccatum*) had been such that, from then on, he could never exercise the episcopal ministry. It was even worse: had Ebo admitted to this sin before his

---

[180] Ebo, *Apologeticum forma prior*, MGH *Conc.* II/2, p. 796, lines 24–7: 'Unde et nequaquam noxia, sed potius saluberrima habenda est illa confessionis meae publica inscriptio, per quam certa perhibetur posse fieri peccatorum remissio.'

[181] Ibid., p. 797, lines 29–38.

[182] Council of Troyes (867), MGH *Conc.* IV, pp. 240–1, lines 39–43. The ring was sent via Framegaudus, presumably the recluse with whom Ebo had sought refuge late February 834.

[183] Ibid., p. 241, lines 10–13.

ordination, he could never have become a bishop.[184] The doors prised open by Judith were closing once more. The court annalist added to this growing publicity by denying any secrecy in Ebo's confession: it had been made in the plenary session of the synod (*in plenaria sinodo*).[185] None of Ebo's enemies dared to disclose the actual sin to which Ebo had owned up. For all their attempts to turn his case into a proper *scandalum* by dark hints and vague intimations, they stopped at divulging the precise nature of this 'moral sin' or 'capital crime'. The boundary between what constituted a secret and a public confession may have been stretched, but it was never violated, either by those (including Louis) eager to have their revenge on Ebo, or by the former archbishop himself, in the interest of his defence. As a result, what Ebo confessed in the presence of three bishops, observed by three others, was to remain the kind of secret nobody was supposed to know about, but on which Ebo's adversaries invited ever more speculation. Which sin of his youth would have prevented him from becoming a bishop, had he publicly confessed to it at the time? A sexual transgression of some sort seems likely, yet to come up with a plausible answer to this question means falling into the trap set by Ebo's opponents in 835. By inviting public speculation on the nature of this grave sin, they hoped to transfer Ebo's secret confession and sin into the domain of public scandal, without actually infringing the secrecy of his confession. The result was decades of debate about Ebo's juridical status, exacerbated by his brief restoration to the see of Rheims by Lothar in 840–1. This is a sad and all too short story: having been reinstated some time after August 840, Ebo was deposed once more by Charles in August 841. Meanwhile, he had managed to ordain several clerics and bishops; the validity of these ordinations was still disputed in the 860s, well after Ebo's death.[186] No wonder that Charles the Bald, who in 867 was at the tail-end of this prolonged controversy, thought one needed to begin at the beginning if one wished to shed any light on this complicated matter.

Yet if this assessment is valid, and the secrecy of his confession was so important for Ebo's long-term survival as a bishop, what are we then to make of his very public declaration in the church of St Stephen, prior to his trial in Thionville? According to the court annalist, on that Sunday, 28 Februrary 835, when all gathered in Drogo's church in Metz, Ebo proclaimed, voluntarily, loudly (*libera voce*), and for all to see and hear, that Louis had been deposed against all the rules of justice (*aequitas*) and had now been justly restored.[187]

---

[184] Council of Thionville (835), MGH *Conc.* II/2, no. 55, pp. 702–3.
[185] *AB*, s.a. 835, p. 17.   [186] Goetting, *Das Bistum Hildesheim*, pp. 69–72.
[187] *AB*, s.a. 835, p. 16.

This was also King Charles's view of the matter: 'In the church of St Stephen [Ebo], mounting the *ambo* in the presence of all, professed that the judgement he imposed on the glorious emperor was not equitable (*equum*).'[188] Apparently there was publicity and publicity. Ebo's proclamation in St Stephen's in Metz became truly public, in the sense of scandalous, only when he repeated it to the entire assembly in Thionville. This was a general and judicial *placitum*, where Ebo's public declaration would have legal consequences. In St Stephen's, however, Ebo freely admitted to having wronged his emperor, seeking maximum publicity of the kind that might earn him the forgiveness of God as well as of Louis. By voluntarily abasing himself, albeit in a grand manner, in front of all those assembled within the sacred precincts of this venerable church, Ebo appealed for the forgiveness Louis had shown so often to others, for worse offences. In Metz, Ebo followed this illustrious precedent by begging for pardon and mercy in a grand manner, in which the emperor himself was the expert *par excellence*: the humility that exalted the one who offered it freely to God and the offended party had saved the day in Attigny (822) and Compiègne (830). Here, magnificently and publicly, Louis showed his true mettle as a Christian emperor. Ebo's public confession in St Stephen's was meant to have a similar effect of dramatic forgiveness, I suspect, but Louis refused to play along. Instead, he wanted to hear Ebo repeat (and eat) his words in the assembly in Thionville, facing the full wrath of royal justice, just as Louis himself, in 833, had submitted to the implacable judgements of bishops who, by turning him into a public sinner, had legitimated his deposition. Given all that had happened, it is amazing that those arguing in favour of the secrecy of Ebo's confession, including Judith, got anywhere at all, and so is the fact that, as his son Charles concluded laconically, Louis never dared to infringe the secrecy he once granted, keeping the see of Rheims vacant until his death.[189] One thing was certain, however: when it came to magnificent and grand displays of humility and forgiveness, from 835 onwards Louis was in charge again, without having his thunder stolen by the likes of Ebo. Authority and atonement were once more the emperor's business.

---

[188] Council of Troyes (867), MGH *Conc.* IV, p. 240, lines 29–32.
[189] Ibid., p. 241, lines 25–36.

Epilogue: The penitential state after Louis the Pious

With hindsight, the revolts of 830 and 833 appeared to have been the work of the devil, who had caused the rebels to take leave of their senses. Through the wiles of his satellites, the Enemy of mankind and peace had persuaded Louis's sons that their father was out to destroy them, without realising that a man who was so mild to strangers would be simply incapable of such savageness.[1] This was the Astronomer's view; as we have seen, it was echoed in a letter sent in 847–9 by Lothar to Pope Leo IV. Here, the emperor referred to the 'time of unhappy discord between us and our father, which, at the instigation of the devil and his satellites, lasted for some time'.[2] Two decades later, Charles the Bald agreed: diabolical inspiration had been behind the attempt of the 'people of the Franks' – that is, Louis's *fideles* – to expel their divinely ordained emperor from imperial rule.[3] These assessments reflect a mixture of sentiments: a recognition of the forces of evil, puzzlement about past actions, and, on Lothar's part, also remorse. But above all, the diagnosis that 'the devil was behind it' conveys the general feeling that the turbulent events of 830–3 had been beyond human control. Blaming the devil in the ninth century had nothing to do with shifting responsibility to some kind of impersonal force. The Old Enemy and his allies prowled around in monasteries as well as in palaces, looking for victims.[4] This was what Dhuoda told her son William, enjoining him to make the sign of the cross over his own forehead and over his bed, lest he be devoured.[5] Einhard's view of the Frankish polity in 828–9 was that of a world infested by Wiggo and other marauding demons;[6] Radbert described the palace at Aachen, dominated by Judith and Bernard, as

---

[1] Astronomer, c. 48, p. 472.

[2] *Epistolae selectae Leonis*, no. 46, MGH *Epp.* V, p. 610: 'cum tempore infelicissimę discordiae, quę operante diabolo per satellites suos inter nos genitoremque nostrum aliquandiu duravit'.

[3] Council of Troyes (867), MGH IV, p. 240, lines 7–9.

[4] On the importance of the devil in the Carolingian world, see Ganz, 'Humour as history'.

[5] Dhuoda, *Liber manualis* IV, c. 5, p. 222; II, c. 3, pp. 128–9. I am grateful to Janet Nelson for this reference, and for making me think harder about the devil.

[6] See above, chapter 4, pp. 162–3.

invaded by the forces of darkness: sorcery, witchcraft and other malign arts were mustered to kill the unwitting emperor.[7] These were real feelings, which stands to reason. Both sides in this conflict had become caught up in an ever-increasing turmoil of suspicion, fear and accusation, which then drove them to consequences which nobody had wanted or foreseen. Where human agency as well as divine assistance failed, the devil and his satellites took over. Einhard's *Translatio* and its dire warnings against diabolical activity in the Frankish polity conveyed the same message: there were forces at work against which even a Christian leadership was powerless, unless it sought the help of the saints in general, and Einhard's martyrs in particular.

Only a detailed study of Louis's government and administration can determine whether the two short-lived but sharp revolts rendered him less effective as a monarch; as far as I can see now, this was not the case. The rebellions did inspire an unprecedented wave of public soul-searching, however. The court annalist, Thegan and the Astronomer all reaffirmed and celebrated Louis's restoration, yet they also sought to come to terms with the causes of their emperor's temporary downfall. Louis's one and only vice was also his chief virtue: he had been excessively merciful to his enemies. Behind the emperor's much-vaunted clemency, which has often been interpreted as a sign of weakness, there was not so much a structural failing as a magnificent claim to transcendent authority: Louis's forgiveness imitated divine mercy. There was also the practical consideration of limiting the damage of the rebellions by getting back to normal as quickly as possible; from this point of view, a protracted revenge on one's enemies was counterproductive. Hence, the number of real culprits identified by those who recorded the rebellions was surprisingly small. Indeed, Matfrid and Hugh were both presented as evil schemers; they were those satellites of Satan to which the Astronomer referred. Yet in 834 they followed Lothar to Italy, alive and well, until they succumbed to the epidemic of 836.[8] When all was said and done, it was Ebo who bore the main brunt of Louis's wrath: his fellow-bishops managed to offload their own part in Louis's penance and deposition on to the unfortunate archbishop of Rheims, claiming that he had been the one in charge. Archbishop Agobard of Lyons was deposed, but could lie low for the time being, awaiting his restoration, which duly came in 839.[9] Four or possibly five bishops fled to Italy with Lothar.[10] Two of these, Elias of Troyes and Jesse

---

[7] See above, chapter 5, pp. 200–2.   [8] Astronomer, c. 56, pp. 512–14.
[9] Boshof, *Agobard*, p. 305.
[10] Bartholomew of Narbonne, Herebold of Auxerre, Jesse of Amiens, Elias of Troyes and possibly Barnard of Vienne; see Boshof, *Agobard*, pp. 260–3; Zechiel-Eckes, 'Ein Blick in Pseudoisidors Werkstatt', pp. 54–9.

of Amiens, died in the Italian epidemic of 836, at a time when Louis had already enlisted Wala's help to effectuate a rapprochement with his eldest son.[11] Had they survived, as their colleague Herebold of Auxerre did, they might have been restored to their respective sees, as Herebold was in 838.[12] All this suggests that in 834–5, Louis's main strategy for recovery was a speedy reconciliation. This was how he had dealt with every revolt until then, including the one instigated by Bernard of Italy in 817–18. The court annalist, Thegan and the Astronomer all followed this approach of collective forgiveness and forgetfulness, and concentrated on the few generally approved culprits. Reflecting on the rebellions of 830–3 with hindsight, when many previous rebels had smoothly returned to the imperial fold, they could hardly afford to do anything else.

The deeply felt wish to put a distance between the present and that turbulent past is visible in the historiography and biography that flourished in the aftermath of the insurrection against Louis: the emphasis was on closure and restoration. The one exception was Radbert's *Epitaphium Arsenii*. Ten to fifteen years after Wala's death, Radbert still felt the need to defend his patron's role in the revolts, and dwelled on an episode that remained confusing and painful to him and others. Radbert's was the lone voice of the court-connected clerics who, together with Louis himself, had tried to build the perfect Christian state, and had then become entangled in the conflicts between the emperor and his sons. Still, this was a voice with a future resonance. From the ranks of these idealistic but disgruntled churchmen, banished from the political arena in 834–5, may have come the collection of false decretals known as 'Pseudo-Isidore'; supposedly, its stance against overbearing royal power reflects Louis's cracking down on his rebellious bishops.[13] This may well be the case, yet to depict the way in which Louis dealt with his episcopate as a 'purge' is surely an exaggeration.[14] Moreover, well before the assembly of Thionville in 835, Frankish bishops had cause to fear their heavy-handed emperor; already at the council of Paris (829), they had clamoured for greater royal respect for their rights and reputation.[15] The false decretals with their strong emphasis on papal authority had a longer prehistory than just the resentment caused by Louis's restoration. They were inspired by a tradition of *correctio* which Louis had inherited from his father and grandfather.

---

[11] Astronomer, c. 55, p. 506.   [12] Depreux, *Prosopographie*, pp. 241–2.
[13] Zechiel-Eckes, 'Ein Blick in Pseudoisidors Werkstatt', pp. 54–9.
[14] Ibid., p. 59 (citing Boshof, *Agobard*, p. 208); also p. 55 ('Vergeltungsaktion oder Revanchefoul').
[15] See above, chapter 4, pp. 179–84.

Significantly, neither Radbert nor the authors backing Louis had much to say about the emperor's public humiliation of 833. Almost all the information on Louis's penance in Soissons comes from the bishops who imposed it. They were intent on showing that they had acted according to canonical authority, affirming the divine judgement that had robbed Louis of his right to rule; as I explained, their narrative was meant to be performative, in that the text itself and the publicity it engendered would preclude the deposed emperor's return to the throne.[16] The discussion after 833 focussed not on Louis's penance, however, but on the question of whether his public atonement had been based on a just verdict. Thegan and the Astronomer ignored the claims that the defection of Louis's men on the Field of Lies had been a *iudicium dei* of any kind. Instead, they contested the episcopal judgement proclaimed by Ebo and the bishops present in 833, maintaining that it had been wrong (Thegan), or that Louis had already atoned for his sins at the assembly in Attigny (822) and should not be judged twice for the same transgressions (the Astronomer). There were other major objections. Lothar was upbraided for having kept his father in strict and therefore demeaning custody (*arta custodia*),[17] rather than in the *libera custodia* which befitted someone of royal status. This may have rankled most with the status-conscious lay magnates; their clerical counterparts, on the other hand, contended that punishment of an excommunication followed by a *paenitentia publica* had been far too heavy for a ruler who had always shown himself so ready to atone for his sins. In Hraban Maur's view, this heavy instrument of ecclesiastical discipline should never have been employed against Louis the Pious.

From this it transpires that the humiliating penitential ritual of 833, which so much offended later historians, was of less concern to contemporaries, who were well aware that a humbling penance had elevated the likes of Theodosius.[18] Their criticism concentrated on the unsoundness of the bishops' judgement, the lack of divine approval, and the demeaning nature of Louis's captivity and excommunication. After all, there was nothing wrong with *voluntary* gestures of royal atonement, of the kind that Louis publicly performed with great effect during two well-attended assemblies, at Attigny (822) and Compiègne (830). Probably this was how Louis intended to swing the mood of the gathering in 833 as well, before he saw that this would be impossible. While the rebellious bishops did their utmost to gloss over the coercive nature of the imperial penance of 833, proclaiming that Louis had confessed freely and publicly, the emperor's supporters emphasised that the force used invalidated the entire

---

[16] See above, chapter 6, pp. 248–9.   [17] Astronomer, c. 48, p. 480, line 4.
[18] Booker, 'Historionic history'.

proceedings. As a consequence Louis's penance in Soissons looked much like the kind of penitential punishment he himself had often imposed on political opponents, as a matter of course. The redefinition of political crime as sin, which began to take shape under Charlemagne, became commonplace during Louis's reign. Accordingly, public penance became one of the instruments of royal justice.

After Louis's death in 840, an excommunication followed by a public penance continued to be one of the methods by which kings disciplined their unruly aristocracy.[19] A telling case in point was the treaty of Meerssen, concluded in 851 between Lothar, Louis and Charles. The brothers promised one another not to shelter anyone who, having committed a 'capital and public crime' (*crimen capitalis et publicus*), fled to another realm in order to avoid the penance imposed, lest 'he infect with his sickness the faithful people of God and of us'.[20] This agreement was not just about criminals fleeing to another kingdom. It was also a joint declaration about not sheltering those who had endangered the public order elsewhere, including political insurgents, in the familiar idiom of the sickness of sin that might infect the entire polity. Something of the sort still existed in 851, in spite of the division into different kingdoms, and fleeing public penitents represented one of the areas in which the kings urgently needed to co-ordinate their policies. Another aspect of the penitential state which remained standard practice during the next generation was the time-honoured method of political tonsure. With varied success, Charles the Bald used this instrument to regulate his succession. In 854, at the age of five, Charles's son Carloman received the clerical tonsure. Having been made a deacon at eleven, his future was that of a powerful lay abbot. Despite concerted efforts to represent Carloman's tonsure as a proper child oblation and a gift to God, this was also part of his father's strategy to limit the number of legitimate successors.[21] In 870, however, when Charles had become king of Lotharingia, Carloman rebelled: he could now hope for a kingdom to which to succeed. His revolt misfired, and Carloman was locked up in what seems to have been the one and only secular prison of the West-Frankish kingdom, the *castrum* of Senlis.[22] The

---

[19] Hamilton, *Practice of Penance*, pp. 184–90.

[20] *AB*, s.a. 851, pp. 61–2; trans. Nelson, *Annals of St-Bertin*, p. 71; MGH *Capit*. II, no. 205, c. 5, p. 73.

[21] *AB*, s.a. 854, p. 70, a chapter that also mentions that Charles, brother of Pippin II, had already become a deacon; Nelson, *Charles the Bald*, p. 174; on the different representations of Carloman's tonsure, see also De Jong, *In Samuel's Image*, pp. 257–8. Charles's son Lothar, who was lame, was made a cleric in 861; cf. *AB*, s.a. 861.

[22] On Carloman's rebellion, see Nelson, 'A tale of two princes' and *Charles the Bald*, pp. 226–30.

captive managed to escape, but not for long; at his father's behest, he was then deprived of his clerical rank. As Hincmar implied, this was not a smart move, for, as a layman, this rebel prince was even more attractive to potential followers rallying to his cause. With this in mind, the synod at Quierzy, chaired by Hincmar, condemned Carloman; he was then blinded and confined to Corbie.[23] The story is not over yet, for shortly thereafter the now blind Carloman escaped from Corbie and was received at the court of Louis the German, as an instrument by which to harm Charles's interests.[24] As Hincmar claimed, Charles the Bald was not greatly upset by the news, and understandably so, for a blind son, however ambitious or vengeful he might have been, could not do much damage.[25] Compared to the outrage caused by the blinding of Bernard of Italy in 818, one can only conclude that this savage punishment had become more accepted during the next generation.

Carloman's fate also shows that depriving a legitimate member of the ruling family of his royal identity by means of political tonsure took time and effort, even when a king and his bishops threw their formidable weight behind it. Another example of the difficulties of unmaking a Carolingian is that of Pippin II of Aquitaine, the son of King Pippin (d. 838), the grandson whom Louis deprived of the succession of Aquitaine in favour of his son Charles the Bald.[26] Prudentius and Hincmar, the successive authors of the *Annals of St-Bertin*, told Pippin's sad story, with deep disapproval for this rebel and his fruitless quest for the kingdom of Aquitaine. In 852 Pippin was delivered up to Charles, who ordered him to be tonsured in St-Médard of Soissons, still a privileged place of monastic exile for members of the royal family.[27] A year later, two monks in orders from St-Médard were defrocked at the synod of Soissons (853) because they had helped Pippin to flee.[28] Even though he was only a tonsured cleric, not a professed monk, Pippin was then accused of having broken his monastic vows. At the same time his brother Charles, who had also been tonsured and was already an ordained deacon at the time, fled from Corbie.[29] Pippin now posed a real danger, and was therefore depicted in the *Annals of St-Bertin* as an apostate monk, whose behaviour

---

[23] *AB*, s.a. 873, p. 190.   [24] Ibid., pp. 192–3; Nelson, *Annals of St-Bertin*, p. 183, n. 11.
[25] *AB*, s.a. 873, p. 193.
[26] To be treated more extensively in Stuart Airlie, *Carolingian Politics*, forthcoming. I am grateful to Stuart Airlie for sending me the text of his paper on Pippin II delivered in Vienna, May 2007.
[27] *AB*, s.a. 852, pp. 64–5.
[28] *AB*, s.a. 853, p. 66; cf. Council of Soissons (853), c. 45, MGH *Conc.* III, pp. 281–2.
[29] *AB*, s.a. 854, p. 69: 'Pippinus … qui in monasterio Sancti Medardi habitum monachum susceperat et iuramentum permansionis fecerat'.

revealed his innate wickedness: he behaved like a king without being one (856), and associated with pagans: first with Danish pirates (857) and then with the Bretons (859). By 864, when Hincmar had taken over from Prudentius, he related that the apostate Pippin, who had left the monastic state to become a layman, was now consorting with Northmen and went along with their pagan customs.[30] Whatever Pippin may actually have done, what Hincmar wanted to get across is clear: this was not a candidate for Christian kingship. In 864 Pippin was captured and led before the assembly at Pîtres. Hincmar prepared a written opinion for the occasion in which, supported by many canonical texts, he argued that Pippin's apostasy and association with the pagan enemy merited a public penance. Once he had completed this, Pippin should receive the clerical tonsure and the monastic habit, and should be guarded by upstanding monastic custodians in 'liberal custody' (*libera custodia*).[31] This was not to say, Hincmar remarked at the end, that Pippin should not be watched over with great care, for 'it should not be forgotten what happened to him in the monastery of St-Médard, and with Carloman in Corbie. What happened then may happen again.'[32] This was Charles's view entirely, so instead of following Hincmar's programme for disciplining Pippin by public penance, the assembly condemned him to death and had him locked up in Senlis under the strictest guard (*artissima custodia*).[33] Nothing more was heard from Pippin, unless 'a certain apostate monk' mentioned in passing in Hincmar's *Annals*, who had forsaken Christianity to live with the Northmen, and was beheaded in 869, was in fact Pippin.[34] Hincmar's emphasis on the dangers this anonymous apostate monk posed to Christendom seems to point in the direction of Pippin II of Aquitaine, but there is no way of being certain.

There was nothing wrong, then, with punishing the rebellious junior competition by public penance and/or involuntary tonsure, but to inflict this on an anointed and crowned monarch, as had happened in 833, proved to be a bridge too far.[35] There was to be no second 'Soissons', with a ruler's *de facto* deposition being confirmed by an excommunication and a *paenitentia publica*, both of which removed him from the political

---

[30] *AB*, s.a. 864, p. 105: 'Pippinus, Pippini filii, ex monacho laicus et apostatus factus, se Normannis coniugit et ritum eorum servat'. Cf. Nelson, *Annals of St-Bertin*, p. 111, n. 3. To my mind, the expression *ritus eorum* does refer, quite pointedly, to the Northmen's paganism.

[31] Hincmar, *Consilium de poenitentia*, col. 1122A. Hincmar distinguished strictly between secret and public sins and their corresponding penances.

[32] Ibid., col. 1122C.   [33] *AB*, s.a. 864, p. 113.

[34] *AB*, s.a. 869, p. 166. Nelson, *Annals of St Bertin*, p. 163, n. 28, makes the connection, without being able to pursue it. As she pointed out to me, beheading was a high-status punishment.

[35] De Jong, 'Humility and power', pp. 50–2.

arena. On the other hand, voluntary and public expressions of contrition on the part of kings and emperors remained part of the political idiom of the next two centuries. The lofty royal example inspired a variety of rituals of begging for pardon and favour by which members of the lay and clerical elites made humble amends to their wronged superiors, without harming their own honour and status.[36] In written representations of such rituals of submission, the secular or religious aspects could be stressed alternately. Whether the ruler acted as a Christ-like figure, extending mercy to the penitent rebel, or whether that rebel threw himself at the feet of his lord, offering satisfaction, was – and still is – mostly in the eye of the beholder. Such gestures of submission were effective precisely because they could mean different things to different audiences. What mattered was that the act of atonement was freely offered to God, and that it met with the kind of manifest divine favour that was generally recognised as such. This made the difference between a royal reputation that was strengthened and one that was undermined. Accordingly, in contemporary historiography, the grand and sweeping public gestures of contrition of the emperors Otto III (983–1002) and Henry III (1039–56) were emphatically presented as initiated by the rulers themselves, as was the atonement of King Robert II the Pious (996–1031) of France.[37] In the eleventh century, royal supplication continued to be perceived as imitation of Christ.[38] The most famous of all royal penances is that of Henry IV in Canossa in 1077. According to modern scholarship, 'Canossa' inaugurated a new era of tension and separation between *regnum* and *sacerdotium*. Yet as Timothy Reuter pointed out, this emperor, who stood barefoot in the snow for three days, belonged to that older world in which rulers enhanced their power and authority by public penitential acts. Additionally, such royal self-abasement might offer a way out of an otherwise insoluble predicament, as it did in 1077 as well. What the Emperor Henry strenuously avoided, however, was a formal and therefore binding public penance of the kind imposed on Louis in 833.[39]

Stripped of its unpleasant connotations of coercion and impotence, Louis's penance of 833 could even become reintegrated in one coherent memory of a penitent emperor associated with the great Theodosius. In a few brisk sentences, Hincmar compared Ambrose's authority over Theodosius with the 'episcopal unanimity' that, 'with sounder counsel and with the consensus of the people, restored him [Louis] to the church

---

[36] Koziol, *Begging Pardon*, pp. 131–213; see above, chapter 6, pp. 245–9.
[37] Reuter, 'Contextualising Canossa', pp. 159–60; Hamilton, 'Otto III's penance' and 'A new model for royal penance?'
[38] Koziol, *Begging Pardon*, pp. 159–73.   [39] Reuter, 'Contextualising Canossa', pp. 60–5.

as well as to the kingdom'.[40] Here we have the bishops in the role of
king-makers, with their part in the attempt to unmake Louis as a ruler
almost completely downplayed. Only Hincmar's reference to the *sanior
consilium* that prevailed hinted at the problematic nature of the emperor's
penance (*satisfactio*). The Astronomer preferred to stress another similarity between Louis and his illustrious predecessor: in 822 the emperor had
chosen to atone for his sins. At least in part, imperial greatness was
predicated on Louis having more options than anyone else, including
his sons. One of these options was to convert to monasticism and enter
the world of the cloister, which was so closely bound up with the
Carolingian court.[41] The Astronomer's portrayal of the tension between
Louis's need to contract a second marriage in 819 and his wish to assume
a religious life is a narrative about a ruler who belonged to both the court
and the cloister, and could choose where he wished to be. This was the key
idea of Carolingian royal authority: to divide the polity into separate but
complementary 'orders', with the ruler transcending these *ordines* and
integrating them, as the head of a body connects the respective limbs
and galvanises them into action.

This ideal of a ruler who was as much at home in the sacred domain as
on the battlefield underpinned Louis's more effective gestures of atonement. Not all those who appealed to this idiom of royal humility and might
managed to get their point across, however. An interesting case of a ritual
that misfired is the self-abasement of the future King Charles the Fat, son
of Louis the German.[42] During the assembly at Frankfurt in 873, Charles
suddenly interrupted the discussions. In a state of agitation, he proclaimed that he wanted to leave the world and renounce his marriage.
Fumbling to rid himself of his sword and belt, and shaking violently, he
was taken into church, where mass was sung; but the young king bit those
who held him, ranting and raving. Four contemporary narrative sources
reported this shocking event, and all four authors agreed that this was an
instance of diabolical possession. As Simon McLean observed, almost all
the elements of this diabolically induced royal madness belong to the
idiom of public penance: the taking off of the sword, sword belt and
'princely clothing', as well as the renunciation of marriage.[43] Building

---

[40] Hincmar, *De divortio*, responsio VI, p. 247, lines 26–9: 'Nostra aetate pium augustum
Hludowicum a regno deiectum post satisfactionem episcopalis unanimitas saniore consilio cum populi consensu et ecclesię et regno restituit.'

[41] Stancliffe, 'Kings who opted out'; de Jong, 'Political coercion'.

[42] The case has inspired two fine articles: Nelson, 'Tale of two princes', and MacLean,
'Ritual'.

[43] *Annales Fuldenses, Bertiniani, Xanteses* and *Vedastiani*; see MacLean, 'Ritual', p. 100, n.
10, and p. 102, for a systematic comparison of the main narratives.

on Philippe Buc's work, McLean makes a good case for the possibility of reconstructing rituals beyond the texts which encapsulate them, arguing that substantial overlap between the four narratives about Charles's penitential gesture constitutes a solid historical base for a reconstruction of what actually happened in Frankfurt. By his spontaneous penitential gesture, in the presence of the entire assembly, Charles had wanted to beg his father's forgiveness for his part in an earlier rebellion, but subsequently the prince's initiative was distorted by those who reported it.[44] To this I would add, however, that the elusive animal we call 'historical reality' is just as present in these distortions (or representations) as in the common ground shared by the four narratives of the prince's strange actions and their possible motives. Here was a son who had rebelled and plotted against his father. For him to adopt the powerful stance of royal humility, with all its implicit claims to authority, was simply not accepted by those contemporaries who witnessed or reported the event. None of the four authors concerned was prepared to tell the story in any way remotely favourable to the rebel son, who, twice over, had assumed a role he had no right to play. What was intended as an instance of intensely emotional reconciliation between father and son, witnessed and approved by the entire assembly, became a scenario with the Old Enemy in the leading part: he made Charles the Fat writhe crazily on the ground, yelling that he wished to abandon the world. Where sons rebelled, the devil was never far away. Moreover, Charles's grand gestures of royal self-abasement and lofty promises to renounce the world represented the kind of claim to royal authority to which no rebellious son was entitled. Obviously, the young man showed signs of diabolical possession.

This general rejection of Charles the Fat's misguided supplication was possible only because by this time there existed an equally general consensus as to what royal and public gestures of atonement should be like, if they were to be interpreted positively rather than negatively. No wonder, then, that the monk Notker, who wrote his *Gesta Karoli* in the early 880s for Charles the Fat, once he had become king, integrated voluntary royal penance into his portrait of Charlemagne.[45] In one of Notker's many stories in which arrogant secular clerics were ridiculed, one encounters Charlemagne transformed into a penitent ruler. There was an effeminate deacon, who, like all southerners, took an unnatural interest in bathing, shaving, skin-polishing and nail-cleaning. While this vain man was reading the Gospel in the presence of the 'most watchful king' (Charlemagne), a spider repeatedly landed on the deacon's shaven head, stinging him and then retreating once more to the

---

[44] McLean, 'Ritual', pp. 99–103; Buc, *Dangers of Ritual*, pp. 1–12; 51–87.
[45] On Notker, see Innes, 'Memory'; McLean, *Kingship*, pp. 199–229.

roof.[46] Always vigilant, Charlemagne saw what happened but pretended not to notice it, and because of the emperor's presence, the deacon did not dare to ward off the spider. Besides, he thought that it was merely a fly tickling him, not a spider attacking him, so having read the Gospel, he completed the rest of the office. Once the deacon had left the church, a swelling appeared, and he died within the hour. 'But the most religious Charles, because of what he saw but did not prevent, gave himself over to a public penance, as if he was guilty of manslaughter.'[47] Charlemagne's resolve to undertake a public penance has been taken to be a vicarious penance for a grave sin 'against nature' on the part of the deacon in question, but this interpretation in terms of homosexuality stretches Notker's story beyond its limits.[48] Charlemagne's readiness to do penance had everything to do with the royal 'ministry' and the ruler's accountability to God for the salvation of his entire people, including the most effeminate and silly deacon. In Notker's view, the royal gaze penetrated all nooks and crannies of the palace and its chapel; nothing escaped Charles's perennial observance and watchfulness.[49] The idea of Charlemagne undertaking a *penitentia publica* as envisaged by Notker would probably have surprised an audience in the 780s, but it had everything to recommend it to his great-grandson and namesake Charles, a century later, and to the monks of St-Gall, who revered pious emperors as much as they loathed vain clerics. This was royal penance as it should be, at its most magnificent: Charlemagne volunteered to do a public penance, which was well in excess of the minor sin of omission he committed; like the ever-vigilant God to whom he was accountable, the king missed nothing of what went on during the divine cult for which he was responsible, but had not wished to disturb it. The sin he thus committed was one of omission, and a typically royal one at that: this was the *negligentia* Louis had been accused of in 833, albeit of a much milder kind. Rather than a people and a realm, Charlemagne's sin involved a deacon and a spider. As a Christian ruler, the historical Charlemagne was no doubt familiar with humility, as a virtue and a royal duty; yet the substance and detail of Notker's story, and the self-evident way in which he wrote of Charlemagne's public penance, all bear the imprint of Louis's reign, and of the penitential state that emerged between 814 and 840.

---

[46] Notker, I, c. 32, p. 44; see the spider (*aranea*) in Ps. 38.12, the image of the soul of the unjust wasting away.

[47] Notker, I, c. 32, pp. 44–5: 'Religiosissimus vero Karolus, pro eo quod vidit et non prohibuit, quasi homicidii reum publica se ipsum penitentia multavit.'

[48] As argued lucidly by Lošek, 'Die Spinne in der Kirchendecke'.

[49] See De Jong, 'Charlemagne's balcony', where I made too little of Einhard, *VK*, c. 26, pp. 30–1 (the ruler who perennially supervised the cult of God in his chapel).

Appendix

The report of Compiègne by the bishops of the realm concerning the penance of Emperor Louis (833)[1]

It behoves those who belong to the Christian religion to know what is the ministry of the bishops, and how those who are evidently Christ's vicars and hold the keys to the kingdom of heaven should be watchful for and concern themselves with the salvation of all. On them such a power is conferred by Christ that, 'what they shall bind on earth, shall be bound also in heaven, and what they shall loose upon earth, shall be loosed also in heaven' [Matth. 18.18]. And in how great a danger will they be, if they neglect to administer the food of life to their sheep, and fail to try with all their might to recall those who are straying to the way of truth by reproving and entreating [them], according to the word of the prophet: 'If you do not announce to the iniquitous man his iniquity and he dies in his impiety, I shall require his blood from your hand' [cf. Ez. 3.18], and many similar [pronouncements] pertaining to the pastoral office, which are dispersed throughout Scripture. Accordingly, these pastors should strive above all to maintain the most circumspect discretion towards the errors of sinners, so that, in accordance with the blessed Gregory's teaching, they will be allies to the virtuous because of their humility, but resolutely set against the vices of sinners in their zeal for justice,[2] so that, having left behind apathy

---

[1] *Relatio* (833). The assembly at Compiègne was convened on 1 October 833 and dismissed on 11 November. Louis's penance fell within this time span, and probably took place in the second half of October. This report must have been composed shortly thereafter, during the assembly; having this document agreed to and signed by all bishops present was a matter of urgency. See above, chapter 6, pp. 234–41. On the transmission of this text, see Booker, 'A new prologue'. A new edition of the *Relatio*, by Courtney Booker, appeared in *Viator* 39/2 (2008), pp. 1–20, too late for me to take into account, but there are no different readings affecting my translation. For this translation I gratefully made use of the English one made by Philippe Buc for teaching purposes, and of the Dutch version I prepared together with students in Nijmegen. As much as possible, I have tried to leave the bishops' long and ponderous sentences intact.

[2] Gregory, *Regula pastoralis*, II, c. 1. 6.

and indifference, human flattery and worldly obsequiousness, they may exercise their ministry thus, that they give salutary counsel to their contemporaries and provide a model of salvation to future [generations]. In fact, since by diabolical inspiration the evil weeds that should be cut up by the pastoral hoe, with root and branch, do not stop sprouting in God's field, that is, Christ's church, and because of the evil-minded who refuse to understand good deeds, or would rather interpret these with malevolent intention than embrace the truth, it is incumbent upon these pastors, whenever they decree something in their assemblies concerning the common good or public order and discipline, to commit it to writing, according to ecclesiastical custom: evidently, with the aim of thoroughly removing any ambiguity for future generations, or the opportunity of legitimately denigrating or contravening [these measures].

Hence, we deemed it necessary that all children of God's holy church, present and future, be notified how we, the bishops placed under the imperial rule of the most glorious lord and emperor Lothar, assembled as a body in the palace of Compiègne, in the month of October of the year of the Incarnation of [our] Lord Jesus Christ 830, in the twelfth indiction, that is, in the first year of this ruler, and listened humbly to the said prince. As befits the ministry committed to us, we carefully clarified to him and to his great men, as well as to the generality of the faithful men[3] who had come together there from everywhere, the nature of the episcopal authority, power and ministry, and the sort of punishment by which he will be struck who refuses to heed episcopal admonitions. Then we did our best to explain to the aforementioned ruler and to his entire people that they should strive to please the Lord with utmost devotion, and not tarry in placating Him concerning those matters in which they had offended Him. Indeed, much was pondered that had occurred in this empire owing to neglect, pertaining, as manifest signs demonstrated, to the church's public scandal, to the people's ruin, and to the kingdom's downfall: of which it was [deemed] indispensable that they be soon corrected and, in the future, avoided in every way.

Among other [business] it was also called to mind by us, and remembered by all, how this realm had been united and nobly enlarged by God through the governance of Charles, the illustrious emperor of good memory, and by the pacifying endeavours of his predecessors; how this realm, entrusted by God to lord Louis the emperor to rule in a state of great peace, would remain safeguarded in this state of peace under the Lord's protection, as long as this ruler worshipped God, carefully followed his

---

[3] I.e. the 'faithful men' (*fideles*) who attended the assembly.

father's example and acquiesced in the counsel of good men; and how, with the passing of time, as was evident to all, through Louis's negligence and lack of foresight, this realm fell into such ignominy and wretchedness that it became not only a source of sadness for its friends but also an object of mockery for its enemies. But because this ruler treated the ministry entrusted to him with negligence, and committed acts – and forced [others] to commit them – that were displeasing to both God and mankind, or allowed such acts to be committed; because he angered God through many unspeakable decisions and scandalised the holy church; and, to omit other innumerable items, because he most recently summoned all the people subjected to him towards a general destruction,[4] and because by God's just judgement the imperial power was suddenly withdrawn from him, we, mindful of God's precepts, our ministry, and His blessings, judged it fitting to send a delegation to him which, with the permission of the aforesaid Emperor Lothar and on the authority of the sacred assembly,[5] would admonish him [Louis] about his faults, in order that he take solid counsel concerning his salvation, so that in his last days he would exert himself with all his vigour to prevent his soul from being damned – since he had lost his earthly power due to a divine verdict and ecclesiastical authority. Louis willingly gave his assent to the counsel of the envoys and their most salubrious admonitions, demanded a delay and set a date on which he would give them a firm answer concerning their salubrious admonitions.

When the aforementioned day arrived, the aforesaid sacred assembly unanimously went to this venerable man [Louis][6] and endeavoured to admonish him diligently, and to bring back to his memory all these matters in which he had offended God, scandalised the holy church, and thoroughly disordered the people entrusted to him. He [Louis] willingly took their redeeming admonition and their fitting and apt rebuke to heart; he promised that he would acquiesce in all these matters to their salutary counsel and submit to their remedial judgement. Next, joyful for so salubrious an admonition, Louis immediately implored his beloved son, the Emperor Lothar, to come to him quickly, so that having overcome any minor delays, he [Lothar] might come with his leading men, to the effect that first of all there would be a reconciliation between them, according to Christian teaching, so that if there inhered in their heart any kind of discord or fault, a pure and humble demand for pardon would expiate

---

[4] Again, by *populus* the *fideles* are meant – Louis's men who were summoned to do battle on the Rothfeld in June 833.

[5] Of the bishops in Compiègne in 833.

[6] Louis is called a *venerabilis vir*, to emphasise his loss of imperial dignity.

it, and that subsequently, in the presence of the entire assembly, he [Louis] would accept an episcopal judgement in the manner of a penitent – which indeed happened not much later.[7]

Thus, lord Louis came into the basilica of God's holy mother Mary, wherein rest the bodies of the saints Médard (the confessor of Christ and pontiff) and Stephen (the most illustrious martyr). There stood the priests and deacons and a large crowd of clerics; there were also present lord Lothar his son and his great men, and the whole assembly of all the people, as many, that is, as this church could hold within its precinct. Prostrate on the ground, over a hair shirt, before the sacrosanct altar, Louis confessed in the presence of all that he had very unworthily handled the ministry that had been entrusted to him, that in so doing he had offended God in many ways and had scandalised the church of Christ, and that by his negligence he had led the people entrusted to him multifariously into disorder. And therefore, in view of the expiation of such grave sins, he declared his intention to ask for a public and ecclesiastical penance, by which he might merit absolution for so many crimes, through God's mercy and with ministry and through the help of those on whom God conferred the power to bind and to loose. In turn, these pontiffs, as doctors of the spirit, admonished him salubriously, asserting that the real remission of sins would follow a pure and straightforward confession, so that he would openly confess these errors by which he professed to have offended God most, lest he hid something inwardly, or did anything deceitful in God's sight, as he was already generally known to have done before, when he was rebuked by another sacred assembly, in the presence of the whole church, in the palace of Compiègne.[8] He should not now, as he had then, through dissembling and the craftiness of a duplicitous heart, come into God's presence, Whom he would provoke to anger rather than to pardon of his sins. For, as the Scriptures proclaim, 'Dissemblers and crafty men prove the wrath of God' [Iob 36.13]. Indeed, after such an admonition, he confessed that he had sinned, primarily in all those matters on which he had been admonished by the aforesaid bishops in a familiar manner,[9] and publicly reproached by appropriate rebuke, be it in writing or in person; moreover, they presented him with a document (cartula) containing the

---

[7] *Iudicium sacerdotalis*, that is, episcopal judgement: the penance in question was a public one, which could be imposed only by bishops. See above, chapter 6, pp. 132–4. As is often the case in Carolingian political idiom, the word *sacerdos* and its derivatives refer to bishops, not to priests as a general category.

[8] At the assembly in June 830, following the rebellion of that spring.

[9] The expression *familiariter* evokes the bishops' proximity to the emperor as advisors and courtiers, and their right to speak freely to him; see above, chapter 3, pp. 117–18.

summary of those faults for which they especially rebuked him, which he
held in his hands.[10]

1. To wit, as this document more fully details, by incurring the guilt
of sacrilege and homicide, he did not heed, as he had promised, his
father's admonition and terrifying exhortation, delivered to him while
invoking God and before the holy altar, in the presence of the bishops
and the greatest crowd of the people.[11] Moreover, he did violence to his
brothers and relatives, and allowed his nephew,[12] whom he could have
freed, to be killed; and forgetful of his solemn promise, he later ordered
[their] entry into religious life[13] for the sake of his own vengeance and
anger.

2. That, as a creator of scandal, a disturber of the peace and a violator of
oaths, he recently broke by an illegal exercise of power the pact that had
been struck, with the counsel and consent of all his faithful men, for the
sake of the empire's peace and concord and the church's tranquillity,
among his sons and confirmed by oaths;[14] and that to the extent to
which he forced his faithful to swear another oath that contradicted this
first pact and oath,[15] by this violation of sworn oaths he lapsed into the
crime of perjury; and how much this displeased God is crystal clear, for
after this neither he nor the people subjected to him deserved to have
peace; subsequently, all have been led into disorder, suffering the punishment for sin because of God's just judgement.

3. Because against the norm of Christianity and his own vow, and without there being any public requirement for it or any evident necessity,
deluded by the advice of wicked people, he gave the order to muster a
general expedition during Lent, and decided that a general assembly would
take place in the farthest reaches of his empire, on Good Thursday, when
the rites of Easter should be celebrated correctly, by all Christians;[16] during
this expedition, in so far as he took part in it, he drove the people to great
grumbling, illicitly removed the bishops of the Lord from their liturgical
offices, and inflicted the heaviest oppression on the poor.

4. That he did violence to many among his faithful who had approached
him humbly for the sake of fidelity to him and his sons and their salvation,
and for the recovery of his tottering reign, and who had given him sound

---

[10] Here and in Agobard's text below I have translated *cartula* neutrally, as 'document';
neither the *Relatio* itself nor the episcopal attestations are charters in the technical sense
used in diplomatics.

[11] Louis's coronation as co-emperor in 813.   [12] Bernard king of Italy (d. 818).

[13] This is the most likely reading of *signum sanctae religionis*: forced tonsure and monastic exile.

[14] The *Ordinatio imperii* (817).   [15] Of 817.

[16] The military campaign of Lent 830 to Brittany, allegedly instigated by Bernard of
Septimania.

information on the plots his enemies prepared against him;[17] and that against every law, divine and human, he deprived these people of their possessions, ordered that they be exiled, and had them condemned to death in their absence, doubtless inducing those judging [them] to a false judgement; and that against divine and canonical authority he infringed upon the rights of God's bishops and monks,[18] and condemned them in their absence; and by becoming guilty of homicide, he had become a violator of divine and human laws.

5. On account of the various and contradictory oaths he ordered and compelled his sons and the people to swear, which were, against reason, sworn frequently, by which he brought to the people entrusted to him a huge defilement of sin, he became guilty of nothing less than perjury: for beyond any doubt [these acts] legally rebound on the author (*auctor*) by whom they have been ordered. Concerning the purgative oath of women,[19] the unjust judgements, false testimonies and perjuries, perpetrated in his presence and with his permission, he himself has known [all along] how much he offended God.

6. That he initiated various military campaigns in the kingdom entrusted to him that were not only useless but also harmful, without counsel and without public benefit. Certainly, during these, many and [even] innumerable public outrages were perpetrated against the Christian people: homicides and perjuries, sacrileges, adulteries, plunders, arsons, which took place either in God's churches or in other places, as well as plunders and oppressions of the poor, wretched perpetrations almost unheard of among Christians; all these reflect on the author, as we just said.

7. With regard to the divisions of the empire undertaken by him arbitrarily and boldly against the common peace and the salvation of the whole empire,[20] and concerning the oath he forced all the people to swear that they would act against his sons as if against his enemies,[21] even though he could have brought them to peace by his paternal authority and with the counsel of his faithful men.

8. That so many evils and public outrages, too many to enumerate, perpetrated in the kingdom entrusted to him because of his negligence

[17] The rebels of 830, who accused Judith and Bernard of adultery and conspiration against Louis's life.
[18] The reference to *monachi* probably concerns Wala and other abbots involved in the rebellion of 830.
[19] *In mulierum purgatione* is usually read as *in mulieris purgatione*, in view of Judith's oath of purgation in 831. But how many women were purged with her, or served as oath-helpers? For the time being, I stick to the plural.
[20] In the aftermath of the rebellion of 830.
[21] In 833, prior to the confrontation on the Rothfeld in June 833; as often, the *populus* referred to here are the *fideles*, the loyal fighting men.

and lack of foresight, from which surely had sprung the endangering of the kingdom and the dishonouring of its king, were not sufficient for him; on top of these miseries he dragged all the people in his power to a common destruction,[22] even though he should have been, to this same people, the leader of salvation and peace, and even though God's mercy had decided to take pity on his people,[23] in an unheard-of and invisible way, to be proclaimed to our age.

Thus, for all these [outrages] and all those recalled above, he [Louis] confessed himself tearfully to be guilty before God and the bishops and all the people, and attested aloud that he had sinned in all these respects; and he asked for a public penance, so that by doing penance he might give satisfaction to the church, which he had scandalised by sinning; and just as he had been a scandal by neglecting many matters, he surely professed his desire to be an example by undergoing a fitting penance. After this confession he handed over to the bishops the document with his sins and his confession, as a record for the future, and they laid it on the altar. Then he took off his belt of office,[24] and placed it on the altar; taking off his worldly habit, he received the habit of a penitent by the imposition of the hands of the bishops.[25] Let no one after a penance of this scope and kind dare to return to his worldly office.

Once this had thus been done, it pleased [the assembly] that each of the bishops would insert in written testimonies of their own how this matter had been transacted, and would confirm it with his own subscription and, thus confirmed, transmit [the documents] to Emperor Lothar in commemoration of what had been done. In the end, all of us who had been present saw fit to summarise all our attestations of this [important] affair in one document, briefly and succinctly, and to confirm this recapitulation with our own subscriptions, as the following [subscriptions] show that it was done.[26]

Agobard's attestation to the penance performed by the emperor (833)[27]

In the name of God and our Lord Jesus Christ. In the year of the Incarnation of our Lord 833, I, Agobard, unworthy bishop of the church

---

[22] To the battlefield in June 833.

[23] The avoidance of bloodshed in June 833 through a divine judgement.

[24] The *cingulum militiae*, a *pars pro toto* for the belt and armour signifying the secular (and military) ministry.

[25] The expression *habitus* refers to the attire in question as well as to the status symbolised by it; hence my translation 'habit', which covers both.

[26] These are the episcopal subscriptions (*signa*), now lost.

[27] Agobard, *Cartula*. Judging by the *Relatio* (see above), Agobard's attestation and those of other bishops were drawn up before their communal report.

of Lyons, attended the venerable assembly at the palace called Compiègne. This assembly consisted of most reverend bishops and most magnificent magnates, as well as a gathering of abbots and counts, and people of differing age and dignity, presided over by the most serene and glorious Lothar, emperor and friend of Christ; with whose protection and help the decisions appended below were made, in the first year of his imperial rule, in the fourth month.

Upon all these [present] weighed heavily the real need to deal energetically with the present danger of the realm and its future state, because this kingdom had already reeled for a long time and was driven to ruin by the negligence and, if truth be told, by the inertia of the venerable lord Louis, one-time emperor, in which he became ensnared by corrupt and corrupting spirits who, according to the apostolic saying, were themselves 'erring, and driving into error' [II Tim. 3.13]. [Concerning] whatever was usefully and commendably found by this assembly through investigating and conferring, and whatever was to be urgently decided, I have not only consented with those judging, but also, consenting, acted as a judge myself. First, that is, those matters which evidently pertained to the integrity and stability of the kingdom and the king; furthermore, what was known [to pertain] most manifestly to the deliverance and purgation of lord Louis's soul. In the aforesaid assembly these [matters] have been faithfully investigated, truthfully uncovered and duly acted upon, namely in this way, that the said assembly decided that lord Louis be admonished by envoys and delegates about his sins, and be exhorted so that he would 'return to his heart', according to the word of the prophet [Is. 46.8] and acknowledge the deeds which he had committed against God while he was hurrying along the road of depravity and injustice; and that he would thereupon accept advice about his way of life and his salvation, so that he might obtain forgiveness and pardon for his iniquities from the Almighty Judge and Lord, who is the most clement forgiver of crimes, so that he, who had lost his earthly kingdom by manifold negligence, would acquire the heavenly kingdom by exceedingly beseeching confessions, through Him with whom 'there is mercy and plentiful redemption'.[28] For this reason, a booklet[29] was drafted by very scrupulous men and given to him to make manifest his crimes, in which, as if in a mirror, he would see clearly the sordidness of his own actions, and to him would happen what is said by the perfect penitent: 'For I know my iniquity, and my sin is always

---

[28] Ps. 129.7 (Old Latin version): 'quia apud Dominum misericordia et copiosa apud eum redemptio'.
[29] On the function of such *libelli* during Carolingian assemblies, see above, chapter 4, pp. 158–64.

before me.'[30] To this end, all the bishops present at the aforesaid assembly then went up to him once more, condoling and commiserating with his weakness and wretchedness, exhorting, longing and praying that the Almighty God, by His merciful hand, would lead him 'out of the pit of misery and the mire of dregs'.[31] Which the most clement Lord not only did not refuse, but also did not delay. And soon, in a spirit reawakened by the contrition of a humble heart, he [Louis], prostrated in front of them, acknowledged his crimes, not once or twice, but for a third time and more, asked for forgiveness, beseeched the assistance of prayers, received advice, requested a penance, and promised to fulfil most willingly the humiliation imposed on him. He was notified of the law and order of public penance, which he did not reject, but accepted in all respects; and then he came to the church, in the presence of a throng of the faithful, facing the altar and the tombs of the saints, and, prostrated over a hair shirt, he confessed – twice, thrice and four times – to all, in a clear voice, in floods of tears; having taken off his armour with his own hands and having flung it at the foot of the altar, with a remorseful mind he undertook a public penance through the imposition of episcopal hands, with psalms and prayers. And having thus cast off his earlier habit, and having assumed the habit of the penitent, gratefully and trustingly he implored to be taken back on the shoulders of the most Pious Shepherd to the unity of the retrieved and redeemed sheep.[32]

When this happened I, Agobard, unworthy bishop, was present, and concurring with better men and assenting, I have judged and subscribed, signing with my own hand.[33]

---

[30] Ps. 50.5 (Old Latin version): 'quoniam iniquitatem meam ego cognosco et peccatum meum contra me est semper'. Agobard replaced *contra* (against) with *coram* (with, in my presence).

[31] David; cf. Ps. 39.3 (Old Latin version): 'et eduxit me de lacu miseriae et de luto fecis'.

[32] Cf. Luc. 15.5; Ioh. 10.11, 14.

[33] The scribe would have written Agobard's name and title, to which he then added the sign of the cross (*signum*) for authentication.

Bibliography: primary sources

Agobard of Lyons, *De cavendo convictu et societate iudaica*, Agobard, *Opera*, pp. 229–34.

De dispensatione ecclesiasticarum rerum, Agobard, *Opera*, pp. 119–42.

De divisione imperii, Agobard, *Opera*, pp. 245–50.

Liber apologeticus I, Agobard, *Opera*, pp. 307–12.

Liber apologeticus II, Agobard, *Opera*, pp. 313–19.

Alcuin, *Epistolae*, ed. E. Dümmler, MGH *Epp.* IV, pp. 18–481.

Ambrose, *De excessu fratris Satyri*, ed. O. Faller, CSEL 73 (Vienna, 1955), pp. 207–325.

Annales Xantenses, ed. B. von Simson, MGH *SRG* 12 (Hanover, 1909).

Ardo/Smaragdus, *Vita Benedicti abb. Anianensis*, ed. G. Waitz, MGH *SS* XV (Hanover, 1887), pp. 200–20.

Augustine, *De civitate Dei libri XXII*, ed. G. Dombart, A. Kalb and G. Bardy (Stuttgart, 1981).

De disciplina christiana, ed. R. van de Plaetse, CCSL 46 (Turnhout, 1969), pp. 207–24.

Benedicti regula, editio altera emendata, ed. R. Hanslik, CCSL 75 (Vienna, 1977).

Boniface, *Epistolae*, ed. M. Tangl, *Epistolarum collectio Bonifatii et Lulli*, MGH *Epp. sel.* 1 (Hanover, 1916).

Brun Candidus, *Vita Aegil abbatis Fuldensis*, ed. G. Becht-Jördens (Marburg, 1994).

Cassiodorus/Epiphanius, *Historia ecclesiastica tripartita*, ed. W. Jacob and R. Hanslik, CSEL 71 (Vienna, 1952).

Chronicon Laurissense breve, ed. H. Schnorr von Carolsfeld, *Neues Archiv der Gesellschaft für ältere deutsche Geschichtskunde* 36 (1910), pp. 13–39.

Chronicon Moissiacense, ed. G. H. Pertz, MGH *SS* I (Hanover, 1826), pp. 282–313.

Concilios visigóticos e hispano-romanos, ed. J. Vives (Barcelona and Madrid, 1963).

Dhuoda, *Liber manualis*, ed. P. Riché, *Manuel pour mon fils*, SC 225bis (Paris, 1991).

Ebo of Rheims, *Apologeticum, forma prior et posterior*, ed. A. Werminghoff, MGH *Conc.* II/2 (Hanover and Leipzig, 1908), pp. 794–806.

Einhard, *Epistolae*, ed. K. Hampe, MGH *Epp.* V (Berlin, 1898–9), pp. 109–41.

Epistolarum Fuldensium fragmenta, ed. E. Dümmler, MGH *Epp.* V (Berlin, 1898–9), pp. 517–33.

Freculf of Lisieux, *Historiae*, ed. M. I. Allen, *Frechulfi Lexoviensis episcopi opera omnia*, CCCM 169A (Turnhout, 2002).

Fredegar, *Chronicae cum continuationibus*, ed. B. Krusch, MGH *SRM* II (Hanover, 1888), pp. 1–193; ed. A. Kusternig and H. Haupt, *Quellen zur Geschichte des 7. und 8. Jahrhunderts*, Ausgewählte Quellen zur deutschen Geschichte des Mittelalters IVa (Darmstadt, 1982), pp. 3–325.

Frothar of Toul, *Epistolae*, ed. K. Hampe, MGH *Epp.* V, (Berlin 1898–1899), pp. 275–298; ed. M. Parisse, *La correspondance d'un évêque carolingien: Frothaire de Toul, ca. 813–847* (Paris, 1998).

Gregory the Great, *Regula Pastoralis*, ed. B. Judic, *Grégoire le Grand, Règle Pastorale*, SC 382 (Paris, 1992).

Gregory of Tours, *Decem libri historiarum*, ed. B. Krusch and W. Levison, MGH *SRM* I (Hanover, 1937–51).

Heito of Reichenau/Basle, *Visio Wettini*, ed. E. Dümmler, MGH *Poet. lat.* II (Berlin, 1884), pp. 267–75.

Hildemar of Corbie/Civate, *Expositio in regulam sancti Benedicti*, prologue, ed. R. Mittermüller (Regensburg, 1880).

Hincmar of Rheims, *Consilium de poenitentia Pippini regis*, PL 125, cols. 1119B–1122C.

De divortio Lotharii regis et Theutbergae reginae, ed. L. Böringer, MGH *Conc.* IV, suppl. 1 (Hannover, 1992).

Epistolae, ed. E. Perels, MGH *Epp.* VIII/1 (Berlin, 1939).

Hraban Maur, *Carmina*, ed. E. Dümmler, MGH *Poet. lat.* II (Berlin, 1884), pp. 154–213.

Commentaria in Libros IV Regum, PL 109, cols. 11–280.

Commentaria in Ecclesiasticum, PL 109, cols. 763–1126.

Epistolae, ed. E. Dümmler, MGH *Epp.* V (Berlin, 1898–9), pp. 381–530.

De institutione clericorum, ed. D. Zimpel, Freiburger Beiträge zur mittelalterlichen Geschichte. Studien und Texte 7 (Frankfurt a/M etc., 1996).

Paenitentiale ad Heribaldum, PL 110, cols. 474–94.

De reverentia filiorum erga patres et subditorum erga reges, ed. E. Dümmler, MGH *Epp.* V, pp. 404–15.

Jonas of Bobbio, *Vita Columbani abbatis discipulorumque eius*, ed. B. Krusch, MGH *SRM* IV (Hanover and Leipzig, 1902), pp. 61–152.

Jonas of Orléans, *De institutione laicali*, PL 106, cols. 121–278.

De institutione regia, ed. A. Dubreucq, *Le métier de roi*, SC 407 (Paris, 1995).

Karolus Magnus et Leo papa, ed. E. Dümmler, MGH *Poet. lat.* I, pp. 367–79.

Laterculus regum Visigothorum, ed. Th. Mommsen, MGH *Auct. Ant.* XIII (Berlin, 1898), pp. 461–70.

Liber Pontificalis, ed. L. Duchesne (Paris, 1886).

Lupus, *Epistolae*, ed. L. Levillain, *Loup de Ferrières, Correspondance*, 2 vols. (Paris, 1964).

Notker Balbulus, *Gesta Karoli* I, c. 30, ed. H. Haefele, MHG *SRG* n.s. XII (Hanover, 1959).

Paschasius Radbertus, *Carmina*, ed. E. Dümmler, MGH *Poet. lat.* III (Berlin, 1896), pp. 38–53.

De corpore et sanguine domini, ed. B. Paulus, CCCM 16 (Turnhout, 1969).

Expositio in psalmum XLIV, ed. B. Paulus, CCCM 94 (Turnhout, 1991).

Paulinus of Milan, *Vita Ambrosii*, ed. M. Pellegrino, *Paolino di Milano, Vita di S. Ambrogio*, Verba seniorum, n.s. I (Rome, 1961).

Pseudo-Cyprian, *De duodecim abusivis saeculi*, ed. S. Hellmann, Texte und Untersuchungen zur altchristlichen Literatur 34 (Leipzig, 1934), pp. 32–60.

Sedulius Scottus, *Carmina*, ed. L. Traube, MGH *Poet. lat.* III (Berlin, 1896).

P. Terentius Afer, *Comoediae: The Comedies of P. Terentius Afer*, ed. S. G. Ashmore (New York, 1967).

Ex translatione Balthechildis, ed. O. Holder-Egger, MGH *SS* XV/1 (Stuttgart, 1887), pp. 284–5.

Venantius Fortunatus, *Carmina*, ed. F. Leo, MGH *Auct. Ant.* IV/1 (Berlin, 1881), pp. 1–240.

Das Verbrüderungsbuch der Abtei Reichenau: Einleitung, Register, Faksimile, ed. J. Authenrieth, D. Geuenich and K. Schmid, MGH *Libri memoriales et necrologia*, n.s. I (Hanover, 1979).

Visio cuiusdam pauperculae mulieris, ed. H. Houben, '*Visio cuiusdam pauperculae mulieris*: Überlieferung und Herkunft eines frühmittelalterlichen Visionstextes (mit Neuedition)', *Zeitschrift für die Geschichte des Oberrheins*, 124, NF 85 (1976), pp. 31–42.

Visio Rotcharii, ed. W. Wattenbach, 'Aus Petersburger Handschriften', *Anzeiger für Kunde der deutschen Vorzeit* 22 (1875), pp. 72–4.

Vita Alcuini, ed. W. Arndt, MGH *SS* XV/1 (Hanover, 1887), pp. 182–97.

Vita Balthildis, ed. B. Krusch, MGH *SRM* II (Hanover, 1888), pp. 482–508.

Walahfrid Strabo, *Carmina*, ed. E. Dümmler, MGH *Poet. lat.* II (Berlin, 1884), pp. 259–423.

Visio Wettini, ed. E. Dümmler, MGH *Poet. lat.* II (Berlin, 1884), pp. 301–33; ed. D. A. Traill, *Walahfrid Strabo's* Visio Wettini: *Text, Translation and Commentary*, Lateinische Sprache und Literatur des Mittelalters 2 (Frankfurt a/M, 1974).

De Imagine Tetrici, ed. E. Dümmler, MGH *Poet. lat.* II (Berlin, 1884), pp. 370–8; ed. M. Herren, 'The *De imagine Tetrici* of Walahfrid Strabo: edition and translation', *Journal of Medieval Latin* 1 (1991), pp. 118–39.

Bibliography: secondary sources

Airlie, Stuart, 'Bonds of power and bonds of association in the court circle of Louis the Pious', in Godman and Collins (eds.), *Charlemagne's Heir*, pp. 191–205.

'Private bodies and the body politic in the divorce case of Lothar II', *Past and Present* 161 (1998), pp. 3–38.

'*Semper fideles?* Loyauté envers les Carolingiens comme constituant de l'identité aristocratique', in Le Jan (ed.), *La royauté*, pp. 129–43.

'Narratives of triumph and rituals of submission: Charlemagne's mastering of Bavaria', *TRHS* 6/9 (1999), pp. 93–120.

'The palace of memory: the Carolingian court as political centre', in S. Rees Jones, R. Marks and A. Minnis (eds.), *Courts and Regions in Medieval Europe* (York, 2000), pp. 1–20.

'True teachers and pious kings: Salzburg, Louis the German, and Christian order', in R. Gameson and H. Leyser (eds.), *Belief and Culture in the Middle Ages: Studies Presented to Henry Mayr-Harting* (Oxford, 2001), pp. 89–105.

'Talking heads: assemblies in early medieval Germany', in P. S. Barnwell and M. Mostert (eds.), *Political Assemblies in the Earlier Middle Ages* (Turnhout, 2003), pp. 29–46.

'Towards a Carolingian aristocracy', in Becher and Jarnut (eds.), *Der Dynastiewechsel von 751*, pp. 109–27.

'"Sad stories of the death of kings": narrative patterns and structures of authority in Regino of Prüm's *Chronicle*', in E. M. Tyler and R. Balzaretti (eds.), *Narrative and History in the Early Medieval West* (Turnhout, 2006), pp. 105–31.

'The aristocracy in the service of the state in the Carolingian period', in Airlie, Pohl and Reimitz (eds.), *Staat*, pp. 93–112.

'The world, the text and the Carolingian: aristocratic and masculine identities in Nithard's *Histories*', in Wormald and Nelson (eds.), *Lay Intellectuals*, pp. 51–77.

Airlie, Stuart, W. Pohl and H. Reimitz (eds.), *Staat im frühen Mittelalter*, Forschungen zur Geschichte des Mittelalters 11 (Vienna, 2006).

Allen, Michael I., *Frechulfi Lexoviensis episcopi opera omnia: Prolegomena: Indices*, *CCCM* 169 (Turnhout, 2002).

Althoff, Gerd, 'Empörung, Tränen, Zerknirschung: "Emotionen" in der öffentlichen Kommunikation des Mittelalters', *FmSt* 30 (1996), pp. 60–79.

'Das Privileg der deditio', in Althoff, *Spielregeln*, pp. 99–125.

'Demonstration und Inszenierung: Spielregeln der Kommunikation in mittelalterlichen Öffentlichkeit', in Althoff, *Spielregeln*, pp. 229–57.

Spielregeln der Politik im Mittelalter: Kommunikation in Frieden und Fehde (Darmstadt, 1997).

'*Ira regis*: prolegomena to a history of royal anger', in B. H. Rosenwein (ed.), *Anger's Past: The Social Uses of an Emotion in the Middle Ages* (Ithaca and London, 1998), pp. 59–74.

Die Macht der Rituale: Symbolik und Herrschaft im Mittelalter (Darmstadt, 2003).

Angenendt, Arnold, 'Das geistliche Bündnis der Päpste mit den Karolingern (754–796)', *HJ* 100 (1980), pp. 1–94.

Kaiserherrschaft und Königstaufe: Kaiser, Könige und Päpste als geistliche Patrone in der abendländischen Missionsgeschichte, Arbeiten zur Frühmittelalterforschung 15 (Berlin and New York, 1984).

'"Mit reinen Händen": Das Motiv der kultischen Reinheit in der abendländische Askese', in G. Jenal *et al.* (eds.), *Herrschaft, Kirche und Kultur: Festschrift für Friedrich Prinz zu seinem 63. Geburtstag* (Stuttgart, 1993), pp. 297–13.

Anton, Hans H., *Fürstenspiegel und Herrscherethos in der Karolingerzeit*, Bonner Historische Forschungen 32 (Bonn, 1968).

'Zum politischen Konzept karolingischer Synoden und zur karolingischen Brüdergemeinschaft', *HJ* 99 (1979), pp. 55–132.

'Pseudo-Cyprian: de duodecim abusivis saeculi und sein Einfluß auf dem Kontinent, insbesondere auf die karolingischen Fürstenspiegel', in H. Löwe (ed.), *Die Iren und Europa im frühen Mittelalter* 2 (Stuttgart, 1982), pp. 568–617.

Arquillière, Henri-Xavier, *L'Augustinisme politique: Essai sur la formation des théories politiques du moyen âge*, L'église et l'état au moyen-âge 2, 2nd edn (Paris, 1955).

Becher, Matthias, *Eid und Herrschaft: Untersuchungen zum Herrscherethos Karls des Großen*, Vorträge und Forschungen, Sonderband 39 (Sigmaringen, 1993).

'*Cum lacrimis et gemitu*: vom Weinen der Sieger und Besiegten im frühen und hohen Mittelalter', in G. Althoff (ed.), *Formen und Funktionen öffentlicher Kommunikation im Mittelalter* (Stuttgart, 2001), pp. 25–52.

Becher, Matthias, and Jörg Jarnut (eds.), *Der Dynastiewechsel von 751: Vorgeschichte, Legitimmationsstrategien und Erinnerung* (Münster, 2004).

Berndt, Rainer (ed.), *Das Frankfurter Konzil von 794: Kristallisationspunkt karolingischer Kultur*, 2 vols., Quellen und Abhandlungen zur mittelrheinischen Kirchengeschichte 80 (Mainz, 1997).

Berschin, Walter, *Biographie und Epochenstil im lateinischen Mittelalter*, III: *Karolingische Biographie, 770–920 n. Chr.* (Stuttgart, 1991).

Beumann, Heinrich, *Ideengeschichtliche Studien zu Einhard und anderen Geschichtsschreibern des frühen Mittelalters*, 2nd edn (Munich, 1969).

'Die Historiographie des Mittelalters als Quelle für die Ideengeschichte des Königtums', in *HZ* 180 (1955), pp. 150–74; reprinted in Beumann, *Ideengeschichtliche Studien*, pp. 40–79.

'Topos und Gedankengefüge bei Einhard', *Archiv für Kulturgeschichte* 33 (1951), pp. 337–50; reprinted in Beumann, *Ideengeschichtliche Studien*, pp. 1–14.

Blattmann, Martina, 'Ein Ungluck für sein Volk: der Zusammenhang zwischen Fehlverhalten des Königs und Volkswohl in Quellen des 7.-12. Jahrhunderts', *FmSt* 30 (1996), pp. 80–102.

Booker, Courtney M., 'A new prologue of Walahfrid Strabo', *Viator* 36 (2005), pp. 93–105.

'The demanding drama of Louis the Pious', *Comitatus: A Journal of Medieval and Renaissance Studies* 34 (2003), pp. 170–5.

'Histrionic history, demanding drama: the penance of Louis the Pious in 833, memory and emplotment', in H. Reimitz and B. Zeller (eds.), *Vergangenheit und Vergegenwärtigung*, Forschungen zur Geschichte des Mittelalters 14 (forthcoming).

Borgolte, Michael, *Die Grafen Alemanniens in merowingischer und karolingischer Zeit: Eine Prosopographie* (Freiburg i. B., 1986).

Boshof, Egon, *Erzbischof Agobard von Lyon: Leben und Werk*, Kölner historische Abhandlungen 17 (Cologne and Vienna, 1969).

Ludwig der Fromme: Gestalten des Mittelalters und der Renaissance (Darmstadt, 1996).

'Einheitsidee und Teilungsprinzip in der Regierungszeit Ludwigs des Frommen', in Godman and Collins (eds.), *Charlemagne's Heir*, pp. 161–89.

Brown, Giles, 'Introduction: the Carolingian Renaissance', in McKitterick (ed.), *Carolingian Culture*, pp. 1–51.

Brown, Peter, *The Rise of Western Christendom: Triumph and Diversity, AD 200–1000*, 2nd edn (Oxford, 2003).

Brubaker, Leslie, and Julia M. H. Smith (eds.), *Gender in the Early Medieval World: East and West, 300–900* (Cambridge, 2004).

Brunner, Karl, *Oppositionelle Gruppen im Karolingerreich* (Vienna, 1979).

Buc, Philippe, 'Ritual and interpretation: the early medieval case' (with an addition of the *Chronicle of Moissac*), *EME* 9 (2000), pp. 183–207.

The Dangers of Ritual: Between Early Medieval Texts and Social Scientific Theory (Princeton, 2001).

'Political rituals and political imagination', in P. Linehan and J. L. Nelson (eds.), *The Medieval World* (London and New York, 2001), pp. 189–213.

'Text and ritual in ninth-century political culture: Rome, 864', in G. Althoff, J. Fried and P. J. Geary (eds.), *Medieval Concepts of the Past: Ritual, Memory, Historiography* (Cambridge, 2002), pp. 123–38.

'The monster and the critics: a ritual reply', *EME* 15 (2007), pp. 441–52.

Buck, Thomas M., *Admonitio und Praedicatio: Zur religiös-pastoralen Dimension von Kapitularien und kapitulariennahen Texten (507–814)*, Freiburger Beiträge zur mittelalterlichen Geschichte 9 (Frankfurt a/M, 1997).

Bühler, Arnold, '*Capitularia relecta*: Studien zur Entstehung und Überlieferung der Kapitularien Karls des Grossen und Ludwigs des Frommen', *AfD* 32 (1986), pp. 305–501.

Bührer-Thierry, Geneviève, 'La reine adultère', *Cahiers de Civilisation Médiévale* 35 (1992), pp. 299–312.

Cabaniss, Allen, *Charlemagne's Cousins: Contemporary Lives of Adalard and Wala* (New York, 1967).

Chazelle, Celia, *The Crucified God in the Carolingian Era: Theology and Art of Christ's Passion* (Cambridge, 2001).

'Exegesis in the ninth-century Eucharist Controversy', in Chazelle and Van Name Edwards (eds.), *The Study of the Bible*, pp. 167–87.

Chazelle, Celia, and B. van Name Edwards (eds.), *The Study of the Bible in the Carolingian Era*, Medieval Church Studies 3 (Turnhout, 2003).

Classen, Peter, 'Karl der Grosse und die Thronfolge im Frankenreich', in *Festschrift für Hermann Heimpel*, 3 vols., Veröffenlichungen des Max-Planck-Instituts für Geschichte 36, 1–3 (Göttingen, 1972), 3, pp. 109–34.

Claussen, Martin A., *The Reform of the Frankish Church: Chrodegang of Metz and the Carolingian Liturgy* (Cambridge, 2004).

Collins, Roger, 'Pippin I and the Kingdom of Aquitaine', in Godman and Collins (eds.), *Charlemagne's Heir*, pp. 363–89.

'Deception and misrepresentation in early eighth-century Frankish historiography: two case studies', in J. Jarnut, U. Nonn and M. Richter (eds.), *Karl Martell in seiner Zeit*, Beihefte der Francia 37 (Sigmaringen, 1994), pp. 227–48.

'The "Reviser" revisited: another look at the alternative version of the *Annales regni francorum*', in A. C. Murray (ed.), *After Rome's fall: Narrators and sources of early medieval history: Essays presented to Walter Goffart* (Toronto, 1998), pp. 191–213.

'Charlemagne and his critics', in Le Jan (ed.), *La royauté*, pp. 193–212.

Contreni, John J., 'Carolingian biblical studies', in U.-R. Blumenthal (ed.), *Carolingian Essays* (Washington DC, 1983), pp. 71–98; repr. in J. J. Contreni, *Carolingian Learning, Masters and Manuscripts* (Aldershot, 1992), ch. 5.

'The Carolingian Renaissance: education and literary culture' in McKitterick (ed.), *NCMH* II, pp. 709–57.

Corradini, R., M. Diesenberger and H. Reimitz (eds.), *The Construction of Communities in the Early Middle Ages: Texts, Resources and Artefacts*, The Transformation of the Roman World 12 (Leiden and Boston 2003).

Corradini, R., R. Meens, C. Pössel and P. Shaw (eds.), *Texts and Identities in the Early Middle Ages*, Forschungen zur Geschichte des Mittelalters 12 (Vienna, 2006).

Coupland, Simon, 'Money and coinage under Louis the Pious', *Francia* 17/1 (1990), pp. 23–54.

Cubitt, Catherine, *Anglo-Saxon Church Councils, c. 650–c. 850* (London, 1995).

(ed.), *Court Culture in the Early Middle Ages: The Proceedings of the First Alcuin Conference*, Studies in the Early Middle Ages 3 (Turnhout, 2003).

Dagron, Gilbert, *Emperor and Priest: The Imperial Office in Byzantium* (Cambridge, 2003).

Davis, Raymond, *The Lives of the Eighth-Century Popes* (Liber Pontificalis), *The Ancient Biographies of Nine Popes from AD 717 to AD 817*, Translated Texts for Historians 20 (Liverpool, 1992).

Delahaye, Hippolyte, 'Note sur la légende de la lettre du Christ tombée du ciel', *Bulletin de l'Académie Royale de Belgique, classe des lettres et des sciences morales et politiques* (1899), pp. 171–213.

Delaruelle, Étienne, 'En relisant le *De institutione regia* de Jonas d'Orléans', in *Mélanges d'histoire du Moyen Age, dédiés à la mémoire de Louis Halphen* (Paris, 1951), pp. 185–92.

Delogu, Paolo, '"Consors regni": un problema carolingo', *Bulletino dell'Instituto Storico per il Medioveo e Archivo Delogu Muratoriano* 76 (1964), pp. 85–98.

Depreux, Philippe, 'Empereur, empereur associé et pape au temps de Louis le Pieux', *Revue belge de philologie et d'histoire* 70 (1992), pp. 893–906.

'Die Kanzlei und das Urkundenwesen Kaiser Ludwigs des Frommen – nach wie vor ein Desiderat der Forschung', *Francia* 20/1 (1993), pp. 147–62.

'Das Königtum Bernhards von Italien und sein Verhältnis zum Kaisertum', *Quellen und Forschungen aus Italienischen Archiven und Bibliotheken* 72 (1992), pp. 1–25.

'Nithard et la *Res Publica*: un regard critique sur le règne de Louis le Pieux', *Médiévales* 22–3 (1992), pp. 149–61.

'Poètes et historiens au temps de l'empereur Louis le Pieux', *LMA* 99 (1993), pp. 311–22.

'Le comte Matfrid d'Orléans (av. 815–836)', *Bibliothèque de l'École des Chartes* 152 (1994) pp. 332–74.

'Louis le Pieux reconsidéré? À propos des travaux récents consacrés à l'héritier de Charlemagne et son règne', *Francia* 20/1 (1994), pp. 181–201.

Prosopographie de l'entourage de Louis le Pieux (781–840), Instrumenta 1 (Sigmaringen, 1997).

'La *pietas* comme principe de gouvernement d'après le *Poème sur Louis le Pieux* d'Ermold le Noir', in J. Hill and M. Swann (eds.), *The Community, the Family and the Saint: Patterns of Power in Early Medieval Europe* (Turnhout, 1998), pp. 201–4.

Deschman, Robert, 'The exalted servant: the ruler theology of the prayer book of Charles the Bald', *Viator* 11 (1980), pp. 385–417.

Dickau, Otto, 'Studien zur Kanzlei und zum Urkundenwesen Kaiser Ludwigs des Frommen', Erster Teil, *AfD* 34 (1988), pp. 3–156; Zweiter Teil, *AfD* 35 (1989), pp. 1–170.

Diem, Albrecht, *Das monastische Experiment: die Rolle der Keuschheit bei der Entstehung des westlichen Klosterwesens* (Münster, 2005).

'Monks, kings and the transformation of sanctity: Jonas of Bobbio and the end of the holy man', *Speculum* 82 (2007), pp. 521–9.

Doherty, Hugh, 'The Maintenance of Royal Power and Prestige in the Carolingian Regnum of Aquitaine under Louis the Pious' (unpublished MPhil dissertation, University of Cambridge, Faculty of History, Cambridge, 1999).

Douglas, Mary, *Purity and Danger: An Analysis of Concepts of Pollution and Taboo* (London, 1966).

Natural Symbols. Explorations in Cosmology (Harmondsworth, 1973).

Duby, Georges, *Dimanche de Bouvines: 27 Juillet 1214* (Paris, 1973).

Dutton, Paul E., *The Politics of Dreaming in the Carolingian Empire* (London and Lincoln, NB, 1994).

Charlemagne's Courtier: The Complete Einhard, Readings in Medieval Civilisations and Cultures 2 (Peterborough and Ontario, 1998).

Charlemagne's Mustache and Other Cultural Clusters of a Dark Age (New York and Basingstoke, 2004).

Engelbert, Pius, 'Papstreisen ins Frankenreich', *Römische Quartalschrift für christliche Altertumskunde und Kirchengeschichte* 88 (1993), pp. 77–113.

Ensslin, Wilhelm, 'Auctoritas und Potestas: Zur Zweigewaltenlehre des Papstes Gelasius I', *HJ* 74 (1955), pp. 661–8.

Erkens, Franz-Reiner, '"Divisio legitima" und "unitas imperii": Teilungspraxis und Einheitsstreben bei der Thronfolge im Frankenreich', *DA* 52 (1996), pp. 423–85.

Ewig, Eugen, 'Zum christlichen Königsgedanken im Mittelalter', in *Das Königtum: seine geistigen und rechtlichen Grundlagen: Mainauvorträge 1954*, Vorträge und Forschungen 3 (Lindau and Konstanz, 1956), pp. 7–73.

Faulhaber, Roland, *Der Reichseinheitsgedanke in der Literatur der Karolingerzeit bis zum Vertrag von Verdun* (Berlin, 1965).

Fees, Irmgard, 'War Walahfrid Strabo der Lehrer und Erzieher Karls des Kahlen?' in M. Thumser, A. Wenz-Haubfliesch and P. Wiegand (eds.), *Studien zur Geschichte des Mittelalters Jurgen Petersohn zum 65. Geburtstag* (Stuttgart, 2000), pp. 42–61.

Feller, Laurent, 'Introduction: crises et renouvellements des Élites au haut Moyen Âge: mutations ou ajustements des structures?', in F. Bougard, L. Feller, R. Le Jan (eds.), *Les Élites au Moyen Âge: crises et renouvellements*, Collection Haut Moyen Âge (Turnhout, 2006), pp. 5–21.

Felten, Franz J., *Äbte und Laienäbte im Frankenreich: Studie zum Verhältnis von Staat und Kirche im früheren Mittelalter*, MMS 20 (Stuttgart, 1980).

Fleckenstein, Josef, *Die Hofkapelle der deutschen Könige I: Grundlegung; Die Karolingische Hofkapelle*, Schriften der MGH 16/1 (Stuttgart, 1959).

'Einhard, seine Gründung und sein Vermächtnis in Seligenstadt', in Fleckenstein, *Ordnungen und formende Kräfte des Mittelalters: Ausgewählte Beiträge* (Göttingen, 1989), pp. 84–111.

Fouracre, Paul, 'Frankish Gaul to 814', in McKitterick (ed.), *NCMH* II, pp. 85–109.

Fried, Johannes, 'Der karolingische Herrschaftsverband im 9. Jahrhundert zwischen Kirche und Königshaus', *HZ* 235 (1982), pp. 1–43.

'Elite und Ideologie oder die Nachfolgeordnung Karls des Großen vom Jahre 813', in Le Jan (ed.), *La royauté*, pp. 71–109.

'Ludwig der Fromme, das Papsttum und die fränkische Kirche', in Godman and Collins, *Charlemagne's Heir*, pp. 231–74.

Ganshof, François L., 'L'échec de Charlemagne (eds.)', in *Comptes rendus de l'Academie des inscriptions* (1947), pp. 248–54.

'Louis the Pious reconsidered', *History* 42 (1957), pp. 171–80; reprinted in Ganshof, *The Carolingians and the Frankish Monarchy* (London and New York, 1971).

'Am Vorabend der ersten Krise der Regierung Ludwigs des Frommen', *FmSt* 6 (1972), pp. 39–54.

'Some observations on the *Ordinatio Imperii* of 817', in Ganshof, *The Carolingians and the Frankish Monarchy* (London and New York, 1971), pp. 273–88.

Ganz, David, 'Humour as history in Notker's *Gesta Karoli Magni*', in E. B. King, J. T. Schaefer and W. B. Wadley (eds.), *Monks, Nuns and Friars in Medieval Society* (Sewanee, 1989), pp. 171–83.

'The *Epitaphium Arsenii* and opposition to Louis the Pious', in Godman and Collins (eds.), *Charlemagne's Heir*, pp. 537–50.

Corbie in the Carolingian Renaissance, Beihefte der Francia 21 (Sigmaringen, 1990).

'Theology and the organization of thought', in McKitterick (ed.), *NCMH* II, pp. 758–85.

'The preface to Einhard's "Vita Karoli"', in H. Schefers (ed.), *Einhard: Studien zu Leben und Werk* (Darmstadt, 1997), pp. 299–310.

'Einhard's Charlemagne: the characterization of greatness', in J. Story (ed.), *Charlemagne: Empire and Society* (Manchester and New York, 2005), 38–51.

'Einhardus peccator', in Wormald and Nelson (eds.), *Lay Intellectuals*, pp. 37–50.

Garipzanov, Ildar H., 'The image of authority in Carolingian coinage: the image of a ruler and Roman imperial tradition', *EME* 8 (1999), pp. 197–218.

Garrison, Mary, 'The social world of Alcuin: nicknames at York and at the Carolingian court', in L. A. J. R. Houwen and A. A. McDonald (eds.), *Alcuin of York*, Germania Latina 3 (Groningen, 1998), pp. 59–79.

'The Franks as the New Israel? Education for an identity from Pippin to Charlemagne', in Hen and Innes (eds.), *The Uses of the Past*, pp. 114–61.

'The Bible and Alcuin's interpretation of current events', *Peritia* 16 (2002), pp. 68–84.

'Les correspondants d'Alcuin', in P. Depreux and B. Judic (eds.), *Alcuin de York à Tours: écriture, pouvoir et résaux dans l'Europe du Haut Moyen Âge: Annales de Bretagne et des Pays de l'Ouest* 111/ 3 (2004), pp. 319–331.

Geary, Patrick J., *Furta Sacra: Theft of Relics in the Central Middle Ages* (Princeton, 1978).

Godman, Peter, *Poetry of the Carolingian Renaissance* (London, 1985).

'Louis "the Pious" and his poets', *FmSt* 19 (1985), pp. 239–89.

Poets and Emperors: Frankish Politics and Carolingian Poetry (Oxford, 1987).

Godman, Peter, and R. Collins (eds.), *Charlemagne's Heir: New Perspectives on the Reign of Louis the Pious (814–840)* (Oxford, 1990).

Goetting, Hans, *Das Bistum Hildesheim: Die Hildesheimer Bischöfe von 815 bis 1221 (1227)*, Germania Sacra, NF 20, 3 (Berlin and New York, 1984).

Goetz, Hans-Werner, 'The perception of "power" and "state" in the early Middle Ages: the case of the Astronomer's *Life of Louis the Pious*', in B. Weiler and S. MacLean (eds.), *Representations of Power in Medieval Germany* (Turnhout, 2006), pp. 15–36.

Goldberg, Eric J., *Struggle for Empire: Kingship and Conflict under Louis the German, 817–876* (Ithaca and London, 2006).

Gorman, Michael M., 'Wigbod and biblical studies under Charlemagne', *RB* 107 (1997), pp. 40–76.

'The commentary on Genesis of Claudius of Turin and biblical studies under Louis the Pious', *Speculum* 72 (1997), pp. 279–329.

Biblical Commentaries from the Early Middle Ages (Florence, 2002).

Guillot, Olivier, 'L'exhortation au partage des responsabilités entre l'empereur, l'épiscopat, et les autres sujets vers le milieu du règne de Louis le Pieux', in *Prédication et propagande au Moyen Âge*, ed. G. Makdisi (Paris, 1983), pp. 87–110.

'Une *ordinatio* méconnue: Le Capitulaire de 823–825', in Godman and Collins (eds.), *Charlemagne's Heir*, pp. 455–86.

'Autour de la pénitence publique de Louis le Pieux (822)', in J. Haoreau-Dodinau, X. Rousseaux and P. Texier (eds.), *Le pardon: Cahiers de l'Institut d'Anthropologie Juridique* 3 (Limoges, 1999), pp. 281–313.

La Guistizia nell'alto medioevo (secoli IX–XI), Settimane 44 (Spoleto, 1997).

Gurevitch, Aaron, 'Popular and scholarly medieval cultural traditions: notes in the margin of Jacques Le Goff's book', in *Journal of Medieval History* 9 (1983), pp. 71–90.

Halphen, Louis, 'La pénitence de Louis le Pieux à Saint Médard de Soissons', in *Bibliothèque de la Faculté des Lettres de Paris XVIII, troisièmes mélanges d'histoire du Moyen Âge* (Paris 1904) 177–185; repr. in Halphen, *A travers l'histoire du Moyen Âge* (Paris, 1950), pp. 58–66.

Charlemagne et l'Empire carolingien (Paris, 1947).

Halsall, Guy, *Warfare and Society in the Barbarian West, 450–900* (London and New York, 2003).

Hamilton, Sarah, 'Otto III's penance: a case study of unity and diversity in the eleventh-century church', in R. Swanson (ed.), *Unity and Diversity in the Church*, Studies in Church History 32 (Oxford, 1996), pp. 83–94.

'A new model for royal penance? Helgaud of Fleury's Life of Robert the Pious', *EME* 6 (1997), pp. 189–200.

The Practice of Penance, 900–1050 (Woodbridge, 2001).

Hartmann, Wilfried, 'Die karolingische Reform und die Bibel', *Annuarium Historiae Conciliorum* 18 (1986) pp. 58–74.

Die Synoden der Karolingerzeit im Frankenreich und in Italien (Paderborn, 1989).

Ludwig der Deutsche (Darmstadt, 2002).

'Neue Texte zur bischöflichen Reformgesetzgebung aus den Jahren 829/31: Vier Diözesansynoden Halitgars von Cambrai', *DA* 35 (1979), pp. 368–94.

Heil, Johannes, 'Agobard, Amolo, das Kirchengut und die Juden von Lyon', *Francia* 25/1 (1998), pp. 39–76.

'"Nos nescientes de hoc velle manere" – "We wish to remain ignorant about this": Timeless end, or: approaches to reconceptualizing eschatology after AD 800 (AM 6000)', *Traditio* 55 (2000), pp. 73–103.

Heinzelmann, Martin, '*Studia sanctorum*: Education, milieux d'instruction et valeurs éducatives dans l'hagiographie en Gaule jusqu'à la fin de l'époque mérovingienne', in M. Sot (ed.), *Haut-Moyen Âge: Culture, éducation et société: études offertes à Pierre Riché* (La Garennes-Colombe, 1990), pp. 105–308.

'Einhards "Translatio Marcellini et Petri": Eine hagiographische Reformschrift von 830', in H. Schefers (ed.), *Einhard: Studien zur Leben und Werk: Dem Gedenken an Helmut Beumann gewidmet*, Arbeiten der Hessischen Historischen Kommission, NF 12 (Darmstadt, 1997), pp. 269–98.

Gregory of Tours: History and Society in the Sixth Century, trans. C. Carroll (Cambridge, 2001; orig. Darmstadt, 1994).

Hen, Yitzhak, *The Royal Patronage of Liturgy in Frankish Gaul to the Death of Charles the Bald (877)*, Henry Bradshaw Society, Subsidia 3 (London, 2001).

'The Annals of Metz and the Merovingian past', in Hen and Innes (eds.), *The Uses of the Past*, pp. 175–90.

'The Christianisation of kingship', in Becher and Jarnut (eds.), *Dynastiewechsel*, pp. 163–78.

Hen, Yitzhak, and M. Innes (eds.), *The Uses of the Past in the Early Middle Ages* (Cambridge, 2000).

Hentze, Wilhem (ed.), *De Karolo rege et Leone papa: der Bericht über die Zusammenkunft Karls des Grossen mit Papst Leo III: in Paderborn 799 in einem Epos für Karl den Kaiser*, Studien und Quellen zur westfälischen Geschichte 36 (Paderborn, 1999).

Herren, Michael, 'The "*De imagine Tetrici*" of Walahfrid Strabo: edition and translation', *Journal of Medieval Latin* 1 (1991), pp. 118–39.

'Walahfrid Strabo's *De imagine Tetrici*: an interpretation', in T. Hofstra and J. North (eds.), *Latin Culture in Medieval Germanic Europe*, Germania Latina 1 (Groningen, 1992), pp. 25–41.

Heydemann, Gerda, 'Text und Translation: Strategien zur Mobilisierung spiritueller Ressourcen im Frankenreich Ludwigs des Frommen', in R. Corradini and M. Diesenberger (eds.), *Zwischen Niederschrift und Widerschrift*, Forschungen zur Geschichte des Mittelalters 15 (forthcoming).

Hofmann, Hartmut, *Untersuchungen zur karolingischer Annalistik*, Bonner historische Forschungen 10 (Bonn, 1958).

Hoymeier, Hélène, 'Zu Walahfrid Strabos Gedicht über das Aachener Theoderich-Denkmal', *Studi Medievali* 12 (1971), pp. 888–913.

Hummer, Hans J., *Politics and Power in the Early Middle Ages: Alsace and the Frankish Realm, 600–900* (Cambridge, 2005).

Hürten, Heinz, '"Libertas" in der Patristik – "libertas episcopalis" im Frühmittelalter', *Archiv für Kulturgeschichte* 45 (1963), pp. 1–14.

Innes, Matthew, 'Charlemagne's will: inheritance, ideology and the imperial succession', *EHR* 112 (1997), pp. 833–55.

'The classical tradition in the Carolingian Renaissance: ninth-century encounters with Suetonius', *International Journal of the Classical Tradition* 3 (1997), pp. 265–82.

'Memory, orality and literacy in an early medieval society', *Past & Present* 158 (1998), pp. 3–36.

'Kings, monks and patrons: political identities and the abbey of Lorsch', in Le Jan, *La royauté*, pp. 301–24.

State and Society in the Early Middle Ages: The Middle Rhine Valley 400–1000 (Cambridge , 2000).

'"He never even allowed his white teeth to be bared in laughter"; the politics of humour in the Carolingian Renaissance', in G. Halsall (ed.), *Humour, History and Politics in Late Antiquity and the Early Middle Ages* (Cambridge, 2002), pp. 131–56.

'A place of discipline: Carolingian courts and aristocratic youths', in Cubitt (ed.), *Court Culture*, pp. 59–66.

'Charlemagne's government', in J. Story (ed.), *Charlemagne: Empire and Society* (Manchester and New York, 2005), pp. 71–89.

Innes, Matthew, and R. McKitterick, 'The writing of history', in McKitterick (ed.), *Carolingian Culture*, pp. 193–220.

Jacob, Walter, and Rudolf Hanslik, *Die handschriftliche Überlieferung der sogenannten Historia Tripartita des Epiphanius-Cassiodor*, Texte und Untersuchungen zur Geschichte der altchristlichen Literatur 54 (Berlin, 1954).

Jarnut, Jörg, 'Chlodweg und Chlotar: Anmerkungen zu den Namen zweier Söhne Karls des Großen', *Francia* 12 (1985), 645–51.

'Kaiser Ludwig der Fromme und König Bernhard von Italien: der Versuch einer Rehabilitierung', *Studi Medievali* 30 (1989), pp. 637–48.

'Ludwig der Fromme, Lothar I und das Regnum Italiae', in Godman and Collins (eds.), *Charlemagne's Heir*, pp. 349–62.

Jarnut, Jörg, Ulrich Nonn and Michael Richter (eds.), *Karl Martell in seiner Zeit* (Sigmaringen, 1994).

Jong, Mayke de, 'Power and humility in Carolingian society: the public penance of Louis the Pious', *Early Medieval Europe* 1 (1992), pp. 29–52.

'Old law and new-found power: Hrabanus Maurus and the Old Testament', in J. W. Drijvers and A. A. MacDonald (eds.), *Centres of Learning: Learning and Location in pre-modern Europe and the Near East* (Leiden, New York and Cologne, 1995), pp. 161–76.

'Carolingian monasticism: the power of prayer', in McKitterick (ed.), *NCMH* II, pp. 622–53.

In Samuel's Image: Child Oblation in the Early Medieval West, Studies in Intellectual history 12 (Leiden, 1996).

'The foreign past: medieval historians and cultural anthropology', *Tijdschrift voor Geschiedenis* 109 (1996), pp. 323–39.

'What was *public* about public penance? *Paenitentia publica* and justice in the Carolingian world', in *La giustizia nell'alto medioevo (secolo ix–xi)*, Settimane 44 (1997), pp. 863–904.

'*Imitatio morum*: the cloister and clerical purity in the Carolingian world', in M. Frassetto (ed.), *Medieval Purity and Piety: Essays in Medieval Clerical Celibacy and Religious Reform* (New York and London, 1998) pp. 49–80.

'Pollution, penance and sanctity: Ekkehard's *Life* of Iso of St Gall', in J. Hill and M. Swann (eds.), *The Community, the Family and the Saint: Patterns of Power in Early Medieval Europe* (Turnhout, 1998), pp. 145–58.

'Adding insult to injury: Julian of Toledo and his *Historia Wambae*', in P. Heather (ed.), *The Visigoths from the Migration Period to the Seventh Century: An Ethnographic Perspective* (Woodbridge, 1999), pp. 373–402.

'An unsolved riddle: early medieval incest legislation', in I. N. Wood (ed.), *Franks and Alamanni in the Merovingian period: An Ethnographic Perspective* (Woodbridge, 1999), pp. 107–25.

'The empire as *ecclesia*; Hrabanus Maurus and biblical *historia* for rulers', in Hen and Innes (eds.), *The Uses of the Past*, pp. 191–226.

'Internal cloisters: the case of Ekkehard's *Casus sancti Galli*', in W. Pohl and H. Reimitz (eds.), *Grenzen und Differenz im frühen Mittelalter*, Forschungen zur Geschichte des Mittelalters 1 (Vienna, 2000), pp. 209–21.

'Transformations of penance', in Theuws and Nelson (eds.), *Rituals of Power*, pp. 185–224.

'Exegesis for an empress', in E. Cohen and M. de Jong (eds.), *Medieval Transformations: Texts, Power and Gifts in Context* (Leiden, 2001), pp. 69–100.

'Monastic prisoners or opting out? Political coercion and honour in the Frankish kingdoms', in De Jong, Theuws and Van Rhijn (eds.), *Topographies of Power in the Early Middle Ages*, pp. 291–328.

'Monastic writing and Carolingian court audiences: some evidence from biblical commentary', in F. De Rubeis and W. Pohl (eds.), *Le scritture dai monasteri: Atti del IIo seminario internazionale di studio "I monasteri nell'alto medioevo"*, Roma 9–10 maggio 2003', Acta isituti Romani Finlandiae 29 (Rome, 2003), pp. 179–95.

'*Sacrum palatium et ecclesia*: L'autorité religieuse royale sous les Carolingiens (790–840)', *Annales: Histoire, Sciences Sociales* 58 (2003), pp. 1243–69.

'Bride shows revisited: praise, slander and exegesis in the reign of the empress Judith', in L. Brubaker and J. M. H. Smith (eds.), *Gender in the Early Medieval World: East and West, 300–900* (Cambridge, 2004), pp. 257–77.

'Charlemagne's church', in J. Story (ed.), *Charlemagne: Empire and Society* (Manchester and New York, 2005), pp. 103–35.

'*Ecclesia* and the early medieval polity', in Airlie, Pohl and Reimitz (eds.), *Staat*, pp. 113–32.

'Queens and beauty in the early medieval West: Balthild, Theodelinda, Judith', in C. La Rocca (ed.), *Agire da donna: modelli e pratiche di rappresentazione (secoli vi–x)*, Collection Haut Moyen Âge 3 (Turnhout, 2007), pp. 235–48.

'Charlemagne's balcony: the *solarium* in ninth-century narratives', in J. R. Davis and M. McCormick (eds.), *The Long Morning of Medieval Europe: New Directions in Early Medieval Studies* (London, 2008), pp. 276–89.

'Becoming Jeremiah: Radbert on Wala, himself and others', in R. McKitterick, I. van Renswoude, M. Gillis and R. Corradini (eds.), *Ego Trouble: Authors and Their Identities in the Early Middle Ages*, Forschungen zur Geschichte des Mitttelalters, Österreichische Akademie der Wissenschaften (forthcoming).

Jong, Mayke de, F. Theuws and C. van Rhijn (eds.), *Topographies of Power in the Early Middle Age*, The Transformation of the Roman World 6 (Leiden, 2001).

Kamphausen, Hans J., *Traum und Vision in der lateinischen Poesie der Karolingerzeit*, Lateinische Sprache und Literatur des Mittelalters 4 (Bern and Frankfurt, 1975).

Kasten, Brigitte, *Adalhard von Corbie: die Biographie eines karolingischen Politikers und Klostervorstehers*, Studia humaniora 3 (Düsseldorf, 1986).
Königssöhne und Königsherrschaft. Untersuchungen zur Teilhabe am Reich in der Merowinger- und Karolingerreich. MGH Schriften 44 (Hanover, 1997).

Keefe, Susan, *Water and the Word: Baptism and the Education of the Clergy in the Carolingian Empire*, 2 vols. (Notre Dame, 2002).

Kershaw, Paul, 'Laughter after Babel's fall: misunderstanding and miscommunication in the ninth-century west', in G. Hallsall (ed.), *Humour, History and Politics in Late Antiquity and the Early Middle Ages* (Cambridge, 2002), pp. 179–202.

King, P. D., *Charlemagne: Translated Sources* (Kendal, 1987).

Koch, Armin, *Kaiserin Judith: Eine politische Biographie*, Historische Studien 486 (Husum, 2005).

Kölzer, Theo, 'Kaiser Ludwig der Fromme (814–840) im Spiegel seiner Urkunden', *Nordrhein-Westfälische Akademie der Wissenschaften. Geisteswissenschaften* (Paderborn, 2005), pp. 5–34.

Konecny, Silvia, *Die Frauen des karolingischen Königshauses: Die politischen Bedeutung der Ehe und die Stellung der Frau in der frankischen Herrscherfamilie vom 7. Bis zum 10. Jahrhundert* (Vienna, 1976).

Kötting, Bernhard, 'Die Beurteilung der zweiten Ehe in der Spätantike und im frühen Mittelalter', in H. Kamp and J. Wollasch (eds.), *Tradition als historische Kraft* (Berlin, 1982), pp. 43–52.

Kottje, Raymund, *Die Bussbücher Halitgars von Cambrai und Hrabanus Maurus: Ihre Überlieferung und ihre Quellen* (Berlin and New York, 1980).

'Buße oder Strafe? Zur "iustitia" in den "libri paenitentiales"', in *La giustizia nell'alto Medioevo (secoli V-VIII)* I, Settimane 42 (1995), pp. 443–68.

Koziol, Geoffrey, *Begging Pardon and Favor: Ritual and Political Order in Early Medieval France* (Ithaca and London, 1992).

'Is Robert I in hell? The diploma for Saint-Denis and the mind of a rebel king (Jan. 25, 923)', *EME* 14 (2006), pp. 233–63.

Krahwinkel, Harald, *Friaul im Frühmittelalter: Geschichte einer Region vom Ende des fünften bis zum Ende des zehnten Jahrhunderts*, Veröffentlichungen des Instituts für Österreichische Geschichtsforschung 30 (Vienna, Cologne and Weimar, 1992).

Krüger, Karl H., 'Zur Nachfolgeregelung von 826 in den Klöstern Corbie und Corvey', in N. Kamp and Joachim Wollasch (eds.), *Tradition als historische Kraft: Festschrift Karl Hauck* (Berlin and New York, 1982), pp. 181–96.

'Königskonversionen im 8. Jahrhundert', *FmSt* 7 (1983), pp. 169–222.

'Neue Beobachtungen zur Datierung von Einhards Karlsvita', *FmSt* 32 (1998), pp. 124–45.

Ladner, Gerhart B., *The Idea of Reform: Its Impact on Christian Life and Action in the Age of the Fathers* (Cambridge, Mass., 1959).

Lammers, Walther, 'Ein karolingisches Bildprogramm in der Aula regia von Ingelheim', in *Festschrift für Hermann Heimpel zum 70. Geburtstag*, Veröffentlichungen des Max-Planck-Instituts für Geschichte 36, 1–3, (1972), 3, pp. 226–89.

Landau, Peter, 'Ursprünge und Entwicklung des Verbotes doppelter Strafverfolgung wegen desselben Verbrechen in der Geschichte des kanonischen Rechts', *Zeitschrift zur Savigny-Stiftung für Rechtsgeschicte, Kanonistische Abteilung* 56 (1970), pp. 124–56.

Lauwers, Michel, 'Le glaive et la parole: Charlemagne, Alcuin et le modèle du *rex praedicator*: notes d'ecclésiologie carolingienne', in P. Depreux and B. Judic (eds.), *Alcuin de York à Tours: Ecriture, pouvoir et réseaux dans l'Europe du haut moyen âge: Annales de Bretagne et des Pays de l'Ouest* 111/3 (2004), pp. 221–44.

Le Jan, Régine, *Famille et pouvoir dans le monde Franc, VIIIe–Xe siècles* (Paris, 1995).

'Justice royale et pratiques sociales dans le royaume franc au IXe siècle', in *La giustizia*, Settimane 44 (1997), pp. 47–87.

'Dhuoda ou l'opportunité du discours féminin', in C. La Rocca (ed.), *Agire da donna: modelli e pratiche di rappresentazione (secoli vi–x)*, Collection Haut Moyen Âge 3 (Turnhout, 2007), pp. 109–28.

Le Jan, Régine, (ed.), *La royauté et les élites dans l'Europe Carolingienne (début du IXe siècle aux environs de 920)* (Lille, 1997).

Le Maître, Philippe, 'Image du Christ, image de l'empereur: L'exemple du culte du St Sauveur sous Louis le Pieux', *Revue d'Histoire de l'Église de France* 68 (1982), pp. 201–12.

Levison, Wilhelm, 'Die Politik in der Jenseitsvisionen des frühen Mittelalters', in Levison, *Aus rheinischer und fränkischer Frühzeit: Ausgewählte Aufsätze von Wilhelm Levison* (Düsseldorf, 1948), pp. 228–46.

Leyser, Karl, 'The German aristocracy from the ninth to the early twelfth century: a historical and cultural sketch', *Past & Present* 41 (1968), pp. 61–83.

'Early medieval canon law and the beginnings of knighthood', in T. Reuter (ed.), *Communications and Power in Early Medieval Europe: The Carolingian and Ottonian Centuries* (London and Rio Grande, 1994), pp. 51–72; orig. in L. Fenske, W. Rösener and Th. Zotz (eds.), *Festschrift für Josef Fleckenstein* (Sigmaringen, 1984), pp. 549–66.

'Nithard and his rulers', in T. Reuter (ed.), *Communications and Power in Medieval Europe, I: The Carolingian and Ottonian Centuries* (London and Rio Grande, 1994), pp. 19–25.

Lobbedey, Uwe, 'Carolingian royal palaces: the state of research from an architectural historian's viewpoint', in Cubitt (ed.), *Court Culture*, pp. 129–54.

Lošek, Fritz, 'Die Spinne in der Kirchendecke: eine St. Galler Klostergeschichte (Notker, Gesta Karoli, 1, 32)', in Scharer and Scheibelreiter (eds.), *Historiographie* (1994), pp. 253–61.

Löwe, Heinz, 'Die Entstehungszeit der Vita Karoli Einhards', *DA* 39 (1983), pp. 85–103.

(ed.), *Wattenbach-Levison: Deutschlands Geschichtsquellen im Mittelalter: Vorzeit und Karolinger 6: Die Karolinger vom Vertrag von Verdun bis zum Herrschaftsantritt der Herrscher aus dem Sächsischen Hause: Das ostfränkische Reich* (Weimar, 1990).

Lugt, Maaike van der, 'Tradition and revision: the textual tradition of the *Visio Bernoldi*, with a critical edition', *Bulletin du Cange: Archivum Latinitatis Medii Aevi* 52 (1994), pp. 109–49.

Lukas, Veronika, 'Neues aus einer Salzburger Handschrift aus Köln: Zur Überlieferung der Episcoporum ad Hludowicum imperatorem relatio (829)', *DA* 58 (2002), pp. 539–48.

McCormick, Michael, 'The liturgy of war in the early Middle Ages: crisis, litanies and the Carolingian monarchy', *Viator* 15 (1984), pp. 1–23.

Eternal Victory: Triumphal Rulership and the Early Medieval West (Cambridge, 1986).

McKeon, Peter R., 'Une année désastreuse et prèsque fatale pour les Carolingiens', *LMA* 84 (1978), pp. 5–12.

'Archbishop Ebbo of Rheims (816–835): a study in the Carolingian empire and church', *Church History* 43 (1974), pp. 437–47.

'The empire of Louis the Pious: faith, politics and personality', *RB* 90 (1980), pp. 50–62.

McKitterick, Rosamond, *The Frankish Church and the Carolingian Reforms, 789–895*, Royal Historical Society, Studies in History 2 (London, 1977).

The Frankish Kingdoms under the Carolingians, 751–987 (London, 1983).

'Knowledge of canon law in the Frankish kingdoms before 789: the manuscript evidence', *Journal of Theological Studies* 36 (1985), pp. 97–117.

The Carolingians and the Written Word (Cambridge, 1989).

'Nuns' scriptoria in England and Francia in the eighth century', *Francia* 19/1 (1992), pp. 1–35.

'Zur Herstellung von Kapitularien: Die Arbeit des Leges-Skriptoriums', *MIÖG* 101 (1993), pp. 3–16.

'The audience for Latin historiography in the early middle ages: text transmission and manuscript dissimination', in Scharer and Scheibelreiter (eds.), *Historiographie*, pp. 96–114.

'Unity and diversity in the Carolingian church', in R. Swanson (ed.), *Unity and Diversity in the Christian Church*, Studies in Church History 32 (1996), pp. 59–82.

'The illusion of royal power in the Carolingian Annals', *EHR* 115 (2000), pp. 1–20.

History and Memory in the Carolingian World (Cambridge, 2004).

Charlemagne: The Formation of a European Identity (Cambridge, 2008).

McKitterick, Rosamond, (ed.), *The Uses of Literacy in Early Medieval Europe* (Cambridge, 1990).

Carolingian Culture: Emulation and Innovation (Cambridge, 1994).

The New Cambridge Medieval History, II: *c. 700-c. 900* (Cambridge, 1995).

The Early Middle Ages, The Short Oxford History of Europe (Oxford, 2001).

McLean, Simon, *Kingship and Politics in the Late Ninth Century: Charles the Fat and the End of the Carolingian Empire* (Cambridge, 2003).

'Ritual, misunderstanding and the contest for meaning: representations of the disrupted royal assembly at Frankfurt (873)', in B. Weiler and S. MacLean (eds.), *Representations of Power in Medieval Germany* (Turnhout, 2006), pp. 97–120.

McLynn, Neil, *Ambrose of Milan: Church and Court in a Christian Capital* (Berkeley, Los Angeles and London, 1994).

Magnou-Nortier, Élisabeth, 'La tentative de subversion de l'État sous Louis le Pieux et l'œuvre des falsificateurs', *LMA* 105 (1999), pp. 331–65, 615–41.

Mähl, Sibylle, *Quadriga virtutum: die Kardinaltugenden in der Geistesgeschichte der Karolingerzeit* (Cologne, 1969).

Malbos, Lina, 'L'annaliste royal sous Louis le Pieux', *LMA* 72 (1966), pp. 225–33.

Mayr-Harting, Henry, 'Charlemagne, the Saxons, and the imperial coronation of 800', *EHR* 111 (1996), pp. 1113–33.

'Charlemagne's religion', in P. Godman, J. Jarnut and P. Johanek (eds.), *Am Vorabend der Kaiserkrönung: Das Epos 'Karolus Magnus et Leo papa' und der Pabstbesuch in Paderborn 799* (Berlin, 2002), pp. 113–24.

Meens, Rob, 'Politics, mirrors of princes and the Bible: Sins, kings and the well-being of the realm', *EME* 7 (1998), pp. 345–57.

'The frequency and nature of early medieval penance', in P. Biller and A. Minnis (eds.), *Handling Sin in the Middle Ages* (Woodbridge, 1998), pp. 35–61.

'Sanctuary, penance and dispute settlement under Charlemagne: the conflict between Alcuin and Theodulf of Orléans over a sinful cleric', *Speculum* 82 (2007), pp. 277–300.

Mersiowsky, Mark, 'Regierungspraxis und Schriftlichkeit im Karolingerreich: das Fallbeispiel der Mandate und Briefe', in R. Schieffer (ed.), *Schriftkultur*, pp. 109–66.

Moeglin, Jean-Marie, 'Harmiscara-harmschar-hachee: le dossier des rituels d'humiliation et de soumission au Moyen Âge', *Archivum Latinitatis Medii Aevi* 54 (1996), pp. 11–65.

'Pénitence publique et amende honorable au Moyen Âge', *Revue Historique* 298 (1998), pp. 225–69.

Monod, Gabriel, *Études critiques sur les sources de l'histoire carolingienne* (Paris, 1898).

Moore, Michael E., 'La monarchie Carolingienne et les anciens modèles Irlandais', *Annales: Histoire, Sciences sociales* 51 (1996), pp. 307–24.

Moos, Peter von, *Consolatio: Studien zur mittellateinischer Trostliteratur über den Tod und zur Problem der christlichen Trauer*, 4 vols., Münstersche Mittelalter-Schriften 3 (Munich, 1971).

Mordek, Hubert, *Kirchenrecht und Reform in Frankenreich: Die Collectio Vetus Gallica, die älteste systematische Kanonensammlung des fränkischen Gallien: Studien und Edition*, Beiträge zur Geschichte und Quellenkunde des Mittelalters 1 (Berlin and New York, 1975).

'Unbekannte Texte zur karolingischen Gesetzgebung: Ludwig der Fromme, Einhard und die Capitula adhuc conferenda', *DA* 43 (1987), pp. 361–439; reprinted in H. Mordek, *Studien zur fränkischen Herrschergesetzgebung: Aufsätze über Kapitularien und Kapitulariensammlungen – ausgewählt zum 60. Geburtstag* (Frankfurt a/M, 2000), pp. 161–85.

Biblioteca capitularium regum francorum manuscripta: Überlieferung und Traditionszusammenhang der fränkischen Herrscherlasse, MGH *Hilfsmittel* 15 (Munich, 1995).

'Karls des Großen zweites Kapitular von Herstal und die Hungersnot der Jahre 778/779', *DA* 61 (2005), pp. 1–52.

Morrison, Karl F., *The Two Kingdoms: Ecclesiology in Carolingian Political Thought* (Princeton, 1964).

Murray, Owen, 'The idea of the Shepherd King from Cyrus to Charlemagne', in O. Murray and P. Godman (eds.), *Latin Poetry and the Classical Tradition* (Oxford, 1990), pp. 1–13.

Nahmer, Dieter von der, 'Die Bibel im Adalhardleben des Radbert von Corbie', *Studi Medievali* 23 (1982), pp. 15–83.

Nelson, Janet L., 'Public *histories* and private history in the work of Nithard', *Speculum* 60 (1985), pp. 251–93 (reprinted in Nelson, *Politics and Ritual*, pp. 195–237).

'Queens as Jezebels: Brunhild and Balthild in Merovingian history', in Nelson, *Politics and Ritual*, pp. 1–48.

'Kingship, law and liturgy in the political thought of Hincmar of Rheims', in Nelson, *Politics and Ritual*, pp. 132–71.

'The Annals of St Bertin', in Nelson, *Politics and Ritual*, pp. 173–94.

Politics and Ritual in Early Medieval Europe (London and Ronceverte, 1986).
'A tale of two princes: politics, text, and ideology in a Carolingian annal', *Studies in Medieval and Renaissance History* 10 (1988), pp. 105–41.
'The last years of Louis the Pious', in Godman and Collins (eds.), *Charlemagne's Heir*, pp. 147–59.
'Literacy in Carolingian government', in McKitterick (ed.), *The Uses of Literacy*, pp. 258–96.
The Annals of St-Bertin, Ninth-Century Histories I, trans. and annotated by J. L. Nelson (Manchester, 1991).
Charles the Bald (London, 1992).
'History-writing at the courts of Louis the Pious and Charles the Bald', in Scharer and Scheibelreiter (eds.), *Historiographie*, pp. 435–42.
'Kingship and empire in the Carolingian world', in McKitterick (ed.), *Carolingian Culture*, pp. 52–87.
'Kingship and royal government', in McKitterick (ed.), *NCMH* II, pp. 383–430.
'Kings with justice, kings without justice: an early medieval paradox', in *La giustizia*, Settimane 44, pp. 797–825.
'The Lord's anointed and the people's choice: Carolingian royal ritual', in Nelson, *The Frankish World*, pp. 99–131.
'Gender and genre in women historians of the Early Middle Ages', in Nelson, *The Frankish World*, pp. 183–97.
'Women at the court of Charlemagne: a case of monstruous regiment?', in Nelson, *The Frankish World*, pp. 223–42.
'Ninth-century knighthood: the evidence of Nithard', in Nelson, *The Frankish World*, pp. 75–87.
The Frankish World 750–900 (London and Rio Grande, 1996).
'The search for peace at a time of war: the Carolingian *Bruderkrieg*, 840–843', *Vorträge und Forschungen* 42 (Sigmaringen, 1996), pp. 87–114.
'The siting of the Council at Frankfort: some reflections on family and politics', in Berndt (ed.), *Das Frankfurter Konzil*, I, pp. 149–66.
'La cour impériale de Charlemagne', in Le Jan (ed.), *La Royauté*, pp. 177–91.
'Carolingian royal funerals', in Theuws and Nelson (eds.), *Rituals of Power*, pp. 131–84.
'Aachen as a place of power', in De Jong, Theuws and Van Rhijn (eds.), *Topographies*, pp. 17–42.
'Nobility in the Ninth Century', in A. J. Duggan (ed.), *Nobles and Nobility in Medieval Europe* (Woodbridge, 2000), pp. 43–51.
'The voice of Charlemagne', in R. Gameson and H. Leyser (eds.), *Belief and Culture in the Middle Ages: Studies Presented to Henry Mayr-Harting* (Oxford, 2001), pp. 76–88.
'Charlemagne – pater optimus?', in Godman, Jarnut and Johanek (eds.), *Am Vorabend der Kaiserkrönung*, pp. 269–81.
'Was Charlemagne's court a courtly society?' in Cubitt (ed.), *Court Culture*, pp. 39–57.
'Bertrada', in Becher and Jarnut (eds.), *Die Dynastiewechsel*, pp. 93–108.
'Gendering courts in the early medieval West', in Brubaker and Smith (eds.), *Gender in the Early Medieval World*, pp. 185–97.

'Dhuoda', in Wormald and Nelson (eds.), *Lay Intellectuals*, pp. 106–20.

Niermeyer, Jan Frederik, *Mediae Latinitatis Lexicon Minus* (Leiden, 1993).

Noble, Thomas F. X., *Louis the Pious and the Papacy: Law, Politics and the Theory of Empire in the Early Ninth Century* (Ann Arbor, 1979) (dissertation, Michigan State University, 1974).

'The revolt of King Bernard', *Studi Medievali* 3/15 (1974), pp. 315–26.

'The monastic ideal as a model for Empire: the case of Louis the Pious', *RB* 88 (1976), pp. 235–50.

'Louis the Pious and his piety re-reconsidered', *Revue belge de philologie et d'histoire* 58 (1980), pp. 297–316.

'Some observations of the deposition of Archbishop Theodulf of Orléans in 817', *Journal of Rocky Mountain Medieval and Renaissance Association* 2 (1981), pp. 29–40.

The Republic of St Peter: The Birth of the Papal State, 680–825 (Philadelphia, 1984).

'Secular sanctity: forging an ethos for the Carolingian nobility', in Wormald and Nelson (eds.), *Lay Intellectuals*, pp. 8–36.

Patzold, Steffen, 'Die Bischöfe im karolingischen Staat: Praktisches Wissen über die politische Ordnung im Frankenreich des 9. Jahrhunderts, in Airlie, Pohl and Reimitz (eds.), *Staat*, pp. 133–62.

'Eine "loyale Palastrebellion" der "Reichseinheitspartei"? Zur "Divisio imperii" von 817 und zu den Ursachen des Aufstandes gegen Ludwig den Frommen im Jahre 830', *FmSt* 40 (2006), pp. 43–77.

Peltier, Henri, *Pascase Radbert, Abbé de Corbie* (Amiens, 1938).

Peters, Edward, *The Shadow King*: rex inutilis *in Medieval Law and Literature, 751–1371* (New Haven, 1970).

Pohl, Walter, 'History in fragments: Montecassino's politics of memory', *EME* 10 (2001), pp. 343–74.

Identität und Widerspruch: Gedanken zu einer Sinngeschichte des frühen Mittelalters, in Pohl (ed.), *Die Suche nach den Ursprüngen: Von der Bedeutung des frühen Mittelalters*, Forschungen zur Geschichte des Mittelalters 9 (Vienna, 2004), pp. 23–36.

Pössel, Christina, 'The itinerant kingship of Louis the Pious' (unpublished MPhil dissertation, Cambridge University, 1998/9).

'Symbolic communication and the negotiation of power at Carolingian regnal assemblies, 814–840' (unpublished PhD dissertation, Cambridge University, 2003).

'Authors and recipients of Carolingian capitularies', in Corradini *et al.* (eds.), *Texts and Identities*, pp. 253–74.

Priebsch, Robert, *Letter from Heaven on the Observance of the Lord's Day* (London, 1936).

Reimitz, Helmut, 'Ein karolingisches Geschichtsbuch aus Saint-Amand und der Codex Vindobonensis palat. 473', in C. Egger and H. Weigl (eds.), *Text-Schrift-Codex: Quellenkundliche Arbeiten aus dem Institut für Österreichische Geschichtsforschung, MIÖG* Ergänzungsband (Vienna and Munich, 2000), pp. 34–90.

'Der Weg zum Königtum in historiographischen Kompendien der Karolingerzeit', in Becher and Jarnut (eds.), *Der Dynastiewechsel*, pp. 277–320.

'*Nomen Francorum obscuratum*: zur Krise der fränkischen Identität zwischen der kurzen und langen Geschichte der Annales regni Francorum' (forthcoming).

Reuter, Timothy, 'Plunder and tribute in the Carolingian empire', *Transactions of the Royal Historical Society* 35 (1985), pp. 75–94.

The Annals of Fulda (Manchester, 1992).

'"Kirchenreform" und "Kirchenpolitik" im Zeitalter Karls Martells: Begriffe und Wirklichkeit', in J. Jarnut, U. Nonn und M. Richter (eds.), *Karl Martell in seiner Zeit*, Beihefte der Francia 37 (Sigmaringen, 1994), pp. 35–95.

'Assembly politics in Western Europe from the eighth century to the twelfth', in P. Linehan and J. L. Nelson (eds.), *The Medieval World* (London, 2001), pp. 95–129.

'Contextualising Canossa: excommunication, penance, surrender, reconciliation', in Timothy Reuter, *Medieval Polities and Modern Mentalities*, ed. J. L. Nelson (Cambridge, 2006), pp. 147–66.

Reydellet, M., *La royauté dans la littérature latine de Sidoine Appollinaire à Isidore de Séville* (Rome, 1981).

Rhijn, Carine van, *Shepherds of the Lord: Priests and Episcopal Statutes in the Carolingian Period* (Turnhout, 2007).

Riché, Pierre, 'La magie à l'époque Carolingienne', in Riché, *Instruction et vie religieuse dans le Haut Moyen Âge* (Aldershot, 1981), pp. 127–38.

Riess, Frank, 'From Aachen to Al-Andalus: the journey of Deacon Bodo', *EME* 13 (2005), pp. 131–57.

Rosenthal, Joel T., 'The public assembly in the time of Louis the Pious', *Traditio* 20 (1964), pp. 25–40.

Scharer, Anton, *Herrschaft und Repräsentation: Studien zur Hofkultur Königs Alfreds des Großen*, *MIÖG* Ergänzungsband 36 (Vienna and Munich, 2000).

Scharer, A., and G. Scheibelreiter (eds.), *Historiographie im frühen Mittelalter*, Veröffentlichungen des Instituts für Österreichischen Geschichtsforschung 32 (Vienna and Munich, 1994).

Schefers, Hermann, *Einhard: Ein Lebensbild aus karolingischer Zeit* (Michelstadt-Steinbach 1993).

Schieffer, Rudolf, 'Von Mailand nach Canossa: Ein Beitrag zur Geschichte der christlichen Herrscherbuße von Theodosius der Grosse bis zu Heinrich IV', *DA* 28 (1972), pp. 333–70.

'Ludwig "der Fromme": Zur Entstehung eines karolingischen Herrscherbeinamens', *FmSt* 16 (1982), pp. 58–73.

'Zwei karolingische Texte über das Königtum', *DA* 46 (1990), pp. 1–17.

'Väter und Söhne im Karolingerhause', in Schieffer (ed.), *Beiträge zur Geschichte des Regnum Francorum: Referate beim Wissenschaftlichen Colloquium zum 75. Geburtstag von Eugen Ewig am 28. Mai 1988*, Beihefte der Francia 22 (Sigmaringen, 1990), pp. 149–64.

Schieffer, Rudolf (ed.), *Schriftkultur und Reichsverwaltung under den Karolingern: Referate des Kolloquiums der Nordrhein-Westfälischen Akademie der Wissenschaften am 17./18. Februar in Bonn*, Abhandlungen der Nordrhein-Westfälischen Akademie der Wissenschaften 97 (Opladen, 1996).

Schieffer, Theodor, 'Die Krise des karolingischen Imperiums', in J. Engel and H. M. Klinkenberg (eds.), *Aus Mittelalter und Neuzeit: Feschrift G. Kallen* (Bonn, 1957), pp. 1–15.

Schmitz, Gerhard, 'Die Kapitulariengesetzgebung Ludwig des Frommens', *DA* 42 (1986), pp. 471–516.

'Die Reformkonzilien von 813 und die Sammlung des Benedictus Levita', *DA* 56 (2000), pp. 1–31.

'*Echte Quellen – falsche Quellen: Müssen zentrale Quellen aus der Zeit Ludwigs des Frommen neu bewertet werden?*', in F. -R. Erkens und Hartmut Wolff (eds.), *Von Sacerdotium und Regnum: Geistliche und weltliche Gewalt im frühen und hohen Mittelalter: Festschrift für Egon Boshof zum 65. Geburtstag* (Cologne, Weimar and Vienna, 2002), pp. 275–300.

Schramm, Percy E., *Kaiser, Könige und Päpste: Gesammelte Aufsätze zur Geschichte des Mittelalters*, Band II: *Beiträge zur allgemeine Geschichte*, 2. Teil: *Vom Tode Karls des Grossen (814) bis zum Anfang des 10. Jahrhunderts* (Stuttgart, 1968).

Screen, Elina M., 'The Early Career of Lothar I (795–855)' (unpublished MPhil dissertation, Cambridge University, 1995).

The reign of Lothar I (795–855), emperor of the Franks, through the charter evidence' (unpublished PhD dissertation, Cambridge University, 1999).

'The importance of being emperor: Lothar I and the Frankish civil war, 840–843', *EME* 12 (2003), pp. 25–51.

Sears, Elisabeth, 'Louis the Pious as *miles Christi*: the dedicatory image in Hrabanus Maurus' *De laudibus sancti crucis*,' in Godman and Collins (eds.), *Charlemagne's Heir*, pp. 605–28.

Semmler, Joseph, 'Karl der Grosse und das fränkische Mönchtum', in F. Prinz (ed.), *Mönchtum und Gesellschaft im Frühmittelalter*, Wege der Forschung 312 (Darmstadt, 1976), pp. 204–64.

'Die Beschlüsse des Aachener Konzils im Jahre 816', *Zeitschrift für Kirchengeschichte* 74 (1963), pp. 15–82.

'Mönche und Kanoniker im Frankenreich Pippins III. und Karls des Großen', *Untersuchungen zur Kloster und Stift*, Studien zur Germania sacra 14 (Göttingen, 1980), pp. 78–111.

'Iussit … princeps renovare … praecepta', *Studia Anselmiana* 85 (1982), pp. 97–182.

'Benedictus II: una regula, una consuetudo', in W. Lourdeaux and D. Verhelst (eds.), *Benedictine Culture, 750–1050*, Medievalia Lovaniensa 1/11 (Louvain, 1983), pp. 1–49.

Siegmund, A., *Die Überlieferung der griechischen christlichen Literatur in der lateinischen Kirche bis zum zwölften Jahrhundert* (Munich, 1949).

Siemes, Helena, *Beiträge zum literarischen Bild Kaiser Ludwigs des Frommen in der Karolingerzeit* (Freiburg, 1966).

Simson, Bernhard von, *Jahrbücher der Geschichte des fränkischen Reichs unter Ludwig dem Frommen*, 2 vols. (Leipzig, 1876).

Smith, Julia M. H., *Province and Empire: Brittany and the Carolingians* (Cambridge, 1992).

'Religion and lay society', in McKitterick (ed.), *NCMH* II, pp. 654–78.

'Gender and ideology the Early Middle Ages,' in R. N. Swanson (ed.), *Gender and Christian Religion*, Studies in Church History 35 (Woodbridge, 1998), pp. 51–73.

'Old saints, new cults: Roman relics in Carolingian Francia', in Smith (ed.), *Early Medieval Rome and the Christian West: Essays in Honour of Donald Bullough* (Leiden, 2000), pp. 317–39.

'"Emending evil ways and praising God's omnipotence": Einhard and the use of Roman martyrs', in K. Mills and A. Grafton (eds.), *Conversion in Late Antiquity and the Early Middle Ages: Seeing and Believing* (Rochester and New York, 2003), pp. 189–223.

'Einhard: the sinner and the saints', *THRS* 6/13 (2003), pp. 55–77.

Smolak, Kurt, 'Bescheidene Panegyrik und diskrete Werbung: Walahfrid Strabos Gedicht über das Standbild Theoderichs in Aachen', in F.-R. Erkens (ed.), *Karl der Große und das Erbe der Kulturen* (Berlin, 2001), pp. 89–110.

Stafford, Pauline, *Queens, Concubines and Dowagers: The King's Wife in the Early Middle Ages* (London, 1983).

Stancliffe, Clare, 'Kings who opted out', in P. Wormald (ed.) with D. Bullough and R. Collins, *Ideal and Reality in Frankish and Anglo-Saxon Society: Studies Presented to J. M. Wallace-Hadril* (Oxford, 1983), pp. 154–76.

Staubach, Nikolaus, 'Das Herrscherbild Karls des Kahlen: Formen und Funktionen monarchischer Representation im Mittelalter' (Phil. Diss.; Freiburg, 1982).

'"*Cultus divinus*" und karolingischen Reform', *FmSt* 18 (1984), pp. 546–81.

'"Des grossen Kaisers kleinen Sohn": Zum Bild Ludwig des Frommen in der älteren deutschen Geschichtsforschung', in Godman and Collins (eds.), *Charlemagne's Heir*, pp. 701–23.

Rex christianus: Hofkultur und Herrschaftspropaganda im Reich Karls des Kahlen, II: *Die Grundlegung der 'religion royale'*, Pictura et poesis 2 (Cologne, Weimar and Vienna, 1993).

'*Christiana tempora*: Augustin und das Ende der alten Geschichte in der Weltchronik Frechulfs von Lisieux', *FmSt* 29 (1995), pp. 167–206.

'*Quasi semper in publico*: Öffentlichkeit als Funktions- und Kommunikationsraum karolingischer Königsherrschaft', in G. Melville and P. Von Moos (eds.), *Das Öffentliche und Private in der Vormoderne*, Norm und Struktur: Studien zum sozialen Wandel im Mittelalter und früher Neuzeit 10 (Cologne, Weimar and Vienna, 1998), pp. 577–628.

Stiegemann, Christoph, and Matthias Wemhof (eds.), *799: Kunst und Kultur der Karolingerzeit: Karl der Grosse und Papst Leo III in Paderborn*, 3 vols. (Mainz, 1999).

Stratmann, Martina, 'Einhards letzte Lebensjahre im Spiegel seiner Briefe', in H. Schefers (ed.), *Einhard: Studien zur Leben und Werk: Dem Gedenken an Helmut Beumann gewidmet* (Darmstadt, 1997), pp. 323–39.

Suchan, Monika, 'Kirchenpolitik des Königs oder Königspolitik der Kirche? Zum Verhältnis Ludwigs des Frommen und des Episkopates während der Herrschaftskrisen um 830', *Zeitschrift für Kirchengeschichte* 111 (2000), pp. 1–27.

Suntrup, Aloys, *Studien zur politischen Theologie im frühmittelalterlichen Okzident: Die Aussage konziliarer Texte des gallischen und iberischen Raumes*, Spanische Forschungen der Görresgesellschaft 36 (Münster, 2001).

Theuws, Frans, and Janet L. Nelson (eds.), *Rituals of Power: From Late Antiquity to the Early Middle Ages* (Leiden, 2000).

Tischler, Matthias, *Einharts 'Vita Karoli'. Studien zur Entstehung, Überlieferung und Rezeption*, MGH *Schriften* 48 (Hanover, 2001).

Toubert, Pierre, 'La doctrine gélasienne des deux pouvoirs: propositions en vue d'une révision', in *Studi in onore di Giosuè Musca* (Bari, 2000), pp. 519–40.

Traill, David A., *Walahfrid Strabo's Visio Wettini: Text, Translation and Commentary*, Lateinische Sprache und Literatur des Mittelalters 2 (Frankfurt a/M, 1974).

Tremp, Ernst, *Studien zu den Gesta Hludowici imperatoris des Trierer Chorbischofs Thegan*, MGH *Schriften* 32 (Hanover, 1988).

Die Überlieferung der Vita Hludowici imperatoris des Astronomus, MGH *Studien und Texte* 1 (Hanover, 1991).

'Thegan und Astronomus, die beiden Geschichtsschreiber Ludwigs des Frommen', in Godman and Collins (eds.), *Charlemagne's Heir*, pp. 691–700.

'Die letzten Worte des frommen Kaisers Ludwig: Von Sinn und Unsinn heutiger Textedition', *DA* 48 (1992), pp. 17–36.

'"Zwischen *stabilitas* und *mutatio rerum*". Herrschafts- und Staatsauffassung im Umkreis Ludwigs des Frommen', in Le Jan (ed.), *La royauté*, pp. 111–27.

Uhalde, Kevin, *Expectations of Justice in the Age of Augustine* (Philadelphia, 2007).

Ullmann, W., *The Carolingian Renaissance and the Idea of Kingship* (London, 1969).

Waldhoff, Stephan, *Alcuins Gebetsbuch für Karl den Grossen: seine Rekonstruktion und seine Stellung in der frühmittelalterlichen Geschichte der libelli precum*, Liturgiewissenschaftliche Quellen und Forschungen 89 (Aschendorff, 2003).

Wallace-Hadrill, John M., *The Frankish Church* (Oxford, 1983).

Ward, Elisabeth, 'Agobard of Lyons and Paschasius Radbertus as critics of the Empress Judith', *Studies in Church History* 27 (1990), pp. 15–25.

'Caesar's wife: The career of the Empress Judith, 819–829', in Godman and Collins (eds.), *Charlemagne's Heir*, pp. 205–27.

Wehlen, Wolfgang, *Geschichtsschreibung und Staatsauffassung im Zeitalter Ludwigs des Frommen* (Lübeck and Hamburg, 1970).

Weinrich, Lorenz, *Wala: Graf, Mönch und Rebell: Die Biographie eines Karolingers*, Historische Studien 386 (Lübeck, 1963).

Wendling, Wolfgang, 'Die Erhebung Ludwigs des Frommen zum Mitkaiser in Jahre 813 und ihre Bedeutung für die Verfassungsgeschichte des Frankenreiches', *FmSt* 19 (1985), pp. 201–38.

Werner, Karl-Ferdinand, 'Die Nachkommen Karls des Grossen bis zum Jahr 1000 (1. bis 8. Generationen)', in W. Braunfels and P. E. Schramm (eds.), *Karl der Grosse: Lebenswerk und Nachleben*, vol. IV (Düsseldorf, 1967), pp. 403–82.

'*Hludowicus Augustus*: Gouverner l'empire chrétien – idées et réalités', in Godman and Collins (eds.), *Charlemagne's Heir*, pp. 3–123.

Wickham, Chris, *The Inheritance of Rome* (London, forthcoming).

Willmes, Peter, *Der Herrscher-'Adventus' im Kloster des Frühmittelalters*, Münstersche Mittelalter-Schriften 22 (Munich, 1976).

Wolfram, Herwig, 'Die Legitimationsformel von Ludwig dem Frommen bis zum Ende des 10. Jahrhunderts', in Wolfram (ed.), *Intitulatio*, vol. II: *Lateinische Herrscher- und Fürstentitel im neunten und zehnten Jahrhundert*, *MIÖG* suppl. 24 (Vienna, Cologne and Graz, 1973), pp. 59–77.

Wood, Ian N., 'Report: the European Science Foundation's Programme on the Transformation of the Roman World and the Emergence of Early Medieval Europe', *EME* 6 (1997), pp. 217–27.

The Missionary Life: Saints and the Evangelisation of Europe, 400–1050 (London, 2001).

'John Michael Wallace-Hadrill, 1910–1985', *Proceedings of the British Academy* 124 (2004), pp. 333–55.

Wood, Susan, *The Proprietary Church in the Middle Ages* (Oxford, 2006).

Wormald, P., and J. L. Nelson (eds.), *Lay Intellectuals in the Carolingian World* (Cambridge, 2007).

Zechiel-Eckes, Klaus, 'Zwei Arbeitshandschriften Pseudoisidors', *Francia* 27/1 (2000), pp. 205–210.

'Ein Blick in Pseudoisidors Werkstatt: Studien zum Entstehungsprozess der falschen Dekretalen. Mit einen exemplarischen Editorischen Anhang', *Francia* 28/1 (2001), pp. 37–90.

'Auf Pseudoisidors Spur: Oder – Versuch, einen dichten Schleier zu lüften', in W. Hartmann and G. Schmitz (eds.), *Fortschritt durch Fälschungen? Ursprung, Gestalt und Wirkungen der pseudoisidorischen Fälschungen*, MGH *Studien und Texte* 31 (Hanover, 2002) pp. 1–28.

Zeddies, Nicole, 'Bonifatius und zwei nützliche Rebellen: die Häretiker Aldebert und Clemens', in M. T. Fögen (ed.), *Ordnung und Aufruhr: Historische und juristische Studien zur Rebellion*, Ius Commune, Sonderhefte 70 (Frankfurt a/M, 1995), pp. 217–63.

Zotz, Thomas, 'In Amt und Würden. Zur Eigenart "offizieller" Positionen im früheren Mittelalter', *Tel Aviver Jahrbuch für deutsche Geschichte* 22 (1993), pp. 1–23.

'Le palais et les élites dans le royaume de Germanie', in Le Jan (ed.), *La royauté*, pp. 233–47.

Index of biblical references

General index

Aachen, palace of 28, 30, 34, 40–4, 47, 49–50, 57, 60, 69–70, 72, 88, 91, 95, 138, 149
  assemblies at
    (802) 23
    (813) 18–19
    (816) 22–3, 131
    (817) 22–3, 26
    (828–9) 107, 157–76
    (831) 45
    (836) 53, 183
  chapel dedicated to St Mary 19, 73, 75, 161
  coronation of Louis at 18–19
  earthquakes in 84, 156–7
  takeover by Louis in 814 19–24, 190–3
  solarium at 185
abbesses 37, 61, 139, 155, 185
abbots 37, 61, 155, 185
  free election of 166
  lay 22, 96, 102, 107, 168, 264
Abel 20
Abu Marwan 39, 150
Achab 178, 229
Adalhard, abbot of Corbie and Corvey 20–1, 23, 35–6, 61, 103–4, 106, 108, 122–6, 129, 142–3, 153–4, 216
  authority of 117, 125–7
  exile of 20–1, 123
  See also De ordine palatii
Adalhard 'the seneschal' 97, 100–1
Adelaid, sister of Louis the Pious 14
Adhemar, monk 29, 82
admonitio 5, 112–42
  and accusation 114, 142–8
  and frank speech 117–18
  and mirrors of princes 117
  by rulers 5, 17, 27, 85, 124–5, 131–5
  of rulers 71, 79, 115–17, 126–7
  and use of biblical texts 117–21
  in visionary literature 135–41
  vocabulary of 118–20
  See also Louis the Pious, criticism of; *correptio*; *increpatio*

Admonitio ad omnis regni ordines (825) 37, 53, 132–3, 152, 155, 182, 249
Admonitio generalis (789) 17, 117, 131–3
adultery 42, 115–16, 162, 195–204, 230, 239
adventus 15, 44, 211, 216–20
  and textual strategies of defamation 47, 62, 216–20
Aethelbald, king of Mercia 115–16
Agobard, archbishop of Lyons 51–3, 61, 115, 131, 142–7, 149, 218, 248, 262, 277–9
  Apologia I 195–6, 203–4
  Apologia II 212, 229–31
  at assembly of Attigny (822) 124–6, 142–3, 153–4, 159, 167, 170, 186–7, 220–1
  at assembly of Compiègne (833) 229–48
  on Jews 144–5, 192
  on Judith 146–7, 188, 194–5
  on Matfrid 144–5, 151
Airlie, Stuart 12, 96, 101
Aizo, rebel in Septimania 39, 148–50
Alberic, blind visionary 161–2
Alcuin 5, 20, 174, 192
Alemannia 30, 41, 46, 52, 215
Alexander the Great 94
Alpais, daughter of Louis 15, 22
Alsace 1, 41, 47, 51, 224
Althoff, Gerd 245
Ambrose of Milan 109, 196
  De excessu fratris 105–6
  and Theodosius I 6, 36, 117–18, 121–5, 129–31, 297
Amorites 229
Angers 30, 91
Angilbert of St-Riquier 96
Anjou 52
Annales Bertiniani 65–6, 82, 250
  authorship of 65, 265
  See also Hincmar; Prudentius
Annales Fuldenses 54
Annales regni Francorum 18, 28, 33, 35, 60, 82, 122–3, 128, 148, 152, 156–7, 163, 206–7, 218